D1491134

RATING THE FIRST LADIES

Lady Bird Johnson, Pat Nixon, Nancy Reagan, Barbara Bush, Rosalynn Carter, and Betty Ford at the Reagan Library

RATING THE FIRST LADIES

━━━━━━━━━━━ ★ ━━━━━━━━━━━

The Women Who Influenced the Presidency

JOHN B. ROBERTS II

CITADEL PRESS
Kensington Publishing Corp.
www.kensingtonbooks.com

CITADEL PRESS BOOKS are published by

Kensington Publishing Corp.
850 Third Avenue
New York, NY 10022

All Kensington titles, imprints, and distributed lines are available at special quantity discounts for bulk purchases for sales promotions, premiums, fund-raising, educational, or institutional use. Special book excerpts or customized printings can also be created to fit specific needs. For details, write or phone the office of the Kensington special sales manager: Kensington Publishing Corp., 850 Third Avenue, New York, NY 10022, attn: Special Sales Department, phone: 1-800-221-2647.

Photo credits
Provided by the Library of Congress: Photos of Anna Harrison, Julia Tyler, Betty Taylor Bliss, Ellen Arthur, Frances Cleveland, Edith Roosevelt, Helen Taft, Ellen Wilson, Edith Wilson, Florence Harding, Grace Coolidge, Lou Henry Hoover, Eleanor Roosevelt, Bess Truman, Mamie Eisenhower, Jacqueline Kennedy, Lady Bird Johnson, Pat Nixon, Betty Ford, Rosalyn Carter, Barbara Bush.

Other photo sources: Photo of Elizabeth Monroe courtesy of Ash-Lawn Highland:
photo of Jane Pierce courtesy of Pierce Manse; photo of Ida McKinley courtesy of Vignos, Canton, Ohio; group photo on Frontispiece, and photo of Nancy Reagan courtesy of the Reagan Library; photo of Laura Bush courtesy of the White House photo office

All other photos were provided from the author's collection.

CITADEL PRESS and the Citadel logo are Reg. U.S. Pat. & TM Off.

First printing: March 2003

10 9 8 7 6 5 4 3 2 1

Printed in the United States of America

Library of Congress Control Number: 2002113399

ISBN: 0-8065-2387-5

To Elizabeth and Ben, for their love, encouragement,
and support.

CONTENTS

— ★ —

Acknowledgments ix

Introduction: Thinking About First Ladies xi

The Ranking of U.S. First Ladies by Siena Research Institute xxiii

Martha Dandridge Custis Washington 3

Abigail Smith Adams 11

Martha Jefferson Randolph and Mary Jefferson Eppes 19

Dolley Payne Todd Madison 25

Elizabeth Kortright Monroe 32

Louisa Catherine Johnson Adams 39

Emily Donelson Donelson and Sarah York Jackson 45

Angelica Singleton Van Buren 51

Anna Tuthill Symmes Harrison 56

Letitia Christian Tyler 59

Julia Gardiner Tyler 62

Sarah Childress Polk 68

Margaret Mackall Smith Taylor 77

Abigail Powers Fillmore 82

Jane Means Appleton Pierce 89

Harriet Lane 97

Mary Todd Lincoln 106

Eliza McCardle Johnson 115

Julia Dent Grant 125

Lucy Ware Webb Hayes 137

Lucretia Rudolph Garfield 145

Ellen Lewis Herndon Arthur 150

Frances Folsom Cleveland	153
Caroline Lavinia Scott Harrison	161
Ida Saxton McKinley	168
Edith Carow Roosevelt	177
Helen Herron Taft	185
Ellen Louise Axson Wilson	193
Edith Bolling Galt Wilson	199
Florence Kling DeWolfe Harding	209
Grace Anna Goodhue Coolidge	220
Lou Henry Hoover	229
Anna Eleanor Roosevelt Roosevelt	237
Elizabeth Virginia Wallace Truman	256
Mamie Geneva Doud Eisenhower	264
Jacqueline Lee Bouvier Kennedy	274
Claudia Taylor "Lady Bird" Johnson	282
Patricia Thelma Catherine Ryan Nixon	292
Elizabeth Bloomer Ford	301
Eleanor Rosalynn Smith Carter	308
Nancy Anne Frances Robbins Davis Reagan	317
Barbara Pierce Bush	329
Hillary Rodham Clinton	339
Laura Welch Bush	351
About the Author	361
Index	363

ACKNOWLEDGMENTS

———— ★ ————

Many political insiders helped me write this book by sharing their insights on the exercise of political power by recent first ladies. Several who agreed to have their observations on the record are quoted throughout the book, yet others insisted on anonymity, particularly when making critical observations or shedding light on previously undisclosed episodes involving first ladies. James Rosebush was particularly generous with his time. Susan Porter Rose, who worked for three first ladies, was extremely helpful and candid. Eleanor Clift of *Newsweek* shared her insights and observations. Eleanor Smeal was helpful in providing a feminist perspective. Michael J. Bayer provided rare candor in discussing the family's role in the 1988 Bush campaign. To every source who helped me get closer to the facts beneath the facade I am especially indebted. To those whose names have not been mentioned because of space, my thanks nonetheless. To those who did not want their names revealed, I am also grateful.

The unique approach taken in *Rating the First Ladies* would not have been possible without the generous assistance of the Siena College Research Institute. I am grateful to Professors Tom Kelly and Doug Lonnstrom for permission to use their expert poll results on first ladies, and for their patience in explaining the methodology and findings to me.

Every work of history builds on the efforts of others who have taken the time to record events as they occur. I am indebted to the countless diarists, memoirists, journalists, authors and White House stenographers who have helped preserve a record of presidencies and first ladies throughout our history. In recounting some of the history of Nancy Reagan's tenure as first lady, I relied on notes taken at the time and conversations with other White House insiders. Such contemporaneous observations have come down to us over the centuries for many first ladies. Let us hope that the fear of having notes subpoenaed by overzealous congressional committees or future independent counsels does not deter future

White House insiders from keeping accurate, contemporaneous journals recording their experiences. Truth will suffer if those who live history are too wary to chronicle their experiences.

I had a great deal of support from staff at the numerous presidential libraries, but Mark Renovitch of the FDR Library stands out as particularly helpful. I would also like to thank the Photo Duplication staff of the Library of Congress for going out of their way to help me circumvent a backlog of orders created by the quarantine of mail in Washington, D.C., during the anthrax attacks of the fall of 2001. Thanks also to The Folio Society for permission to cite extensive passages from Esmond Wright's *The Fire of Liberty,* an outstanding chronicle of the American Revolution.

Bob Shuman, my editor, gave sage guidance that helped me avoid many errors of fact and judgment and sharpened each account of a first lady. Any remaining omissions, mistakes, or biases are mine and mine alone. Of course, I am grateful to my agent, Mike Hamilburg, for his consistent support not only in this endeavor but also those in the past as well as others yet to come.

Introduction: Thinking About First Ladies

★

Eleanor Roosevelt represents a watershed in the history of first ladies. Their public role was expanding at a very gradual pace before her, typically limited to the social confines of being White House hostesses. Then it changes. Greatness in a president tends to be associated with great national crises; the same is true of Eleanor Roosevelt and her ability to rise up with the American people and face the Great Depression. In desperation, the country welcomed Eleanor's extensive involvement in New Deal policy making and her political activism. Without the crisis atmosphere, she would no doubt have been criticized for usurping powers that did not belong to her. Yet after Eleanor Roosevelt, first ladies were free to be as active in the job as they wanted to be and to achieve as much as they wanted, subject to the sole limitation every politician faces: They have to be able to maintain public and political support for their efforts.

The job of first lady has no formal definition in the Constitution. It has evolved informally, with the powers of each new first lady building upon the last, or suffering setbacks because of a previous first lady's political blunders.

At the beginning of the republic, it had no definition at all, formal or informal. The role literally had to be created. The world had few democracies in 1789 from which to draw examples of how political, social, and diplomatic protocols should be practiced in the newly independent United States. The fledgling republic also had to be taken seriously as a new member of the family of nations. This posed a problem. The simplest way to establish legitimacy was to copy the customs of established powers, but this meant patterning the job of first lady along the lines of a European court. The more difficult path was to create customs reflecting the unique nature of the revolutionary new country, etiquette that emphasized equality over aristocratic rank, and showcased democratic virtues instead of replicating the court manners of kings and queens.

This tension between following the fashions of European courts and creating new American customs has plagued the job from the beginning. Early first ladies such as Elizabeth Monroe and Louisa Adams were criticized for entertaining at the White House as though it were a royal court. More than a century later, Nancy Reagan came under attack when her redecorating of the White House and extravagant inaugural celebrations were too regal for the public's tastes. Yet other first ladies, like Jane Pierce and Sarah Polk, were criticized because the White House was too plain, the entertaining too bland, during their tenure. Not every first lady who focuses her activities solely on glamorous public events and redecorating the White House is criticized, either. Jacqueline Kennedy was widely revered as a first lady, yet she was one of the most traditional of them all.

As ambiguous and contradictory as public attitudes may be regarding the first lady's handling of social duties, when it comes to open involvement in policy making the limits of public acceptance are even less clear. The vast majority of the women who have served as first ladies have been politically active in their husbands' careers. They have used their power to champion causes, effect policy, urge declarations of war, and hire and fire presidential advisers. Often this has been done in private, not in public.

Immediately after the Revolution, the country's first ladies were strong women who had been through a war and had definite views about their country's political future. Abigail Adams sought an open political role, but social customs prevented women from playing an overt part in politics. As the country grew, first ladies came to resemble Victorian gentility. After women got the vote in the twentieth century, first ladies took on more active political roles, especially in campaigns. It seems only a natural evolution that if a first lady is involved in campaigning for her husband's election on a platform that involves clear policy issues, she should have a role in implementing those policies. Yet this last step in the evolution toward full power sharing between president and first lady has proven elusive. Twentieth-century first ladies like Edith Galt Wilson and Lady Bird Johnson were publicly active in both political campaigning and policy making. Nancy Reagan was openly assertive in the political management of the White House and in helping achieve her husband's policy objectives, but was heavily criticized for transgressing her boundaries as first lady. Hillary Clinton took office functioning almost as co-president, but the failure of her ambitious initiative to overhaul the nation's health care insurance system was a setback from which she never recovered as first lady. During the remainder of the Clinton presidency, she had to publicly retreat to more traditional activities for a first lady, although in private she continued to exercise her influence over the administration's policies.

In this book, I have approached first ladies from the perspective of a political insider. In writing about them, I emphasize each woman's involvement, to the extent that it can be known, in the vital affairs of the presidency. Although it is not always an equal one, the presidency is a political partnership. It is as political partner that the first ladies are of greatest interest.

Putting first ladies on pedestals does a disservice to our understanding of them in presidential politics and as human beings. Julia Grant not only served twenty-five-course meals at her White House functions, but also took secret cash payments to help pay for the lavish entertainment and then used her power as first lady to block corruption investigations. Jane Pierce held séances in the White House to try to communicate with her dead son Benny. Mary Lincoln bought gloves as compulsively as Imelda Marcos collected shoes—and even went so far as to issue orders on War Department letterhead signed "Mrs. President." Each had some degree of political influence over her husband.

America's greatest first lady was a bisexual whose lesbian lover lived with her in the White House. There are eighteen boxes of Lorena Hickok's personal papers documenting her affair with Eleanor Roosevelt at the Franklin D. Roosevelt Presidential Library. These revealing archives not only broaden our understanding of this remarkable first lady who consistently rates No. 1 in expert opinion polls, but—given Eleanor Roosevelt's continuing popularity and great contributions to modern America—ought to help promote tolerance and vanquish homophobic attitudes as well. One might think that such a discovery would be a welcome addition to our knowledge.

Yet when Doris Faber, a former *New York Times* reporter researching a biography of the first lady, discovered their contents, she lobbied officials to keep the Hickok files secret until the year 2000! Faber, who wrote for the *Times* in the 1940s and covered Eleanor Roosevelt's appearances, thought that by hiding the truth she would protect Eleanor's legacy as first lady.

"Pedestal reporting" is a relic of the nineteenth century, but the relic lives on today. Beginning with Martha Washington, the press and public have been interested in the president's wife and the hostess of the White House. As soon as newspapers began circulating nationally, first ladies began to set fashion trends by the clothes they wore or the way they styled their hair. When newspaper and magazine editors realized their influence over women readers, they began to assign female reporters to cover first ladies. Merchandisers caught on quickly, too, and used first ladies to advertise every kind of product imaginable, from soap and perfume in the nineteenth century to paint colors and automobiles in the twentieth. The social influence of first ladies was recognized long before their political importance was realized.

We owe much of our contemporaneous information about first ladies to the women correspondents who first began reporting on them. Unfortunately, women didn't have the right to vote in the nineteenth century. Newspaper coverage of first ladies tended to reflect society news. The rare exception was during political campaign season, when a controversial first lady could draw unfavorable coverage. Rachel Jackson was said to have died brokenhearted after she was attacked as a bigamist in the presidential campaign of 1828. Rachel, however, was the exception. Newspaper reporting normally told in great detail how the tables were set at a White House dinner, what order the courses were served in, and what the first lady wore to greet guests.

Laura Holloway wrote one of the first comprehensive books about first ladies. *The Ladies of the White House* was published in 1880 and provides a detailed account of the lives of the first ladies from Martha Washington through Lucretia Garfield. Holloway's book marks the first serious effort to chronicle the contributions of first ladies, and it remains a classic.

Long after women finally got the vote and became a powerful political force, covering first ladies was still thought of as a beat for women reporters. The first female correspondent assigned by one national newspaper to cover the White House told me, on condition that I wouldn't quote her, that she fought against covering the first lady because she didn't want to be pigeonholed into "girls' work." This was in the mid-1980s.

The action and drama was with the presidents; the pomp and ceremony was the first lady beat. Even Eleanor Roosevelt, who held regular news conferences for the reporters she called "the girls," was primarily covered by women like the *New York Times*'s Doris Faber. When it became clear that Eleanor was no average first lady, and male reporters began asking for access to her press briefings, the men were denied the privilege. The East Wing was for girls, the West Wing was for boys.

Of course, this neat gender division never really existed. White House women have always had power and influence over affairs of state, political campaigns, and presidential appointments. Pedestal reporting merely cloaked it, on the presumption that the American public wasn't ready for a presidential spouse to play a significant role in government. Those who did, from Edith Galt Wilson to Nancy Reagan, became lightning rods for criticism. The lesson many first ladies have drawn is that it is safest to limit their nonceremonial public activities to noncontroversial causes. These have ranged from promoting traditional charities to highway beautification to drug abuse prevention and literacy projects. As a result, the twenty-first-century public image of a first lady is an amalgam of the pre-liberation White House hostess role with advocacy for "soft" political issues chosen to alienate as few voters as possible. They write books about White House dogs and child rearing and make utterly unbelievable public pronouncements like Barbara Bush's claim that "he doesn't fool around with my household, and I don't fool around with his office."

Take such words in light of the fact that women have had the vote for eighty years. At colleges and universities, women make up the majority of students. This is also true for many graduate schools and in professions ranging from medicine to veterinary science and law. Nobody in America believes that a political spouse has no significant involvement in the power exercised by the officeholder in the marriage. *Rating the First Ladies* is not a book about the public images of first ladies. Rather, it is about the women who have shared the White House with presidents.

WHAT IS A FIRST LADY?

There seems to be some confusion about definitions. Some books feature only the wives of presidents as first ladies. This leads to absurdities such as the inclusion of President Andrew Jackson's wife, Rachel, who died between the election of 1828 and the presidential inauguration of 1829 and, therefore, never functioned as first lady in her life! By limiting the scope to presidential spouses, others who did serve in the role of first lady—like the wildly popular Harriet Lane or Martha Randolph Jefferson—are omitted.

The answer seems clear to me.

She is the woman who handles the duties of first lady during the presidency.

But what is the job of a first lady?

This question has caused confusion throughout all of America's history. Usage of the term *first lady*, in fact, became common only in the twentieth century. Just as frequently, the women in the White House have been referred to as "Mrs. President," "Lady Presidentress," "Madame President," or simply "Lady," as in "Lady Washington." As recently as the turn of the twentieth century, Marian West titled her magazine profile of first ladies "Our Four Year Queens."

James Rosebush, who was chief of staff to Nancy Reagan for four years, described the job as political partner to the president. "It's a two-person job," he said. "It takes two people to do it."

Susan Porter Rose, who worked for first ladies Pat Nixon, Betty Ford, and Barbara Bush, agrees that the official and political duties of the modern presidency are so demanding that it requires a couple to handle them.

Even the least activist of first ladies has some political involvement. Anyone who has tried to arrange the seating at a wedding appreciates the intricacy of hosting a White House event in which political rivals, allies, and potential allies have to be accommodated in the same room. Now imagine handling seating charts on the eve of the Civil War! Or in an impeachment crisis. A first lady doesn't have to give public speeches or champion a political cause for her to be a political partner in the presidency. This is because all her actions—almost everything that happens at the White House—is political.

Some men have resisted including first ladies in their political affairs, while others have leaned heavily on them. With the exception of President Chester Arthur, however, all have had women in the White House to help manage the affairs of the presidency.

In this volume, the biographical essays do not give a comprehensive account of each woman's life, or even every aspect of her role as first lady. Instead, my focus is on her political performance. This includes whether she was a political asset to the presidency, her advocacy of issues, her skills in diplomacy and statecraft, and her role in political campaigns and elections. Not every first lady has been enthusiastic about politics, but all have been political partners whether they wanted to be or not.

RATING FIRST LADIES

Eleanor Smeal of the Feminist Majority Fund notes that those first ladies who use their power to champion women's rights have been rated the highest. In an interview for this book, she told me that the first lady's visibility gives her "a real opportunity to help people." Women who seize that opportunity rank among the most popular. Smeal's advice to first ladies is to "be somebody who does something!"

Susan Porter Rose dislikes the concept of rating first ladies, especially when college professors are the ones doing the rating. "I have to confess to you the idea of rating first ladies really turns me off," she told me in an interview. "The idea of academics rating them almost makes me laugh. They're so far out of reality. To be descriptive of first ladies, to be historical about it, that's one thing, but to rate them, I don't see the value of it."

Political insiders like to say that "perception is reality," meaning that what people believe to be true is what matters most in politics. Ratings are just another form of perception. When it comes to first ladies, the matter of perception is complicated.

First ladies, like presidents, are perceived differently over time. The first impression is the contemporaneous perception. It is largely created by what is known and reported as it happens during the first lady's tenure. Every modern White House tries to control this image, just as it does with the presidency itself, although some succeed better than others. Florence Harding had a great public image, because she understood the power of the media and adopted World War I veterans as her "cause" as first lady. This made her widely popular during the Harding administration. If her job performance had been judged during his presidency, she would rate near the top of the scale.

But public relations and political spin, no matter how effective in the short run, rarely endure unless they reflect the underlying political reality. After President Harding died in office, a series of corruption scandals were exposed to public view. Florence went into semiseclusion and spent a month burning incriminating documents—she said they could be taken out of context and misunderstood—but no amount of shredding could preserve Harding's legacy. Today, Florence ranks near the bottom of the scale. Some presidencies and first ladies rise in public esteem over time, too, as the significance of their accomplishments becomes clearer and can be measured against the presidencies that follow. When Bess Truman left the White House, the popularity of the Truman presidency was very low. In hindsight, it is clear that Truman played a major role in winning the Cold War. The positive reevaluation of Harry and Bess Truman took place before her death in 1982.

A final period of reevaluation comes later, usually long after a president and first lady leave office. During the first few years after a presidency ends, White House insiders and cabinet secretaries write their memoirs. It can take decades, however, before the canned memoirs are replaced by candid memoirs, and lifetimes for real secrets like the identity of Deep Throat, for example, to be revealed. Eleanor Roosevelt had been dead for almost two decades before Lorena Hickok's papers were made available to researchers. We will not learn what George H. W. Bush—and Barbara—knew about the Iran-Contra affair so long as the Bush progeny remain active in their own political careers. This is because political insiders have a stake in preserving their access to power. Sometimes documentary evidence surfaces to clear up history's mysteries, but just as often it is destroyed. Many nineteenth-century first ladies burned their political correspondence. Edith Roosevelt, who handled sensitive diplomatic business for Teddy, for example, routinely destroyed her papers. Therefore, a historical reevaluation of a first lady's role, such as the one I am writing, cannot be as complete as we would wish.

Subjectivity is inevitable in assessing a first lady's performance. Political bias has the greatest potential for distorting how a first lady is viewed. Partisan Democrats will view Democratic first ladies more favorably, while partisan Republicans will prefer Republican first ladies. Issues advocates will like those first ladies who champion their causes. Those who believe first ladies should stay out of policy making will favor women whose public interests are apolitical and who pay more attention to White House entertaining and setting fashion trends.

As a former political strategist and White House insider, I have a bias that is job-centered and based on the bottom line. If a first lady is part of a one-term presidency that ends in a failed reelection bid, her job performance can't be judged successful, no matter how much popularity she enjoys. Conversely, she can be extremely controversial, but if she helps her political partner survive an impeachment crisis or achieve a policy objective, she deserves credit. Readers will note that my account of a first lady's accomplishments may, from time to time, seem out of sync with the ratings assigned by the Siena Research Institute poll. This is because my perspective as a political insider differs from that of the academics who were polled by the institute.

Polls have peaks and valleys, and political approval ratings are fleeting; I consider them meaningless unless attached to the uses of power. If popular presidents or first ladies use their political equity to get important things done, that matters. High poll ratings that aren't deployed to achieve results mean nothing, unless one considers popularity in and of itself to be an important achievement. Betty Ford had very high poll ratings, but the Ford presidency was mediocre and ended in a failed reelection bid. George H. W. Bush had great poll ratings following the Gulf War, but he failed to capitalize on them and ended up losing his reelection campaign. Politics is a bottom-line business, and one has to judge both partners by the end result. What did they accomplish? Were they a political success?

Did they achieve the things they thought most important? The answers to these questions are how I evaluate the role of first ladies.

I also take women in politics seriously. In 1994, I had the privilege of running Bernadette Castro's campaign for the same Senate seat Hillary Clinton won in 2000. I like to think Bernadette helped pave the way for New Yorkers to accept a woman in the Senate.

THE SIENA COLLEGE RESEARCH INSTITUTE RATINGS

A woman came up with the idea of polling academic experts to rank first ladies. Professors Doug Lonnstrom and Tom Kelly of the Siena College Research Institute at Siena College, New York, had done several polls of presidential ratings when Lonnstrom's wife suggested they do the same for first ladies.

The result was the 1982 Siena College Research Institute poll. The survey was repeated in 1993 to rate new first ladies and to provide a trend analysis of how first ladies are evaluated over time.

The survey measures the opinions of academic experts. The methodology relies on a written questionnaire that is mailed to a representative cross section of college and university history department chairpersons. They are in turn asked to send the questionnaire to the individual in their department whom they believe is most qualified to evaluate the first ladies.

Each questionnaire contains ten key criteria that Professors Kelly and Lonnstrom have identified, and which they believe pertain to first ladies throughout history. The ten factors that are surveyed are the first lady's intelligence, background for the job, her value to the country, value to the presidency, the extent to which she is her own woman, her integrity, her accomplishments, her leadership, her courage, and her public image. The academic experts assign scores for each first lady on each factor. The composite scores determine the first lady's overall placement.

A "perfect" score is 100 on this scale, but the median score is 60. It is important to note that the first lady who ranks dead last at No. 37 on the 1993 Siena survey scored a composite 52.62 while the first lady who rated No. 8 scored 69.61 points. That means that all twenty-eight first ladies who fell between the bottom and the top ten were evaluated in a range of only 15 points' difference.

What does this mean?

It means that even academic experts have a hard time making distinctions among first ladies. The majority are rated very closely; relatively minor differences in ratings separate the majority from the top ten. Eleanor Roosevelt is the exception. As No. 1, she rates 16 points higher than Rosalynn Carter's No. 5 place showing and almost 10 points above Abigail Adams's No. 3 rating.

Professor Kelly cautioned that surveys of academic experts have hidden weaknesses. The survey respondents are college professors who tend to be more ideologically liberal and more Democratic than the overall population. Another factor is what Professor Kelly called "presentism." Recent first ladies tend to be rated higher because they feature in the "vital memories" of the respondents. Very recent first ladies seem to do well. In the survey's top ten, only 30 percent are from the eighteenth and nineteenth centuries, and 10 percent from the early twentieth century; the remaining 60 percent date from the depression onward.

"The survey tells you more about the professoriate than it does the first ladies," said Professor Kelly.

One hundred twenty-five experts responded to the questionnaire in 1993. One can presume that as interest in first ladies grows, and scholarship in the field evolves, the body of experts responding to future surveys will be larger. As this book was being written, the Siena College Research Institute was about to begin its third first lady survey.

FUTURE OF THE FIRST LADY

Newsweek's Eleanor Clift believes the twenty-first century could mean new vitality in the job of first lady. "Future first ladies are going to be more like Hillary than Barbara Bush or Laura Bush," she told me in an interview, "because more women are working as professionals. The Hillary-type first lady will come back into vogue."

Hillary Clinton was the first first lady to hold a professional degree, but it's unlikely she will be the last. In the future, a presidential spouse may want to continue in her profession.

"One potential Democratic presidential candidate's wife is a physician," Clift said, "and he has suggested that if he wins the presidency, she'll be a practicing physician in Washington."

Nancy Reagan's chief of staff James Rosebush agreed in part: "It does reflect to a certain extent the role of women in American society." He also noted, however, that each individual woman brings her own style to the job.

The role of presidential spouse is bound to change when the first woman is elected president, especially if her husband has an independent career of his own. Will we expect him to confine his role to overseeing White House social events? Or should his wife be free to tap his expertise in policy making? Will he have to find a politically noncontroversial cause to support, or can he take over part of his spouse's political agenda, as Hillary attempted to do with health care reform in 1993? Finally, if Americans accept the idea of a presidential spouse in an equal political role when a man has the job, will the next first lady who follows him have the same degree of freedom?

Hopefully, the answer will be learned sometime in the twenty-first century. Women, it should be noted, are advancing throughout the ranks in politics, although at a very slow pace. One day a woman will become president. Then there is one final question to confront: What will we call her husband?

The Ranking of U.S. First Ladies by Siena Research Institute, 1993 Survey

──── ★ ────

1. Eleanor Roosevelt
2. Hillary Clinton
3. Abigail Adams
4. Dolley Madison
5. Rosalynn Carter
6. Lady Bird Johnson
7. Jacqueline Kennedy
8. Barbara Bush
9. Betty Ford
10. Edith Wilson
11. Bess Truman
12. Martha Washington
13. Lou Hoover
14. Edith Roosevelt
15. Lucy Hayes
16. Louisa Adams
17. Mamie Eisenhower
18. Pat Nixon
19. Grace Coolidge
20. Sarah Polk
21. Ellen Wilson
22. Frances Cleveland

23. Elizabeth Monroe
24. Eliza Johnson
25. Helen Taft
26. Julia Grant
27. Julia Tyler
28. Lucretia Garfield
29. Caroline Harrison
30. Letitia Tyler
31. Abigail Fillmore
32. Ida McKinley
33. Margaret Smith Taylor
34. Jane Pierce
35. Florence Harding
36. Nancy Reagan
37. Mary Lincoln

Rating the First Ladies

★

Martha Dandridge Custis Washington

First Lady: 1789–1797
1st Presidential Administration

Siena Research Institute Rating: 12

". . . the greater part of our happiness or misery depends upon our dispositions, and not upon our circumstances."

British redcoats tried to escape from their encounter with colonial Minute-men at Lexington green. Clouds of black smoke billowed from burning homes. The British, accustomed to the orderly rules of eighteenth-century warfare in which men formed in open lines to shoot at one another en masse, were terrified by the cacophony of unceasing gunfire from behind stone walls, trees, and houses.

Lieutenant John Barker of the Queen's Own Regiment wrote:

> We were fired on from all sides, but mostly from the rear, where peo-ple had hid themselves in houses till we had passed and then fired. The country was an amazing strong one, full of hills, woods, stone walls, which the rebels did not fail to take full advantage of, for they were all lined with people who kept an incessant fire upon us . . . we marched between nine and ten miles, their numbers increasing from all parts, while ours was reducing by deaths, wounds and fa-tigue, and we were totally surrounded with such an incessant fire as it's impossible to conceive.*

From the very first day of the war women became revolutionaries. "Even women had firelocks," wrote an anonymous British observer of the retreat. "One was seen to fire a blunderbuss between her father and her husband from their windows. There they three, with an infant child, soon suffered the fury of the day."*

Women also became targets. Hannah Adams was in bed recovering from childbirth when the retreating British troops broke into her home:

> ". . . three of the soldiers broke into the room in which I was laid on my bed, being scarcely able to walk from my bed to the fire and not having been to my chamber door from my time being delivered in childbirth to that time. One of the said soldiers immediately opened my [bed] curtains with his bayonet fixed and pointing . . . to my breast. I immediately cried out, "For the Lord's sake, don't kill me!"
>
> He replied, "Damn you."
>
> One that stood near said, "We will not hurt the woman if she will go out of the house, but we will surely burn it."
>
> I immediately arose, threw a blanket over me, went out, and crawled into a corn-house near the door with my infant in my arms . . . they immediately set the house on fire, in which I had left five chil-

---

*Indicates text first published in *The Fire of Liberty,* The Folio Society, 1983.

dren and no other person; but the house was in the utmost danger of being utterly consumed.*

The Pennsylvania County of Safety reported after British troops under the command of Lord Cornwallis passed through Pennytown.

Besides the sixteen young women who had fled to the woods to avoid their brutality, and were there seized and carried off, one man had the mortification to have his wife and only daughter (a child of ten years of age) ravished ... another girl of thirteen years of age was taken from her father's house, carried to a barn about a mile [away], there ravished, and afterwards made use of by five more of these brutes.*

The Revolution was, until Vietnam, the longest war in American history. Its scars, human and physical, lie long buried beneath our landscape and in our collective psyche. In 1789, when Martha Washington became our first first lady, these images were fresh and vivid. Their memory animated Martha's sense of public service and patriotic duty. As first lady, fulfilling the promise of the Revolution was foremost in her mind.

She was the first presidential spouse to stand in for the president at a public ceremony. The event was a memorial service in tribute to General Nathanael Greene, a hero of the Revolution. When George Washington was too ill to make an appearance, Martha went in his stead, joining the ranks of dignitaries and members of Congress in attendance.

Most historians depict Martha Washington as a reluctant first lady who found the duties of being the president's wife oppressive and tiresome. This is a misreading of history. Martha Washington was enthusiastic about some duties of the office—just not the social obligations of hosting receptions, dinners, and other state events later thought to be the prime duties of the White House hostess. Anything involving the troops who fought the Revolution kindled her spirit.

Her grandson Custis Washington recalled that war veterans who came to see General Washington but had to be turned away would gladly meet instead with Lady Washington. She often gave small gifts of money to veterans, and enjoyed swapping war stories with them. Sometimes she interceded with her husband on behalf of veterans with legal troubles, urging presidential pardons.

Martha Washington's concern over the plight of Revolution veterans reveals a social consciousness that transcended the shallow life of society drawing rooms to which many women of her social standing were consigned by traditional sex roles. But Martha had never been a traditional female.

She was born to a prominent Virginia family in 1731. Martha was the eldest daughter of John and Frances Dandridge. The family owned a plantation near Williamsburg, the seat of the British colonial governor.

Like many women of her era, she was well schooled in social graces but received little formal education. Poor grammar and spelling plagued her throughout life, but that was little impediment to her. When she had to manage her own business affairs as a young widow, she employed a secretary to take dictation, and then copied the letters in her own hand. As first lady, she read a variety of newspapers daily. This reveals a tenacity of purpose in her character, a trait that manifested itself when she was still just a teenager.

At age seventeen, Martha audaciously pursued Daniel Parke Custis, an eligible bachelor more than twice her her age. They married when she was eighteen, and over the next eight years had four children. Two died as babies, and the two survivors—Patsy and Jack—were just past infancy when Daniel Custis died in 1757.

Suddenly a wealthy widow, Martha's inheritance included hundreds of slaves and seventeen thousand acres of tobacco-growing land. She took charge of her own business affairs, handling commercial correspondence about her tobacco crops with distant business contacts in London despite the limitations of her formal education. She might well have been speaking about herself when she gave advice about independence to her niece many years later:

> I very sincearly [sic] wish you would exert yourself so as to keep all your matters in order yourself without depending upon others as that is the only way to be happy—to have all your business in your own hands without trusting to others. . . . I wish you to be as independent as your circumstances will admit, and to be so, is to exert yourself in the management of your estate. If you do not no one else will.

Martha Dandridge Custis did not remain a widow long. In 1759, she married George Washington. For the next decade and a half, they enjoyed domestic peace, tending to their plantations and participating in the social life of colonial Fredericksburg and Alexandria and Williamsburg.

Until the Revolution.

If there is one concept that summarizes the lives of George and Martha Washington, it is *reluctant duty*. This theme radiates from a letter George wrote to Martha from Philadelphia, where the Second Continental Congress had proclaimed him commander of the Continental army.

> My Dearest,
> I am now set down to write you on a subject which fills me with inexpressible concern, and this concern is greatly aggravated and increased, when I reflect upon the uneasiness which I know it will cause you. It has been determined in Congress that the whole army raised for the defense of the American cause shall be put under my care, and that it is necessary for me to proceed immediately to Boston to take upon me the command of it.
> You may believe me, my dear Patsy, when I assure you in the most solemn manner that, so far from seeking this appointment, I have used every endeavor in my power to avoid it, not only from my unwillingness to part with you and the family, but from a consciousness of its being too great a trust for my capacity, and that I should enjoy more real happiness in one month with you at home. . . . But as it has been a kind of destiny that has thrown me upon this service, I shall hope that my undertaking it is designed to answer some good purpose.*

When the war came, Martha did not wait idly at Mount Vernon. Instead, and despite his qualms, she joined her husband in the field. She is said to have boasted that she had heard the cannon roar for the opening engagements of the war and was there at the close to hear them fall silent, a boast not far removed from fact.

We have a word portrait of Martha Washington with the army in 1777, provided by a visitor, Mrs. Martha Dangerfield Bland, who wrote in a letter to her sister-in-law:

> His worthy lady seems to be in perfect felicity, while she is by the side of her "Old Man," as she calls him. We often make parties on horseback, the General, his Lady, Miss Livingston, and his aides-de-camp . . . at which time General Washington throws off the hero and takes on the chatty agreeable companion. He can be downright impudent sometimes, such impudence, Fanny, as you and I like.*

At her "Old Man's" side, Martha helped transcribe military correspondence, a copious chore in an age before photocopiers and e-mail. This made her privy to matters of military intelligence and strategy, the conditions of the army, and the adequacy—more often inadequacy—of supplies, clothes, ammunition, food.

Martha threw herself into the war. She formed organizations of women to support it. They met in places like Fredericksburg's Kenmore Inn, built originally as a town residence in 1752 for George Washington's sister Betty. The women assisted in bandage making, packaging gunpowder into precise quantities so it could be speedily used to charge a rifle or musket in the heat of battle, and operating hospitals for the injured. They also provided relief for the families left behind and those destituted by British depredations such as the burning of homes, the killing of livestock, and the destruction of crops. For her efforts, "Lady" Washington earned the enmity of the British, who threatened at one point to take her hostage.

Should it be surprising, then, that this woman of action found the daily social duties of the presidency tedious? During Washington's two terms of office, the President's House moved from New York to Philadelphia. In each city, not only did Martha have to meet the obligations of presidential hostess, but she and her husband had to create the traditions appropriate to the new republic.

It would have been simplest to copy the courts of Europe, with their easily imitated stylized mannerisms and well-delineated social etiquette. Her youthful experiences growing up just outside colonial Williamsburg certainly gave Martha exposure to courtly graces. The General and the Lady, however, chose to set different standards in presidential entertainment.

Establishing the young republic's legitimacy was their chief aim, accomplished through their first presidential protocols, an uneasy blend of plebeian equality and an aristocratic attention to rank.

On the plebeian side, they opened the President's House to the public for New Year's Day. This tradition, which lasted until 1930, meant a willingness to mingle, literally, with the people of the land.

On the aristocratic side, Fridays were set aside for formal, invitation-only receptions. Guests were announced as they entered. Hierarchy dictated the seating, with President Washington passing by the seated guests to say a few words. The women moved off into a separate room for refreshments, while the men talked politics. The atmosphere was deliberately austere. There were no amusements or merriments as would be found at a European court. They were dignified occasions meant in large part to impress European ambassadors with the seriousness of purpose of the young republic. The receptions ended promptly at nine in the evening.

Martha dressed simply, ignoring prevailing fashion trends. Her preferred form of transportation was, however, a gilded coach, in which she performed daily rounds of returning calls from visitors.

Soon fractious newspapers criticized her for acting like a queen. Others complained that the presidential protocols weren't courtly enough, and that a European monarchess would have a much more impressive royal retinue. The press criticism of Lady Washington formed another presidential precedent.

Martha is said to have expressed opinions on policy matters, especially foreign affairs. The Washington presidency was characterized by a suspicion of foreign "entanglements" that would today be called isolationist. Washington made formal peace with Britain through Jay's Treaty, signed a proclamation of neutrality to avoid being drawn into European wars, and signed Pinckney's Treaty establishing relations with Spain. In her correspondence, Martha then expressed the view that it was time to put the turmoil and animosities of the Revolution to rest by restoring good relations with England.

Determined to see that the executive power of the presidency was kept within its proper limits, Washington neither expanded the power of the chief executive imperiously nor allowed it to be encroached upon during his two terms of office. He was wary of Congress's tendency to erode presidential power, especially in matters of foreign policy. He also had to assert the authority of the federal government over the states. He sent troops into Pennsylvania to crush the Whiskey Rebellion, the first real test of the federal government's powers. After eight years, he left behind a solid foundation that showed that the new Constitution worked as designed, a stark contrast to the fate of most revolutionary governments.

For George and Martha, the Revolution and the presidency were duties, solemn obligations. For them, the concept of liberty and self-determination for America became more than a dream. We will never know with certainty the extent to which Martha's views may have influenced the Washington administration's policies. She kept her counsel private, so much so that little of it creeps into her surviving correspondence. It is hard, if not impossible, not to think of her as a committed political partner. The thought of her sitting by candlelight copying military orders and correspondence during the darkest days of the Revolution, or riding horseback across wintry fields at the general's side, are too vivid. After George's death in 1799, she destroyed the private letters between them, written over the course of a tumultuous two decades in public life. Had these letters survived, we would have a fuller understanding of this unique partnership. But even without them, it is clear that Martha Washington embraced her fate.

These words from this supposedly unlettered woman echo lines from Shakespeare's *Hamlet*. "I cannot blame him for having acted according to his ideas of duty in obeying the voice of his country," she wrote to a friend. "I am still determined to be cheerful and to be happy, in whatever situation I may be."

Martha herself died on May 22, 1802, leaving us too little autobiographical record of her political life. After she was no longer first lady, she expressed her political views openly to friends who called on her at Mount Vernon. We can only guess what she may have said to George privately when she was first lady.

Today, we take for granted America's emergence from a colonial power to a superpower; we tend to underestimate the challenges the country's founders faced. If modern historians had a more complete appreciation of the difficulty of winning a revolution and establishing a functioning new government, Martha Washington would rate in the top ten first ladies. She was not a bystander at the nation's emergence.

Abigail Smith Adams

First Lady: 1797–1801
2nd Presidential Administration
Siena Research Institute Rating: 3

"All men would be tyrants if they could."

Abigail Adams is America's first modern first lady. If television talk shows or talk radio had existed in her era, she would have been a frequent, and outspoken, guest. While her predecessor, Martha Washington, preferred to cloak her political beliefs from public view during the eight years of the Washington administration, Abigail was the opposite.

Abigail wanted to have a voice in the fledgling republic's political dialogue. She wrote letters on policy and politics to leading newspapers of the day, with the clear intention of having her views published.

These were not letters-to-the-editor in the modern sense. Today, a politician who wants to make an impact on an issue would do so in an interview with a journalist or by holding a news conference. The eighteenth-century equivalent was to send a letter for publication. In turn, political opponents would write rebuttals; sometimes the cycle of point and counterpoint would continue for months. The great debate over the revolutionary nation's new government, published as the *Federalist Papers*, appeared originally as newspaper columns. Sometimes authors used their real names, and just as frequently they wrote under pseudonyms.

Abigail Adams's letters were published under a pseudonym or anonymously, as was typical of newspapers of that period. In the tight-knit community of Philadelphia, where President Adams remained until the last four months of his one term in office, editors knew who authored the columns they published, and in short order so did all the politicians in town, friend and foe alike. This was political activism in the purest sense.

As first lady, Abigail set important precedents in other ways. She listened regularly to floor debates in the House of Representatives. She became involved in personnel decisions, making recommendations to her husband concerning political appointments. She was politically active in the partisan sense, too, so much so that Anti-Federalist congressman Albert Gallatin called her "Mrs. President not of the United States, but of a faction." Two centuries later, Republicans made similar complaints about another first lady, Hillary Clinton.

It is true that there are important differences between Abigail Adams's political activism and that of twentieth- and twenty-first-century first ladies. She did not have the right to vote. She could not run for political office. It was impossible for her to emerge as a public political power in her own right. The fact that her power derived from her husband's career, however, doesn't diminish the corresponding fact that she did exercise influence in party politics, domestic and foreign policy, and political patronage.

If she had had it her way, she might have done far more. While her husband was drafting the Constitution, Abigail lobbied him to include women's rights. "I desire you would remember the ladies and be more generous and favorable to them than your ancestors," she wrote. "Do not push such unlimited power into the hands of the husbands. Remember, all men would be tyrants if they could. If particular care and attention is not paid to the ladies, we are determined to foment a rebellion and will not hold ourselves bound by any laws in which we have no voice or representation."

Understanding this woman who overtly used her power and seems so at odds with her times calls for a close look. Born in November 1744 at Weymouth, Massachusetts, Abigail Smith came into the world with a political pedigree. Her mother, a Quincy, came from one of New England's leading families. Her grandfather held office in the Massachusetts legislature and was a justice of its supreme court. Her father, William Smith, was a Quaker parson whose enlightened views extended to the education of his daughter.

Although she did not attend school in any formal sense, Abigail Smith's homeschooling was thorough. She learned Latin, history, and literature, and read Shakespeare and Molière. Contemporary political philosophy also formed part of her education. While she was still a teenager, she was exposed to the thinking of John Locke by reading the lively political exchanges published in *The Spectator,* a widely read London magazine of arts and letters.

She met her future husband, John Adams, when she was eighteen. She is described by her contemporaries as a tall and thin girl, with intelligent eyes. For two years, the couple carried on a courtship marked by strong will and wit. At one point, John Adams sent Abigail a none-too-gentle letter chronicling her faults. She replied that she enjoyed reading it as much as other people would relish reading about their strong points, and then went on to list his shortcomings. This pattern of point, counterpoint, and a willingness to debate show Abigail's independent streak.

John Adams actually lacked the family pedigree of the Smiths. His training as a Harvard lawyer was not viewed as prestigiously in the eighteenth century as it is today. Still, Abigail and John married in 1768. Their first home together was a place in Boston they called "The White House"; perhaps it was a premonition. Thirty-two years later, Abigail Adams would become the first first lady to occupy the President's House, known today as the White House.

Despite her family's misgivings about the marriage, young John Adams soon rose to political prominence in ways the old Quincy clan would have envied. He was one of the planners behind the Boston Tea Party. He served in the First Continental Congress in 1774. He was on the drafting committee for the Declaration of Independence and the Constitution. During the Revolution, Adams negotiated aid from France and the Netherlands. He negotiated the terms of the peace treaty between Great Britain and the new United States in 1783, and stayed on for another five years as minister to the Court of St. James. He was George Washington's vice president from 1789 until 1797, and then he assumed the mantle of the presidency.

During his early career, when Adams served as member of the Continental Congress during the Revolution, Abigail managed the family farm and home in Quincy, Massachusetts, while he commuted between Philadelphia and Massachusetts. Abigail was often alone for the nine years between 1774 and 1783. She effectively raised the couple's four children almost alone.

Like Martha Washington, she aided in the Revolution as well. Abigail melted pewter to make bullets for the underequipped colonial troops at the battle of Bunker Hill. She certainly must have known about the Boston Tea Party plot. In every other way, Abigail had her husband's confidence. She was truly a revolutionary.

During his absences, Abigail sent John as many as three letters in a single day. Imagine what she might have done with e-mail! These weren't letters about ordinary household news. She reported political trends, the public mood, hot issues—the kind of political intelligence good politicians crave. In addition to news, she offered her own insights and judgment, prompting John Adams to remark that they contained "more good thoughts, fine strokes, and mother wit in them than I hear in a whole week."

After England and the United States made peace in the treaty of 1783 (under the Articles of Confederation, the new republic had no president and was governed by the Continental Congress; it would take half a decade before the new Constitution was ratified and George Washington unanimously elected president in 1789), John served as minister to the Court of St. James and Abigail journeyed to London with him. Aside from Boston, she had never been to a city, much less the capital of a world power. London doesn't seem to have intimidated her, however. She scouted for a suitable ambassadorial residence and found one at Grosvenor Square, where the U.S. embassy is still located today. Over the next decade and a half, she lived in Paris, New York, Philadelphia, and finally the newly built federal city we know today as Washington, D.C.

When she was first lady, Martha Washington considered the younger woman a valuable ally. Abigail had had time to polish her social skills in Europe's diplomatic circles, making her a useful adviser on etiquette and politics to Lady Washington. During the Washington administration, Martha kept Abigail close at hand on social occasions, always reserving a seat to her right for Mrs. Adams. Given Abigail's outspokenness, can there be any doubt that she was also a political adviser to Lady Washington?

The tradition of weekly presidential receptions established by the Washingtons was continued under the Adams administration, but changed to Tuesday and Thursday nights. Because there was as yet no official entertainment budget, the cost came straight from the president's pocket. As with Mrs. Washington, Abigail's time as first lady included the tiresome necessity of returning social calls. In a letter to her daughter, Abigail wrote that she had returned fifteen calls in one day, despite the difficulty of travel in "the wilderness city" of Washington where she said callers came from as far as three or four miles away and "the return of one of them is the work of a day." Like Mrs. Washington, too, Abigail enjoyed military affairs. In New Jersey, she toured a federal military encampment and later boasted that she had reviewed the troops as a stand-in for the commander in chief!

Days as first lady were arduous. Abigail awakened at five in the morning to devote her first several hours to family affairs. By eleven, the official day began. Sometimes as many as sixty visitors would call on Abigail in a day. In the late afternoon, she made her calls, returning to the presidential mansion around seven in the evening. Often there were official dinners to be hosted for important congressmen or senators, the cabinet and the diplomatic corps.

One of the greatest challenges facing the Adams administration was remaining neutral in the growing Napoleonic Wars between England and France. Because the French had rendered invaluable assistance to the United States during the Revolution, they expected American support in return. President Adams's instinct mirrored the one that Washington would have had. Foreign entanglements, he felt, were best avoided. To pressure Adams into fighting with them, however, the French began seizing American merchant ships and demanding the payment of bribes. By interfering with the shipping on which America's economy depended, the French hoped to force Adams to accept their terms. The ploy backfired badly. Adams refused to negotiate with the French diplomats, and instead of meeting their demands for loans to the French government and payment of bribes, Adams created the Department of the Navy and ordered American merchant ships to be armed. It was this episode that prompted the now-famous line, "Millions for defense, but not one cent for tribute."

In response to the growing threat of entanglement in the Napoloenic Wars, with their complex international alliances and intrigues, Congress passed the Alien and Sedition Acts. The laws gave the federal government the power to deport aliens, arrest citizens, and close newspapers by order of the president. Abigail especially feared the influx of French immigrants fleeing the chaos of the French Revolution. She suspected many were secretly plotting to overthrow the new American republic. Adams signed the controversial law, which had a sunset provision requiring Congress to renew the acts at the end of two years or they would automatically expire. After September 11, 2001, this same kind of legislation was debated by Congress regarding powers to be granted to President Bush to deal with terrorism.

Abigail Adams was among those who thought war with the French was inevitable. The record of her correspondence shows that she wanted a declaration of war in 1798, when tensions were highest. Abigail had been horrified at the excesses of the French Revolution, particularly the indiscriminate use of the guillotine and the descent into the Reign of Terror. Abigail loathed what she described as "king-killing" and "anarchy, chaos, murder" running rampant. She believed that France, which then had a formidable presence in North America extending through the entire Mississippi basin down into New Orleans, intended to take over the entire continent by fomenting a slave rebellion. Her fears were not entirely unfounded. The threat of a slave uprising in coordination with a French military invasion of the southern United States prompted President Adams to appoint Charles Pinckney, his minister to France, to head up federal troops in Georgia, although some progress was being made in negotiations with France. If Abigail's political judgment had prevailed, the United States would have been drawn into the Napoleonic Wars. On this subject, she and her husband disagreed. History has shown that she was clearly wrong about French aims in North America, which lowers her ranking substantially in the diplomatic arena.

Adams managed to avoid getting entangled in Europe's wars and, ultimately, concluded a peace treaty with France that respected American neutrality. Some historians believe that this ranks as one of the most important accomplishments of the Adams administration, and helped prevent the fragile new republic from becoming ensnarled in a war that could have meant its destruction.

Adams's contemporaries were not so appreciative of his crowning accomplishment. His reelection bid failed, and America's second president became its first one-term president.

John and Abigail Adams retired from power. Despite Abigail's protestations (Martha Washington made them, too) that political life robbed her of precious time, it is clear that the trade-off between private life and public power was not entirely one of self-sacrifice. As Abigail wrote:

> I can truly and from my heart say that the most mortifying circumstance attendant upon my retirement from public Life is, that my power of doing good to my fellow creatures is curtailed and diminished, but tho' the means is wanting, the will and the wish remain.

These are words of a true activist. Thomas Jefferson's correspondence from the period of his semiretirement at Monticello echoes similar themes to that of Martha Washington and Abigail Adams. They all speak about their personal sacrifices and "lost years" of public service, and their preference for the pleasures of attending to their private affairs. Jefferson in particular complained about the burdens of public office, the impossibility of tempting him to return public life, and his absolute contentment to remain at Monticello enjoying the life of a gentleman farmer. He was most outspoken on these points shortly before returning to power as Adams's vice president!

Many historians writing about Abigail Adams have focused on her laments about the high personal cost of public service. In this she isn't unusual. Most people who devote years to politics have the same love-hate relationship with power. They crave a zone of privacy that the media, fellow politicians, and the public simply will not give them—but some crave power more.

Abigail Adams's statement that her will to use power remained although the means were no longer within her reach reveals the modern nature of this unusual woman. Unlike Martha Washington, for Abigail Adams her view of her role was about power and equality, an equal voice in shaping the new nation's affairs.

"If a woman does not hold the Reigns [sic] of Government," she had written to John, "I see no reason for her not judging how they are conducted." Abigail believed that a woman had every right to have and to voice an opinion about how government was run, even if she was barred from voting and blocked from holding office.

Both among the political elite of Philadelphia and the people, there is little disagreement about the fact that Abigail Adams was a popular first lady. She even had a company of Massachusetts infantry, the Lady Adams

Rangers, named in her honor. She was less successful as a social trend-setter—something she had hoped to be. Abigail had been impressed in Europe by the fineness of European cloth and tailoring and the social refinement of courtly manners. She tried to set these trends in her presidential protocol and entertaining, but the political backlash of the election of 1800, which branded John as a monarchist, and the self-consciously plebeian tone set in the Jefferson administration pointed to the fact that in this matter, she had been unsuccessful.

Abigail Adams's political influence and activism, however, rank her high among first ladies of any era. Her diplomatic judgment, especially regarding the handling of the tension between France and the United States and her desire for a declaration of war at the height of the crisis, was wanting, but she possessed formidable skills in politics and statecraft as well as international experience, and she didn't hesitate to use her influence on questions of foreign policy.

As a role model, she ranks at the very top. Abigail Adams set a high standard not only for herself but for other women as well, and she would have set an even higher one had she been successful in removing the legal restrictions that limited her and other women to subsidiary social roles. In a different century, she might have been an Eleanor Roosevelt or a Hillary Clinton. For any time, however, she is a role model for independence, self-assertion, and political activism. Abigail Adams's high standing in the Siena Research poll reflects her strong advocacy on behalf of women's rights. Eleanor Smeal of the Feminist Majority Fund observed that first ladies of any era who stand up for women tend to rate higher than those who do not.

Martha Jefferson Randolph and Mary Jefferson Eppes

First Ladies: 1801–1809
3rd Presidential Administration
Siena Research Institute Rating: 19*

Martha Jefferson Randolf

Well accomplished women
—Reverend Manasseh Cutler

19

For the two terms of the Jefferson administration, two daughters took upon themselves the duties of first lady. When Thomas Jefferson became president in 1801, he had been a widower for nineteen years.

The Revolution had taken its toll on the Jefferson family, affecting the pregnancies of Martha Wayles Skelton, Thomas's wife. Concerned about his wife's frailty during the period, Jefferson resigned from the Continental Congress after serving in the crucial days of 1775–1776, the most intense period of revolutionary fervor. He had authored the Declaration of Independence, a document that seems almost divinely inspired in its ability to express sweeping political concepts with such economy of language. To stay closer to his family, he had had to turn down a diplomatic post in Paris serving alongside Benjamin Franklin. Instead, he threw himself into Virginia politics, drafting the famous Statute on Religious Liberty he considered one of his three crowning accomplishments in life—ranking alongside his authorship of the Declaration of Independence and founding of the University of Virginia, and becoming governor of the colony in 1771.

When the British invaded Richmond in the winter of 1781, Martha fled the capital with a newborn baby just a few weeks old. The child died less than two months later. Barely a month after that, the family had to flee British troops again, this time when they raided Monticello. Martha died in September 1782, only a few months after giving birth to a baby daughter. Jefferson's account book for September 6, 1782, said only:

> My dear wife died this day at 11:45 A.M.

This normally loquacious man never committed his memories of that marriage to writing. To his oldest daughter, also named Martha, we owe the observation of his grief; she wrote about it fifty years after her mother's death. For three weeks, Jefferson closeted himself at Monticello, pacing agitatedly, until physically spent.

"He kept his room for three weeks and I was never a moment from his side," Jefferson's daughter wrote. "He walked almost incessantly night and day only lying down occasionally when nature was completely exhausted. . . . When at last he left his room he rode out and from that time he was incessantly on horseback rambling about the mountain in the least frequented roads and just as often through the woods; in those melan-

---

*The Siena Research Institute poll for 1982 rated only Martha Jefferson Randolph. Neither Martha nor Mary was included in more recent Siena polls, which are limited strictly to presidents' wives.

choly rambles I was his constant companion, a solitary witness to many a violent burst of grief. . . ."

His redheaded ten-year-old daughter subsequently went with him to France when Thomas finally returned to the Continental Congress in 1783–1784 and accepted a diplomatic posting to France to replace Benjamin Franklin. For the next five years, Martha was educated at the Abbaye Royale de Panthemont, outside Paris. At the age of seventeen, she married a cousin, Thomas Randolph Mann Jr. Although she had her own family by the time her father became president, Martha managed to spend seven weeks in the winter of 1801–1802, at the beginning of her father's term of office, handling the social duties of first lady.

They were crucial weeks for Jefferson. The capital was badly polarized between the Federalists and Republicans, the dominant political parties of the day.

A staunch Republican, Jefferson's political views were anathema to the Federalists, who had held the presidency for the first twelve years under the new Constitution. The split between the two factions had grown intense by the time of Washington's retirement from the presidency, resulting in the electoral college selecting Federalist Adams as president and Republican Jefferson as vice president in 1797.

The chief difference between the two parties concerned the power of the federal government. Federalists like Washington and Adams wanted a strong central government. To the Republicans, this seemed monarchical, an effort to reimpose the powers of the British Crown that the colonists had so recently broken free of, but under an American guise. The Federalists in turn were deeply suspicious that the Republicans, with their idealistic faith in the people, would turn out to be dangerous social levelers who could unleash the powers of mob rule. The historical backdrop for this rivalry was the French Revolution, which began with an antimonarchical political revolution in the name of liberty. Many Americans at first sympathized with the French cause. As it degenerated, however, into class warfare and a reign of terror by guillotine, and then spiraled even further into counterrevolution and the dictatorship of Napoléon Bonaparte, the Federalists concluded that common people simply could not be trusted with too much self-government. French intrigues and the war scare during the Adams presidency intensified these concerns.

The presidential election of 1800 was the first negative political campaign, it should be noted. Adams's supporters warned that Jefferson and the Republicans would unleash anarchy. Jefferson newspapers carried the preposterous rumor that Adams planned to marry one of King George III's daughters and bring America back under royal dominion. The result was an election so hotly contested that it produced a tie for the presidency and required thirty-six votes by the House of Representatives before Jefferson was declared the winner.

Jefferson, therefore, wanted to create a tone of bipartisanship from the beginning. Outgoing president John Adams, however, did not come to the Senate to hear Jefferson's inaugural address, considered one of the greatest speeches in American political history. Had he done so, Adams would have been as surprised as others in the audience to hear Jefferson emphasize common ground between the two factions, declaring, "We are all republicans; we are all federalists."

This is the context in which Martha began her newly found role. Her decision to leave her own family and young children to act as first lady for her father and help him set the new tone in Washington could not have been easy. Her own husband had a raging temper and most probably resented the absence.

Aided by his Martha, Thomas set about transforming the social style set by Washington and Adams. The formal receptions that Republicans had criticized as too similar to those of royal courts were phased out in favor of informal entertaining. Jefferson also began rarely dining alone. In fact, he usually had the company of eight to ten people with Martha acting as hostess.

In place of the stiff formality and strict hierarchical rules set by Washington and Adams, Thomas Jefferson introduced a degree of egalitarianism into these dinners. To avoid rigidity of seating arrangements, Jefferson ordered a round dining table, which allowed all his guests to engage equally in conversation.

This is not to say that dining was less elegant. Jefferson had a French chef and a French steward and served his guests a sophisticated cuisine. His expenses for entertainment and alcohol were enormous. He also insisted on paying all the costs associated with Martha's stay in Washington himself, including new clothes, which Dolley Madison helped pick out.

Jefferson's younger daughter Mary, often called Maria by the family, also stayed with him periodically in Washington. In the winter of 1802–1803, the two girls played the role of "first lady" together. They made a good impression even with Federalists such as the Reverend Manasseh Cutler, who attended Jefferson's first formal White House dinner of the social season and found the two to be "well-accomplished women, very delicate and tolerably handsome."

Across the Potomac River at Mount Vernon, on the other hand, Martha Washington made no pretense about her dislike for Jefferson. Any restraint about open expression of her political views vanished after her husband's death. To visitors, she described Jefferson as a vile demagogue.

Still, the tone set by Jefferson's embrace of bipartisanship seemed to temper "factionalism." Aside from openly partisan Federalist newspapers, which maintained an unrelenting barrage of attacks on Jefferson throughout his political career and spawned the myth of his fathering children with Sally Hemings, a slave, the opposition seemed to melt away when met by Jefferson's charming daughters.

In addition to having Martha and Mary with him at the President's House, Jefferson also had the extended company of his sons-in-law. Both Martha's husband Thomas Randolph Mann and Mary's husband John Eppes were elected to Congress in 1802. They stayed with Jefferson when Congress was in session.

In 1804, Mary died. She was twenty-five years old. She had often expressed anxiety about her older sister Martha, who was physically stronger and emotionally closer to Jefferson. He himself considered them equals, writing in mourning to a friend that "half of all I had" is now gone.

Martha continued to stay at the President's House for extended periods. At the start of Jefferson's second term of office in 1805, she remained with him for several months. It was during this visit that she established a precedent for a first lady when she gave birth to her eighth child. James Madison Randolph was the first baby born in the White House.

Today, the Jefferson administration is considered one of the country's great presidencies. Concerned about French encroachments on the new United States, Jefferson persuaded Congress to secretly give him two million dollars to negotiate with Napoléon Bonaparte. He used the money to open the bargaining in what would become the Louisiana Purchase, doubling the size of the United States by buying the vast lands stretching from the Mississippi basin to the Rockies at a price of about three cents an acre. Jefferson sponsored the Lewis and Clark expedition to the Pacific, to chart these new territories and open them to commerce and eventual settlement. Then, close to the end of his second term, Jefferson signed legislation abolishing the slave trade.

Deeply in debt from the expense of entertaining over the eight years of his presidency Jefferson ultimately retired to his Virginia home, Monticello. There, to gain money, he negotiated the sale of his precious collection of books. They became the basis of the Library of Congress.

Martha and her family also moved to Monticello in 1809. Her father died in 1826, and her husband died two years later. Monticello was subsequently sold to satisfy the debts of their estates, and Martha spent her remaining life staying at the homes of her twelve living children. She died at the age of sixty-seven.

Dolley Payne Todd Madison

First Lady: 1809–1817
4th Presidential Administration

Siena Research Institute Rating: 4

"And now, my dear sister, I must leave this house, or the retreating army will make me a prisoner in it . . . when I shall again write to you, or where I shall be tomorrow, I cannot tell!"

In 1985, when the White House facade was stripped for restoration and repainting at the beginning of Reagan's second term, workers found vivid reminders of the Madison administration. Around the edges of windows were long black stains, indelible scorch marks left from the British when they sacked and burned the President's House—and other Washington landmarks—during the War of 1812.

This is how we remember Dolley Madison best, saving artworks and national treasures from destruction while British troops advanced in 1814. Commander in Chief James Madison had left Dolley to direct troops in the field that August. It must have been a poignant parting. The British commander had been threatening to take Dolley hostage and parade her through the streets of London, just as victorious Roman generals had done with captives centuries before.

The new federal city was thought to be well fortified. Down the Potomac from the Capitol, Fort Washington and Fort Hunt straddled a narrow stretch of the river. Their artillery batteries were a classic barrier against invasion by a foreign fleet, part of Pierre L'Enfant's design to make Washington an impregnable city. The British, however, circumvented the static fortress defenses entirely by landing in Maryland. Following the defeat of U.S. troops at the battle of Bladensburg, the city was virtually defenseless.

Dolley watched with a spyglass from the roof as panicked Washingtonians left the city in all directions. She had in her possession the Constitution, the Declaration of Independence, and as many cabinet papers—the official records of President Madison's cabinet meetings as well as the confidential advice of cabinet officers—as she could cram into a carriage trunk. She collected these priceless manuscripts along with the Gilbert Stuart portrait of George Washington, some red curtains, and a few pieces of silverware. She managed to flee the White House, guarded by one sword-waving officer, just before the British arrived. The White House would have burned to the ground, but rain saved the four external walls, leaving a gutted shell. Today, the Stuart portrait of Washington is the only furnishing that remains from the original White House.

Dolley Madison's act of bravery earned her immortality. Renowned before the war as a gracious hostess and fashion trendsetter, her heroism revealed that she was much more than a society doyenne.

Dolley was born to John and Mary Coles Payne, a Quaker couple, in 1768 in North Carolina. She was fifteen when her father moved the family to cosmopolitan Philadelphia. Here she met a Quaker attorney named John Todd. They married in 1790. Soon the couple had two children.

Philadelphia was thriving as the nation's capital, but the city's vitality was short-lived. In 1793, an epidemic of yellow fever struck. Five thousand people died in five months. Among them were Dolley's husband and youngest child.

At age twenty-five, she was a widow and a single mother. Her brother-in-law administered her husband's estate, forcing Dolley and her son Payne into near poverty before it was finally relinquished to her.

Soon the tall, full-figured widow with the piercing blue eyes and black hair had suitors. Among them was James Madison, a hero of the Revolution and one of the principal writers of the U.S. Constitution. Congressman Madison was seventeen years older and several inches shorter than Dolley Todd. The seemingly odd match was encouraged by first lady Martha Washington, by marriage a distant relative of Dolley. She summoned the young woman to meet her and pointedly asked about the courtship. Then before giving Dolley her leave, Martha let her know that she and George looked on the match favorably.

James and Dolley Madison were married a few months later, in September 1794. Because "Jemmy" was not Quaker, Dolley was ousted from the Society of Friends. Yellow fever had already severed many of her family ties to the faith in any event. She accepted her excommunication as a form of emancipation that freed her to indulge in pleasurable social pastimes, dress stylishly, and embrace life fully. This liberating impulse included a new sense of her own independence. Instead of subordinating her property rights to her new husband, for example, Dolley kept the Todd house in her name. The rental income she received as a result was hers alone, and she spent it on fashionable clothing and to indulge her passion for snuff.

Marrying a congressman brought Dolley Madison inside Philadelphia's political and social circles. She was gifted with social graces, had a knack for remembering names and faces, and compensated for James's inability to engage in small talk and put people at their ease. She was a natural hostess.

In 1801, Jefferson made Madison his secretary of state. Dolley now ably entertained diplomats as well as politicians, and as her social skills grew Jefferson frequently called on her to assist in entertaining his guests at the President's House. By the time she became first lady in 1809, Dolley Madison was already well known in political circles and had ample experience in the demands of the job.

Dolley made a splash from the start of the Madison administration, beginning with a presidential first—an inaugural ball. She dressed for the occasion, reported Margaret Bayard Smith at the time:

She had on a pale, buff-colored velvet, made plain, with a very long train, but not the least trimming, and beautiful pearl necklace, earrings, and bracelets. Her head dress was a turban of the same coloured velvet, and white satin (from Paris) with two superb plumes, the bird of paradise feathers.

Margaret Smith, a novelist and writer who became Dolley's friend, was to play an important role in making Dolley Madison a national celebrity. Margaret's husband, Samuel, published the *National Intelligencer,* the country's first newspaper with nationwide distribution. As the *Intelligencer* reported on Dolley Madison's entertaining, taste in fashions, and even favorite pets, women across the country emulated her style. The publicity made her a national trendsetter, the way movie and television celebrities are today.

Dolley's first innovation in White House entertaining was to bring back weekly receptions like the ones Martha Washington and Abigail Adams had held, but which Thomas Jefferson had jettisoned in favor of smaller dinner parties. The first of Dolley's "levees," as they were called, was held on Wednesday, March 30, 1809. She dressed regally, preferring the latest Parisian fashion, but she also managed to put guests so much at ease that her "crushes," as they soon became known, were fun affairs.

Dolley circulated freely among her guests while her less sociable husband huddled off into a corner of one of the reception rooms deep in political conversation. One delicacy that Dolley served at her reception has become an American favorite. It was ice cream, a French dish some say Jefferson introduced her to, which she served in pastry shells buffet-style to the guests. Dolley shared the recipe willingly when guests asked for it. Soon the ice cream rage swept the country.

The Madisons also hosted dinners limited to twenty or thirty guests. These exclusive affairs gave the president an opportunity to sound out political foes and allies in an intimate atmosphere. Dolley Madison sat at the head of the table for these events, reportedly because her husband prized her tact and finesse in drawing out conversation among the guests. But surely James also knew that an attractive and vivacious wife was a political asset, and placing her prominently among the guests only added to the allure of a White House invitation.

Just as Jefferson often relied on Dolley's help as hostess when he entertained women at the White House, a staple of her duties as first lady involved socializing with the wives of the officials who peopled Washington. This was especially important when Congress was in session.

Dolley called these occasions "dove parties." They may have served more than a social purpose by enabling Dolley to sound out the women in order to learn about their husbands' political leanings on issues of the day.

All this entertaining came at a price. Dolley redecorated the White House at a cost of eleven thousand dollars, a fortune at the time. The domestic staff was doubled to handle her extensive guest lists, and she added new silver and china. Her wardrobe was costly as well. The American consul in France complained of the amount of time he spent searching for the latest fashion items on "Lady Presidentress" Madison's shopping lists.

From her taste for snuff to her love of ice cream to her pet parrot, Dolley was copied by women everywhere. Abigail Adams had tried to be a fashion trendsetter, self-consciously choosing silk over the plain muslin Martha Washington preferred for her wardrobe. Nevertheless, she failed to ignite interest in the way Dolley managed without even trying. The outward trappings of her appearance and preferences might be what the women were copying, but what they really wanted to achieve was Dolley Madison's natural ebullience.

Despite this flair for life, Dolley's passions apparently did not extend to politics. While she did attend Senate and House debates and encouraged other women to do the same, there is little record of any effort to exercise political influence in her own right.

Abigail Adams left an unmistakable record of political activism in her correspondence with her husband. Martha Washington was discretion itself as first lady, to the point that she burned all her correspondence with her husband after his death. Later visitors to Mount Vernon, however, found her unrestrained in her political views, which she expressed so freely that there can be little doubt politics was a lifetime interest. This is not the case with Dolley Madison. It is true that she had some influence on matters of patronage, urging the political appointments of social friends. Compared with Abigail Adams, however, who eagerly embraced her power over political patronage, Dolley used it sparingly. The writer Washington Irving, for example, was disappointed when she made no effort to help him secure a diplomatic sinecure.

His presidency dominated by the hostilities that came to a head in the War of 1812, James Madison took office as the Napoleonic Wars raged across Europe. France and England, the two prime antagonists, were pitted squarely against one another with America uncomfortably in the middle. At the inaugural ball, a minor diplomatic incident involving all three countries was avoided when both the French and English ambassadors sought to be seated next to Dolley Madison. She coolly avoided a gaffe by taking control of the situation and seating herself squarely between the two competitors.

President Madison, however, was unable to accomplish the same trick. He tried to achieve a balancing act between France and England, but American diplomacy and trade sanctions failed. Three days before Jefferson's term expired, he signed the Non-Intercourse Act of 1809 barring trade with France and Britain in retaliation for their interference with American merchant ships. Madison enforced the new law but it had little effect, so trade relations with France and Britain were restored on the condition that they respected American neutrality. The French agreed, but Britain's refusal led to new trade sanctions imposed against only it. In 1811, the British instigated a Shawnee Indian uprising. Although the Shawnees, along with other allied tribes, were decisively defeated by General—and future president—William Henry Harrison at the battle of Tippecanoe, the provocation drew President Madison into a declaration of war. An American attack on Canada gave the British an excuse for their invasion and the destruction of Washington. The battle of New Orleans in 1815 created a new national hero and restored the American pride battered so badly by the sacking of Washington. General Andrew Jackson's defenders were outnumbered two to one by the British troops advancing on New Orleans, but the seasoned Indian fighters and frontiersmen under Jackson's command were more than a match for the redcoats. They routed the British army in a battle in which twenty-six hundred redcoats were killed, while Jackson lost only eight men. "The Battle of New Orleans" became a popular ballad that is still played by bands today in Irish American pubs while crowds sing along.

Dolley Madison gave Andrew Jackson a hero's reception when he came to Washington in 1816. Her guests barely had room to move. To provide better lighting, so she said, she had slaves serve as human candleholders throughout the reception rooms.

It can be argued that in important respects Dolley Madison expanded the role of presidential spouse. She was the first first lady to grant a formal newspaper interview. During the war, she gave short patriotic speeches, setting another important precedent. After the war, she undertook a civic role as trustee of the Washington City Orphans Asylum and rallied other society ladies to the cause. Dolley not only donated twenty dollars and a cow, but took up sewing clothes for the orphans as well; she encouraged other women to do the same. This is the first documented instance of a first lady using her influence and leadership position to advance a charitable cause.

Ceremonially and commercially, the role of first lady also broadened under Dolley Madison. A ship, the *Lady Madison*, was named for her. A minuet was composed in her honor, and the music sold throughout the country. The baron of the beaver trade, John Jacob Astor, knowing of her interest in fashion and his vital business interests in shipping, lavished gifts upon her, including furs. Dolley Madison awakened the country to an unspoken fact: Women of position could have influence not only on— and sometimes over—their husbands, but on the whole of society. Clever people began cultivating the first lady. This, too, was a precedent.

When James Madison's second term ended, he was at the peak of his political popularity. Historians concur he would handily have won a third term had he sought it. Instead, like Washington and Jefferson before him, he chose not to run for reelection. He and Dolley retired from the nation's capital until she returned to Washington, D.C., after James's death. She remained as popular as ever.

During the Polk administration, guests frequently left the White House receptions early to make a call on Dolley. Sarah Polk did not believe in serving alcohol at the White House, but Dolley had no such compunctions about showing her guests liquid hospitality!

When she attended her last White House reception in 1849 at the age of eighty-two, Dolley wore her trademark plumed turban. She died a few months later. Her funeral was as lavish as a state affair, said to be more impressive than that of any president. She was the only first lady ever awarded a place of honor in Congress.

Elizabeth Kortright Monroe

First Lady: 1817–1825
5th Presidential Administration
Siena Research Institute Rating: 23

La Belle Americaine
—Popular title for Elizabeth Monroe conferred by French

Nothing better illustrates Elizabeth Monroe's troubled tenure as first lady than her youngest daughter's wedding. It was the first in the White House and the low point in what Secretary of State John Quincy Adams called a "senseless war of protocol. " On his part, it took urgent diplomacy to quell rebelliousness among Washingtonians for whom it alternately intrigued and incensed.

Seventeen-year-old Maria Monroe was betrothed to her cousin, and junior presidential aide, Samuel Lawrence Gouverneur. In the status-conscious world of Washington politics, everyone who thought themselves to be anyone of consequence eagerly anticipated an invitation. Then, as the wedding date neared, expectations soared out of control.

Where Dolley Madison would have used the occasion to throw a wedding party on a grand scale, the more reticent Monroes favored a small, intimate affair. Maria's elder sister Elizabeth, called Eliza by the family, became the wedding planner. Eliza was put in charge of many White House social events during the Monroe presidency, helping her mother who was said to be in poor health. There is some evidence to support the theory that Elizabeth Monroe may have had epilepsy. Eliza ruled out invitations for foreign diplomats, and even went so far as to suggest that they not send gifts. To accommodate public interest and political demands, the couple would host a serene reception at the White House after returning from a five-day honeymoon. Several balls were planned to fete the young couple, including one at Commodore Stephen Decatur's home on Lafayette Square just across Pennsylvania Avenue from the White House.

It appeared a good compromise. What the Monroes failed to grasp was the extraordinary sensitivity of Washington's new political class to any hint of a snub, intentional or otherwise. As word of the growing disaffection reached into the White House, Secretary of State Adams was dispatched to make the rounds, personally explaining to each offended dignitary that the Monroe wedding was a family affair.

He might as well have saved his breath. By the time the wedding took place, first lady Elizabeth Monroe was plainly detested in the city's social circles. Prominent Washingtonians expected to be present at the nuptials, not a formal reception nearly a full week after the wedding. Even the ball plans were marred unexpectedly, when Stephen Decatur was mortally wounded in a duel two days after the ball at his home; all parties in the capital were canceled during the mourning. The unpolitical White House wedding was a social catastrophe. The Monroes failed to grasp that every action in Washington—even a family wedding—has political significance, and that the sphere of privacy in the White House is very small.

It is a strange failing for a woman whose life before she entered the White House suggests ample experience in entertaining and social graces. Elizabeth Kortright came from a prominent New York family that had grown rich off legalized piracy. Her father was a privateer during the French and Indian Wars, seizing ships that sailed under the French flag and keeping the proceeds from the plundered cargo and vessels.

When she was still in her teens, she met James Monroe, then serving in New York as a member of the Continental Congress. The tall Revolutionary War veteran must have been a dashing figure. He saw service under Washington in several campaigns and was badly wounded at the battle of Trenton. By the end of his military service, he had risen to the rank of lieutenant colonel and had earned Washington's confidence. He married Elizabeth in 1786. She was just seventeen.

All of Elizabeth Monroe's adult life was subsequently spent in political and diplomatic circles. In 1794, Washington named Monroe minister to France, and the couple moved to Paris. Here Elizabeth Monroe distinguished herself by helping to keep the Marquise de Lafayette's wife from being beheaded on the guillotine.

It was the height of the Reign of Terror. In a six-week period, more than fifteen hundred people had been executed, including Madame Lafayette's mother. The marquise himself was imprisoned in Austria, and his wife was behind bars in Paris. Outright intervention by the newly appointed American minister might have been counterproductive, and was certainly not in keeping with President Washington's instructions to maintain a cautious neutrality in French affairs.

There is little doubt that Elizabeth and James jointly concocted what turned out to be an ingenious solution. Relying on public opinion and their ability to create a stir, they had a carriage brightly painted to attract attention. The young Elizabeth went unaccompanied to the prison, her carriage moving slowly through the streets of Paris, drawing curious crowds as she passed. With her fair skin and dark curls, she cut a striking figure. By the time she reached the jail, Elizabeth had an entourage.

She announced herself loudly to the jailers, taking pains to make sure the crowd knew this was the wife of the American minister. The jailers complied with her request to have Madame Lafayette brought out to greet her. The two women embraced in full view of the curious Parisians. As the Monroes had hoped, word of their concern about Madame Lafayette spread through Paris quickly. Soon, Monroe was able to meet with the Committee on Public Safety that had authority over prisoners, and Madame Lafayette was freed. The Monroes' clever manipulation of public opinion is credited with Madame Lafayette's safe release. Thirty years later, when Lafayette visited America, he gave the Monroes two marble mantelpieces in appreciation. They can be seen today in Ashlawn-Highland, the Monroe plantation outside Charlottesville, Virginia.

Elizabeth was dubbed *la belle americaine*—the beautiful American—by the French. She was by all accounts a popular hostess in Paris, widely admired for her social graces. The Monroes became close to their French hosts—so close, in fact, that President Washington recalled Monroe as minister in 1796. In 1803, President Jefferson named Monroe envoy extraordinary and minister plenipotentiary to France, and James and Elizabeth returned to Paris. It was a brief appointment. Although Monroe performed ably in negotiating the purchase of the Louisiana Territory from Napoléon, Jefferson feared that Monroe was becoming too close to the French emperor and could compromise the neutrality Jefferson coveted for the new nation. Monroe was minister to France only six months before being named minister to England.

By 1810, however, James Monroe was appointed secretary of state by President Madison, and the Monroes moved to Washington. Elizabeth seems to have performed well as a hostess for the diplomatic corps, and circulated satisfactorily among Washington's social set.

Her stunning success in Paris and seemingly successful debut in Washington make Elizabeth Monroe's unpopularity as first lady all the more enigmatic. To be fair, following Dolley Madison was to be set up for failure. Dolley's success in making herself and the White House the social center of Washington had raised expectations for future presidential spouses extraordinarily high. She set a standard few would ever meet. But Elizabeth Monroe's problem was not simply that Dolley was a hard act to follow. The trouble began when she didn't even try.

Upon assuming the duties of first lady, Elizabeth Monroe let it be known immediately that she would no longer engage in the tiresome chore of returning social calls that her predecessors had all suffered. In practice, returning a social call meant traveling hours each day by coach over bumpy roads or slogging through the mud of unpaved streets to show reciprocity to the wives of senators and congressmen or diplomats. It was an important social courtesy in an era before telephones, but also a very inefficient use of time and a haphazard way to establish contact. A caller would just as likely find a lady gone from the premises making calls herself as waiting at home to receive guests. Nineteenth-century socialites could go around and around, leaving their printed calling cards and receiving a caller's card in return, before making contact. Think of it as phone tag, but much more time-consuming and labor-intensive.

People in the nineteenth century were little different than people today when it comes to social standing, especially in status-conscious Washington. Modern Washingtonians measure their standing in the political hierarchy by their ability to get their phone calls returned. By declaring that she would no longer return calls, Elizabeth Monroe struck at the deepest social insecurities of the political classes. Although she continued the tradition of regular "levees," it must have been like a dentist hitting an exposed nerve.

"The drawing room of the President was opened last night to a row of beggarly chairs," one socialite wrote. "Only five women attended. . . ." Some commentators believe that the president's wife was being deliberately snubbed.

The excuse offered for the change in protocol was Elizabeth's health. It has been speculated that Elizabeth Monroe was an epileptic, prone to unpredictable seizures. If so, this may account for her desire to limit her public schedule. Yet Washingtonians noted, on those infrequent occasions of her public engagements, that her appearance belied poor health. She was beautiful and seemed younger than her age. Whether or not health was a factor in the curtailed public activities of first lady Monroe, the excuse was not widely accepted.

Soon unfavorable comparisons to Dolley Madison evolved into accusations of assuming the airs of royalty. These worsened when the White House, under reconstruction since its burning in 1814, was opened to the public for a New Year's Day reception in 1818.

Congress had voted the sum of twenty thousand dollars for the building's restoration and redecoration. It was a project Elizabeth pursued with vigor. She hired the French firm of Russell and La Farge to handle the interior design, and furniture from France soon replaced the simpler Colonial style, with bronze adornments on dark glossy woods. Some pieces arrived still bearing the emblem of Louis XVIII. There was also a new china pattern, made in France, with an American eagle in the center of the plate.

The overall effect was a transformation away from Dolley Madison's cheerful style into a more regal and austere Empire style. It must have looked alien to most Washingtonians. In their haste to furnish the house, the Monroes used some of their own furniture, compensating themselves to the tune of nine thousand dollars from the treasury. This action, coupled with overspending on the White House restoration and the need for numerous supplemental appropriations from Congress to make up the shortfall, created a minor scandal and required a special congressional commission to sort out the finances.

Presiding over the grand reopening of the White House, Elizabeth wore the latest French fashion. It was rumored that she spent as much as fifteen hundred dollars on one imported outfit. But instead of being a fashion trendsetter, she was derided for putting on monarchical airs. One guest at the New Year's reception criticized her for greeting guests with a "royal" nod of the head. It was another unfavorable contrast with the more energetic Dolley Madison. The former first lady had spent lavishly on her own clothes, amassing a two-thousand-dollar tax bill for one shipment of imported clothing, but Elizabeth Monroe's every action was now ammunition for her critics in Washington's wars of protocol.

By the end of her second year as first lady, Monroe's White House social functions had devolved into stag affairs. With a few notable exceptions, including a dinner for the marquise of Lafayette, the Monroe presidency was socially inept.

This is in contrast to the fact that the Monroe administration was exceptional politically and diplomatically. To reduce tensions, President Monroe's statesmanship set in motion a series of agreements with Great Britain regarding the United States and Canada, beginning with the Rush-Bagot Treaty of 1818 in which the United States and Britain agreed to limit their naval forces on the Great Lakes. Other agreements involved fishing rights in the waters and the boundary demarcation at the forty-ninth parallel. Future presidencies built on Monroe's accomplishments to further demilitarize the U.S.-Canadian border. The end result is one of the world's longest borders without a substantial military presence on either side. We take for granted now the peaceful relationship with Canada, but during Monroe's presidency this state of affairs was far from a foregone conclusion.

In domestic affairs, Monroe tried to maintain the uneasy balance between free states and slave states by signing the Missouri Compromise, which simultaneously admitted Maine as a free state while Missouri was admitted as a slave state. His view toward slavery was enlightened for his time, and he favored the emancipation and resettlement of blacks in Africa. It was during the Monroe administration that Liberia was formed as a haven for freed slaves, with the capital Monrovia named in his honor.

His crowning accomplishment, however, is the Monroe Doctrine. It is neither a treaty nor a multinational convention; rather, it is simply a presidential declaration. Its force, however, prevented European meddling in our hemisphere. More than a century later, the Monroe Doctrine remained a vital component of our Cold War policy of containing communism in Latin America.

Monroe was reelected in 1820 without any political opposition. He had no opponents, and every member of the electoral college except one—who decided to cast a vote for John Quincy Adams even though he was not campaigning for the presidency—voted for Monroe. His electoral college landslide stands as a record today. His two terms in office also saw partisanship decline so dramatically that the Federalists literally disappeared as an organized political force. The time became known as the "Era of Good Feelings" as a result.

Elizabeth Monroe's political influence during the two terms is difficult to measure. Snippets of correspondence hint at a political role, including a hand in shaping the Monroe Doctrine. Unlike the prolific Abigail Adams or the outspoken Martha Washington, the retiring Elizabeth Monroe left few direct traces. It is impossible to say with certainty where she did—or didn't—exercise political influence over her husband's policies.

Independently minded in matters of White House protocol, determined to have a say over the handling of her schedule, guarded in matters of family privacy, Elizabeth Monroe, nevertheless, remains an enigma. How can a woman so cognizant of the power of public opinion, as evidenced by her rescue of Madame Lafayette, also have been so blind to it?

Presumably, it was a conscious choice. For reasons that may never be fully understood, Elizabeth Monroe chose not to try to compete with Dolley Madison. Future first ladies might thank her for the precedent she established over taking control of her own time.

Elizabeth Monroe died at Oak Hill, the Monroes' Virginia home in Loudoun County, on September 23, 1830. Her husband outlived her by ten months. In his autobiography, he gave her credit for sharing in the public duties imposed on their marriage by the Revolution and its aftermath.

> It is a remark, which it would be unpardonable to withhold, that it was improbable for any female to have fulfilled all the duties of such a partner (as myself) of such cares, and of a wife and parent, with more attention, delicacy, and propriety than she has done.

James died on July 4, 1831.

LOUISA CATHERINE
JOHNSON ADAMS

FIRST LADY: 1825–1829
6TH PRESIDENTIAL ADMINISTRATION

SIENA RESEARCH INSTITUTE RATING: 16

"The nature of our institutions, the various turns of policy to which an elective government is ever liable, has long occupied my thoughts. . . ."

She excelled as a campaign manager. Without her, John Quincy Adams might never have become president. Throughout his long career, which spanned their fifty years of marriage and included diplomatic postings in Europe, service as secretary of state under President Madison, the presidency, and Congress, Louisa Adams was a consummate political spouse.

Louisa Johnson was born in London, one of seven daughters of the American consul Joshua Johnson. Her mother was English, and Louisa was twenty-six years old before she ever saw America. At the age of eighteen, she was betrothed to John Quincy Adams, who was ten years her senior. The couple were married in 1797, when his father was president. Then, as now, nepotism played a strong role in politics, and President Adams appointed son John to be minister in Berlin.

Adams's young bride was, by all accounts, a success on the diplomatic circuit. This is unsurprising. Louisa was, after all, a consul's daughter and had grown up in diplomatic circles. She spoke French fluently. She was educated. Her childhood in London gave her a cosmopolitan outlook, one that was particularly suited to dealing with Europe's courtly social fashions. After she was presented to Queen Louise, Berlin society embraced her. She must have been a novelty in Berlin, where the president's daughter-in-law was sometimes introduced as "Excellency" or "Princess Royal."

The honeymoon ended in 1801 when President Adams lost his reelection bid and retired to Massachusetts. John returned home with Louisa. It was her first exposure to the United States. She was literally a stranger in her own country. Matters were made more difficult because the young couple, now with a baby, lived with their in-laws while waiting for their own home in Boston to be built.

The outspoken former first lady Abigail Adams was a critical mother-in-law. She felt Louisa to be too genteel, mistaking her London manners for snobbery. Apparently former president Adams disagreed on that count, and peace was kept in the family.

Elected to the Senate in 1804, John Quincy Adams and the family split their time between Washington and Boston. Although Washington was still a city in its rudimentary stages of development, during Senate recesses Louisa preferred to stay in the capital rather than return to Massachusetts. Her husband preferred to be with his family in Quincy. The result, predictably, was stress on their marriage, which recurred at various times throughout their five-decade union, yet never deeply strained their political partnership.

When Adams was named secretary of state by President Monroe in 1816, Louisa made her grand debut in Washington's political circles. She aided her husband's career by entertaining socially. She hosted Tuesday-night receptions that acquired a reputation for elegance and refinement, although the couple complained that they felt restrained by finances in their ability to entertain in the style they would have wished.

But Louisa was far more than the gracious hostess. At a time when presidents were nominated by Congress and chosen by the electoral college—in a political sphere that would seem very foreign to us—the inside game of politics was of the utmost importance. A candidate needed the support of members of Congress, and potential supporters had to be wooed one-on-one. In the closely contested election of 1824, which pitted four candidates against one another for the presidency, it was Louisia who became her husband's campaign manager.

Her political role began when he was still secretary of state. During the Washington social season, which tracked the sessions of Congress, she held her Tuesday-night receptions unfailingly, featuring fine food and entertainment. She hosted dinners for sixty-eight members of Congress in the run up to the election. After a visit to Philadelphia, where she met with politicians to discuss the Monroe administration and her husband's prospects, she encouraged her husband to make a campaign visit to the city to shore up his support. To stay current, she attended debates in the Senate. By the end, she was calling it "my campaign."

The 1824 election pitted John Quincy Adams against Henry Clay, William Crawford, and war hero Andrew Jackson. The Era of Good Feelings under Monroe had temporarily obliterated political parties, and all the candidates ran as "Democratic-Republicans." It became a contest of personality. Jackson won more popular support and electoral college votes than any of the other three contenders, but failed to secure a majority. This left the election's outcome to be decided by the House of Representatives.

Then Henry Clay gave his backing to Adams and Congress chose him over Jackson. Jackson partisans were infuriated when Adams subsequently appointed Clay as his secretary of state. They believed that the presidency had been stolen from Jackson in a corrupt backroom deal between the two victors. It was an immediate end to the Era of Good Feelings. Jackson's supporters spent the next four years fighting to take back the White House.

Louisa Adams had worked hard to see her husband win the election. Her assiduous courtship of likely congressional allies no doubt paid off. Unlike Elizabeth Monroe, Louisa spent many hours calling on congressional wives. It may have been as crucial to Adams's victory as any deal with Clay. On some days, she made up to twenty-five social calls during the campaign.

"It is understood that a man who is ambitious to become president of the United States must make his wife visit the Ladies of the members of Congress first," Louisa wrote in her diary. "Otherwise he is totally inefficient to fill so high an office."

Louisa's words let us see the role of first lady taking its modern shape. The first lady was expected to be a political partner in campaigning for office, if not in shaping policy after the election. She was subject to attention from the press, favorable and otherwise. She was expected to be a gracious hostess in performing the functions of state. She might become a social and fashion trendsetter. Her influence could extend to charitable causes, if she chose.

Louisa Adams may have been the first presidential spouse to complain of the rigors of campaigning as well, but she would certainly not be the last. Nor did Louisa's political activism end once the election was decided. Because of the bitterness of Jackson backers, the four years of the John Quincy Adams administration were a constant political struggle. When the *Daily Telegraph*, a pro-Jackson newspaper, attacked Adams for procuring his own family servant to perform sexual favors for the czar of Russia when Adams was a diplomat in St. Petersburg in 1809, it was Louisa who answered the allegation. She chose a gazette widely read by women, *Mrs. A. S. Colvin's Weekly Messenger,* for her detailed rebuttal. Change the medium to television and the time to the twentieth century, and Louisa Adams' s defense of her husband is not so different from that of another first lady, Hillary Rodham Clinton. Louisa took the offensive, calling herself the daughter of an "American republican merchant" and her husband John a paragon of virtue, whose character was falsely under attack by a conspiracy of political foes.

There is little evidence of Louisa's influence on the Adams administration's policies, but that could be because the Adams presidency left little in the way of a legacy. Like his father, Adams believed in a strong federal government. He felt that expanding the country's transportation system was a proper role for federal support. Although he wanted federal funding for a more extensive transportation infrastructure, Adams scored only a partial success when he persuaded Congress to fund the development of the Cumberland Road and the Chesapeake & Ohio Canal system.

When he imposed a tariff to protect domestic manufacturers against competition from European importers, Adams inadvertently dealt the concept of a strong federal government a serious setback. The tariff was so unpopular in the South that Adams's own vice president, John C. Calhoun, declared it unconstitutional and subject to nullification by the states! The crisis that this precipitated would linger for Adams's successor to resolve. Measured solely by his own criterion of strengthening the national government, Adams has to be judged a failure.

On the other hand, Louisa Adams's keen political instincts had her independently traveling to cities such as Baltimore and Philadelphia, confirming her belief that her husband needed to get out and campaign actively in order to win a second term of office. She developed a detailed campaign travel itinerary, including stops with local political leaders her husband needed to court in order to shore up his political base and carry swing states like Pennsylvania. Her husband did not follow her advice.

Jackson's overwhelming victory in the election of 1828, against the backdrop of the unpopular tariffs, suggests that most Americans of the day shared the view of the Adams presidency as a failure. The former president returned to Massachusetts. In 1830, he was elected to Congress, and he went on to a fairly distinguished career as a legislator. In 1848, he died after a stroke felled him during a speech on the floor of Congress protesting the Mexican War.

Many historians have suggested that Louisa Adams suffered from depression when she was first lady, citing notes and letters in which she complained about the loneliness of life in the White House and the oppressive burdens of office. Before her husband became president, she wrote to one correspondent that she had no ambition to higher office for herself, because she knew the constraints would be a kind of prison. Some writers have suggested that the four years of the presidency strained the Adams's marriage, too, and they have depicted the couple as barely on speaking terms, each reading the newspapers they preferred without conversing with one another during meals.

Whatever private ordeals she faced as first lady, Louisa kept them private at the time. With regard to her public image, she is remembered as a gracious first lady who met the social expectations of the time and was a valuable political partner to her husband.

Later in her life, Louisa became an advocate for women's liberation. She corresponded with women's rights activist Sarah Grimke and studied the Old Testament for signs regarding the proper role of women. Louisa's own reading of the Bible contradicted the then prevailing view that Scripture justified the subordinate role of women. Man may suppress women, Louisa wrote Grimke, but man "cannot degrade her in the sight of God. . . ." Louisa considered the discovery of her late mother-in-law's letters about women's empowerment a true treasure that gave her new respect for Abigail Adams.

Although kindled late in life, perhaps this interest in the writing of her mother-in-law inspired Louisa to write an account of her journey by carriage from St. Petersburg to Paris. It was at a time when the ravages of the Napoleonic Wars were still fresh on the landscape. Although Louisa's story was written many decades later, it has a vivid quality of high adventure.

John Quincy Adams had been posted to Paris and gone ahead of his pregnant wife and six-year-old son Charles, leaving Louisa to make her way accompanied only by a maid and a token Russian military escort. She recounted the arduous trip in her *Narrative of a Journey From Russia to France, 1815.*

Their carriage was equipped with runners and filled with spares so they could travel the ice-covered roads. They had barely crossed the frozen Vistula River when the ice broke up behind them. The Russian escort, fearful of entering French territory, deserted upon learning the news that Napoléon had escaped from his exile on the island of Elba, leaving Louisa alone to deal with bands of roaming French troops. She was nearly dragged from the carriage by one mob of soldiers, but saved herself by shouting "Long live Napoléon" in French. Her attackers relented long enough to listen to her plead that she was American, not Russian, before finally leaving her alone.

It was the adventure of a lifetime. The journey took weeks and featured major and minor tribulations, but in retrospect it must have been exhilarating to Louisa. She wrote that her purpose in publishing the memoir was to knock down "the fancied weakness of feminine imbecility" by telling her tale. It is the portrait of an independent woman managing by herself a difficult and sometimes dangerous trek.

Louisa Adams was the first and only foreign-born woman to become first lady, a fact her husband's political rivals used against her in campaigns. In assessing her role, she deserves credit for stretching the boundaries of a presidential spouse's political involvement. By assuming an active role in her husband's campaigns for office, she expanded the precedents set by other first ladies and shaped the role along the modern lines we recognize today.

Emily Donelson
Donelson and
Sarah York Jackson

First Ladies: 1829–1837
7th Presidential Administration
Siena Research Institute Rating: 26*

★

Mistress of the Hermitage and Hostess of the White House.

45

Rachel Donelson Robards Jackson would have been the country's first cigar-
and pipe-smoking first lady had she lived long enough. General Andrew
Jackson easily defeated John Quincy Adams in the election of 1828, but
the triumph was bittersweet. His wife Rachel died a few months before
the presidential inauguration of 1829. Jackson never remarried during his
two terms in the White House.

The couple had been childless, but young relatives of Rachel's often
lived with them at their home, the Hermitage, in Nashville. They formally
adopted one nephew, Andrew Jackson Jr. Another of Rachel's nephews,
Andrew Donelson, was raised by the couple as well. Andrew Donelson
then married his first cousin, Emily Donelson. When Jackson won the
presidential election, he brought Andrew Donelson with him to serve as a
private secretary, and Emily took on the duties of White House hostess.

She was slender, with dark hair, and just twenty-one years old when
she became Jackson's first lady. She had a young child to raise, and would,
after the raucous start to the Jackson presidency, give birth to three more
children over the next two terms.

On Inauguration Day, thousands of Jackson supporters mobbed the
streets of Washington and converged on the White House. Many were
backwoodsmen and common people whose idea of a social celebration
differed significantly from that of Washington's elite. As many as twenty
thousand passed through the White House that day, jostling to see their
hero, drinking freely and devouring the food, shoving and occasionally
breaking into fistfights, and even breaking the furniture.

Washingtonians like Margaret Bayard Smith were horrified: "A rabble,
a mob, of boys, negroes, women, children, scrabbling, fighting, romping,
what a pity, what a pity!"

It was the first people's inaugural, a spontaneous populist outpouring
for a popular president. Daniel Webster observed: "Persons have come
five hundred miles to see General Jackson, and they really seem to think
that the country has been rescued from some dreadful danger."

Then it changed. Jackson's first inauguration may have been homespun, but his tenure in the White House revealed a taste for refinement.
He spent freely to make the White House a true mansion. Over eight
years, fifty thousand dollars was spent redecorating the building. There
were new chandeliers and drapes, rich carpets from Belgium, new china
and tableware.

White House receptions sometimes featured a thousand guests.
Official dinners were formal affairs with lavish menus. Jackson's southern-

style hospitality was reminiscent of Dolley Madison, and Emily Donelson won praise throughout the city for her social graces.

Jackson was known as the People's President. The two terms of the Jackson administration were characterized by a strong emphasis on egalitarianism, with Jackson championing the interests of the working class and poor against wealthy elites. The primary battlefield for this class warfare was over the national bank, which Jackson believed placed public money at the disposal of private shareholders. He fought against Congress's renewal of the bank's charter, believing that its owners would use public funds to enrich themselves. By placing public funds in private banks, the shareholders benefited by being able to profit from interest on short-term loans while they had control over the public deposits. When Congress renewed the bank's charter, Jackson vetoed the legislation.

Tariffs remained a source of friction between the states, as well as between Jackson and his own vice president, John C. Calhoun. Jackson inherited from his predecessor not only the tariff of 1828 but also a brewing constitutional crisis. The tariff was unpopular in the South, which had little manufacturing of its own, because it imposed higher costs on goods the southerners imported from Europe. Northern merchants liked the tariff because it made their own manufactured goods more competitive with the less expensive European imports, and southerners deeply resented being forced to pay higher prices for the benefit of the North. Southern politicians questioned whether the federal government had the power to impose the tariffs, threatening a constitutional showdown.

Calhoun, who came from South Carolina, supported his state's right to nullify the federally imposed tariff. In 1832, the tariff was adjusted downward, but not enough to satisfy South Carolina.

When the state legislature passed an Ordinance of Nullification voiding the tariff in South Carolina, Calhoun supported the act as within the rights of a state. Jackson saw it as an act of treason and got Congress to authorize him to use the army to enforce the federal tariff.

Henry Clay defused the simmering crisis by proposing a compromise tariff that was acceptable to South Carolina. Congress enacted it as the tariff of 1833, and Jackson avoided a military showdown over states' rights. His decisive show of leadership at a time of political crisis—and subsequent willingness to strike a compromise—typified his presidency.

Loyalty mattered to Andrew Jackson. Angered by Calhoun's defiance and his role in escalating the tariff crisis to the point of civil war, Jackson dumped Calhoun in favor of Martin Van Buren, who served as his vice president throughout the second term of office. Jackson extended his view of the importance of loyalty to all political patronage decisions.

"If you have a job in your Department that can't be done by a Democrat," he once told a cabinet member, "then abolish the job."

Jackson wanted loyal political supporters in every government post. As a result of his attention to political patronage and loyalty, Jackson is credited with founding the modern two-party system. Known as the "spoils system," the awarding of government jobs and contracts to party loyalists created a strong incentive for partisanship.

With regard to Emily Donelson, there is little on record to demonstrate that she had any influence over Jackson in political affairs. Nevertheless, she was clearly a strong-minded woman who didn't flinch at disagreeing with her revered uncle over a matter of principle.

The episode that reveals this trait has its roots in the bitter first Jackson election of 1828, in which his wife, Rachel's, character was questioned with charges of adultery. Before she married Andrew Jackson, Rachel was married for six years to Lewis Robards. He is reported to have been obsessively jealous and abusive. When she could stand it no longer and they separated, Robards told her that he was filing for divorce—but didn't. In 1791, she married Andrew Jackson, apparently without realizing that she was not yet legally divorced. The exact chronology is difficult to determine because the records regarding the events before Robards finally filed for divorce disappeared after Jackson's election to the presidency.

Two years later, in 1793, Lewis Robards did finally sue for divorce—this time on grounds of adultery. The discovery must have come as a shock to both Andrew and Rachel Jackson. Their first marriage was utterly invalid. Not only was Rachel still legally wed, but her marriage to Andrew had taken place in Spanish territory where Protestants could not legally be married under any circumstances. After the divorce became final, Rachel and Andrew Jackson renewed their vows in a legal ceremony in 1794.

In the presidential campaign of 1824, the circumstances of Rachel's first marriage led to a whispering campaign alleging adultery and bigamy. Enduring these aspersions on her character was hard on a woman like Rachel, who despite her free-spiritedness was quite traditional regarding morality. But they were only a hint of what was to come in 1828.

John Quincy Adams may not have followed Louisa's advice to campaign vigorously for the presidency by getting out of the White House and traveling around the states to build political support, but he didn't hesitate to participate in what would become one of the nastiest, most negative presidential campaigns of the time. Newspapers loyal to Adams began attacking Rachel Jackson as an adulteress in print. Her fitness to be first lady became a campaign issue. "Ought a convicted adulteress and her paramour husband," an Adams campaign broadside read, "be placed in the highest offices of this free and Christian land?"

The negative campaign didn't actually help Adams's prospects for re-election, but it did wound Rachel Jackson. When she had a heart attack just before Christmas 1828, Andrew Jackson attributed it to her despair over the character attacks against her during the presidential contest.

When similar character attacks were launched against the wife of his secretary of war, John Eaton, it provoked a rift within his inner circle and his acting first lady. He saw in Peggy Eaton's treatment at the hands of Washingtonians a bitter reprise of the political savagery suffered by his beloved Rachel.

Peggy Eaton's social origins were distinctly plebeian. Her father was a tavern keeper, and it was rumored that she had other dalliances with navy men before marrying. Socially, her husband's political rank in the cabinet dictated a degree of deference, and she should have been welcomed into Washington society. Other wives—of senators, congressmen, and even Jackson's own cabinet—shunned her.

The treatment of Peggy Eaton, who had been a social acquaintance of both Rachel and Andrew Jackson, infuriated the president. Then Emily Donelson sided with the rest of Washington society and refused to entertain Peggy Eaton in the White House.

Emily's stand on principle met with an equally strong response from her uncle. She was sent away from the White House, and the role of first lady was transferred to Sarah York, the wife of Jackson's adopted son and heir Andrew Jackson Jr. She had married the son shortly after President Jackson's inauguration, and the younger woman was always in Emily Donelson's shadow except for the brief period of Emily's exile over the Peggy Eaton affair. Jackson himself had determined which woman would fill the role of first lady, according to Laura Holloway. "You, my dear, are mistress of the Hermitage," Holloway reported Jackson as saying to Sarah shortly after he was elected president, "and Emily is hostess of the White House."

Emily had not been singled out for harsh treatment. Jackson's own cabinet was also brought into his line of thinking. When most of their wives continued to refuse to recognize Peggy Eaton, Jackson sacked the appointees with the exception of his postmaster general. They were not his closest advisers in any event. In one of Jackson's innovations, he relied upon personally loyal, and often objective, advisers outside the government. They became known as the Kitchen Cabinet and are a staple of modern presidential government.

It should be pointed out that Jackson clearly missed Emily. He wrote and begged her to come back to the White House, provided she would yield and be sociable to Peggy Eaton. Emily would not yield, and the standoff was resolved only when Jackson appointed John Eaton governor of Florida. The Eatons moved south, Emily returned to the White House, and the impasse was over.

Emily Donelson died in 1836, shortly before Jackson's second term ended. For the remaining months of the Jackson administration, Sarah once again took over the duties of first lady. She continued to help Jackson socially in his later years of declining health after he left the presidency and returned to his beloved Kentucky home, the Hermitage.

Emily didn't extend the role of first lady beyond the scope she inherited from Louisa Adams. She refrained from becoming involved in policy or political affairs. Laura Holloway gave her high praise, however, for handling the social duties of first lady with aplomb at a time of intense partisanship.

"It was a day of fierce party spirit," Holloway wrote in 1881, "political animosity spared neither sex nor condition, yet the voice of detraction was never raised against her honored name. Friend and foe alike paid homage to her charms."

*As rated in the Siena Research Institute poll of 1982. Subsequent Siena polls have not rated Emily Donelson because she was not a president's spouse. Sarah Jackson has not been rated in any Siena poll.

Angelica Singleton Van Buren

First Lady: 1837–1841
8th Presidential Administration
Siena Research Institute Poll: 36[*]

"A lady of rare accomplishments, perfectly easy and graceful in her manners, and free and vivacious in her conversation."
—*Boston Post*, January 2, 1839

Another widower, the "Little Magician," followed Andrew Jackson to the White House in the election of 1836. Martin Van Buren had been vice president during the second term of the Jackson administration and had Jackson's backing in winning the Democratic nomination.

More important, Peggy Eaton had Van Buren's backing. When Jackson sacked his cabinet over the dour wives' snubbing of Mrs. Eaton, Martin Van Buren was among those handing in their resignations. But Jackson knew Van Buren was on his side in the affair. He promptly nominated Van Buren as minister to Great Britain, a post that required Senate confirmation. When Jackson's political foes blocked Van Buren's nomination by a single vote, the wily general outflanked his rivals. He chose Van Buren as his vice presidential running mate in 1832, and gave his loyal ally full backing in the election of 1836.

During his first year in office, in fact, the widower relied on Peggy Eaton to fill the role of White House hostess. Van Buren's first term coincided with the panic of 1837, an event that today would be called a deep economic recession or even a depression. The sluggish economy lasted until the presidential election of 1840, and no doubt made Van Buren a one-term president.

Under the circumstances, a show of White House austerity would seem politically prudent. Unlike Jackson, Van Buren did not hold receptions for a thousand guests or serve lavish dinners. Like that other White House widower—Thomas Jefferson—he favored small dinner parties with influential senators or congressmen. Even these were somewhat parsimonious. Whereas the Jackson White House had never been dry, Van Buren sometimes didn't serve wine or punch for his dinner guests. Peggy Eaton acted as hostess for these affairs, reviving some of the old criticism, but given the limited social agenda of the new presidency there were few opportunities to snub a White House invitation!

It lasted twelve months. Just across Lafayette Square from the White House, Dolley Madison once again was holding court as Washington's leading lady. During the twelve years of the Adams and Jackson presidencies, she had stayed away from the federal city. In 1837, she returned, in a nearly destitute condition, eager to strike a deal for Congress to acquire her late husband's papers in return for a handsome sum.

Her much younger cousin, Angelica Singleton—refined, strikingly beautiful, and single—was visiting her. Dolley paid a call on the new president

---

*As rated in the Siena Research Institute poll of 1982. Angelica Van Buren was not included in subsequent Siena polls.

to introduce her kin; the widower Van Buren had four grown sons who lived with him at the White House.

Angelica began being courted by one of them, Abraham. He served in the same capacity of private secretary to his father that Jackson's nephew Andrew had in the previous administration. Soon Angelica and Abraham were betrothed, then married within months of their first meeting. Dolley Madison's cousin took on the same responsibilities that Emily Donelson had as first lady. The country had two wives of presidential private secretaries in a row serving in the role of first lady.

A newspaper correspondent who encountered Angelica in a White House receiving line for New Year's Day in 1839 gave us this observation: "Graceful in her manners, and free and vivacious in her conversation . . . she is said to have borne the fatigue of a three hours' levee with a patience and pleasantry which must be inexhaustible to last one through so severe a trial."

With Dolley Madison for a mentor, there should have been little doubt that Angelica would impress White House visitors. She was also well prepared in her own right. Educated at a Philadelphia boarding school, Angelica came from a courtly South Carolina lineage. Her family plantation, Home Place, featured a racetrack, landscaped lawns, and a baronial house. Angelica Singleton Van Buren was no newcomer to refined society or to wealthy elites.

After her marriage to Abraham Van Buren, the couple honeymooned in Europe. The extensive trip was studded with royal encounters. In England, the de facto first lady and the president's son dined with Queen Victoria. In France, they were entertained by King Louis Philippe, who restored aristocratic etiquette for France's revived monarchy.

Pomp and ceremony greeted the young couple everywhere. Angelica Van Buren was the first "first lady" to travel abroad. Foreign courts were not sure how to receive the American dignitaries. They weren't quite heads of state, just closely related to a president. As his relatives, they were dignitaries, but not quite in the same way a royal heir or heiress to the throne would be. The young republic presented problems of protocol to the old European courts.

King Louis Philippe chose to receive Abraham and Angelica as he would have done for visiting royalty. They were greeted by a queen seated on an elevated platform, surrounded by ladies-in-waiting, as guests were announced by a doorman. The queen and her royal retinue did not mingle and shake hands with their guests in the style Dolley Madison had made popular at the White House, but maintained a strict decorum dictated by social hierarchy. By some accounts, the young Angelica was deeply impressed with these ritualistic receptions.

Whether it was due to Angelica's influence or to the urbane Martin Van Buren's real preferences, when the young couple returned from their extended European honeymoon the era of White House austerity was over. At dinners, guests ate from menus with a distinctly European flavor. Expensive wines and liquors were again in abundance. While there was opulent entertainment at the Van Buren White House, the rest of the country remained mired in recession.

White House "levees" or receptions also returned to favor. Angelica decided to copy the royal style of receiving guests. She would remain on a dais, dressed in a long purple gown and a bejeweled headdress sporting three long feathers, and surrounded by a small retinue of female retainers dressed in flowing white gowns, while guests were announced to her. Angelica may have meant for her plumed headdress to evoke Dolley Madison's trademark feathered turbans, but to outside observers it seemed distinctly regal.

As the panic of 1837 wore on into 1840, the Van Buren White House's ostentation inevitably became a political target. Van Buren had persuaded Congress to allocate twenty-seven thousand dollars for new White House furnishings and decoration. Dolley Madison, it should be mentioned, had received only thirty thousand from Congress for James Madison's papers. Van Buren spent the funds to repaint the White House, add new carpets, and reupholster furniture.

It was too much for Pennsylvania congressman Charles Ogle. "Your house glitters with all imaginable luxuries and gaudy ornaments," he said in a speech on the floor of Congress. "Will they [the people] longer feel inclined to support their chief servant in a Palace as splendid as that of the Caesers, and as richly adorned as the proudest Asiatic mansion?" It was a campaign speech for William Henry Harrison, who would run against Van Buren in the election of 1840. It became known as the Golden Spoon speech.

"Harrison would scorn to charge the people of the United States with foreign cut wine coolers, liquor stands," Ogle railed, "and golden chains to hang golden labels around the necks of barrel-shaped flute decanters with cone stoppers." To most of the public, the imagery of Ogle's speech conveyed an exoticism that depicted the Van Buren White House as indulgent and decadent.

Although she wasn't mentioned directly, Angelica Van Buren also came under Ogle's attack. His speech implied that she had tried to get Congress to appropriate money allowing the White House to copy the royal gardens she had seen on her European tour.

The Golden Spoon speech set the theme for the presidential campaign. It was "Log Cabin" Harrison versus "Golden Spoon" Van Buren. It isn't an exaggeration to say that Angelica Van Buren's tastes had a major political influence on the election. Otherwise, she didn't have great influence over the policies or politics of the Van Buren administration.

Van Buren lost to the Whig Party's William Henry Harrison in the 1840 election. Harrison was a war hero. In 1848, Van Buren again ran for the presidency as the candidate of the Free Soil Party.

He lost both reelection bids. Angelica and her husband left Washington and split their time between Europe, South Carolina, and New York. The 1982 Siena College Research Institute poll rated Angelica No. 36, seventh from the bottom. Her disregard for the harsh economic realities most Americans faced during the recessionary times of Van Buren's administration demonstrated the political perils of acting as though the White House was a royal court, and the ease with which a first lady can become a political liability by seeming to be insensitive to the voters. Angelica would not be the last First Lady to make this mistake.

Anna Tuthill Symmes Harrison

First Lady: March 1841–April 1841
9th Presidential Administration
Siena Research Institute Rating: 23*

"I wish that my husband's friends had left him where he is, happy and contented in retirement."

Sudden death and secret marriages marked the tenure of the three first ladies who presided at the White House between 1841 and 1845. Anna Harrison may be the only president's wife who never saw the inside of her White House. Unlike Rachel Jackson, who died after her husband was elected president but before he was officially sworn in, Anna Harrison was married to a sitting president. Delay in traveling to Washington cost her the chance to live in the White House.

"Log Cabin" Harrison easily defeated Martin Van Buren in the presidential campaign of 1840, but the triumph was short-lived. Less than a month after his inauguration in March 1841, William Henry Harrison died of pneumonia.

Anna Harrison learned of her husband's death at their Ohio home. She had decided to wait until the weather improved in May before joining her husband at the White House. She was packing the household belongings for the journey to Washington when she received word.

Harrison's untimely death deprived the country of what would undoubtedly have been a politically active first lady. Anna Harrison was then a mature woman of sixty-five who read the newspapers avidly and was outspoken in her political opinions. She later pronounced her husband's successor a weak president.

Anna came from a prominent family and was educated at a boarding school in New York City. When she was courted by the young Lieutenant William Henry Harrison, her father opposed the romance, fearing his daughter would spend her life in military forts at remote frontier outposts. ". . . the young man has understanding, prudence, education, and resource in conversation," Anna's father wrote in 1795, "about 3,000 pounds in property, but what is to be lamented is, that he has no profession but that of arms."

She displayed a rare streak of independence by opposing her father. She waited until he was out of town, and then married William behind his back. Harrison shortly began what would become a distinguished political career, and Anna's father soon reconciled to her choice.

By 1800, Harrison was governor of Indiana. He became a war hero in 1811 by defeating the Shawnee Indians, who were allied to the British, in the battle of Tippecanoe. He later became a member of Congress, a state senator, a U.S. senator, and ambassador to Colombia during the Jackson presidency. Harrison was sixty-eight when he was sworn in as president, a

---

*As rated in the 1982 Siena Research Institute poll. Subsequent Siena polls did not include Anna Harrison because of the brevity of her tenure as first lady.

record not superseded until Ronald Reagan was inaugurated in 1981 shortly before his seventieth birthday.

Harrison's inaugural address, delivered on a wet and windy March day, lasted for two hours. He wore neither a coat nor a hat. This is probably why he contracted pneumonia and died one month later.

Anna decided not to make the journey to Washington for the funeral, opting instead to have his body sent home for burial in North Bend overlooking the Ohio River. She outlived her husband by more than twenty years, and reportedly remained an avid consumer of political journals and newspapers, before being buried next to him in 1864.

Despite her brief tenure as first lady, she managed to set a posthumous precedent. When Benjamin Harrison was elected in 1889, she became the only first lady to have a grandson serve as president.

Letitia Christian Tyler

First Lady: April 1841–September 1842
10th Presidential Administration
Siena Research Institute Rating: 31

★

"Beau ideal of a perfect gentlewoman."
—Actress Priscilla Cooper Tyler

William Henry Harrison's unexpected death catapulted Vice President John Tyler into the White House, literally. Tyler had hoped to serve his term as vice president from his home in Williamsburg, Virginia. For his wife, Letitia, it would undoubtedly have been a blessing.

Letitia Tyler had been born in the eighteenth century and grown up at Cedar Grove, a Tidewater, Virginia, plantation. She had little formal education but was more than competent at managing a large estate. She married John Tyler in 1813, and the couple had seven children who survived into adulthood.

She preferred domestic life to the duties of a political spouse. During the years that John served as a member of Congress, Letitia only once joined him for the winter social season in Washington.

Letitia had even more reason to prefer Williamsburg to Washington in the spring of 1841. Two years earlier she had suffered a stroke and was left a quasi-invalid. During her seventeen months as first lady, she was largely confined to a second-floor bedroom in the White House. The only record of her attending a White House social event was the occasion of the marriage of a relative in 1842.

Letitia's twenty-four-year-old daughter-in-law, Priscilla Cooper Tyler, took over the role of first lady during Letitia's convalescence and confinement. Fortunately, the young woman was tutored in her new duties by the irrepressible Dolley Madison. One stern admonishment from the former first lady: Return all calls. Three days each week Priscilla did so, spending hours in a carriage jostling about Washington's streets dutifully meeting her social obligations.

President Tyler hosted two White House dinners each week while Congress was in session. One was an intimate affair mainly for visitors to the capital; the second, for groups as large as forty made up of the city's political elite. On a monthly basis, there was also a "levee" for as many as one thousand guests. The New Year's Day and Fourth of July celebrations were by now additional permanently ingrained annual events.

Presiding over the entertainments was a role Priscilla clearly liked. "I have not had one moment to myself since my arrival," she wrote to her sister, "and the most extraordinary thing is I feel as if I had been used to living here always: and receive the Cabinet, ministers, the diplomatic corps, the heads of the army and navy, etc. etc. with a facility which astonishes me.

"I am plainly born to it," she continued. "I really do possess a degree of modest assurance that surprises me more than it does anyone else."

While the young Priscilla thrilled to her new duties as de facto first lady, her mother oversaw details of the entertainment and management of the presidential household from her second-floor rooms. This teamwork was an innovative move on Letitia's part, in some ways presaging the future in which every first lady would employ ample staff to help her manage her White House role. She also apparently read the newspapers, giving pointers to her family to avoid drawing too much press attention and following current events with sufficient interest to have been said to be able to engage in lively conversation with visitors. Among those who visited were distinguished writers such as Washington Irving and Charles Dickens. Whether she served as a political adviser to her husband is unclear, although he does make reference to her as a trusted confidante.

The first politician to assume the powers of the presidency through death, Tyler was referred to by political opponents as "His Accidency." Many expected him to serve as a caretaker president only until the next election. Instead, Tyler immediately took over full presidential powers and governed in every sense of the word. Priscilla Cooper Tyler's social facilities and assiduous courtship of Washington's diverse power centers no doubt helped smooth Tyler's assumption of his unexpected new role.

Death again stalked the White House in 1842. That September, with the new administration still less than halfway through its first term of office, Letitia Tyler succumbed to illness. Once again, the White House had a widowed president and a stand-in for first lady.

Julia Gardiner Tyler

First Lady: June 1844–March 1845
10th Presidential Administration
Siena Research Institute Rating: 27

Lovely Lady Presidentress
—Popular title and toast made to Julia Tyler

A president had died in office and now, in 1842, a first lady had. What resulted was another secret marriage before the Tyler administration came to an end. But this secret wedding, unlike that of Anna and William Harrison, would attract national attention.

For more than a year, Priscilla Cooper Tyler and her younger sister Letitia Tyler Semple shared the duties of first lady after their mother's death. Julia Gardiner arrived on the scene in December 1842 as well. She was a New York socialite from an extremely wealthy family whose nickname was "the Rose of Long Island." She had met President Tyler at a White House reception that January, during a visit to Washington, and she recalled that he paid her many compliments and seemed infatuated by her presence.

This time the fifty-two-year-old newly widowed President made no secret of his interest in the twenty-three-year-old Julia, who apparently had half the town, including several members of Congress, a Supreme Court justice, and at least one navy officer, courting her. Although he was more than twice her age, Tyler had the advantage of having what Henry Kissinger would later term the greatest aphrodisiac of all—power. He was, after all, president, and in an excellent position to court a trophy wife.

When he invited her to play cards with him privately at the White House, Julia readily agreed. While other young women might have thought this was a dangerous and compromising liaison, she clearly relished the attention. By the end of the evening, John and Julia were chasing around the furniture and frolicking around the White House. Several weeks later he proposed marriage to her at a White House ball.

She firmly put him off. "I had never thought of love," she wrote later, "so I said 'No, no, no' and shook my head with each word, which flung the tassel of my Greek cap into his face and with every move. It was undignified, but it amused me very much to see his expression as he tried to make love to me and the tassel brushed his face."

Letitia Tyler had been dead less than six months. It didn't stop the president. He raised marriage again, this time within earshot of Julia's sister. Soon the entire family knew. Julia's parents were pleased at the prospect of the match, although they delayed a firm wedding date, insisting that their daughter needed more time. They did not delay using the relationship to seek a political appointment for their politically ambitious son, Alex Gardiner.

Death and Dolley Madison intervened. In early 1844, Dolley arranged a social outing for the president, the Gardiner family, and other prominent Washingtonians on the naval vessel *Princeton*. The ship was fitted with a naval cannon called "Peacemaker," an impressive armament for the time. As it sailed down the Potomac past Mount Vernon, the *Princeton* fired demonstration shots for the president and his entourage.

While Julia and President Tyler listened to music on a deck below, her father was standing near the secretary of state and the secretary of the navy waiting to see the Peacemaker fire again. This time the gun barrel shattered, blowing shrapnel into the guests, killing eight men and wounding more. The dead included Julia's father.

Tyler had intended to be above deck to watch the cannon fire, but he tarried below while his son-in-law William Waller broke into a sea chanty with the band. Julia was spared being present at her father's death; she could possibly have even been killed herself, if she had not gone below deck with Tyler and Dolley Madison. Tyler is said to have carried Julia off the ship in his arms after she fainted.

The day's dead were given a state funeral in the East Room of the White House, where only eighteen months earlier Letitia Tyler had died.

The tragedy had the effect of hastening the marriage between Julia and John Tyler. In June of that year, the president traveled to New York without any fanfare and checked into a local hotel. On June 26, 1844, he and Julia were married at the Church of the Ascension on Fifth Avenue. Not even Tyler's children knew of the secret wedding until he told them about it afterward.

The bride was only twenty-four years old. Most of his children were older than their new stepmother. Tyler himself was nine years older than Julia's mother. Predictably, the newspapers mocked the May-September wedding, but the public seemed fascinated by it.

"Wherever we stopped, wherever we went," Julia wrote later, "crowds of people outstripping one another, came to gaze at the President's bride; *the secrecy of the affair* is on the tongue and admiration of everyone. *Everyone* says it was the best-managed thing they ever heard of."

If secrecy appealed to Julia before the wedding, publicity appealed to her afterward. Her mother had cautioned her not to take criticism from the press too seriously, but Julia was not one to simply endure the vagaries of media coverage. Instead, she sought to shape the coverage she received. She is the first first lady to use a press secretary—called a press agent in the parlance of the day—to get her favorable media coverage. This revealed a keen instinct for politics and public relations.

Fanfare was very much in Julia's mind as she set about putting her imprint on White House social events. Another of her lasting innovations involved having the Marine Band play "Hail to the Chief" whenever

President Tyler entered an event. This has become a White House custom still in use today.

The young socialite had been sent away to Europe for almost a year after causing her parents social embarrassment by becoming a model for an advertisement for Bogert & Mecamby's, a clothing emporium on Ninth Avenue in New York. It was unheard-of behavior for a young lady of her class. There, she had been introduced to the same French court that had so impressed Angelica Van Buren—and with the same effect. Julia imitated the monarchical manners in her receptions.

Congress, caught in political struggles with Tyler over his refusal to sign legislation authorizing a national bank (he vetoed two separate bills), had refused to appropriate money to refurbish the White House. Using her mother's money, Julia set about repainting the building, reupholstering the furnishings, and updating the decoration. Once the president's mansion was presentable, she set about making her mark.

"I intend to do something in the way of entertaining," the young bride wrote, "that shall be the admiration and talk of all the Washington world."

Toward that end, she threw herself a White House wedding reception. She revived Angelica Van Buren's custom of receiving guests while seated on a raised platform, surrounded by a retinue of young female retainers who were referred to by one newspaper as the "twelve vestal virgins." These female friends followed her like an entourage, accompanying her at White House events and even to parties in private homes.

Dolley Madison became a close companion, mentoring the young Julia in the social ways of Washington and the subtle interplay between politics and entertainment in the nation's capital. It would have been familiar advice. Her own mother is supposed to have told her to pay attention to politics and affairs of state as well, but now she was hearing it from the woman who wrote the book. Some authors, such as Melba Porter Hay and Dorothy and Carl Schneider, maintain that Julia's White House events were carefully calculated to curry political favor from powerful members of Congress whose support the Tyler administration needed. There is ample evidence that Julia became involved in matters of political patronage, the business of deciding who will receive presidential appointments or plum government jobs. Julia was especially involved in New York patronage decisions, where her brother's aspirations to launch his own political career through New York's Tammany Hall Democratic machine depended on creating a political network. Presidential appointments would be particularly useful.

She also did something no other first lady had done. In Europe Julia had learned the latest dance crazes, including the energetic polka. Now she danced in public at White House receptions, and started a national dance craze in the process. "Julia Waltzes" and the polka spread across the country now that the first lady had legitimized public behavior that the prudish still viewed as scandalous.

It is a mark of her impact that society soon began to refer to Julia as the "Lovely Lady Presidentress." No first lady had earned a popularly conferred title in many years. This is even more remarkable in light of the fact that the title was planted in the newspapers by her press agent. It stuck.

Julia quickly accumulated political power and put it to use in support of her husband's controversial proposal to annex Texas to the United States. Disputes between proslavery and antislavery factions had stalled action until Julia went to work. She courted the necessary votes among members of the Senate and the House, even to the point of persuading Supreme Court Justice John McLean, a former suitor, to make a toast to "Texas and Tyler" during a Washington dinner. Julia drew the men out on their opinions at White House social events, sometimes flirting or using flattery, always advocating the Tyler administration's views.

The newspapers noticed Julia's activism. The first political cartoon linking a first lady and a policy issue featured Julia and the Texas annexation proposal. Editorialists opined that the issue might cost Tyler his chances of being elected in his own right. Some implied that it was Julia who had annexed Tyler. Then it actually happened.

When Tyler's annexation of Texas was approved by Congress, he gave Julia the commemorative gold pen used for the signing ceremony. She wore it proudly around her neck like a hunter would a trophy claw.

Then, as the papers had predicted, the election was lost. Tyler had alienated many key supporters of his own political party. At one point his entire cabinet, with the exception of Secretary of State Daniel Webster, resigned en masse. The annexation of Texas was a contentious issue between free states and slave states, and it energized his political opponents. Julia's glory was short-lived. Tyler lost the election of 1844 to James K. Polk. The Lovely Lady Presidentress had had a mere eight months as first lady, but she left an indelible mark. From her innovative use of the press to the new tradition of playing "Hail to the Chief," Julia Gardiner Tyler was a trendsetter. We can only speculate what she might have done with more time in the White House.

Historians rate the Tyler administration's greatest accomplishments in foreign affairs. The annexation of Texas is among President Tyler's most notable domestic policy accomplishments. Julia played an open and active role in lobbying for congressional support of the annexation bill, making her a political partner in the fullest sense.

Her last White House ball was an affair to remember. Three thousand guests were invited. The rooms were lit by six hundred candles. Wine was served in open barrels, and ninety-six bottles of champagne were consumed in toasts.

Julia paid several calls on incoming first lady Sarah Polk in the interval between the election and the inauguration. Mrs. Polk was a stark contrast to Mrs. Tyler. She was pious, thought dancing at public functions was improper, and disapproved of hard liquor. This latter trait earned her the nickname "Sahara Sarah" because she preferred her dinners and receptions to be "dry."

Julia invited President-elect Polk and his wife, Sarah, to attend her farewell ball, but they chose not to come.

After leaving the White House, John and Julia Tyler had seven children together. John Tyler died in 1862. Julia lived until 1889. She never remarried.

In 1982 and again in 1993, the academics polled by the Siena College Research Institute ranked Julia No. 27 among first ladies. This seems a low rating in view of the ways in which Julia expanded the role of first lady. She was the first to understand the value of public relations and to employ a press secretary. She was active in successfully lobbying Congress on her husband's top priority of bringing Texas into the Union. She was not only a full political partner in the presidency but also a public trendsetter. Her standing among first ladies deserves reevaluation.

SARAH CHILDRESS POLK

FIRST LADY: 1845–1849
11TH PRESIDENTIAL ADMINISTRATION
SIENA RESEARCH INSTITUTE RATING: 20

"The scepter shall come back to Tennessee before very long and your own fair self shall be the queen."
—President Andrew Jackson

It seems to have been manifest destiny that made Sarah Childress Polk a politician's wife. She and her husband, James K. Polk, functioned as a political partnership throughout the entire twenty-five years of their marriage, culminating in a presidency that historians rate as among the top twenty administrations in our history. To this day, she remains one of the most politically influential women to have occupied the White House.

Sarah Childress's childhood set the stage for a career in politics. Her father, Captain Joel Childress, was a prominent Tennessee planter involved in the state's political circles. General Andrew Jackson was a family friend. Sarah's childhood home was the scene of political gatherings; overnight guests included congressmen and candidates passing through the area during political campaign seasons. From the start she was exposed to politics and politicians.

When it came to his daughters, Captain Childress had an enlightened view of education. Sarah received her primary education at the Daniel Elam School in Murfreesboro. She and her older sister were tutored by the principal of the Bradley Academy, where her future husband, James Polk, was also a student. Next, Captain Childress sent his girls to a boarding school in Nashville.

Sarah's exposure to the wider world of Nashville included being entertained as a guest at the home of Andrew and Rachel Jackson. The War of 1812 had only just ended, and Jackson was at the pinnacle of his popularity as a war hero. The talk around the Jackson household would have been heady for a young woman just entering puberty, and although it would be another ten years before Jackson would first run for the presidency, members of the press were already comparing him with George Washington. No doubt the impressionable young Sarah was caught up in the excitement of political speculation—and her personal acquaintance with a real American hero.

Captain Childress's ambitions for his daughters did not end in Nashville, however. The preeminent school for young ladies in the region was the Moravian Female Academy in Salem, North Carolina. In 1817, Sarah and her sister made the five-hundred-mile journey together. For the next two years, she studied history, geography, English, music, and the Bible. Then her studies at the Moravian Academy were cut short when her father died in 1819.

Although she was only sixteen years old, Sarah had already gotten an education far beyond what was available to most of her contemporaries. By the time of her father's death, she had been exposed to politics at home and in Nashville. It's no surprise that she met James Polk, then a young attorney with political ambitions, at a political reception for Tennessee's governor.

Their courtship lasted for four years. Andrew Jackson is said to have advised the young James to make Sarah his bride. "Her wealthy family, education, health, and appearance are all superior," the general is supposed to have remarked. It may not have been a romantic endorsement, but by putting his imprimatur on the couple Jackson helped forge an enduring political alliance among the three of them.

The couple were married on New Year's Day in 1824. She was twenty years old, and he was twenty-eight. Contemporary legend has it that she agreed to marry James only on the condition that he would run for the state legislature. This story is most likely apocryphal, but its mere existence illustrates the fact that in her own time Sarah Polk was recognized as a driving political force in the couple's life. If it is true, it has to be one of the more unusual prenuptial agreements.

Whatever their arrangement, James did run for the legislature in 1823, while the couple were planning their wedding. He won his election a few months before they married. From their first wedded day, they were a political pair. Two years later, James ran for Congress, and Sarah joined him in Washington during the second year of his first term. They lived in a boardinghouse with congressmen from other states. It may not seem like an ideal arrangement for a young couple, but it had its advantages. Cooking and cleaning were handled by the proprietor, liberating Sarah from many domestic duties. Two slaves she brought with her from Tennessee further relieved Sarah of the Polks' personal chores.

At breakfast, lunch, and supper, the table talk in the boardinghouse inevitably turned to politics, given the occupations of the inhabitants. Sarah took part in the political dialogue as an equal, sometimes openly disagreeing with Congressman Polk's views.

It may have been at the boardinghouse that Sarah developed an aversion to hard alcohol. In the nineteenth century, whiskey was a common breakfast beverage. Social drinking began in the morning and continued throughout the day. The annual per capita alcohol consumption far exceeded today's quantities, and an inescapable conclusion is that nineteenth-century Americans were, by current standards, legally drunk most of the time. No doubt Sarah observed how liquor loosened men's tongues, compromised political confidences, and confounded reasonable discussion of political differences. Many commentators attribute "Sahara Sarah's" dislike of drinking to her religious views, but it seems equally likely that she objected to it on practical grounds.

She attended sessions of the House of Representatives, not for the purpose the young and flirtatious Julia Gardiner had—to attract male admirers—but to listen avidly to the debates on the floor. She devoured the newspapers, noting stories for James to read, and helped craft his political speeches.

Sarah was also a hit socially. She gratefully attended receptions, levees, dinners, and all the other obligations of political careers that so many spouses view as an insufferable burden. Along the way, she won many friends through her intelligence, social graces, and dark beauty that one admirer said was like a Spanish *dona*, or lady.

In 1835, Polk became Speaker of the House. Andrew Jackson was president, and Polk bore the burden of seeing that his agenda was enacted into legislation. He was effective and earned the nickname "Young Hickory" in recognition of the role he played in the success of the Jackson administration. It was more than a flattering nickname. With "Old Hickory" Jackson in the White House and "Young Hickory" Polk ramrodding his legislation through the House, the comparison marked Polk as a political rising star.

Sarah understood the importance of the Speaker's job. "The Speaker," she astutely observed, "if [it is] the proper person . . . with the correct idea of his position, has even more power and influence upon legislation, and directing the policy of parties than the President or any other public officer."

Her husband was potentially this single most powerful politician in the land. It would no longer do for the couple to live among junior congressmen at a boardinghouse. Polk foresaw awkward situations arising, and Sarah agreed. They moved to private rooms on Pennsylvania Avenue.

In a move that superficially seems a political misstep, Polk abandoned his Speakership and the accompanying politically safe congressional seat to run for governor of Tennessee in 1838. Sarah became his campaign manager, handling his schedule, speaking appearances, campaign literature mailings, and political correspondence. He won. For the next two years, Mr. and Mrs. Polk enjoyed the governorship of Tennessee. Sarah became a social surrogate for her husband, accepting invitations he couldn't and attending them in his stead. Again, her superior social and intellectual skills won many supporters.

Then, in 1841, Polk lost his reelection bid. He ran for governor again in 1843, and again lost. Between campaigns, Polk supported the two with legal work. It must have seemed to Sarah that they had left the pinnacle of power only to end up in a self-imposed political exile.

Chance intervened. The Democratic convention of 1844 deadlocked over the choice of a presidential candidate. Polk became the compromise candidate. No one had foreseen this development. A new phrase—*dark horse*—entered the political lexicon.

The couple's home in Columbia, Tennessee, quickly was converted into a campaign headquarters. Again, Sarah was instrumental in directing the efforts of political workers. She oversaw the issuance of news releases regarding the campaign, in effect becoming a campaign press secretary.

This time Polk won. During the campaign, he made an unusual promise. Polk laid out his political agenda in clear terms, and declared that he would be a one-term president. He intended to accomplish his agenda in four years. It was an unusual step. A century later it still earned accolades from the likes of Harry Truman, who praised Polk as a president who told the people what he would do, and then did it.

Sarah Polk now had to meld two roles. She was her husband's political partner in the fullest sense of the word—and she also was first lady. By the middle of the nineteenth century, the term had begun to develop the connotation of a queen in the sense that first ladies were perceived primarily in terms of their ceremonial duties as spouse of the head of state. In the early days of the republic, the title *Queen* would have been applied as an insult, implying that the occupant of the White House was assuming courtly airs or, worse, trying to restore the monarchy. In another fifty years, the term would freely be applied, without any sense of irony, to the role. Marian West, writing about first ladies for *Munsey's Magazine* at the turn of the twentieth century, titled her work "Our Four Year Queens."

If she was to be queen as well as political partner, the duties of the White House would require all her energy. The Polks had no children. To outside observers, this was fortuitous. "You are not the one, Madam," a sympathetic judge told her, "to have the charge of a little child; you who have always been so absorbed in political and social affairs."

Sarah Polk decided to economize on time in other ways, too. She refused the tedious duty of returning calls, a time-consuming affair that kept other first ladies carriagebound from house to house for three or four hours in a day.

There was one important exception to this rule. She developed a genuine friendship with the now-septuagenarian Dolley Madison. On one occasion, first lady Polk pulled up in her carriage outside Dolley's house while the dowager was entertaining a group of wives of congressmen and senators. They pushed their hostess to gently reprimand the first lady for her failure to return calls. Dolley outfoxed them instead. Whether she believed it or not, she diplomatically noted that it was much easier to return calls in her day, when Washington was still a new and sparsely populated town.

Sarah forbade dancing at White House parties, explaining that she thought it indecorous for dancing to go on in one room while important political and diplomatic conversations went on in the next. One wonders whether this was a mere pretext. First lady Polk knew she could command the attention of Washington's prominent men in a cerebral conversation. She may have felt less certain of her dominance when viewed together with younger women on the dance floor. No doubt the participants in the important state conversations in the adjoining rooms would have been distracted, and probably lured away by the sounds of a lively dance in the next salon vying for their attention. Banning dancing was simply Sarah's way to ensure that White House receptions were politically productive.

Sarah kept Julia Tyler's innovation of having the Marine Band play "Hail to the Chief," but she did away with other White House pretensions. Gone were the "vestal virgins," the raised dais, and the announcement of guests as done in royal courts. The Polks held White House "levees" twice a week, in which the president and first lady shook hands and mingled freely with their guests. No alcohol or food was served at these affairs. This may have reflected Sarah's determination to manage the White House on the twenty-five-thousand-dollar annual salary her husband made as president. Guests who preferred more lavish entertainment are said to have gone to nearby Dolley Madison's house afterward, but the revered widow was again near poverty, thanks largely to Payne, her spendthrift grown son. It is hard to imagine Dolley's budget stretching to supply Washington's political elite with the free drinks and food they had become accustomed to during the Tyler administration, but she did it.

While most accounts of Sarah suggest that she was against drinking, one passage from the diary of a congressional wife belies the notion. The woman wrote in her journal that during a four-hour White House dinner, there were multiple wineglasses for different hues of wine with each course of the meal that "formed a rainbow around each plate." There were glasses for the champagne, a Sauternes, and ruby port for after dinner. In all they totaled six glasses—just about the right amount, over four hours, to stay at the legal sobriety limit for driving, but apparently to nineteenth-century guests this quantity of alcohol was deemed insufficient.

Similarly, her reluctance to entertain callers at the White House on

Sundays has been reported as excessive piety. Her husband, James, who never had as robust a constitution as Sarah, was in fact frail. Doctors prescribed rest, suggesting a prolonged stay by the seashore and a diet of oysters and lobster to restore his strength. Polk refused to take their advice. Throughout his presidency, he never took a vacation. Sarah's desire to preserve one day in the week out of the hectic presidential schedule seems equally explainable for the practical reason that Polk needed rest. She would certainly not be the last first lady to try to exercise some restraint in presidential scheduling.

We get a sense of Sarah's view of a first lady's domestic duties from an exchange with a niece: ". . . If I should be fortunate enough to reach the White House," Sarah told the young woman, "I expected to live on $25,000 a year, and I will neither keep house nor make butter."

Instead she followed her passion for politics, immersing herself in state affairs. She wrote and rewrote her husband's speeches, reported to him after sounding out the opinions of influential members of Congress at political receptions and official dinners, and traveled with him on presidential trips. She was a combination of political strategist and policy consultant, press secretary, and speechwriter. This unique political partnership yielded impressive results.

The Polk administration embraced the concept of manifest destiny. This held that the young republic was ordained to expand as far in all directions as possible—northward toward Canada, south and west into Mexican territory—until it stretched from the Atlantic to the Pacific.

Polk made manifest destiny a reality during his one term in office. He, like Monroe, settled a simmering border dispute with Britain, this time in the Pacific Northwest; it resulted in the Oregon Treaty of 1846. As a result, waves of American immigration to the territory flowed in wagon trains along the Oregon Trail.

When Mexican troops crossed the Rio Grande, Polk got Congress to declare war. Two years later, the treaty Polk concluded with Mexico gave the United States undisputed claim to Texas, all of California and New Mexico, and parts of seven southwestern states in exchange for a payment of fifteen million dollars. Polk's successful negotiations with Mexico built on former president Tyler's prescient annexation of Texas. Polk's announcement of the discovery of gold in California in his 1848 State of the Union address contributed to the gold rush fever, and advanced the settlement of California and the newly acquired territories of the Far West by American immigrants.

The Polk presidency even laid the groundwork for Teddy Roosevelt's Panama Canal. In 1847, he negotiated a treaty with Colombia giving the United States rights to create a passageway across the isthmus of Panama. In domestic affairs, the Polk administration maintained a strict constructionist view of the Constitution that emphasized the rights of individual states to act as sovereign entities. Strict constructionists believed that the Constitution should be followed closely, not expanded to meet the demands of the times by judicial interpretation. Polk fostered the independence of the treasury to prevent public funds from being accumulated in private banks. His administration's theme was "New Democracy," which in reality was a continuation of the Jacksonian concept of democracy. It placed an emphasis on the rights of common people over the privileges of social and political elites.

True to his word, Polk did not campaign for reelection. Within three months of leaving the presidency, he died of dysentery-like symptoms. It is likely that he was exposed to a typhus epidemic during a visit to New Orleans. He was fifty-three when he died at home in Tennessee on June 15, 1849.

Sarah Polk lived for another forty-two years. After his death, however, she no longer took a public role in political affairs. Although she was a slaveholder and kept a plantation the couple had purchased in Mississippi until just before the outbreak of fighting, during the Civil War she declared her neutrality between North and South. Politicians from both sides are said to have respected this stance, and her home became a staple for political visitors during and after the great conflict. She was left to become an icon of the more tranquil days of the early republic.

She must have exercised a kind of nostalgic attraction, for prominent politicians continued to pay her calls throughout her lifetime. Her mind remained keen, and she indulged her lifelong love of politics and statecraft in the discussions with her visitors but refused to engage in public political activities. Sarah Childress Polk chose to rest her laurels on the accomplishments she and John had made together as political partners. She died in 1891.

In the 1993 Siena College Research Institute poll, Sarah was rated No. 20. This is an improvement over the 1982 poll, in which she ranked No. 22. Like other first ladies who served in the period immediately before the Civil War, her ratings seem too low. It is as though Sarah Polk's accomplishments have been overshadowed by the looming national crisis, at least in the view of modern academics. Because being "her own woman" was a criterion used in rating the first ladies, Sarah's reluctance to use her prominence after her husband's death also depresses her score. But these factors are probably less important in accounting for her low rating than the simple fact that many people, even the experts, are unaware of the nuances of Sarah's political involvement and achievements. Familiarity may breed contempt; ignorance breeds low ratings.

Margaret Mackall Smith Taylor

First Lady: March 1849–July 1850
12th Presidential Administration
Siena Research Institute Rating: 33

Margaret Taylor's daughter, Betty Bliss, often acted as First Lady. There is no known portrait or photograph of First Lady Margaret Taylor.

"A plot to deprive me of his society, and shorten his life by unnecessary care and responsibility."

—First Lady Margaret Taylor

To prevent her husband from becoming president, Margaret Taylor prayed every night. During the campaign of 1848, she wanted Henry Clay to win the election. The prayer ploy didn't work. General Zachary Taylor, the hero of the battle of Buena Vista in the just-ended war with Mexico, became the nation's twelfth president and the second to die in office. His term lasted just sixteen months.

There are several accounts of how Margaret Smith and Zachary Taylor met. In one she was only fourteen years old when Taylor, with an injured foot, rode onto the family farm while traveling from Maryland to Washington by horse. She supposedly bound the wound and continued to carry on a long-distance, long-term courtship with the dashing young officer. Some six years later, he is supposed to have returned to marry her. More prosaic accounts hold that the two met while she was visiting a cousin in Kentucky in 1809. Whichever is true, the two married in 1810, when Margaret was twenty-one years old.

Margaret came from a prominent Maryland family, while Zachary grew up on the Kentucky frontier. His father was a wealthy plantation owner. For a wedding present, he gave the young couple a 324-acre farm.

Margaret's father, Walter Smith, had been an officer in the Revolutionary War. He also was a prosperous planter. He gave his daughter many advantages, and Margaret by all accounts displayed the grace and manners to be expected from a member of Maryland's social elite. But by marrying a military officer, she had relatively little opportunity to display them. A military career in the nineteenth century meant a life spent at remote outposts far from the refinements and social life of towns and cities.

For most of their marriage, the Taylors lived in a succession of military posts, often on the ever-expanding republic's new frontiers. They were posted at Fort Knox, Kentucky, Fort Snelling, Minnesota, and Fort Crawford, Wisconsin. Zachary fought in wars against the Seminole Indians, the British in 1812, Chief Black Hawk in the 1830s, and finally against the Mexicans in 1846. His combat career earned him the nickname "Old Rough and Ready." The many military campaigns frequently meant long months of separation from his family.

Two of their daughters died in infancy from a "violent bilious fever" in Louisiana. Three other daughters and a son survived the hardships of frontier posts. Both parents wanted their children well educated and sent them to boarding schools in the East. Nevertheless, all seem to have been entranced by military life. Their only son became a lieutenant in the Confederate army, and all three daughters married military men.

When she could, Margaret accompanied her husband on campaigns. In the Second Seminole War, she went with him to Florida.

"She superintended the cooking of his food; she ministered to the sick and wounded," wrote one chronicler. "She upheld the morale of the little army by the steadfastness of her own self-possession and hope. . . ."

Margaret could not go with Zachary on the Mexican campaign; it was a war reported to have filled her with the opposite of self-possession and hope. She was allegedly overcome by superstitious dread that Zachary would die fighting the armies of Santa Anna. Legend holds that Margaret made a compact with God. She prayed that if he would return her husband unharmed, in repayment she would never go out in society again.

It was an odd bargain, if true, and apparently she intended it to apply only to socializing outside the house such as accepting party or dinner invitations or attending musical recitals or theatrical performances. Zachary not only survived the Mexican War but also emerged a hero after a series of battles culminating in the spectacular Buena Vista victory. The war cemented President Polk's plans to expand the American frontier to the Pacific, and it catapulted General Taylor to unexpected political prominence.

Nothing in his life had prepared him for a political career. Zachary was in his midsixties when he was nominated to be the Whig Party standard-bearer in the 1848 presidential election. Margaret was sixty-one. They were a mature couple who had devoted almost four decades of their lives to national service, sometimes in hardship posts, sometimes in real danger, at a time in their lives when it would only be reasonable to look forward to well-deserved leisure. It's not surprising that Mrs. Taylor might have prayed for the election to go in favor of Henry Clay, or that the outcome seemed more of a punishment than a reward—and she made no pretense about it. From the beginning, Margaret did not want to be an active first lady. When the outgoing president and Mrs. Polk invited her to dinner at the White House, she sent her twenty-four-year-old daughter Betty in her place.

When Betty married Colonel William S. Bliss shortly before Christmas 1848, she had undertaken many of the social functions of the first lady. Her husband also served as an aide to President-elect Taylor.

Margaret was reportedly in "feeble" health, although whether this served as a socially acceptable excuse or was true isn't clear. Unlike Sarah Polk, she had not spent years honing the combination of social and political skills necessary to success in Washington. In this she was not alone.

Some historians believe that, despite his undisputed military prowess, President Taylor also lacked a keen grasp of the workings of the American political system.

Bereft of their accustomed social access, Washington's elite soon spawned rumors to account for Margaret's inattention to the duties of first lady. It was reported that she smoked a corncob pipe and had to kept from public view because of her scandalous habit. She was said to be a "poor white of the wilds" who simply lacked the social skills to entertain. Both rumors were false. In fact, tobacco smoke made her "actively ill."

Betty Bliss greeted guests at White House levees and the larger social affairs, but Margaret was hardly the recluse depicted by the rumors. She did entertain visitors and guests in the more intimate family quarters upstairs at the White House. Some were said to be surprised to find not the pipe-smoking lady of the wild frontier they had imagined, but a gracious, intelligent, and refined woman.

"I always found the most pleasant part of my visit to the White House to be passed in Mrs. Taylor's bright pretty room," wrote Varina Davis, "where the invalid, full of interest in the passing show in which she had not the strength to take part, talked most agreeably and kindly to the many friends admitted to her presence."

Margaret's relationship with Varina Davis is particularly interesting. The young woman was the second wife of Jefferson Davis, who had served with President Taylor in the Mexican War and would go on in a few years to lead the Confederacy. Davis's first wife was the Taylors' daughter Knox.

Knox had married Jefferson Davis against her parents' wishes. Knowing too well the rigors of military life, they preferred that their daughters not marry military men. Their opposition softened when Knox seemed truly contented with Davis, yet the marriage lasted only a few months before Knox died from malaria. That Margaret Taylor welcomed Varina Davis into her company at the White House belies the notion that she was a recluse. To the contrary, it suggests an openness of spirit completely at odds with the rumors about her.

She did attend some public events, and regularly went to services at St. John's Episcopal Church just across Lafayette Square from the White House. She entertained political visitors who called on her husband at eight o'clock at night, and she stayed close to her husband during political discussions. Although she preferred her smaller White House dinners, she took an active part in them. A guest recalls her "capably sharing in her part of the conversation."

If the myth of the recluse was false, however, its existence does reflect the fact that Margaret Taylor was not the kind of first lady to wow Washington. She disappointed the political socialites who expected to be invited into her company, even if it was only as one of a thousand guests at a reception. She set no fashion trends, sparked no controversy for introducing dances at the White House, as Julia Tyler did—nor for banning them either, as did Sarah Polk—nor for pouring alcohol freely, or prohibiting it. She didn't use the newspapers to advance an image, nor did she do so to defend herself when the deprecatory rumors began.

Perhaps she would have grown into the role of first lady, or the role might have grown on her, but we will never know. On July 4, President Taylor attended a ceremony for the laying of the cornerstone of the Washington Monument. When he returned to the White House he ate cherries and ice milk, and soon after fell ill. By the ninth he had died.

Margaret Taylor was too grief-stricken to attend his funeral. She lay in her bed wordlessly and "trembled from head to foot as one band after another blared the funeral music." Within a day she moved out of the White House. No portrait, daguerreotype, or engraving of her has ever been discovered.

Her low ranking in the Siena Research Institute poll reflects both her brief tenure as first lady and her reluctance to engage in the political and social aspects of the job.

Abigail Powers Fillmore

First Lady: 1850–1853
13th Presidential Administration
Siena Research Institute Rating: 31

"What Mrs. Fillmore most enjoyed was to surround herself with a choice selection of congenial friends in her own favorite room—the library."
—lifelong friend and intimate of the first lady

The first teacher to become first lady arrived at the post against all odds. It took President Taylor's untimely death to elevate Vice President Millard Fillmore to the presidency, a rare enough event but not unprecedented. What is remarkable about the Fillmores' political ascendancy is that it happened at all.

Millard Fillmore was not born to wealth or power. He did not capture glory on the battlefield. His beginnings were remarkably humble. He was a farmer's son, born in a frontier log cabin. At the age of fourteen, he apprenticed to learn a trade.

Millard met Abigail when he enrolled in a school where she taught. He was nineteen, and she was twenty-one. She hadn't been born with a silver spoon in her mouth, either. Her father, a Baptist preacher, died when she was a child. Her widowed mother raised the family, educating Abigail largely from the library of books that were her father's legacy. Today, we would call Abigail Powers a bookworm. She developed a lifelong love of books and reading, and created the first White House library.

There was nothing in the pedigree or future prospects of young Abigail and Millard to remotely suggest the likelihood that one day they would become president and first lady. Their horizons ought to have been limited to achieving a comfortable degree of prosperity as the frontier towns developed into cities. They had few advantages other than those they could give themselves through education. That would turn out to be more than enough for this determined young couple.

Abigail had begun working as a teacher when she was sixteen. She was teaching at the New Hope Academy in Sempronius, New York, when the tall young carpenter became her pupil. They were engaged in 1819, but seven years passed before they were married. Millard Fillmore was too poor to support a wife, and Abigail's family objected to her marrying someone who was beneath them socially. Mrs. Powers may not have had much money to raise her children, but as a preacher's widow she and her brood had a higher social standing in the frontier community than a farmer's son. Nevertheless, in 1826 the couple finally married, and moved to the Fillmore family homestead.

For the next two years, Abigail continued to teach school to help support the young couple. This makes her the first first lady who kept working after marriage. For himself, Millard set up a law practice and studied for the bar, supported in part by Abigail's income. She also encouraged him to run for the state legislature. In 1828, he was elected. The couple had known each other for nine years, had supported each other's interests and dreams, and he was only twenty-eight. It was the beginning of a long political partnership.

Abigail worried that when Millard attended legislative sessions in Albany, he might be seduced. She feared the women he encountered would be "fairer and more accomplished females," and that he might be tempted to stray from her. But his responses were reassuring. Millard wrote to his wife every day when they were separated, telling her about the latest political developments and details of his daily activities. The constant contact relieved Abigail's anxiety.

"I am happy and proud in the thought that your heart is firm," she wrote in a letter of 1830, "and that no fascinating female can induce you to forget her whose whole heart is devoted."

That same year they moved to Buffalo, where Millard opened a law partnership. Abigail helped establish a lending library in the town, and studied French and music. She also began accumulating and reading books. Soon their horizons began to expand beyond Buffalo. In the elections of 1832, Millard ran for Congress as an Anti-Mason Party candidate. It was America's first third-party movement, and it owed its existence to a nineteenth-century conspiracy theory that Freemasons in public office were colluding for mutual benefit. After the author of a popular book purporting to reveal Masonic secrets mysteriously disappeared, the Anti-Mason movement gained steam. Its first national political convention was held in 1832. Millard was elected to Congress on the Anti-Mason ticket, which promised to drive all Freemasons out of public life. Ironically, George Washington had been a Freemason.

Abigail did not accompany him to Washington. By now the couple had several children, and she stayed in Buffalo while he boarded in the federal city during legislative sessions. At the end of two years, he returned to his law firm, but in 1836 he ran for Congress again, this time as a candidate of the newly created Whig Party. The Whigs had formed in 1834 in opposition to Andrew Jackson's populism. They favored a national bank and greater federal involvement in economic matters, although on the issue of slavery they were in agreement with the Jacksonian Democrats that the rising tension between free and slave states was best kept off the political agenda.

Winning the election, he left for Washington; Abigail went with him. The children were left with relatives, and for the next six years the couple spent legislative sessions together in the capital. This was Abigail's first exposure to Washington. She adhered to the norms for a politician's wife of the time, immersing herself in the tiresome daily rounds of making and returning social calls, and attending ceremonial affairs.

Abigail made sure her intellect was not confined. She read the newspapers avidly, attended debates in the House, and kept abreast of political developments. Millard consulted her for political advice, which she gave freely and thoughtfully.

Politics was not all that Washington offered a curious mind, either. There were galleries, theaters, concerts, and lectures to attend. Abigail plunged into the city's offerings as she would have done with a good book, wringing from it every available ounce of interest and stimulation.

Millard rose to become chairman of the House Ways and Means Committee, a powerful leadership post. This in turn endowed Abigail with higher ranking than other congressional wives whose husbands lacked a committee chairmanship. The couple with such humble backgrounds found themselves more than midway up the congressional hierarchy. But it was not enough to satisfy Millard's ambition.

In 1842, he left Congress to seek the governorship of New York or the Whig vice presidential nomination, but didn't win either. He returned to his law practice and family for the next five years. The couple's children were now teenagers, and domestic matters occupied their attention until 1847, when Millard was elected comptroller of New York State.

After moving to Albany, the couple sent their daughter Abby to a boarding school in Massachusetts while their son Powers went to Harvard. Abigail, now more worldly, sought out the city's intellectual life and socialized freely in its political circles. But her health suffered. She had injured her foot half a decade earlier, and it never fully recovered. Standing for long periods became torturous. Soon Abigail developed hip and back problems, a common side effect from favoring an injured limb.

Millard's ambitions continued to climb. In 1848, he won the vice presidential nomination for the Whig Party, and when Zachary Taylor won the election that fall Millard was on his way back to Washington. Abigail, however, decided to stay in Buffalo and nurse her ailments. Although her health was suffering, she remained active, welcoming visitors, returning calls, and staying on top of state and now national political trends.

When President Taylor died, Abigail knew she should move to Washington. She filled the role of first lady graciously, despite the real physical difficulty imposed by her injury. The Friday-evening White House receptions typically lasted at least two hours, and the president and first lady were expected to remain on their feet greeting guests and mingling throughout the entire time. Abigail bore the ordeal with grace, although she preferred the smaller White House dinners where she could sit and converse without physical pain.

Her daughter Abby filled in as hostess at some of the larger White House events and receptions, relieving her of some of the physical distress. But it was Abigail who attended most of the official state dinners, the Tuesday-morning open houses for guests and visitors, and the politically important dinners for key congressmen and senators.

She was reportedly appalled to find that the White House had no library. Congress gave her an appropriation of two thousand dollars, and she went to work building an ideal library of classics in all fields. She invited writers like William Thackeray and Washington Irving to meet with her, and cultivated performing artists such as the celebrated soprano Jenny Lind, the "Swedish Nightingale." In effect, she used her position as first lady to create a White House literary salon. She was reportedly a witty and even erudite conversationalist, the most intellectual of the early first ladies.

Millard apparently appreciated his wife's mind. During their absences when he was away at legislative sessions, he wrote to her about politics on a daily basis. Her letters in reply offer political counsel.

"Mrs. Fillmore was a woman who had read much and was well-informed on all the topics of the day," a friend recollected after her death, "and Mr. Fillmore had the highest respect for her attainments, and has been heard to say he never took any important step without her counsel and advice."

Unfortunately for President Fillmore, he didn't heed his wife's good advice regarding the Fugitive Slave Law, which required federal officials to pursue runaway slaves even if they were apprehended after reaching free states. The bill was part of a series of legislative measures that collectively formed the Compromise of 1850, an unsuccessful effort to contain the growing tensions between proslavery and antislavery forces and forestall armed conflict between the states. The compromise's main components admitted California to the Union as a free state, and in return gave slave states the Fugitive Slave Act. President Fillmore personally opposed slavery, but he mistakenly believed a civil war could be prevented through negotiation and compromise. Abigail feared, correctly, that stronger fugitive slave laws would undermine Fillmore's political support in the Northeast. The Compromise of 1850 was a delicate balancing act of competing interests so sharply drawn that former President Zachary Taylor had spoken openly of using military force to impose a blockade against the South. The Civil War was still a decade away, but the political forces that created it were raging.

Historians consider the Compromise of 1850 to be a crowning legislative achievement. In the decades before the Civil War, each time a new state was admitted to the Union there was a battle over whether it would be a free state or a slave state. Quite naturally, the slave states wanted more slave states admitted, to strengthen their voting power in the Congress. At the same time, free states wanted statehood only for those territories that would enter as nonslave states. Although there were high moral principles involved in these disputes, it was also a matter of which side would accumulate more power in Congress. In the Compromise of 1850, while California was admitted as a free state, other western territories were left to choose for themselves whether or not to permit slavery. The slave trade—although not slavery itself—was outlawed in the District of Columbia. To appease proslavery states, the Fugitive Slave Law was given new talons in the form of enforcement by federal marshals. Now runaway slaves could no longer be safe anywhere in the Union, even in antislavery states.

Abigail warned Millard that his signature on the Fugitive Slave Law would undermine his northeastern political base, which was heavily reliant on support from abolitionists. It was an astute observation. Millard lost the Whig nomination in 1852, becoming a one-term president.

He had won his position as Zachary Taylor's running mate because the Whig Party wanted a geographically balanced ticket at a time when sectionalism was rife. Taylor's Kentucky roots and long residency in the South during military postings dictated someone from the North. Millard, a staunch New Yorker, filled this requirement. By signing the Fugitive Slave Law, he in essence pulled the rug out from under himself by eroding his political base.

The president may have felt he had no choice. Without having a clear idea how it would come about, many politicians who were antislavery hoped the nation would find a way to gradually, and painlessly, end the institution of forced servitude. Fillmore fell into this category. The Compromise of 1850 in some respects embodied the hope that a gradual evolution away from slavery could be achieved.

Ironically, had Taylor lived he might have vetoed the entire series of bills that made up the compromise. He and Fillmore disagreed on the issue. Fillmore told President Taylor that if the legislation was deadlocked in the Senate, he intended to use his vice presidential prerogative to cast the tie-breaking vote in favor of the legislation. This split within Whig ranks was avoided when Taylor died soon before the legislation passed Congress.

In foreign policy, the Fillmore administration is remembered best for dispatching Commodore Perry to open Japan to trade, and for the appointment of Daniel Webster as secretary of state.

Abigail was the first first lady recorded as attending the inauguration of the new president-elect. She and Millard attended the lengthy ceremony on a blustery March day. Afterward she returned to her rooms in the Willard Hotel, where the couple stayed after vacating the White House for President Franklin Pierce. Abigail caught a chill during the ceremony and parade, though it didn't seem serious at first. She busied herself packing her books and other belongings. She and Millard discussed traveling now that they were free of the burdens of office, possibly to Europe. On a shopping trip with her daughter Abby, she collapsed. Her cold had developed into bronchitis, and from there progressed to pneumonia. Three weeks after the end of the Fillmore administration, Abigail died in the Willard Hotel.

Although he remained active in politics and ran unsuccessfully for the presidency in 1856 as the candidate of the Know-Nothing Party, Millard Fillmore had reached the pinnacle of his political career. Without Abigail at his side, he never attained the same degree of political influence he had achieved as part of a couple.

Jane Means Appleton Pierce

First Lady: 1853–1857
14th Presidential Administration
Siena Research Institute Rating: 34

"Inclined to pensive melancholy."
—Laura C. Holloway

Jane Pierce made so little mark as first lady that not only is her tenure in the White House shrouded in mystery, but even her physical characteristics are clouded by history's mists. She is an enigma, and will probably always so remain.

Modern historians and biographers report that she didn't attend a single White House social affair for the first two years of her husband's term as president. They say she had little influence over or interest in political or social events in Washington, a city she is claimed to have detested. She is portrayed as a grief-stricken woman of great beauty who pined away in the upstairs rooms of the White House mourning for her dead children, while her husband entertained guests in the reception rooms below.

Of her physical appearance, one modern writer, Carl S. Anthony, said she was "a beautiful woman, with finely chiseled features, pale ivory skin, and raven hair," while another called her "pretty" and yet another modern chronicler, Margaret Brown Klapthor, noted that "in looks . . . she resembled the heroine of a Victorian novel."

Jefferson Davis's wife Varina, who was a social companion (some say social rival) of Jane's during her tenure as first lady, offers a less flattering view of Mrs. Pierce's physical appearance. "She was very small," Varina wrote, "and never could have been pretty. . . ."

Was the recluse a beautiful woman, or not? Was the recluse even a recluse? Here again, contemporary and modern accounts differ.

Nineteenth-century writer Laura Holloway chronicled Jane Pierce's life in her 1881 book, *The Ladies of the White House*. Holloway asked one of Pierce's contemporaries, a J. D. Hoover, about Pierce's activities as first lady. Hoover sent Holloway a detailed letter refuting the contention that she was reclusive.

"The idea has somehow gone out that Mrs. Pierce did not participate in the receptions and entertainments at the White House," he wrote. "This is an inexcusable blunder. . . . The fact is, Mrs. Pierce seldom omitted attendance upon the public receptions of the President.

"She was punctually present also at her own Friday receptions," Hoover continued, "although at times suffering greatly. Often in the evening of the President's levee, she would allow herself to be conducted into the Blue Room, and there remain all the evening receiving, with that quiet ease and dignity that characterized her always: a duty which few ladies, indeed, would have had the courage to perform in her then delicate state of health."

The answer to the contradictory accounts regarding Jane Pierce may lie in the tragedy that befell the Pierce family before their move to the White House. She entered her husband's term of office a first lady in mourning for her eleven-year-old son Benny, and was probably in a state of clinical depression. He had died in a train accident two months before the presidential inauguration.

Jane, her husband Franklin, and their last surviving child Benny—two other sons had died previously—were traveling between Boston and Concord on the Boston & Maine Railroad when an axle broke on one of the passenger cars. The train cars derailed and plunged down an embankment.

Although badly bruised in the accident, President-elect Pierce recovered his senses sufficiently to start searching through the wreckage for his family. He found Jane in the shattered passenger compartment and carried her in his arms away from the wreck.

Benny was pinned under a heavy metal beam, his forehead crushed, and either already dead or in his death throes when his father found him. As with most aspects of the Pierce presidency, accounts differ. Some say that Jane and Franklin witnessed Benny's final agony; others that she could never forget the sight of her son's crushed skull.

Her bereavement was apparently so strong that she was unable to attend the March inauguration of her husband and Vice President Rufus King. In deference to the Pierces' mourning, there were no inaugural balls to celebrate the new administration.

Few events in life are so powerful as death. It causes a broad range of psychological phenomena among, not only the grief-stricken but also those who observe them, ranging from denial to projection. Jane Pierce's tragic loss no doubt still causes many historians to see, and then report as fact, what they imagine ought to have been her circumstances. And so she becomes the mysterious, reclusive, beautiful, tragic, Victorian heroine of mythic proportions.

Jane Means Appleton was born in 1806. Her father, a reverend, became the president of Bowdoin College when she was only a year old. She was well educated and intelligent and enjoyed literature. But from childhood, she is described in terms that today would suggest chronic depression.

"Naturally inclined to pensive melancholy," Holloway wrote, "the result, partly of her physical condition, she was from her childhood the victim of intense sensibilities and suffering, and was during her life the unfortunate possessor of an organism, whose every vibration was wonderfully acute and sensitive.

"The world of suffering locked up in the hearts of such persons it is impossible to estimate," Holloway continued, "but happier by far is the day of their deaths than the years of their lives."

Jane and Franklin Pierce met in 1826. At twenty-two, he was two years older than she, and from a politically active family. His father, Benjamin Pierce, became governor of New Hampshire.

Jane's mother—her father died in 1819 when she was thirteen years old—disapproved of Franklin. Her Calvinist beliefs disdained drinking, while Franklin plied the taverns drinking freely and talking politics. The Appletons had been Federalists, distrustful of Democrats such as Pierce, whom they perceived as part of a dangerous rabble. No doubt the mother's opposition played an important role in stretching out the young couple's engagement, which lasted an epic eight years!

During the interval, Franklin began his political ascent. He served two terms in the New Hampshire House of Representatives while his father was governor. After that, he ran as a Jackson Democrat and won election to the U.S. House of Representatives.

They married in 1834. He was twenty-nine and a newly elected congressman. She was twenty-eight and eagerly accompanied him to Washington.

The young couple lived in a boardinghouse during his first session of Congress. Jane was introduced to the life of Washington's political elite. Andrew Jackson was president, and Congressman Pierce and his wife were invited to White House affairs and entertained by the city's political insiders.

At the end of the session, the Pierces bought a house in Hillsborough, New Hampshire. Franklin established a law practice where he worked when Congress was not in session, and Jane became pregnant with their first child. When Congress reconvened, Franklin Pierce returned to Washington and Jane stayed behind in New Hampshire. Their son Franklin Pierce Jr. was born in February 1836. He lived for only a few days.

The following autumn Jane returned to Washington, where the couple again settled in a boardinghouse. In November, Franklin won the race for senator. Jane continued to alternate her time between New England and Washington. A second son, Frank Robert Pierce, was born in 1839, and Benjamin arrived in 1841.

The boys are said to have given Jane Pierce an excuse to urge her husband to abandon politics. She reportedly wanted to raise them in a healthier climate than Washington, D.C., afforded, but didn't want them (or presumably herself) to endure long separations from their father. Pierce resigned his Senate seat in 1842, and practiced law in Concord, New Hampshire.

When President Polk offered him the post of attorney general, he declined it in pointed language. "Although the early years of my manhood were devoted to public life, it was never really suited to my taste," Pierce wrote. "I longed, as I am sure you must have often done, for the quiet and independence that belong only to the private citizen, and now, at forty, I feel that desire stronger than ever."

Pierce pleaded that he could not settle matters at his law firm or rearrange them so as to be able to take up the new post in a timely fashion. Then he added a personal touch to underscore his decision.

"Besides, you know that Mrs. Pierce's health, while at Washington, was very delicate," he said. "It is, I fear, even more so now; and the responsibilities which the proposed change would necessarily impose upon her, ought, probably, in themselves to constitute an insurmountable objection to leaving our quiet home for a public station in Washington."

Jane's wish for a healthful climate in which to raise her sons backfired badly. Despite Concord's healthier climate, in 1843 Frank Robert died, a victim of typhus. He was just four years old. Now Jane had only one surviving child—Benjamin.

When war with Mexico broke out in 1846, Franklin Pierce felt compelled to join in the fight. He enlisted in a company of infantry in Concord and sailed for Mexico from Newport, Rhode Island, in 1847. During the nine months he spent in the Mexican campaign, ex-senator Pierce distinguished himself sufficiently to make the rank of brigadier general.

Although he returned to private life seemingly contented, Franklin schemed secretly to return to national politics. In 1852, he was nominated as the Democratic Party's presidential candidate. He protested to his wife that he didn't really want the presidency but felt compelled to run out of loyalty to his party. Like Margaret Taylor, a previous reluctant potential "presidentress," Jane actually prayed for her husband to lose the election. Catching her mood, even young Benjamin reportedly prayed that his father would not win.

Jane's and Benny's prayers went unfulfilled. Pierce won in an electoral college landslide. It was in the interval between the election and the inauguration that Pierce took his family to Boston to attend a friend's funeral. The derailment that killed Benny resurrected a streak of fatalism in Jane.

In her grief, she offhandedly told her husband that the Almighty had taken their child's life so he would suffer no distractions from his duties as president. Franklin was reportedly wounded by the remark, which he construed to mean she believed his political ambitions had cost him his last child's life. Jane's fatalism mirrors Franklin's own beliefs regarding Frank Robert's earlier death from typhus; he had mused that God had taken the boy's life because believers are commanded not to worship "idols," even in the fleshly form of loved ones. There is little doubt both Jane and Franklin searched their religious convictions for the meaning of their loss, and if her comments hurt him it is probably because they reflected his own misgivings.

Disconsolate is too weak a word to describe the mood both Pierces must have felt on becoming the White House's newest occupants. The sense of tragedy that preceded them must have colored the perception of all that followed. Believed to be in deep mourning, she was said by some historians to be holed up in the upstairs rooms of the White House, writing letters to her dead child, consulting psychics, and trying to contact his spirit.

That is the enigma of Jane Pierce. Albert Einstein said that theory decides what we manage to observe. To those who wanted to see a grief-stricken, dysfunctional first lady, there is the gloomy and star-crossed Jane Pierce, the tragic heroine of Victorian literature. To those who wanted to see Jane Pierce rise above her personal tragedies, there is the reluctant but dutiful first lady.

"He has but three large dinners yet, " Jane wrote to her sister of her new duties as mistress of the White House, "at all of which I have appeared, but not at the evening receptions. . . ."

Nathaniel Hawthorne took her on boat outings along the Potomac. She attended private White House dinners at which she talked politics with Senator Stephen Douglas. She appeared in the Senate to hear debates.

Yet her "woe begone face," as one woman cruelly remarked, "banished all animation in others. . . ." Even when she began appearing regularly at the White House "levees," observers couldn't see beyond their own expectations. One claimed to see "traces of bereavement legibly written on a countenance too ingenuous for concealment."

In all likelihood she was all of these things—present at White House events, but virtually unnoticeable because of her dampened mood, there but not really there—desperate for contact with Benny, to the point of seeking solace through religion or the occult, whichever delivered the goods, but able to rally to the occasion and go through the empty motions of dealing with temporal political concerns—unreconciled to Washington's social and political trivialities, but reconciled to the belief that God had taken her son from her so that she and her husband could fill some divine intention without distraction.

The Pierce presidency is rated as undistinguished by most historians today. That is a fate shared by all three presidents who served in the decade before the Civil War. The judgment against them is perhaps colored more by the events that followed their administrations. None, after all, was able to devise a political solution to prevent the war that ultimately killed more Americans than any other war in our history. None was able to peacefully end slavery, quell sectarian and regional strife, or resolve the Constitution's inherent tension between states' rights and a strong federal government without bloodshed. To the modern mind, this marks them all as failures.

Judged solely on its accomplishments, however, the Pierce presidency fares somewhat better. Pierce was a believer in manifest destiny, and by carrying out the Gadsden Purchase of 1853 he peacefully expanded America's border with Mexico so that the railroads could link Texas to California. In 1855, he tried to purchase Cuba from Spain to add it as another state. He had to abandon his plan when antislavery advocates feared Cuba would enter the Union as a slave state. Had he succeeded, the United States might have averted the war of 1898, the Bay of Pigs fiasco, the Cuban Missile Crisis of 1960, and forty years of anti-American activism spawned by Castro in Central and South America.

Pierce also had a strong fiscal record. When he took office, the national debt stood at sixty million dollars. It had fallen to only eleven million when his term concluded. Pierce believed in limited government, but he was capable of being an activist president. He gave land grants to encourage the expansion of the country's fledgling but state-of-the-art transportation system, the railroads. He backed construction of a transatlantic telegraph cable—the Internet of its day—to build a stronger communications infrastructure between the United States and Europe.

Overshadowing it all, however, was the looming conflict between North and South. Perhaps the prevention of the Civil War was what Jane considered her husband's divine duty to achieve without distraction. Perhaps her despondency and the cheerlessness of her tenure as first lady owes to the conviction that this was their true calling—a calling in which they ultimately failed.

Franklin Pierce might have met his calling if he had won a second term in office, but he didn't even get the nomination. His own party passed him over, and the title of Democratic Party presidential candidate passed to James Buchanan.

Jane Pierce and her husband spent the next two years traveling, first in the United States and then in Europe. She carried Benny's Bible with her, and a box containing lockets of hair of all her beloved family dead, her sons, her sister, her mother. She died in 1863, possibly of tuberculosis, or perhaps pneumonia, passing into history as she had passed through life, enigmatically.

She ranks among the lowest of the first ladies, largely because she so often failed to make a mark—and when she did make one, it was generally in the negative. Her political impact, for example, registers in the form of opposition to her husband's career. She was not so much a political partner as she was a political impediment. We do not know what she would have become had her children not died.

She did not set or seemingly want to set any social trends. She doesn't register as a force in foreign policy. She was most certainly not a role model. The most she can be credited with is that, given her circumstances, she went through the motions.

HARRIET LANE

FIRST LADY: 1857–1861
15TH PRESIDENTIAL ADMINISTRATION
SIENA RESEARCH INSTITUTE RATING: 28*

The Democratic Queen

An orphan who played White House hostess for the only bachelor president became one of the country's most popular first ladies. James Buchanan raised his niece Harriet Lane after the young girl was orphaned at the age of nine. In his youth, Buchanan had loved a woman named Anne Coleman. After what he later described as a trivial lover's quarrel, they separated. Then she died suddenly, perhaps by suicide. Buchanan considered her the love of his life, and never married.

He was almost fifty years old, a bachelor well set in his ways, with a busy political career when Harriet literally thrust herself into his life. Harriet's mother had died when she was only seven. Her father died two years later, leaving the children with an estate but no guardian. Harriet wanted to live with her bachelor uncle at his Lancaster, Pennsylvania, home. By the time she turned eleven, he had become her lifelong legal guardian.

Buchanan was already launched in a political career in which he would ultimately serve as state legislator, congressman, senator, secretary of state, minister to Russia and to the Court of St. James, and finally president. But if he had any misgivings about young Harriet's intrusion into his life, they were short-lived.

The blond-haired girl with the violet-blue eyes apparently livened up his life. Laura Holloway described her as "a fun-loving, trick-playing romp, and a willful domestic outlaw." Others called her "tom-boyish." She was certainly spirited. At a time when women didn't engage in athletic sports, and certainly didn't compete in them against men, Harriet not only challenged a young man to a footrace but left him gasping for air in the dust behind her.

This capacity for mischievous charm stayed with her for life. The young orphan would one day use it to enchant the older politicians who surrounded Uncle Buchanan, charm royal admirers, captivate Queen Victoria, and fascinate Washington, D.C., and the nation.

Until the age of twelve, Buchanan educated his niece at a day school near his Lancaster home. For three years, she attended a boarding school in Charlestown, West Virginia. She spent her vacations with her uncle, and went with him to a fashionable spa resort at Bedford Springs. When she was fifteen, he enrolled her in the Visitation Convent school in Georgetown.

Buchanan had just resigned his Senate seat to become Polk's secretary of state. Harriet was free to leave the school and stay with her uncle on weekends. He encouraged his niece to stay with his guests when he entertained for dinners, listening to their political and diplomatic conversations. She was an attentive audience, soaking up the exposure to powerful politicians.

When Buchanan asked about her favorite subjects at school, her reply was "history, astronomy, and especially mythology." She also excelled in music, presaging a fondness for dance.

When he was named ambassador to the Court of St. James in 1854, he took Harriet with him. She was now a polished young woman of twenty-four and something of a beauty. She was tall, with thick blond hair, whose "deep violet eyes, with the strange dark line around them, could glance cold, stern rebuke. . . ." Laura Holloway thought that "of all her features, her mouth was the most peculiarly beautiful.

"Although in repose it was so indicative of firmness," she wrote in 1881, "it was capable of expressing infinite humor and perfect sweetness."

It helped make her a hit in London. She was introduced to Queen Victoria and made a strong impression on the royal assemblage. The train of her dress contained a hundred yards of white lace. She wore a diamond tiara with white ostrich plumes, and evidently managed the occasion with perfect composure.

"Well, a person would have supposed you were a great beauty, to have heard the way you were talked of today," her uncle said to her that night. "I was asked if we had many such handsome ladies in America.

"I answered, 'Yes, and many much handsomer,' " he teased her. " 'She would scarcely be remarked there for her beauty.' "

At the Court of St. James, diplomatic protocol required that the female relative of an ambassador be assigned a social ranking below his. Harriet, however, was a special case. Queen Victoria herself determined that Harriet should be assigned the same rank as an ambassador's wife. As word spread that she was a favorite at the court, English society opened its doors to embrace Ambassador Buchanan and his niece.

If the English were impressed by Harriet, the mesmerization was mutual. She was courted by young aristocrats, welcomed at great country houses, and entranced by London's cultural attractions.

"She loved England, English people, and English habits," wrote Laura Holloway. "Upon every occasion Miss Lane was most graciously singled out by the Queen, and it was well known that she was not only an unusual favorite with her majesty, but that she was regarded with favor and admiration by all the royal family."

Young, with riveting blue eyes, strikingly tall—Harriet Lane was the Diana of her day.

At age twenty-seven and fresh from her European debut, she watched

Buchanan, now sixty-six, be inaugurated president in March 1857. She quickly dazzled Washington as thoroughly as she had London.

Harriet presided over the now-customary White House events—the open receptions, the official dinners, the smaller private ones whose purposes were principally political, and the ceremonial occasions such as New Year's and Fourth of July parties. Buchanan's international service and wide number of foreign acquaintances added many more social obligations, as visitors from abroad came to call on him motivated by friendship as well as politics.

Under Harriet's guidance, the White House took on an elegant tone. Congress appropriated twenty thousand dollars to replace aging furnishings, and she supervised the expenditures. The domestic staff were English servants. Even as a bachelor, in the days before Harriet became his social hostess, Buchanan had always been an elegant entertainer. Between the two of them, the White House quickly became known for the lavish entertainment.

Not everyone was pleased with the Buchanan style.

"The White House, while under the administration of Buchanan, approached more nearly to my idea of a republican Court," Jefferson Davis complained to an associate. Harriet was soon referred to as the "Democratic Queen," and the Buchanan administration became known as the "gayest Administration."

She was popular. The song "Listen to the Mockingbird" was dedicated in her name, perhaps because she had from childhood displayed a talent for mockery, which as a young woman she expressed in flirtatious teasing. The *Harriet Lane*, a naval vessel, was named for her. Women followed her taste in fashion, copying her "Bertha" style low-cut lace collar that exposed her ample cleavage. *Harriet* became one of the most popular names for baby girls.

She was not merely a fashion and social trendsetter. Harriet and Buchanan read the newspapers together each morning in the White House, and discussed the political events of the day. She attended cabinet meetings. Influenced by the social activism of Victorian England, Harriet made several causes her own as first lady. She was an activist for Native Americans, intervening selectively on their behalf. She loved the arts, and was the first first lady to invite painters to White House dinners. She helped launch the movement to fund a national art gallery. Her activism was distinct from her uncle's political agenda, and Harriet Lane can therefore be considered to have set the precedent for first ladies pursuing separate social agendas—a model that has been followed by the majority of first ladies ever since.

She and the president may have shared similar political views on slavery as well. Buchanan so disliked slavery that he sometimes bought slaves in Washington just so he could set them free in his antislavery home state of Pennsylvania. Because he didn't think slavery was an issue that merited a civil war, however, he bitterly blamed abolitionists—especially women abolitionists—for stirring up animosities that would lead to one.

Harriet abhorred both slavery and the prospect of secession. Moreover, she believed that a sudden emancipation of slaves, rather than a gradual phasing out of slavery followed by the slow integration of freed slaves into society, would be socially disastrous. An early biographer records her view that millions of newly freed slaves unprepared to become citizens could "increase the rate of poverty and disease which would not only cripple the Negro but could devastate the nation as a whole."

Buchanan was a strict constructionist who believed in following the literal meaning of the Constitution when it came to the division of powers between the federal government and the states. His was the last presidency on the eve of the Civil War, and, like Harriet, he fervently believed the correct course of action was compromise between proslavery and antislavery forces. He felt that this would enable a gradual solution to ending slavery.

Because friction between the North and South was increasing, Harriet carefully arranged the invitations and seating of dinner guests to keep the peace. She kept hotheads on either side separated to avoid bitter political arguments at her tables. She is also said to have intervened when discussions became heated, urging her guests to turn the conversation to other topics.

There was plenty to avoid in Buchanan's era. Two days after his inauguration, the Supreme Court handed down the famous *Dred Scott* decision, which infuriated northern abolitionists. The Court ruled that slavery was constitutional and that African Americans whose ancestors had been slaves, even when freed, did not share full rights of citizenship. The Court also ruled that Congress could not ban slavery, nullifying several vital political compromises between slave states and free states, and held that escaped slaves had to be returned even if they had successfully negotiated the passage via the Underground Railroad to a free state.

That same year, Kansas was under consideration for admission to statehood. The *Dred Scott* decision greatly complicated the political maneuvering between southern and northern factions in Congress, with proslavery and antislavery forces locked in a two-year struggle to get Kansans to ratify a state constitution favoring their side. The balance of power in Congress between slavery and antislavery states was delicate. Slave states feared that if new states were admitted to the Union only under the condition that they were free, the South would eventually be outnumbered in Congress. The issue of statehood for Kansas was guaranteed to keep tensions at a high boil for the first three years of Buchanan's term.

Two years into Buchanan's presidency, the abolitionist John Brown struck at southerners' primordial fears when he tried to organize a slave rebellion. Brown and a handful of conspirators raided the federal arsenal at Harpers Ferry, Virginia (now West Virginia), in a forlorn quest to steal weapons to arm a slave uprising. Every slave owner knew of the history of slave insurrections, including particularly bloody uprisings in the French Caribbean. Few doubted that their slaves would be capable of slaughtering them in their beds. Even Martha Washington, in her dotage, feared being poisoned by her slaves, because she had promised to set them free when she died.

Brown's raid was a dismal failure. It ended in a prolonged standoff, with Brown and his followers barricaded in a warehouse. They eventually surrendered to federal troops after killing six people, including a free black man. After a trial they were duly hanged. But as with all acts of political terrorism, the impact went far beyond the actual events into the realm of symbolism. Brown's raid meant the abolitionists had a martyr, and that slave owners could never be completely certain they were beyond the reach of the abolitionists. No matter how many political victories they might win in Congress or the courts, slave owners now feared the next time abolitionists instigated a slave rebellion, it might succeed.

Given the events of the era, there must have been a sense of surrealism in the Buchanan White House, where the elegant young Harriet tried to minimize dinner conversation over issues that would ultimately cost more than 640,000 young American white men their lives.

Buchanan, following the precedent set by the Polk administration in which he'd served as a cabinet officer, banned dancing at White House receptions. That didn't stop Harriet. She simply commandeered the navy ship that was, after all, named for her, using the *Harriet Lane* as a floating ballroom where she and her guests could party while cruising the Potomac River.

Harriet's misuse of a government ship, however, aroused the ire of the press. After a New York newspaper criticized her, her uncle told her he felt that using the ship for a leisure excursion was a "fair subject" for public criticism. This was not the only occasion when Harriet came under the scrutinizing gaze of the press.

In 1860, Buchanan invited the nineteen-year-old Prince of Wales, who was then touring Canada, to extend his North American excursion to include a visit to the White House. Queen Victoria readily accepted, and Harriet Lane set about preparing a royal reception. The event was important because it marked the first time that an heir apparent to the British throne had visited the capital of the United States.

The royal visit lasted five days. It was one of the two occasions in which Harriet used the *Harriet Lane* as a floating ballroom, as she tried to impress the young Prince Edward with the cosmopolitan ways of Washington. Her White House reception for the prince was one of the coveted events of the season. Then, as now, Americans fawned over their royal visitor and fought for invitations.

In other respects, the entertainment she arranged for the royal visit was quite imaginative. Harriet took Edward to a school for teenage girls, where he watched the nubile young ladies as they performed calisthenics. At the time, it was controversial enough for young women to engage in athletics; to do so under the royal eye bordered on voyeurism to nineteenth-century sensibilities. Yet Edward enjoyed himself immensely, and the occasion was seen as evidence of Harriet's enlightened attitudes. The duo also visited Mount Vernon, now a bit dilapidated, to see the graves of George and Martha Washington.

Queen Victoria wrote from Windsor Castle to express her gratitude for the treatment accorded her son in Washington. "He cannot sufficiently praise the great cordiality with which he has been everywhere greeted in your country, and the friendly manner in which you have received him," the queen noted, "and whilst, as a mother, I am grateful for the kindness shown him. . . ."

The trouble began when the prince presented, through the auspices of one Lord Lyons, an engraving of the royal family. It was hung in the White House for the remainder of Buchanan's term. He had declined to run for reelection and was a lame duck by the time of the prince's visit. When the Buchanan presidency ended, Harriet packed the engraving and took it with her when they left. Buchanan was nearly seventy years old and worn out from a lifetime in politics. He had no desire to seek reelection for another term.

Shortly after Lincoln was inaugurated, someone noticed the missing print. Newspapers picked up the story, which in essence accused Harriet of stealing a gift that was intended for the American people, not for her personal use. The propriety or impropriety of gifts to the occupants of the White House was to be a perennial one, whether it was Harriet Lane's keepsake engraving, Nancy Reagan's borrowed designer dresses, or Hillary Clinton's furniture.

In 1862, the prince—as if to make clear where he stood on the matter of the gift—gallantly sent Harriet an oil painting portrait of himself done by the artist Sir John Watson Gordon. Writing from Jaffa in Israel, he said:

> Dear Mr. Buchanan:
> Permit me to request that you will accept the accompanying portrait as a slight mark of my grateful recollection of the hospitable reception and agreeable visit at the White House on the occasion of my tour of the United States. . . . I venture to ask you at the same time to remember me kindly to Miss Lane. . . .

Buchanan had been out of the presidency for just over a year when Edward penned his note. The first great battles of the Civil War were already being fought. In 1860, Lincoln and the Republican Party had campaigned on an open platform promising that if any states seceded from the Union, their rebellion would be met with war. If the ultimatum was intended to have the effect of discouraging secession, it failed miserably. Between the November election of 1860 and Lincoln's March 1861 inauguration, seven states—South Carolina, Louisiana, Alabama, Texas, Mississippi, Florida, and Georgia—seceded. The "gayest Administration" was over.

Harriet Lane heeded her uncle's admonition to marry late in life. She was thirty-six when she became Mrs. Harriet Lane Johnston. She had two sons; both of her children and her husband predeceased her. She returned to live in Washington, and attended White House events, now dressed in a widow's black velvet, adorned in pearls and diamonds. When she died, she donated her art collection to the Smithsonian's National Gallery of Art and left a legacy to the fledgling Johns Hopkins hospital for children.

The "Democratic Queen" was America's Princess Diana. Young, beautiful, audacious, Harriet Lane was a popular first lady who set the standard for fashion and was widely emulated. She was politically involved in her uncle's presidency, and embraced social causes of her own. Her skills at diplomacy are evident from her friendship with Queen Victoria and her adept handling of America's first state visit from a British royal heir. She managed something few first ladies ever achieve—to be simultaneously popular with the public and the Washington elite.

No doubt the years when Harriet Lane was first lady looked even better to Americans in hindsight, as a distant dreamlike time of music and glamour now obscured by the din and smoke of battlefields and the anguished cries of the wounded and the dying.

*As rated in the 1982 Siena Research Institute poll. In subsequent Siena polls, Harriet Lane was not rated because she was not a presidential spouse.

Mary Todd Lincoln

First Lady: 1861–1865
16th Presidential Administration
Siena Research Institute Rating: 37

"I had an ambition to be Mrs. President . . ."

Tempestuous, violent, greedy, driven by ambition and a supernatural belief in destiny, Mary Todd Lincoln is among the most complex women to have occupied the White House. Journalist Marian West, writing in *Munsey's Magazine* at the turn of the twentieth century, called her the "unfortunate Mrs. Lincoln, of whom the less said, perhaps, the better," but then went on to add:

> She was a handle for Lincoln's enemies, an offense to his friends . . . the violent, jealous, vulgar "first lady of the land." Society frankly showed its estimate of her, and all her rage and insolence could not make her queen in anything but name. That she was not quite sane is her best excuse.

Had she lived today, she would have been arrested for domestic violence. In her rages, she battered Abraham Lincoln by throwing stovewood at him and on one occasion chasing him with a butchering knife. Modern analysts would have called him codependent, an enabler of rages and mood swings that oscillated between manic delusions of grandeur and bottomless depression.

She wanted to be the president's wife. She wanted to be a fashion trendsetter. She wanted to be admired by Washington's elite. She wanted to be a full political partner in running the government. She wanted to decide which generals should run the army, and how the war should be fought. Above all, she wanted power.

"He is to be President of the United States some day," Mary Lincoln said early in his political career, "if I had not thought so I never would have married him, for you can see he is not pretty. But look at him. Doesn't he look as if he would make a magnificent President?"

Mary Ann Todd was born in 1818 to Eliza Parker and Robert Smith Todd, an affluent Kentucky couple who ranked among the state's social elite. She was six years old when her mother died in childbirth. She never got along with the woman her father remarried, and her relationship with her stepmother was probably a major factor in Mary's later characterization of her childhood as "desolate."

Well educated by the standards of her time, Mary received the equivalent of a grade school education at the Shelby Female Academy, followed by four years at Madame Charlotte Mentelle's boarding school. She could recite passages from Shakespeare from memory, spoke good French, and had been exposed to history, geography, and natural science in addition to mathematics and English.

As a protégée of Madame Mentelle, Mary came out as a debutante on the cotillion and party circuit with Lexington, Kentucky's, social elite. She was evidently fetching in her youth. Although short by today's standards, her five-feet, two-inch height was well in the average range for the mid–nineteenth century. She had a full figure, alabaster shoulders, clear blue eyes, and light brown hair tinged with gold highlights. A male relative remarked that she was so entrancing that she "could make a bishop forget his prayers."

She left school at the age of eighteen and went to stay for the summer with a sister who lived in the state capital of Springfield, Illinois. Politics had fascinated Mary from childhood, and in the summer of 1836 the heady talk in her sister's home was whether her brother-in-law should run for Congress. In order to remain in Springfield when the summer ended, Mary took a job as an apprentice teacher at Ward's Academy.

Even at this early age, Mary told her friends she would marry a future president. When she was twenty-one, she met Abraham Lincoln, then a practicing attorney and state legislator. Among her other suitors was Lincoln's political rival, Stephen Douglas, who was quickly brushed aside.

"I can't consent to be your wife," she told Douglas bluntly after meeting Lincoln. "I shall become Mrs. President, or I am the victim of false prophets, but it will not be as Mrs. Douglas."

Lincoln was nine years older than her and, at six feet, four inches, towered over her physically. Socially, however, the roles were reversed; in the hierarchy of the times, she towered over him, so much so that her parents considered any match between them ill advised. Lincoln had come from a farm family that ranked far below the social circles enjoyed by the Todds. He was self-educated, often ill clothed, and socially awkward. Her parents vigorously opposed their budding romance.

For two years, they carried on their courtship secretly. When they announced their plans to marry, her parents finally realized the hopelessness of their opposition to the match and consented to hold the wedding in their home. Abe and Mary were wed on November 4, 1842. After the birth of their first son the following year, any remaining parental opposition relented further, and Mary's father helped the young couple purchase a house.

In 1846, Lincoln was elected to Congress, and Mary and their sons went with him to Washington. It was her first introduction to the capital city. As a congressional spouse, she would have attended the White House levees hosted by first lady Sarah Polk; the grande dame of Washington society, Dolley Madison, was still on the scene, although she was now a dowager. Mary fell in love with Washington. Her sister, Elizabeth, gives us the reasons: "Mary loved glitter, show, pomp and power."

This woman, driven since youth to call the White House her own because of a premonition that she would marry a president, must have sized up the city as an invading general analyzes the path to conquest. No doubt she carefully studied the art of cultivating power, projecting a carefully crafted political image, massaging potential supporters, building and then enlarging upon a political base. These are all fundamental survival skills for politics, then and now, and were all the more so for Mary and her spouse. He was not born to privilege, power, or wealth, like so many occupants of the White House. He did not come from a politically prominent family. He was not an heir to a political network, as John Quincy Adams had been earlier in the century or George W. Bush would be in the twenty-first century.

Lincoln, in fact, had poor prospects for advancement and knew it. He often despaired that his political career would ever rise. After his one term in Congress, his career did indeed stall. He sought a sinecure as commissioner of the Land Office but was passed over, although he was offered the post of territorial governor of Oregon. Mary thought it was a bad career choice, and he turned it down.

They went back to Springfield. With her father's financial assistance, Mary oversaw the transformation of the home they had purchased earlier into a fashionable Greek Revival–style house suitable for the upper classes. Mary hosted receptions for as many as five hundred guests at their Springfield home, boosting Lincoln's political prospects. The food was served buffet-style, as was often the fashion in the White House. She was copying the mode of entertainment the political elite used in Washington to cultivate followers.

It paid off in 1860. Lincoln had earned wide exposure in the debates with Mary's former beau Stephen Douglas in 1858, but he was still a long shot for the presidency. In the balloting for the Republican nomination in 1860, he won on the fourth vote as a compromise candidate.

"We are elected!" he is reported to have said when he raced home to give her the news that he was chosen to run. She set to work at once managing his campaign. She wrote letters to political supporters to communicate his policies and platform. She gave interviews to journalists. She attended campaign rallies and debates. She chose the campaign materials and the portrait she considered best, no doubt bearing in mind the angle that made him seem most presidential, the look she had seen on him when they first met twenty years earlier.

Lincoln won the presidency in a four-way race with only 40 percent of the popular vote. What should have been Mary's hour of triumph became an hour of crisis as seven southern states seceded between the November 1860 election and the March 1861 inauguration. Lincoln and the Republican Party had campaigned on a platform that openly called for the abolition of slavery. No president had done so before Lincoln. Rather than face further political battles over slavery, the southern states seceded to form the Confederacy, declaring that Lincoln and the North were a separate political entity with no power over the South.

Nonetheless, the inaugural ball was a splendid affair. Mary led off with a briskly performed dance called the quadrille. The festivities went on two hours longer than scheduled. Never mind that the president now ruled only half the country that had existed before secession; Mrs. President was not to be denied her rendezvous with destiny. Two months after Lincoln's inauguration, the Civil War began.

Mary set about redecorating the White House with a twenty-thousand-dollar appropriation from Congress. In less than a year, she not only spent the entire four-year allowance, but promptly overspent it by 30 percent. She purchased two sets of purple Haviland china—one for official White House entertaining and another entire set for her private use. She bought custom carpets, curtains, wallpaper, and even a seven-hundred-piece set of Bohemian cut glassware. Friendly officials hid the cost overrun in other budgets to spare her from criticism by Congress. Privately, Lincoln fumed. He was having difficulty equipping the rapidly growing Union army and couldn't understand how she could spend on "flub dubs" for the White House when he couldn't ensure that every soldier had a blanket. He wanted to reimburse the government for the cost overruns from his own salary, but Mary refused.

Extravagance didn't trouble Mary. She continued to host dinners and White House receptions for as many as four thousand guests while the casualties mounted on the battlefield and Union generals suffered setback after setback. Predictably, there was criticism. She and Lincoln discussed whether to scale back the entertainment, but Mary refused to sacrifice her grandiose receptions. It was her turn to be the "Republican Queen," and a queen requires a court. Lincoln's instinct was to forgo the weekly receptions, but Mary persuaded him otherwise, and in compromise they agreed to cut back on official White House dinners. She didn't seem to understand that a civil war dictated new boundaries of taste and impropriety.

The Lincoln White House receptions were held on Thursday nights and ended at eleven o'clock. After these soirees, Mary and Abe would generally retire to their quarters and discuss the political intelligence they had gleaned until about one o'clock in the morning. They began their day at breakfast together around eight-thirty in the morning. She spent much of the morning handling correspondence and carefully studying the newspapers for political and war news.

Mary's letters were exercises in political power. She made job recommendations, signing her correspondence "Mrs. President Lincoln." Sometimes she used official War Department stationery to send directions regarding appointments and promotions, ending her letters "By Order of President through War Department" under her own signature. Mary had no constitutional authority to do so, but that was no impediment to her use of power. She didn't hesitate to send such "requests" to cabinet officers, who customarily obliged her. Nor did she hesitate to promote relatives. Lincoln was aware of her political activities, and he did consult her about cabinet appointments. Later, as the war progressed and the strategies of Union generals seemed to generate only more deadlock and high casualties, they discussed top military appointments. Here they came to disagreement.

"Well, mother, suppose we give you command of the army," Lincoln chided her gently. "No doubt you would do much better than any general that has been tried."

No matter. Whether they disagreed on personnel decisions or not, the important fact is that Lincoln consulted Mary. He also frequently left decisions on minor political appointments entirely in her hands.

Mary Lincoln took kickbacks in exchange for her help, too. They were always couched as "gifts," and included diamonds and a carriage with four black horses. She needed the money. Mary was a spendaholic.

She had an appetite for clothes that rivaled that of Imelda Marcos. In just four months, she bought three hundred pairs of gloves. That averages out to the purchase of between two and three pairs of gloves every day, including Sundays. She loved to shop at Galt's, one of Washington's fine purveyors of jewelry, silver, and even weapons for the newly minted officers of the Army of the Potomac. They often had custom-made swords mounted with gold and inlaid with silver. Among the items carried under the Galt name was a finely engraved little handgun with a herringbone pattern on its barrel, the Derringer.

If her famed intuition registered alarm at the presence of the diminutive guns in the glittering showcases at Galt's, it didn't deter Mary's shopping sprees.

In one season alone, she spent twenty-seven thousand dollars—more than Lincoln's presidential salary for a year—on clothes. She fretted as the election drew near that if he weren't reelected, they would face a financial crisis. Mary had hidden most of her spending from Abe by inducing merchants to extend credit to her. He didn't know it, but they were deeply in debt. She often tried to manage the debt by pressuring merchants to make her purchases "gifts." When that didn't work, she dispatched intermediaries to try to negotiate reduced prices, and presumably to bargain for bribes, taking sums off her credit accounts in exchange for political favors. She is said to have taken kickbacks from the White House gardener, a man named Watt. After a falling out, he threatened to expose three incriminating letters written by Mary Lincoln unless he was paid twenty thousand dollars. A political supporter paid off the blackmailing Watt with the lesser amount of fifteen hundred, and the letters were destroyed. Their contents remain mysterious.

Lincoln, fortunately, won reelection in 1864, and Mary made a triumph of the 1865 inaugural ball by keeping her spending spree going at full speed. Her gown cost two thousand dollars, a huge sum at the time. In equivalent terms today, it is as if a first lady were to wear a forty-five-thousand-dollar gown for her inauguration. Shortly thereafter, she acted on her lifelong impulse to be ready for what destiny held in store. She spent a thousand dollars on black mourning clothes, a widow's wardrobe.

During the election campaign, Lincoln had premonitions himself. He once awakened from a nap to see a double image in a mirror. The other face was clearly his, but it was about an inch or so higher than his own profile. It was also several shades more pale, ghostlike. He drew Mary to him, but the apparition would not reappear. She had interpreted the vision as an omen that he would win the campaign, but not survive his second term in office.

She was correct. While attending a play at Ford's Theatre, Lincoln was fatally shot just behind the ear by John Wilkes Booth's Derringer. Mary Lincoln was so distraught that she could not see to his funeral arrangements or attend the procession. Her sister Elizabeth came to her comfort.

She was self-absorbed to the end.

"Did ever woman have to suffer so much and experience so great a change?" she wailed in her grief. "I had an ambition to be Mrs. President; that ambition has been satisfied, and now I must step down from the pedestal."

Historians rate the Lincoln presidency as the best in our history. He oversaw a great crisis, preserved the Union, and emancipated the slaves. The cost, however, was horrific. More than half a million Americans lost their lives; an entire region of the country was plunged into poverty for a century. Lincoln ran roughshod over the Constitution, and the Supreme Court later ruled that some of his wartime expediencies, such as putting private citizens on trial in military courts, were unconstitutional. Draft riots in New York cost a thousand lives as new immigrants to the country, largely Irish, protested against conscription in a war that they felt was alien to them. As many as one man in every four in Lincoln's conscript armies was a foreign-born immigrant—German, Irish, Scandinavian— who had come to America not to expunge the evil of slavery, but simply to build a better life. Instead, scores of thousands would die on battlefields. It was a conflict that ultimately set the nation on a new course. And it may have been destiny's hand signaling that there was no gradual political solution, no series of creeping compromises that would end the moral evil of slavery.

Mary Lincoln saw her husband's political potential from the beginning. Theirs was—at least from her perspective—a calculated political partnership. To the extent that his presidency was great, she deserves an enormous amount of credit. Without her drive and determination, Abraham might never have risen above the level of a congressman. They campaigned together, and they governed together. Whatever her flaws—Lincoln attributed them to "partial insanity," her sister to excessive personal ambition—they were partners.

She failed in becoming a social trendsetter, one of her desires. She was never a popular first lady, but that may have been a function of the times. When one of the Lincoln sons, Willie, died of typhoid fever in 1862, her grief was pronounced. She canceled social events for months, and kept the White House draped in black mourning cloth. It was an excessive display at a time when America's bloodiest battle ever—Antietam—was fought and families across the country suffered the loss of their sons. This self-absorption caused others to resent her and blunted any public popularity.

Nor did national crisis make her grow into a role model, as it would for other first ladies who followed. Mary Lincoln couldn't seem to grasp that war imposed boundaries on the displays of pomp and ceremony she so loved. Although she visited soldiers' hospitals and became interested in the plight of newly freed slaves, these were not concerns that preoccupied her most of the time. Rather, she was interested in political patronage, the conduct of the war, her own privileges and perks, and of course personal extravagances and luxuries. Had the public known the full extent of her financial dealings, the scandal might have cost Lincoln his prospects for reelection.

Financial problems dogged her throughout the rest of her life. She carted away as much as she could from the White House, but was now pressed by her many creditors. She tried to return the jewels and clothing she had purchased, but most wanted cash. She sold items that had belonged to her husband and tried to organize a high-profile auction of her White House wardrobe, but found few takers. Lincoln's estate was ample, and she ought to have been able to manage very well on the money left to her in trust, but she couldn't control her spending.

Her reputation then came under attack. Her late husband's law partner told the press that Lincoln's life had been hellish, and that he had always loved another woman despite his marriage to Mary. Newspapers published stories that she had taken kickbacks in the White House. She began to suffer stress-induced afflictions, and traveled to Europe's spas and watering holes seeking cures.

In 1870, Congress voted her an annual stipend of three thousand dollars. It was a generous sum, except for a profligate like Mary Lincoln. Money problems continued to dog her. Denied the public respect she craved, out of favor and out of power, her general decline continued.

In 1875, her own son, Robert, had her declared insane. She was involuntarily committed to the Bellevue Sanatorium in Batavia, Illinois. After four months, she was released into the custody of her sister. She returned to her European wanderings for a few years, and then settled with her sister in Springfield. There she remained until her death in 1882.

Eliza McCardle Johnson

First Lady: 1865–1869
17th Presidential Administration
Siena Research Institute Rating: 24

"Plain people from Tennessee"
—Martha Johnson Patterson

Some are born to privilege, others to poverty. For every advantage that her predecessor, Mary Todd Lincoln, had in life, Eliza McCardle Johnson was equally disadvantaged. Even the conditions under which she became first lady—during the disastrous Civil War and due to the country's first presidential assassination—were formidable handicaps.

Eliza and her family were already war refugees. Her husband, Andrew Johnson, had been the only southern senator to pledge loyalty to the Union at the war's outbreak. His home state, Tennessee, was quickly divided into Confederate and Union zones as the clashing armies ground to a stalemate in 1862. The Johnson family home was in the Confederate-occupied western region of the state, but when Lincoln named him military governor of Tennessee in return for his loyalty to the North, Andrew moved to Nashville. Eliza and the children remained behind to run the household, hoping that as civilians they would be left in peace. Instead, the Johnson family became pariahs. The family home and all their possessions were commandeered by the Confederates, and Eliza and her family were given thirty-six hours to leave the territory. Her husband, Andrew, was safely across the lines in Union territory. Eliza and her children were on their own. She bought some extra time because of illness, but soon had to flee.

Homeless and dispossessed, the war refugees made their way to the Union lines. It was a laborious effort, the most daunting journey made by a future first lady since Louisa Catherine Adams's carriage trip from Russia to France across territory ravaged by the Napoleonic Wars. Many times the Johnson family came close to being able to cross the lines to find refuge, only to be turned back by local Confederate commanders. In some towns, they found sympathy and shelter, but in others they were treated with scorn and contempt. They frequently slept outdoors in poor weather. Finally, after a month of wandering, they managed to reunite with Andrew Johnson in Nashville, Tennessee.

Clearly, Eliza Johnson had pluck. Given her start in life, she had to be tough.

She was born in 1810, the daughter of Sarah Philips and John Mc-Cardle. He was a frontier shoemaker. The family was poor, but Sarah's parents valued education and taught her to read and write and do arithmetic.

Eliza was fifteen years old when she met Andrew. He was only slightly more than a year older than she was, and had learned a trade. Andrew Johnson was a tailor. He was five feet, ten inches tall with piercing dark eyes. She must have been a beauty. "I have heard persons say her mother was the handsomest lady in all that region of the country," Laura Holloway reported in 1881, "and her old neighbors stoutly maintain that Mrs. Johnson is the image of her." Within a year, the teenage couple married. She was just sixteen, and he only eighteen.

Andrew had ambition but almost no education. He was born in a log cabin to a poor family in Raleigh, North Carolina. He knew the alphabet and could manage some reading, but he didn't know the rules of grammar, composition, or mathematics.

Eliza had the capacity to teach, and her husband, eager to advance, was a willing pupil. To the extent of her ability, she filled in the gaps in his knowledge. While he sewed garments in their small shop, Eliza read books and articles to him. Together, the couple explored the worlds of geography, history, and literature. She encouraged him to learn the art of public speaking by joining a local debating society.

By sheer willpower and hard work, this couple educated themselves and expanded their horizons beyond the narrow confines of a tradesman's existence on what was then the western frontier. Eliza would later fondly recall these as the happiest times of their lives.

Andrew learned well. Armed with education, he ran for town alderman and was elected. It was just the beginning of his political career. Next he was elected mayor of Greeneville, Tennessee. The Jackson Democrats, who emphasized the workingpeople and common man over the social elites, appealed strongly to this young couple, and Andrew ran for the U.S. House of Representatives under their party banner in 1842. After representing Tennessee in Congress, he ran for and was elected governor of the state in 1853.

It was a meteoric rise from such humble beginnings, but it came at a price. The couple were frequently separated. While Andrew pursued his political career, Eliza stayed in Greeneville, managing the family household and raising their growing family.

It was a rare, but not unique partnership. During the Revolution and its aftermath, Abigail Adams and her husband, John, had endured frequent separations because of his political obligations, while she managed their household affairs in Quincy, Massachusetts. As a consequence, both Eliza and Abigail developed a greater degree of independence than other women of their era. They managed the family business affairs, handled contracts, and controlled money to an extent most women of the time never experienced. There was no simplistic sex stereotyping in the division of labor in these families either; businesswomen who had a good deal of autonomy, they were, in fact, more liberated than women in many households today.

Eliza might have liked to move to Nashville when Andrew became governor in 1853, but her health intervened and she remained at their Greeneville home. Sometime in the early 1850s, she contracted tuberculosis. It was a debilitating disease for which there was, at the time, no cure.

In 1856, Andrew was elected to the U.S. Senate. Because of her continuing health problems, Eliza didn't join him in Washington until the end of his four-year term in 1860. The secession crisis drove them together. By the time Lincoln was inaugurated in March 1861, it was clear that the country was headed irrevocably for war.

Eliza was in Washington less than a year before the couple's pathway led back to her Tennessee home. Johnson's declaration of allegiance to the Union was personally courageous, but dangerous. When Lincoln appointed Johnson wartime military governor of Tennessee in 1862, the danger didn't lessen and may have actually increased. Eliza chose to stay at the family home while Andrew again went to Nashville, which was controlled by Union forces. Now they were kept apart by warring armies instead of politics.

When Lincoln campaigned for reelection in 1864, he chose Johnson to run with him as vice president under the National Union Party banner. Lincoln had surprised his supporters by choosing Johnson, a Tennessee Democrat, to replace incumbent vice president Hannibal Hamlin. Lincoln may have wanted Johnson as vice president during his second term because he knew the Confederacy was near collapse, and the task of reconciliation would be easier with a southerner on the National Union Party ticket. Johnson had been vice president for only one month when John Wilkes Booth assassinated Lincoln and elevated him to the presidency.

The White House was a shambles after the Lincoln funeral. The lower floors had been opened to the public. Souvenir hunters cut strips from the carpets and draperies, leaving them in shredded ribbons. What the crowds didn't carry away, Mary Lincoln did in her sixty-five trunks of cargo.

Eliza was an invalid in her midfifties. She gathered the family—five grandchildren, two daughters, and three sons—and moved them all into the White House. There was much to do to make it livable. Tobacco juice stains covered the remaining carpets and peeling wallpaper. Bugs infested the furniture. It was clear there needed to be major refurbishing.

Congress granted an appropriation of thirty thousand dollars, and Eliza oversaw the remodeling and purchases of new furnishings.

There were, however, no cost overruns to be hidden in other expense accounts this time. There were no kickbacks from contractors, no indebtedness to creditors to be paid off in political patronage. Eliza Johnson was practical, thrifty, and utterly unpretentious. Milk cows grazed on the White House lawns. Every morning, one of her daughters attended the cows so the family could have fresh milk.

To relieve their invalid mother of the burden, Eliza's daughters, particularly Martha Patterson, took over many of the social obligations of the White House. This allowed Eliza to concentrate her energy on the tasks she felt were important. Each morning, she met with her husband for half an hour, and they jointly went over the day's schedule. She read the newspapers avidly, following all political developments closely.

Soon White House visitors on official business noticed that Eliza, from her room directly opposite the Oval Office, had a good intellectual grasp of the business of the presidency and served as a political adviser to her husband. Tuberculosis may have prevented Eliza from fulfilling all the now-customary social duties of first lady, but she kept her eye on the political affairs of state.

Martha Patterson handled the obligations of White House receptions and official dinners, which were in any event curtailed out of respect to the martyred Lincoln during the first year of the Johnson administration. Eliza did attend particularly important social events, even if she had to greet visitors while seated in a chair. Breathing could be laborious for her, making prolonged standing and walking about difficult.

Martha, for her part, was well prepared for her role as social stand-in for the first lady. When Andrew Johnson served in Congress, he enrolled Martha in a school in Georgetown. Polk, also a Tennessean, was then serving as president. Martha was often invited to visit the White House and to stay as a guest during school vacations. She knew Washington, D.C., and the White House, and she knew what it meant to be a member of a political family. She had grown up from the daughter of a politician to also become the wife of a senator at the time of Lincoln's assassination.

Martha made a wise and disarming statement upon Johnson's assumption of the presidency. "We are plain people from the mountains of Tennessee," she said, "called here for a short time by a national calamity. I trust too much will not be expected of us."

It was masterful understatement, if far from the truth. The entire aftermath of the war would now fall upon Johnson's shoulders. Much indeed would be expected from him. The impossible burden of healing a war-torn nation was about to be thrust upon the Johnson administration. It would provoke a civil war within his own political party, one that threatened his presidency with the first-ever impeachment trial in the country's history.

New Year's Day of 1866 marked the first White House event hosted by President Johnson. His two daughters, Mary Stover and Martha Patterson, handled the duties of hostess, decorating the reception rooms for the occasion and greeting the guests. Martha continued the pattern of understatement, wearing no ostrich plumes in her headdress or ostentatious fashions, but only "attired in blue velvet, a white lace shawl, and point lace collar."

When interviewed by a reporter from the *Albany Evening Journal*, Martha Patterson explained the simplicity of the Johnson administration's ethos: "We do not propose to put on airs because we have the fortune to occupy this place for a little while."

The "plain people from Tennessee" theme struck a chord with the press, but was also seen as a swipe at war profiteering by some of Washington's political elite. In a celebrated corruption trial involving two politically connected Boston businessmen, Benjamin and Franklin Smith, accused of defrauding the navy, most members of Massachusetts's congressional delegation signed a petitition in their defense despite the Smith brothers' conviction in a court-martial. The brothers won a reprieve after Senator Sumner and Congressman Rice of Massachusetts brought political pressure to bear on the White House. In another case involving an Englishman who had swindled soldiers out of their pay, Congressman Odell of New York interceded with Lincoln to plead for his release. There were dozens of such cases, with prominent politicians shielding, and perhaps being paid off by, corrupt businessmen during the war.

"The reference of Mrs. Patterson to the mountain home of her family," one paper editorialized, "is suggestive of the fact that when the tornado of war was sweeping over Tennessee, President Johnson's kin dwelt where its ravages were most dreadful, and that while some who are now leading the shoddy aristocracy of the metropolis were coining their ill-gotten dollars from the sufferings and blood of brave men, they were being hunted from point to point. . . ."

In war, the spoils belong to the victor, and it was on this point that President Johnson clashed severely and repeatedly with the Radical

Republican faction of his party. In the Johnson cabinet, they were represented most prominently by Secretary of War Edwin M. Stanton. The Radical Republicans also dominated Congress. Johnson clashed with them over Reconstruction. At issue was whether the southern states that comprised the Confederacy were to be reconciled for the sake of a stronger Union, or looted by profiteers.

Stanton and the Radical Republicans wanted the spoils of war. During the fighting, the Confiscation Act had given Lincoln the power to seize Confederate property, including private property. But he had resisted pressure to use this power. Stanton had even proposed in a cabinet meeting with Lincoln that control over all commerce and business in the South be given to his War Department. He favored running state governments with federal officials, confiscating land and businesses, and even combining the states of North Carolina and Virginia to dilute their strength in the Senate after reunification. Lincoln had kept Stanton and the Radical Republicans at bay, and they were actively trying to undermine him politically at the time of the assassination. Now Johnson tried to oppose them by vetoing the First Reconstruction Act, warning that it imposed an "arbitrary despotism" on the defeated South. Congress ignored his warnings, with long-lasting political implications. The South was ruled for a decade by military government. Local business owners and entrepreneurs were dispossessed by northern "carpetbaggers" awarded lucrative contracts due to their political connections. Nor was there any sound strategy for giving four million newly freed slaves help in becoming self-sufficient, independent people. As a result, when the military occupation ended and angry white southerners resumed a degree of self-government, they vented their resentment against African Americans. Denied equal rights and access to education, many newly freed slaves ended up as impoverished sharecroppers or hired field hands. The failure of Reconstruction created a culture of African American poverty that endured for a hundred years before another President Johnson—Lyndon Baines Johnson—passed the Great Society programs and civil rights laws to attempt to undo the damage.

In 1865, President Andrew Johnson had angered the Radical Republicans by granting an amnesty to all Confederates who would take an oath of allegiance to the Union, with the exception of the political leaders who had begun the insurrection through secession and run the Confederacy during the fighting. Johnson, who had a populist hatred of the southern plantation aristocracy, didn't want to punish ordinary southerners by stripping them of their rights. Had he been president at the end of World War II, Johnson would likely have had the vision to embrace the Marshall Plan for war-ravaged Germany and Japan. He was that kind of visionary.

Johnson knew that reconciliation was crucial to the country's future, but the Radical Republicans were blind to all but revenge and reaping the spoils of victory. The Radical Republicans moved to constrain Johnson's presidential powers. After having placed the South under the control of the army through Reconstruction, the Radical Republicans in Congress passed a law limiting Johnson's control over the army. They also passed the Tenure of Office Act, which forbade the president from firing any presidential appointee who had already been confirmed by the Senate.

It was both a constitutional crisis and a battle of political wills. The final showdown came over Secretary of War Edwin M. Stanton. Johnson fired him from the cabinet. Stanton refused to acknowledge the president's authority and barricaded himself in his office. Johnson remained steadfast, appointing the popular war hero Ulysses S. Grant to replace the recalcitrant Stanton. The House of Representatives promptly voted articles of impeachment against Johnson for violating the Tenure of Office Act and Command of the Army Act. In February 1868, the Senate initiated his impeachment trial.

Eliza Johnson may have left much of the White House entertaining to daughters Martha and Mary, but impeachment was a different matter. Rallying her strength, she discussed every aspect of legal and political maneuvering with Andrew. Together they plotted his defense against the charges and his political counterattack on the Radical Republicans. She studied the newspapers assiduously, compiling a massive dossier of clips on the trial, watching the shifts of public opinion. All the while she remained optimistic and encouraging to Andrew, counseling him to remain true to his principles and not to doubt his eventual triumph.

On May 26, the trial was over and the Senate gave its verdict. President Johnson prevailed. He had asserted important constitutional principles in defense of the powers of the presidency, preserving the president's prerogative of picking—and firing—senior government officials. We take for granted today that presidents have the ability to choose or dismiss cabinet officers, largely because Andrew put up a fight and won by defeating those who wanted him impeached. Subsequent Supreme Court decisions would affirm that his interpretation—that Congress had no constitutional authority to limit his power to fire cabinet officers—had been correct, and the Radical Republicans wrong in their effort to unconstitutionally wrest power from the White House and take it for themselves.

Eliza Johnson deserves credit for this successful defense of the Constitution's arrangement of powers, a delicate design intended to balance competing power centers against one another. It was a landmark achievement, and this self-made couple from Tennessee who rose from poverty to the pinnacle of power against all odds won accolades for their grit.

In her triumph, Eliza began to attend more White House events. The first state dinner in honor of visiting royalty was for Queen Emma of Hawaii. Eliza greeted the queen standing, but had to be seated in a chair as she greeted the rest of the guests that night.

According to journalists, the final White House reception given by President Johnson was a huge success. ". . . Never before, since receptions were inaugurated, has there been such an ovation as was last night at President Johnson's closing reception," one paper reported. "The attendance comprised not only an unusual number of our own citizens, but also a greater multitude of visitors from all parts of the world. . . . The crowd here was fearful. . . . Those in front were pushed on by those behind, and the position of everyone was most uncomfortable, while at one time persons were in actual danger of being crushed. . . ."

Martha Patterson stood behind her father for this final White House levee. She was dressed in "Lyons black velvet, handsomely trimmed with bands of satin and black lace," with a lace shawl falling in folds over her dress. From eight in the evening until past eleven, President Johnson shook hands with his well-wishers. He wanted to run for reelection and had sought the backing of both the Democratic and Republican Parties, but lacked the support in either to win the nomination.

"President Johnson held his farewell reception at the White House, and certainly in a blaze of glory," another newspaper reported. "Perhaps the whole history of the Presidential Mansion gives no record of such a crowded reception. It is estimated that some five thousand people sought admittance in vain, while fully as many must have gained an entrance. . . ."

Meanwhile, the newspapers were criticizing Mary Lincoln for taking White House property with her when she left. The widowed former first lady responded professing her own innocence, and blaming Harriet Lane for any missing White House property. In this context, one newspaper praised Eliza and Andrew Johnson.

"They have received no expensive presents, no carriages, no costly plate," the paper editorialized. "They will be remembered in Washington as high-minded and honest people."

In 1875, Andrew Johnson was elected to the Senate. He died after serving only a few months of his term. It was the end of a marriage that had lasted nearly fifty years, the majority of which embodied an enduring and successful political partnership. He held office, she was his political counselor, and together they prevailed over the odds in life and in politics.

Eliza died in 1876, about six months after Andrew.

Julia Dent Grant

First Lady: 1869–1877
18th Presidential Administration
Siena Research Institute Rating: 26

"Life at the White House was a garden spot of orchids, and I wish it might have continued forever."

The Gilded Era was an age of gargantuan excess, the heyday of the Robber Barons—ruthless business tycoons like Jay Gould and Jim Fisk, who exploited their political connections for profit and for whom the phrase *Robber Baron* was coined—and first lady Julia Grant was a woman of her times. State dinners at the Grant White House were prepared by an Italian chef and featured up to twenty-five courses for each guest served over an interval of two hours, complemented by six varieties of wine. For the visit of Queen Victoria's son Arthur, a twenty-nine-course dinner was served at a cost of fifteen hundred dollars, excluding wine. By way of contrast, in the year before the Civil War began Ulysses Grant's total annual salary as a clerk in his family's store was less than a thousand dollars.

Julia Grant's average White House dinners cost seven hundred dollars, and they were weekly affairs. On an annual basis, the dinners alone cost more than the president's yearly salary, but thanks to the generosity of well-heeled political friends, the Grants could afford to entertain on a scale commensurate with the expectations of the age. The two terms of the Grant administration were ridden with scandal and corruption, extending throughout the cabinet and reaching directly into the White House itself. After four years of the Civil War, followed by four years of the corruption-free Johnson administration, there were spoils to be had—and Grant was the victor.

Riches, however, had not come easily to Julia and Ulysses Grant. He was a man made for war whose peacetime business ventures—from farming to real estate to brokering stocks—floundered badly. No wonder she spoke of their eight years in the White House as a time of exceptional happiness, when life was like "a garden spot of orchids."

They met in 1844 at White Haven, her family plantation, near St. Louis, Missouri. Grant was then a twenty-two-year-old lieutenant. He was short, with blue eyes and brown hair, but as a West Point graduate had a promising future before him.

Julia was just eighteen. Her brother had been a classmate of Ulysses at West Point, and when Grant was stationed at nearby White Haven, the family invited him to visit. When Ulysses called at the plantation, he was evidently charmed by the slightly cross-eyed young woman with a tomboy's reputation. Soon he became a regular caller, visiting three or four times a week, accompanying the family on outings, and escorting Julia to balls.

Julia was the daughter of Frederick and Ellen Bray Dent, affluent plantation owners. Frederick Dent clashed with Ulysses on the question of slavery, which Grant opposed, and disapproved of the young man's ardent courtship of his daughter. Julia and her mother disagreed. Julia thought her young man was destined for great things. When Grant proposed to her in 1845 just before he was sent to fight in the Mexican War, surprisingly, she gave her consent.

Her father did not. He agreed to the betrothal only if she agreed to wait until Grant's return from Mexico before marrying. The engagement lasted a full three years while Grant was away in the fighting. Laura Holloway, who corresponded with Julia Grant in the 1880s, reported that Grant saved her brother's life in one battle, no doubt an aid in endearing him to the family. In 1848, they were finally married at White Haven. His parents did not attend the wedding ceremony. They were unhappy that Ulysses had married into a slave-owning family.

For the next six years, Julia lived the life of an army wife. In 1854, Ulysses resigned his officer's commission. His promising career had presumably been cut short by heavy drinking. Over the following six years, he tried his hand at a number of trades to support Julia and his growing family. He farmed a sixty-acre plot of land her father had given them as a wedding present. His own father pitched in a thousand dollars to buy livestock. Nevertheless, it was difficult making a living from the uncleared land. Ulysses had to borrow money after farm prices dropped in a recession, and eventually gave up on the homestead he and Julia had nicknamed "Hardscrabble."

Next he tried his hand at selling real estate in a business owned by one of Julia's cousins. That, too, faltered. He got a sinecure at a customs warehouse, but lost it after two months. The family moved to Galena, Illinois, to work for Ulysses' two younger brothers in a thriving leather goods shop. He still had a hard time making ends meet and needed his salary increased from the initial six hundred dollars a year not once, but twice. Meanwhile, he chafed at his dependence on his younger brothers, who had built the business and taken him in as a family obligation.

The Civil War came along at the right time to rescue Grant's prospects. After Fort Sumter was shelled in April 1861, Lincoln called for an army of volunteers. Ulysses' military experience resulted in his being appointed to raise a troop of volunteers in Galena. In August, he was reappointed to the army—this time with a brigadier general's commission.

Over the next four years of the war, Julia joined her husband in the field whenever possible, staying in commandeered homes, quartered with hostile southerners, in boardinghouses, and even in tents. Once when she was traveling by steamboat taking the children to meet him, they came under Confederate artillery fire. On another occasion, she was almost taken prisoner by Confederate troops. She even encouraged Ulysses to allow their thirteen-year-old son Fred to join him at the front, likening him to the young Alexander the Great accompanying Philip of Macedon on his conquests. She was on a boat at Ulysses' side when the Union ironclad ships were shelled during Grant's siege of Vicksburg.

Julia shared not only the dangers and hardships of the war, but also the secrets of military strategy with her husband. Yet she found time to minister to sick soldiers in the military encampments and to mingle with the officers and men around the campfires, utterly without pretension.

She also shared in the glory. Her first taste of public acclaim came in 1863 when Grant captured Vicksburg. A crowd gathered where she was staying in St. Louis, and they sang and cheered when she appeared on the balcony. Rising steadily in rank as a result of his success on the battlefield, Ulysses was appointed commander of the Army of the Potomac by Lincoln.

Julia moved the family to Washington and was plunged into the city's social and political life. Because of her husband's rank and accomplishments, she was recognized throughout the city, and she enjoyed status and attention. Julia dedicated herself to volunteer duties, helping wounded and convalescing soldiers, visiting military hospitals, and attending social events at the Lincoln White House.

On one such occasion, she encountered Mary Todd Lincoln's pathological insecurity. Mary often tried, unsuccessfully, to undercut General Grant with President Lincoln. His popularity, and therefore his political fortunes, were rising with each battlefield victory. Mary Lincoln sensed in Julia a potential rival.

"I suppose you think you'll get the White House to yourself, don't you?" Mary Lincoln baited Julia in one encounter.

Mrs. Grant demurred, claiming to be perfectly satisfied with her position in life.

The first lady was unpersuaded. "Oh, you had better take it if you can get it," she scolded, " 'tis very nice."

On another occasion, Julia was in a military camp when Mary Lincoln visited. She imperiously commanded Julia to leave the room as is done in royal courts—Mary ordered Julia to back away from her so that Julia never turned her back on the first lady, as if the first lady were a queen and Julia a mere commoner. If the humiliating treatment was intended to provoke an outburst, Mary Lincoln failed. Julia later denied she had any ill feeling about her treatment at the hands of the first lady.

Julia Grant was canny, capable of keeping a confidence, and personally courageous in the presence of danger. Ulysses had urged her to sit out the war safely in Detroit, which he considered far enough north to be safe from Confederate forces, but she refused to be separated from him whenever it was possible. If such a thing can be said, she appears to have taken the war almost in stride, maintaining a semblance of family life, roughing it in the camps with the troops, and remaining by her husband's side in battle. Like other "camp followers"—women and children who remained close to the troops during military campaigns—Julia took to the rigors of military campaign life with gusto.

She also apparently saw no contradiction in bringing her maid, a slave, with her on these wartime jaunts. She may in fact have been oblivious to the politics of the war, slavery, and secession. In her memoirs, she wrote about an episode when she was quartered in the home of a Confederate family. The women of the household confronted her about the constitutionality of the war.

"I did not know a thing about this dreadful Constitution and told them so," Julia wrote. "I would not know where to look for it even if I wished to read it."

It is an astonishing admission. Julia had been decently educated, attending school at the Philip Mauro Academy in St. Louis until she was seventeen years old. She was married to a man at the center of a conflict whose very essence was a constitutional crisis over whether or not states had a right to permit slavery and to secede from the Union, yet she herself professed ignorance of its fundamental cause.

It would be a mistake, however, to consider Julia Grant apolitical because she knew nothing about American government. She was deeply political in a primitive way, keen to the nuances of power, personalities, and the perks and privileges of political prowess.

Grant was already a popular war hero when President Andrew Johnson elevated him by proposing Grant as a replacement for War Secretary Edwin Stanton. It was a move that triggered the impeachment crisis, which culminated with Johnson's Senate trial and acquittal in May 1868.

For herself, Julia understood that the impeachment proceedings could erode presidential power and might permanently weaken the presidency. She thought impeachment "savored of persecution"—by which Julia meant that Johnson's impeachment was driven by a political vendetta and differences over Reconstruction—and could establish "a dangerous precedent." Although she sympathized with President Johnson's view of Reconstruction, Julia and Ulysses' shared instinct was to remain cautiously neutral in the protracted political fight between the Johnson White House and the Radical Republican–dominated Congress. If Ulysses was to be nominated for the presidency, he couldn't afford to alienate the Radical Republicans. Staying above the fray was, in fact, a smart move for Grant, who consciously avoided comment on the unfolding political drama.

Julia and Ulysses, however, did find an ingenious way to show support for Johnson. Julia publicly attended White House receptions—without Ulysses—which allowed Johnson supporters to interpret her presence as evidence of Grant's support, while the Radical Republicans could interpret the general's absence as evidence of support withheld. The stratagem shows considerable political cunning.

In 1868, only a few months after Johnson's impeachment ordeal ended, Grant received the Republican presidential nomination. He was elected by a wide margin. Julia turned to one of the Radical Republican kingmakers who dominated the Congress that had given former president Andrew Johnson to much trouble, New York senator Roscoe Conkling, for help writing Grant's inaugural address. It was a shrewd gesture of conciliation that showed that Grant would work with the Radical Republicans instead of against them. In her own words, Julia became an "enthusiastic politician," just as she had cheerfully shared in her husband's soldiering life during the Civil War.

She was also an enthusiastic entertainer. Once a week, she held two-hour White House receptions, in addition to one each morning in the Blue Room. The lavish Grant dinners quickly drew favorable attention. Many of Washington's newspapers now featured society reporters, primarily women, who wrote on the details of White House entertainment, decoration, and the first lady's fashion tastes.

Julia also gained favor among Washington's political elite by involving their wives in formal White House events. She thought it proper when receiving a military dignitary to have the wives of the war secretary and top brass participate in greeting their counterparts. She extended this concept to the diplomatic corps, visiting legislators and governors. This allowed a role for the spouses of the political elite in almost every White House receiving line.

Some believe that her poor eyesight—she was partly cross-eyed with one eye that fluctuated uncontrollably—made this innovation a practical necessity. She sometimes had difficulty recognizing guests and was well known for forgetting names and the trivial personal touches that made conversation flow. Surrounding herself with other Washington women to prompt her when required may have helped; politically, it was very clever. By sharing the glory, Julia made friends and allies everywhere.

The first lady frequently joined President Grant in newspaper interviews. When they traveled away from the White House, she met with the
local press alongside Ulysses and was quoted in print in her own right.
Julia exercised her power when it came to political appointments. Like
others before her, Julia was oblivious to charges of nepotism and lobbied
for relatives to get government jobs. She also didn't hesitate to try to
shape Grant's cabinet.

Attorney General George Williams came under Julia's fire for spreading suspicions that Grant misused government funds. Williams's wife in-
discreetly told another cabinet wife that she thought Grant had used
federal funds to help his political ally Roscoe Conkling win reelection to
the Senate. Grant had nominated Attorney General Williams to the Supreme Court, but the Senate was reluctant to confirm him for the post.
Julia was convinced that the attorney general had offered the tip about
Grant's misuse of federal money to the Senate in a desperate bid to revive
his prospects for Senate confirmation. Williams had made a sworn enemy
of Julia. The Senate did not confirm him for the Supreme Court. Julia
pressed Grant to fire the disloyal attorney general, and within five months
he lost his cabinet post. Julia also lobbied Ulysses to fire Postmaster
General Marshall Jewell for political disloyalty. Within a year, he was
gone. When Interior Secretary Jacob Box proposed reforming the civil
service as an anticorruption measure, Julia agitated for his removal. She
had learned the power of patronage, urging government appointments for
relatives as well as political supporters. Her brother John was appointed to
a post that controlled the Indian trade in New Mexico. Another brother,
George, got a customs appointment in San Francisco. Her son Fred was
made an assistant to General Sherman. Julia's brother-in-law Dr. Alexander Sharpe was appointed a federal marshal in Washington, D.C.; another brother-in-law, James Casey, was made collector of customs in New
Orleans. Secretary Box's proposal, if enacted into law, would have hin-
dered Julia's power. He resigned after eighteen months, prompting the
New York Herald to observe that the first lady had some influence in the
matter.

If Julia had been woefully ignorant of the Constitution only a few years
earlier, she appears to have been determined not to miss a trick in Washington's power corridors. She attended Senate hearings, met with members of the cabinet, and intervened with the White House staff on matters
ranging from presidential appointments to interrupting meetings when
she wanted to know more about their substance. She took the initiative to
learn firsthand about prospective presidential appointees, legislation that

should be signed or vetoed, and the day-to-day political dealings of the administration.

In some arenas, Julia wisely knew her limits. She was in midlife, portly, and had no intention of being measured as a fashion trendsetter. She apparently understood the political art of framing public expectations—subtly letting the public know where your interests and disinterests lie so that people focus on the areas of activity that matter most to you. To frame expectations, she shrewdly let the press know she didn't want to be a "fashion dictator."

In other more substantial matters, Julia should have realized there were other kinds of limits. As the eight years of the Grant presidency unfolded, the administration became tainted by case after case of high-level political corruption.

Julia had her hand in too many of these scandals for comfort. The first happened early in the administration and concerns an event known as Black Friday. Julia's brother-in-law Abel Corbin teamed up with two New York financiers, Jay Gould and Jim Fisk, to try to corner the gold market and make huge speculative profits. Gould and Fisk were among the first lady's social set. They entertained her in New York and met with the first lady and president during their summer vacations at the Jersey shore.

Who was using whom is not entirely clear. By using his access to the White House, Corbin served as the political insider for Gould's and Fisk's moves to corner the market. Corbin urged Grant to build up the government's gold reserves, thus driving up the value of the precious metal. Gould and Fisk had cornered the market on gold at lower prices and stood to make a fortune. Julia herself was cut in for a piece of the action. A later congressional hearing into the affair established that she had a half-million-dollar position in the trades—money that was not her own but had been advanced to her—and came out of the affair with a twenty-seven-thousand-dollar "profit," which by today's standards would have constituted illegal graft.

The affair ended with a market collapse known as Black Friday. When Grant announced a change in fiscal policies on September 24, 1869, to appease silver-producing western states by building silver reserves, there was a massive sell-off of gold on Wall Street. Before he announced the change of policy, Grant warned Julia to alert her brother-in-law Corbin that he would be ruined if he continued speculating in gold. Grant dictated a letter for Julia to send to her sister, Mrs. Corbin.

"The General says, if you have any influence with your husband," Julia obediently wrote, "tell him to have nothing whatever to do with [Gould and Fisk]. If he does, he will be ruined. . . ."

Some historians have interpreted this letter, which Julia signed "Sis," rather than Mrs. Grant or Mrs. President Grant, as exonerative. It may have been a tip-off intended to preserve Corbin's financial fortunes, for Grant ruined Gould's and Fisk's insider plot by flooding the market with the government's gold reserves, driving down the price of gold and ruining those who had speculated on higher prices. Julia's letter and warning of being "ruined" could have been a simple insider tip-off to Corbin to cash out while he could. Just as Enron insiders sold their own holdings while urging employees to buy more of the company's stock, people of the nineteenth century weren't immune to the lure of making money at the expense of others. Unfortunately, many traders besides Gould and Fisk suffered from Grant's decision to sell the reserves. Thousands were wiped out on Black Friday.

The advance notice enabled Corbin to get out before the panic. Had the affair not ended in the market collapse, congressional testimony indicated that Julia Grant's cut would have been at least five hundred thousand dollars.

If this were the only corruption scandal involving the first lady, it might be excused as an error in judgment. But it was not. The Whiskey Ring affair reached directly into Grant's office. The scandal involved Internal Revenue Service agents giving false reports that understated by fifteen million gallons the amount of liquor production in the United States. Meanwhile, the revenue collectors received tax revenues on the far higher real volume. The agents were skimming the difference and splitting it between a ring of insiders and political appointees. When investigators began to suspect that some scheme was afoot, Grant directed them to work with John McDonald at the St. Louis office of the IRS. Grant may not have known it, but McDonald was one of the scheme's ringleaders. Next, Treasury Secretary Benjamin Bristow discovered evidence that Grant's White House private secretary, Orville E. Babcock, had gotten kickbacks from the Whiskey Ring.

Julia insisted that Babcock be shielded. His probe stymied by the first lady, Treasury Secretary Bristow resigned his cabinet post. The question of Julia Grant's involvement has never been settled. Was she simply protecting Babcock because she thought him an honest and loyal White House staffer? Or was she doing so because he knew too much and he could implicate others in the White House, possibly the president and first lady themselves?

Whether he was part of it or not, Grant's administration is considered one of the most corrupt in the nation's history. Grant's vice president,

Schuyler Colfax, was caught in a scandal that involved misappropriated federal construction funds diverted to the Union Pacific Railroad's Robber Baron owners. When the scandal became the focus of a congressional inquiry, railroad executives responded by trying to bribe the members of Congress handling the investigation with shares of steeply discounted stock—the nineteenth-century equivalent of stock options. Grant's first treasury secretary in his second term, William Richardson, was caught skimming some two hundred thousand dollars in tax money and forced to resign. Secretary of War William Belknap took kickbacks from merchants who needed government licenses to sell their goods at the Indian reservations whose creation Grant had championed during his inaugural address.

When the attorney general's wife sent Julia letters warning about corruption allegations involving another of her brothers-in-law, James Casey—who had a government appointment at the New Orleans Customs House—Julia's response was to lobby Grant to have the attorney general fired. Finally, there was a mysterious event in which someone mailed the first lady twenty-five thousand dollars in cash. The money raised suspicions, and even Grant supporters questioned why a legitimate sum hadn't been paid by check, but the riddle was never resolved even though one White House clerk tried to be helpful to the first lady by later suggesting that maybe the sum had only been twenty-five dollars—and the decimal was misplaced in the record books!

If the Grants themselves were not participants in the corruption, their actions set a moral tone. With the first lady circling the wagons to protect those suspected of wrongdoing, tipping off relatives to sell their gold shares before the bottom fell out of the market, pressing to fire officials who raised concerns about corruption, and receiving unexplained cash payments, the least that can be said is that the Grants turned a blind eye to financial wrongdoing. More likely is the case that the president and first lady profited handsomely from their eight years in the White House and took their share of graft.

Julia wanted Ulysses to campaign for a third term in office, but when he called an unusual Sunday meeting of his cabinet and invited Julia to attend, she knew something was seriously amiss. At the meeting Grant disclosed that he had sent a letter to the Republican state convention in Pennsylvania saying he would not make a third bid for the presidency, and for good measure had given the press copies of the letter. Grant wanted a third term as president, but Republican Party leaders had warned him that the scandals had undermined his support and could cost him his reelection prospects. Rather than risk defeat, Grant withdrew. Julia felt betrayed that he hadn't discussed the matter with her beforehand.

Grant's status as a war hero may have spared him. Ultimately, he didn't become the focus of the media, and those around him served as lightning rods to absorb the damage. In a different era, with a more adversarial press, Grant would doubtlessly have fared differently. Grant seems to have emerged with his personal reputation for integrity intact—although there were no public opinion polls in the nineteenth century to give us a true reading of the facts—but the scandals hurt Grant's legacy.

The eight-year Grant administration was largely a caretaker presidency. There were no dramatic policy initiatives, no Grant presidential agenda that made its mark on history. Grant maintained the Radical Republicans' punitive Reconstruction policies, guaranteeing that the South would remain an economically disadvantaged region for a full century following the Civil War.

As do many eras of excess, the Grant administration ended with a nasty depression when the speculative bubbles burst. The panic of 1873 started shortly after Grant's second term began and lasted five years, overshadowing everything else.

"Mistakes have been made, as all can see and I admit," he said in his final State of the Union speech. It is an astonishing admission to modern ears. It may be a harsh verdict, but Grant never succeeded in any civilian ventures and failed miserably in most—including the presidency.

When Julia and Ulysses left the White House, it wasn't to settle down. Instead, they set out on a two-and-a-half-year world tour. When they returned to the United States, Grant became a partner in a stock brokerage firm that failed, leaving him saddled with sixteen million dollars in debts. Not long thereafter he developed throat cancer, attributable to his habit of smoking up to twenty cigars in a single day. He feared leaving Julia destitute and, after Mark Twain persuaded his publisher to agree to a book contract, Grant wrote his memoirs literally racing death. He finished the book shortly before cancer took his life. It was a success, and combined with a small widow's pension from Congress, Julia was able to live comfortably.

Some historians have detected in Julia Grant's actions a budding feminism and a strong belief in the equality of men and women. There is also ample evidence to contradict it. In 1891, the aging Mrs. Grant visited the

Chicago World's Fair and had an exchange of views with Enid Yandell, a twenty-two-year-old sculptress. Julia told the young woman bluntly that she didn't approve of women working, even in the arts.

"I think every woman is better off at home taking care of husband and children," Julia said. "The battle with the world hardens a woman and makes her unwomanly."

For the remainder of her days, she looked back on her years as first lady as the most wonderful period of her life aside from the carefree days of her childhood. She died in 1902 and was buried next to her Ulysses in Grant's Tomb.

Lucy Ware Webb Hayes

First Lady: 1877–1881
19th Presidential Administration
Siena Research Institute Rating: 15

"Mr. Hayes will, during the absence of Mrs. Hayes, be acting president."
—contemporary newspaper

War isn't all battle. There are long periods of tedium and waiting. During the Civil War, fighting virtually ceased in wintertime. To alleviate camp life's boredom, soldiers often played practical jokes.

James Saunders was a young recruit with the twenty-third Ohio Volunteers, whose colonel was future president Rutherford B. Hayes. James repeatedly fell for the tricks his fellow soldiers played on him. Like many other Union soldiers in the early years of the war, he soon found that his uniform was falling to pieces. Crooked contractors were bilking the government by using cloth made of leftover scraps from other garments—called "shoddy" in the trade—to make uniforms. Jackets and pants made of shoddy didn't last long, and Jim had complained to his campmates that he needed someone to mend his uniform.

"Why Jim," Laura Holloway reported a fellow soldier as saying, "didn't you know there is a woman in camp whose business it is to mend the boys' clothes?"

"No," Jim answered, astonished. "Where is she?"

"Up at the Colonel's tent," said another. "I was there and had her fix my coat yesterday, and she did a smackin' good job, too."

Jim innocently marched up to the colonel's tent and asked about the seamstress. Instead of bawling out the trooper for his audacity, Colonel Hayes went quietly inside his tent and brought the woman out. The young man bowed awkwardly and asked for her help. Jim went back to his camp blissfully ignorant of his breach of military protocol.

His mates could barely conceal their laughter when they asked if he'd found his female tailor. When Jim said yes, and that she was going to finish his jacket that afternoon, they broke out in howls.

"Jim, didn't you know that woman is the colonel's wife?" one asked.

They knew that Colonel Hayes's wife, Lucy, was staying at the camp. Like Julia Grant, Lucy Hayes took her sons to join their father in the field when they could. Camp followers were common during the Civil War. Women who joined their husbands in military encampments, children, merchants who followed to sell goods and "sundries" to the troops, and even prostitutes were all lumped together under the catchall description *camp follower.*

Rutherford Hayes was wounded four times during the war, once very seriously, and Lucy not only tended to his recovery but also looked out for the welfare of the soldiers under his command. She once earned the enmity of upper-class passengers on a train by leading a group of wounded soldiers into the Pullman carriages when there was no room for them elsewhere.

Word of the incident spread, earning Lucy the immediate affection of the Twenty-third Ohio Volunteers. They knew this attractive, college-educated woman would have grasped immediately that the gullible Jim Saunders was intended to be the butt of a practical joke. She turned the tables on them, displaying her trademark sense of humor and a complete lack of pretension. They were traits that served her and her husband well throughout a long political lifetime.

Lucy Ware Webb was born in 1831 in Chillicothe, Ohio, to an affluent family. Her father, a doctor, died of cholera on a trip to Lexington, Kentucky, when she was only two years old. He had been trying to arrange transportation to Liberia for newly freed slaves.

Lucy's grandfather was a judge and an Ohio state legislator. Her father's estate left the family with ample money. In 1844, her mother moved Lucy and her brothers to Delaware, Ohio, so that the children could attend Wesleyan University.

The young Lucy studied with Wesleyan professors alongside her brothers. She excelled at academic work and went on to higher studies at the Wesleyan Female College at Cincinnati. It was the first chartered college for women in the United States, and when Lucy graduated, her degree would make her the first college-educated first lady in the country's history.

Lucy was only fifteen years old when she first met Rutherford Hayes, a twenty-four-year-old attorney. His family felt Lucy would make a good match. A few years later, he began courting her in earnest, and in 1852 they married. His political ambitions became evident early in their life, when he ran for and won election as city attorney for Cincinnati, Ohio.

The Civil War elevated Hayes to prominence. He rose on the battlefield to the rank of brigadier general, then won election to the U.S. House of Representatives. After serving in Congress, Hayes was elected governor of Ohio.

Lucy embraced the life of a political spouse, just as she had done with the Twenty-third Ohio Volunteers during the war, when she eagerly helped her husband look after the welfare of the men in his command. The nation was still bleeding from its wounds. Six-hundred-forty thousand men had died, and many more were left injured or crippled. Everywhere there were orphans, widows, elderly parents left destitute without support from the sons they had lost in war in an age before social welfare programs or Social Security pensions. It was a time that called for social activism to deal with the immediate and urgent relief of those victimized by the war.

Lucy took full advantage of her position as the governor's wife to rally support for relief efforts. She threw herself into fund-raising to establish an orphanage for soldiers' children. After she succeeded in starting the orphanage, she lobbied the legislature to turn it into a state institution, thereby assuring its continued financial support. Another of her causes was the education of the handicapped. She championed an institution called the Reform Farm that helped deaf and dumb boys learn to be self-sufficient.

Behind the scenes, she was a political adviser to her husband, who from the beginning of their relationship had admired her intellect as much as her beauty and personality. She influenced his views on prison reform and social welfare policies, and through him had an effect on lawmaking in these areas.

She also entertained at the governor's executive mansion, honing her political and public relations skills. Lucy and Rutherford had formed a successful partnership, and Rutherford was reelected to the governorship for a second term. In 1872, he campaigned unsuccessfully for the Senate. A brief hiatus from politics followed, and in 1875 he ran for governor for a third time and won.

Hayes was now poised to be the Republican nominee in a hotly contested presidential election. The 1876 campaign was among the most contentious ever. Hayes's opponent was Democratic governor Samuel J. Tilden of New York. After the scandals and excesses of the Grant administration, voters in both parties were looking for reform. Hayes had a reputation for fighting corruption as governor of Ohio, and Tilden was nationally known for fighting corruption in New York.

The battle of the reformers was closely fought. Tilden was the popular winner by more than 250,000 votes, but he fell a single electoral college vote short of victory. The electoral college votes of Florida, Louisiana, and South Carolina were in dispute. The Radical Republican machine controlled all three states under Reconstruction policies. The stage was set for a stolen election.

It began with a series of certification and recertifications exercises in the contested states, with Democratic officials ruling in favor of Tilden and Republicans in favor of Hayes. Next the Republicans sent a blue-ribbon delegation to Louisiana to examine the state's balloting. The result was a shift of thirteen thousand votes in favor of Hayes, allegedly after payoffs to the state election board. Then came a flawed congressional inquiry. It was initially designed to be evenly balanced between Democrats and Republicans, with one independent member, but just before it began deliberations the independent member—under either pressure or financial inducement—abruptly resigned and was replaced by a Republican. Predictably, the Republican majority voted to confirm Hayes as the winner.

Lucy and Rutherford Hayes were en route to Washington when they heard that Rutherford had been declared the winner. It had taken months to resolve the election, and he was hurriedly sworn in as president in March at the White House with Grant standing by, amid rumors that Tilden supporters intended to storm the building and install their man as president.

If the carpetbaggers expected Hayes to permit them to continue looting the South and turn a blind eye toward the corruption that had enriched so many of the Radical Republicans, they were quickly given a dose of reality. He set about cleaning house with a vengeance.

Hayes's first measure was to fire all Grant cabinet appointees. He ruled out political appointments to satisfy party supporters, opting instead to make appointments based on qualifications for the job. He was mocked by Democrats as "his Fraudulency" because of the crooked election, but Hayes's anticorruption agenda gave him a needed popular boost. Because the election had been so contentious, Hayes tried to soothe bitter partisans by promising to stay in office for only one term. He also ended the military occupation of the South, pushing for financial aid to help rebuild the region's war-torn railroads, bridges, and ports. Hayes appointed a southern Democrat to his cabinet. To curb corruption, Hayes supported the reform of the civil service. Before Hayes, it was customary to award government jobs to political supporters without regard for merit or qualifications. Under this "spoils system," government jobs and contracts were spoils that the winning political party had the right to dispense as it wished. Hayes's goal was to professionalize government service by creating a career bureaucracy along the lines of the modern civil service we recognize today.

After Hayes, the Robber Barons and the Radical Republicans would no longer have the defeated South to plunder, but their ability to loot was far from over. The West, resource-rich but sparsely populated and politically underrepresented in Washington, would make another generation of Robber Barons rich before Teddy Roosevelt's trust-busting against monopolists broke up the party two decades later.

Lucy Hayes quickly distinguished herself from Julia Grant. She announced that she would not support jobs for relatives or do favors for office seekers. In so doing, she was relinquishing a use of power that previous first ladies, beginning with Martha Washington, had exercised freely. Others who followed Lucy would not be so squeamish about using their office to help friends and relatives find jobs.

She also suspended the weekly White House public receptions that had been a tradition since Martha Washington. During her tenure, the events were transformed to invitation-only affairs. It was a small step along that creeping incremental path toward today's imperial presidency, where the average citizen stands a better chance of winning the lottery than gaining entrance to a White House social function or official reception.

Lucy's most controversial change to White House entertainment involved alcohol. Sarah Polk had earned Washington's ire by banning hard liquor, but she still allowed wine to be consumed. Lucy was a supporter of the Women's Christian Temperance Union and had taken vows against alcohol. She proposed banning all liquor and wine from White House events, but the secretary of state objected that foreign dignitaries expected to enjoy wine with their meals.

Against her better judgment, Lucy deferred to the State Department. The result was a calamity for social drinkers. The first foreign guests to be entertained at the Hayes White House were Russians, a nationality known at the time for hard drinking and alcoholic excesses.

The state dinner for Grand Dukes Alexis and Constantine began elegantly enough. Flowers decorated the reception, in the halls and on the dining tables, where oval mirrors, meant to resemble the clear reflecting surface of a tranquil lake, were set along with Sevres china. The mirrors at the center were surrounded by ferns and vines, with mounds of fruit intended to look like foothills. At each end were glazed cakes decorated with azaleas and tea roses.

The Marine Band played the Russian anthem as Lucy led Grand Duke Alexis into the reception. The secretary of state's wife took Constantine in tow. What happened next has never been completely chronicled, but the Russian guests became inebriated and a scene ensued. It was the last straw.

The Hayeses never even served wine at their entertainments after that, although it has been reported that sympathetic White House stewards would secretly spike the punch of guests with alcohol upon request. It was a far cry from Julia Grant's formal dinner for President-elect Hayes and first-lady-to-be Lucy, in which six varieties of wine were poured to accompany a twenty-one-course meal. As a courtesy, Grant had the White House wine cellars amply stocked in readiness for Hayes. Now the bottles would remain in storage. The First Lady herself earned the nickname "Lemonade Lucy" for keeping the White House dry. Enterprising Washington proprietors, however, sensed an opportunity, and saloons near the White House advertised new names like "Last Chance."

Soon the temperance movement began to metamorphose into a broader women's movement, suggesting not only prohibition but also the more controversial notion of women's suffrage. It was an inevitable development. The Civil War and Reconstruction had given voting rights to black men—many still illiterate, because slave laws had made it a crime to educate an African American—so why not voting rights for white women, too?

Suffragists appealed to Lucy to publicly embrace their cause, but she maintained a careful neutrality. Invited to give a commencement speech at a women's college of medicine, she declined, probably because she felt it would draw her too deeply into the debate over women working. Instead she chose to visit the college, showing her support without plunging the White House directly into the debate.

Modern biographers have seized upon these events to criticize Lucy for failing to aggressively promote women's rights. However, these modern commentators fail to appreciate that Lucy's subtlety may have been a more effective tactic for changing entrenched nineteenth-century attitudes about sex roles. They miss the point that Lucy accomplished something more zealous advocates could never have achieved—she managed to be a leading role model for women's causes without simultaneously becoming a polarizing and alienating figure. She led by example. There can be no doubt that Lucy's brand of quiet social activism had a deeper and more far-reaching impact than outspoken social protest could have accomplished in the context of the times.

The distinction was not missed by Lucy Hayes's contemporaries. They understood that this college-educated woman had broken barriers for all women.

"Mrs. Hayes is the most widely known and popular president's wife the country has known," a contemporary female writer gushed. "She is an element in the administration that is strongly felt, and her influence is most potent and admirable. In her successful career as the first lady of the land is outlined the future possibilities of her sex in all other positions and conditions. She represents the new woman era. . . ."

Laura Holloway admired the first women to hold the position of first lady—Martha Washington, Abigail Adams, Dolley Madison—but derided the wave of occupants who followed after the John Quincy Adams administration as mere "social queens."

"They aspired to supremacy in the drawing room," she wrote acidly, "and were content to acquire it."

Holloway thought this pertained to all first ladies until the arrival of Lucy Hayes. To nineteenth-century female eyes, there was something about this woman that conveyed liberation and seemed to usher in an era of limitless prospects.

"She has given the world a fair example of the power for good which a woman of mental culture and social opportunities can exercise," Holloway wrote. "Mrs. Hayes has called forth, through her successful efforts in placing herself beside her husband in his official rank, a more just appreciation of her womanhood. . . ."

Besides the political partnership that Holloway witnessed between the president and the first lady, Lucy adopted several causes—for example, pushing for completion of the Washington Monument. Like her interest in the Reform Farm for deaf and mute boys in Ohio, she now championed the Deaf Mute College in Washington, D.C. She also showed an interest in the education of newly freed slaves through her visit to Hampton College, one of the few institutions of higher education then open to African Americans.

Organizations like the Women's Christian Temperance Union, which raised funds to commission a formal portrait of the first lady without her consent, adopted her as a standard-bearer the way social causes today would try to enlist a celebrity endorsement. The mere fact that Lucy's support was solicited by a wide variety of groups demonstrates that her contemporaries recognized her influence and saw her as a leader.

Lucy Hayes established the precedent of the White House Easter egg hunt, too. Before the Hayes administration, the event had been held on the Capitol grounds, but in a moment of political ineptitude Congress banned the event because the members were tired of having the grounds littered with broken eggshells. The First Lady eagerly opened the White House lawns to Washington's children, and the White House has been the venue for the popular Easter egg hunt ever since.

The Hayes presidency embraced public policies that were many years ahead of their times. Hayes supported penal reform in order to rehabilitate prisoners, favored federal aid to the states for public education, and advocated civil service reform. His presidency wasn't able to accomplish much in these policy areas, but he did manage to restrict civil servants' open participation in political campaigns and election drives on behalf of candidates. Lucy Hayes's views also helped shape her husband's policies After her tenure in the White House, she became president of the Woman's Home Missionary Society, and was the first former first lady to routinely give public speeches.

She died in 1889.

Lucretia Rudolph
Garfield

First Lady: March 1881–September 1881
20th Presidential Administration

Siena Research Institute Rating: 28

"She will have a most beneficent influence upon society in Washington. She loves truth and despises shams."

—Laura C. Holloway

Lucretia Garfield was the second first lady to become widowed by an assassin's bullet when her husband, James, was shot and fatally wounded in July 1881, only four months into his term of office.

Nineteenth-century writer Laura Holloway's book *The Ladies of the White House* had appeared in print shortly before the assassination. She wrote of Lucretia's handling of the role of First Lady before the tragic event:

> ... Mrs. Garfield is in the prime of her life. She is forty-three years old, and is slight in figure and piquant in manner. Her pretty brown hair is streaked with silver, and there are care lines in her face wrought there by thought and endeavor and suffering ... for the next four years Mrs. Garfield will preside over the White House, and entertain in its historic apartments as her predecessors have done. The administration is but entered upon its career. . . .

In fact, Lucretia Garfield was forty-eight years old when she became first lady. She was born in Garrettsville, Ohio, in 1832, to a prosperous but not wealthy farming family. Like Lucy Hayes, Lucretia Garfield was a college-educated woman. She graduated from Hiram College (then known as Western Reserve Eclectic Institute) before becoming a teacher. She was fluent in several modern languages and conversant in Latin and Greek.

She met her future husband, James, at Hiram College, where he taught. He was the last of the presidents to be born in a log cabin, to a not-so-prosperous farming family. Campaigning for him in the 1880 election, President Rutherford Hayes claimed that he had risen farther from humble origins to high office by dint of hard work and talent than any other president, including Abraham Lincoln. After a four-year engagement with Lucretia, the couple married in 1858. James had shown an interest in politics and been elected to the Ohio Senate, but war broke out before he took office. In response to Lincoln's call for volunteers, James raised and trained a company of troops, drilling them in military tactics through knowledge he gained by reading books and manuals. Before long, he and his men were engaged in combat in neighboring Kentucky. By the age of thirty, he had become the youngest general in the Union army. Illness, described as a recurrence of "fever and ague, contracted on the towpath when he was a boy," however, cut short his promising military career.

Then, in 1863, Garfield was elected to the House of Representatives. The following year, Lucretia joined him in Washington. It was her first exposure to Washington, D.C., and she attended debates in Congress and joined in the social life of the city as a congressman's wife.

As Garfield won reelection after reelection campaign, the family moved from boardinghouses to their own home in Washington at Thirteenth and I Streets, only a few blocks from the White House. The Garfields began splitting their time between Washington and Ohio.

Garfield rose through the party leadership ranks to become Republican minority leader in the House. In 1880, he was elected to the Senate. Lucretia's prospects, however, didn't seem particularly bright. She was an intelligent woman interested in politics, fulfilling the domestic duties of a wife raising a growing family of young children. "It is horrible to be a man," she wrote in a moment of frustration, "but the grinding misery of being a woman between the upper and nether millstone of household cares and training children is almost as bad. To be half civilized with some aspirations for enlightenment, and obliged to spend the largest part of the time the victim of young barbarians keeps one in a perpetual ferment!"

James Garfield was a dark-horse presidential candidate in the 1880 election, winning the Republican nomination only after convention delegates balloted thirty-six times. His Democratic opponent was another Civil War general, Winfield S. Hancock, who lost no time spreading rumors that Garfield intended to undermine the workingman by importing Chinese laborers willing to work for "coolie wages." Garfield barely won the popular vote.

Lucretia remained an asset throughout the close campaign. She didn't want merchants trafficking in her likeness, refusing to allow photographs to be taken of her during the campaign. Still, she studiously engaged the political supporters necessary to win the race, and avoided becoming ensnarled in any campaign controversies. Garfield later remarked that she had never made a misstep that required him to divert attention from his political goals in order to rectify her mistakes. She was, in effect, a perfect political partner.

There were domestic issues hidden in the couple's past that might have been problematic in a campaign. James Garfield was a womanizer. Their four-year engagement was marred with various interludes in which James openly courted other women, and may have gone further. During his first term in Congress, he carried on an indiscreet affair with a twenty-year-old correspondent for the *New York Tribune*, Lucia Gilbert Calhoun. Lucretia knew about and had forgiven James's marital infidelity, but perhaps her reluctance to be photographed during the presidential campaign stemmed from fear that raising her own profile might simply invite James's mistresses to come forward to the press. She may have reasoned that if his campaign featured them as a couple too prominently, a mistress might find the political hypocrisy an irresistible target, and try to embarrass them both by coming forward with charges of marital infidelity. Fortunately for Garfield, the 1880 election turned on economic issues, and their domestic affairs remained private.

Lucretia gave interviews to the press. She advised James on the selection of cabinet officers, weighing in heavily—and successfully—on behalf of James Blaine as secretary of state. Her diary entries show that she not only understood the implications of each appointment on the rival factions within the Republican Party but also carefully calculated their effects. In particular, she foresaw a bitter struggle with the "Stalwart" faction of the Republican Party, whose chief figure was none other than Garfield's own vice president, Chester A. Arthur.

"You will never have anything from these men but their assured contempt, until you fight them dead," she warned James. "You can put every one of them in his political grave if you are a mind to & that is the only place where they can be kept peaceable."

It was an ominous and revealing premonition. Lucretia was a woman who knew what it took to wield power successfully in the furtherance of statecraft.

She also knew that there was a lighter side to the duty of first lady as hostess of the White House. She eagerly held reception times when she received visitors, but enforced her schedule with iron determination. When one self-righteous socialite demanded to see Lucretia outside the appointed visiting hours, she was turned away by the staff. In official reception lines, Lucretia stood right beside her husband, in the fashion of modern first ladies. At state dinners, she revived the practice of serving wine. When ardent temperance advocates rebuked her, she refused to yield to their criticism, earning praise from her husband for her steadfastness. When the navy wanted to demonstrate new techniques for generating power for steamships, it was President and Mrs. Garfield who attended.

Where other first ladies had complained about the White House for one reason or another, Lucretia Garfield was fascinated by the history of the "old house." She had plans to make it the cultural center of Washington, D.C., by creating a salon. She collected the names of writers and artists she wanted to meet with and solicited more names from other prominent Washington women.

It all came to an abrupt halt in May, when Lucretia fell ill with malaria. For a while she was in serious condition, possibly near death, but she finally began getting better. She left Washington for the New Jersey seashore in an effort to speed her recovery. Her husband accompanied her to the Washington railway depot a few blocks from the White House on June 18, 1881, where a crowd had assembled to see the president and his wife. Among them was Charles Guiteau, a deranged postal clerk. He is usually described in history texts as a disappointed job seeker, but that hardly does justice to this cold-blooded political killer. Guiteau was stalking Garfield. Lucretia had met him earlier at the White House, when Guiteau had come to a public reception and started a conversation with her. At the train station that day, Guiteau, in a chilling display of chivalry, chose not to shoot James because Lucretia looked so frail and thin from her bout with malaria.

On July 2, 1881, as Garfield was preparing to travel by train to New Jersey to visit his convalescing wife, Guiteau struck. At close range he fired at the president, shouting "I am a Stalwart! Arthur is now president!"

His proclamation was premature. Garfield was fatally hit, but it took more than eighty days before he died. In an age before X rays and MRI machines, doctors could not locate and remove the bullet that lodged in his back.

Although she had barely recovered herself, Lucretia nursed James daily. When he spoke of dying, she encouraged him to persevere. When his surgeons told her only a miracle would save him, she chose to hope for one. In the humid Washington summer, Garfield's torments were terrible. To cool his sickroom in the White House, they brought ice into the basement and tried to fan the cooler air upward through a lead pipe. Finally, to escape the torrid heat, Lucretia moved him to the seashore town of Elberon, New Jersey.

Under her care, he clung to life until September 19, 1881. If Guiteau was part of a political conspiracy, no proof was ever found.

Through it all, Lucretia Garfield remained a model of grace and strength. Public drives to raise money for her and their children struck an immediate chord. She received a gift of $360,000 from the American people, along with another $50,000 onetime grant from Congress and a pension of $5,000 annually.

For the next eighteen years, she split her time between Ohio and California. She is said to have found her own young children to be trying "barbarians" at times, but she reportedly blossomed in the role of grandmother and then great-grandmother to an expanding and adoring clan. She died in 1918, just a few weeks short of her eighty-sixth birthday.

Ellen Lewis Herndon Arthur

First Lady: 1880
21st Presidential Administration
Unrated

One of the best specimens of the Southern woman.
—Anonymous Friend of President Arthur

To those who believe a first lady is essential to any Presidential administration, Chester A. Arthur's term of office stands in contradiction. Arthur's wife, Ellen, had died on January 12, 1880, of pneumonia. His presidential campaign was hardly under way, and it would still be months before Arthur was chosen to be the running mate for James Garfield.

Although other widowed presidents, such as Andrew Jackson and Thomas Jefferson, chose to have female relatives fill the role of first lady, Arthur said he didn't want any other woman to have the honored position that he felt rightfully belonged to Ellen.

She might have been an interesting first lady. Ellen Arthur was a distinguished soprano who performed with the New York Mendelssohn Glee Club. She was the first artist to become first lady. Born to an aristocratic Virginia family, she was familiar with Washington's political and social elite. Her father was a naval officer who moved the family to Washington when he was assigned a post that involved the founding of the U.S. Naval Observatory, now the grounds for the vice president's residence.

Ellen had shown promise as a singer even as a child. She joined the choir at St. John's Episcopal Church—known now as the church of the presidents in Washington—while still a teenager. When her father was assigned command of a naval steamship, the family moved to New York, where she continued to study music. She was nineteen when a cousin introduced her to a promising young attorney just starting to practice law in New York. He was Chester Arthur, and within a year the couple were engaged.

She might have become a patron of the arts had she lived to be first lady. But in 1880, after a winter performance in New York, she became chilled waiting to catch a carriage. The cold progressed into pneumonia, and Ellen died.

Chester Arthur turned to his sister Mary to assist with some of the social duties of the White House, but he didn't let her become a full-fledged first lady in the same sense that Andrew Jackson had done with Emily Donelson. Mary's real role was to aid Arthur raising his ten-year-old daughter, also named Ellen. When Mary stood in a receiving line, it was with many other wives of administration officials, preventing her from standing out in her own right.

Arthur was known for his impeccable taste and style, and he managed his own White House entertaining without any special help from the opposite sex. Social functions at the Arthur White House were known for their elegance. It can't be said, however, that the White House was without Ellen's presence.

The president kept a small portrait of her in his room, placing a fresh flower in front of it each day. He also gave St. John's Church a special stained-glass window depicting angels in Ellen's memory. It was kept illuminated all night. From the upstairs rooms at the White House, he could glimpse its colors across the grassy expanse of Lafayette Square. When Arthur left the White House at the end of Garfield's term, he was still a widower. Arthur remained a widower. He died on November 18, 1886.

FRANCES FOLSOM
CLEVELAND

FIRST LADY: 1886–1889 AND 1893-1897
22ND AND 24TH PRESIDENTIAL ADMINISTRATIONS
SIENA RESEARCH INSTITUTE RATING: 23

White House Bride

President Cleveland's life was a tabloid reporter's dream. As a young man, Cleveland and a group of male friends, including his law partner Oscar Folsom, were frequently entertained by a young widow named Maria Halpin. When she became pregnant, Cleveland—the only bachelor among the group of otherwise married men—took responsibility for the child, although as far as anyone knew the paternity was in question. Although he refused to marry the widow Halpin, Cleveland nevertheless paid regular child support for the boy, who was named Oscar Folsom Cleveland, until his adoption by an affluent New York family.

The affair didn't come to light for almost ten years, but when Cleveland won the Democratic presidential nomination in 1884 the press quickly exposed the story. "A Terrible Tale, a Dark Chapter in a Public Man's History," read one banner headline typical of the media coverage. It was the beginning of a political campaign that would feature the issue of character. He barely squeaked by Republican opponent James G. Blaine at the election, winning by a popular-vote margin of only 62,683 votes, although his margin in the electoral college was a healthy 37 votes.

When Cleveland entered the White House in 1885, he was a father and a middle-aged bachelor. For the first year of his first term, therefore, Cleveland turned to his sister Rose to handle the social affairs of the White House.

Rose was a professional woman. Unmarried, seemingly "masculine" in her manners to some observers of the time, she was a teacher and a writer. A book she authored, *George Eliot's Prose and Other Studies*, was a literary success. It ultimately earned her almost twenty-five thousand dollars in royalties. It was a stopgap measure. Queried by one friend about when the president would marry, Cleveland quipped that he was still waiting for his future wife to grow up. No one knew it, but he meant the remark earnestly. Cleveland had his eye on his future wife before he won the presidency. In fact, he had had his eyes on her from the time she was twelve years old.

Frances Folsom was the daughter of Cleveland's law partner. When Oscar Folsom was killed in a carriage accident, Cleveland took the young girl and her widowed mother as his wards. Throughout her teens, he nurtured her education, sent her correspondence, and, as she grew older, showered her with flowers and gifts from the governor's mansion in New York.

She called him "Uncle Cleve," and he called her by her despised nickname "Frankie." When Frances and her mother came to visit Grover and Rose at the White House during her spring break from Wells College in

1884, rumors arose that Cleveland was romancing her mother. But it was the daughter he was romancing.

In 1885, Cleveland proposed to his ward, who by then was a young woman of twenty-one. He was more than twice her age. She was tall and thin, with a full figure, blazing blue eyes, and wavy chestnut hair. At 260 pounds, he was obese, weighing almost twice as much as Frances.

It was a match destined to draw attention. The couple decided to keep their engagement secret. Frances and her mother went on an extended European tour so that the first lady to be could acquire additional polish and worldliness. It was Cleveland's finishing touch in his attendance to cultivating a perfect mate for himself.

When their ship docked in New York at the end of the European travels, Cleveland's sister Rose and a White House aide were waiting to greet the returning Frances and her mother. So was the press. Rose hurried her charges wordlessly through the waiting reporters, but it was too late to stifle the story. Gossip pages had begun reporting that Cleveland was secretly engaged to marry not Frances, but her mother, Emma Folsom.

To avoid further embarrassment to the widow, the White House released an official announcement the day after Emma and her daughter returned to the States. It announced the engagement of her daughter to the president. Cleveland's administration felt the record had to be set straight.

Immediately, Frances became a sensation. Cleveland wanted the first wedding of a president in the White House to be a small, private affair, but it nonetheless began involving the entire city of Washington. True to the couple's desire, there were only thirty-one guests in attendance for their marriage in the Blue Room of the White House on June 2, 1886. At six-thirty in the evening, the Marine Band struck up Mendelssohn's "Wedding March." Outside, cannon saluted their nuptials and every church bell in the city rang to herald the union.

Frances had hoped her grandfather would give her away, but he died during her European grand tour. President Cleveland escorted his bride down the hallway to the Blue Room.

Frances' train was four yards long, and her satin gown was short sleeved, ivory colored, trimmed in white silk. The Parisian fashion mogul Worth had designed the bridal outfit. A coronet of flowers held her five-yard-long silk veil in place. On the main table at the dinner following the ceremony was a ship made of roses and pansies, resting on a mirror meant to look like the sea. The guests received a souvenir slice of cake, along with a card bearing the autographs of the president and first lady.

When the wedding dinner ended at about nine o'clock, they changed and left the White House by a rear exit. A special train was waiting to take them to a secluded honeymoon retreat at Deer Park, Maryland. On their way to the resort, however, the couple found themselves under the scrutiny of what can only be described as the paparazzi of the day. Reporters watched them through binoculars and stalked them with cameras, prying into every aspect of the couple's behavior. Even their breakfast menu was considered newsworthy enough to print.

To the Clevelands, especially Grover, it was an unwelcome intrusion into their privacy. What was undeniable was the fact that Frances was quickly becoming a celebrity. The press was interested in her every move. When she tied her hair back in a bun, the style became known as "a la Cleveland" and set a trend. Later, when it was falsely reported that she no longer wore a bustle on her dress because it was going out of fashion, women across the country stopped wearing bustles.

Merchants freely used her image to peddle wares of every description. It was nothing less than a mania, a craze of the sort that might have disoriented many others, but Frances took her instant fame in stride. To compensate for the exclusivity of the wedding, for example, she obligingly took part in two receptions after their honeymoon. One was an invitation-only affair for Washington's political elite, but the other was open to the public. In each reception, Frances wore her full wedding outfit.

She was in fact an accomplished young woman. She could read Latin and spoke French and German. She was the third first lady in the White House who was a college graduate. Initially, the public was intrigued with her youth and her beauty, but the love affair between first lady and the people only grew stronger when they came to know her character.

Cleveland's concept of the ideal wife, however, did not include a woman who was a political partner in the full sense of the word. He believed that "a woman should not bother her head about political parties and public questions." He had risen through politics without a partner at his side, and the middle-aged bachelor had no intention of changing his modus operandi because of a wedding ceremony. Frances' influence was not felt in cabinet affairs or political patronage. For example, when Julia Grant—never one to shy away from nepotism—came to visit her at the White House, she urged Frances to intercede with Grover so that her son could get a political appointment. If Frances mentioned Julia's interest, it had little effect. Cleveland did not make the appointment.

Still, as a role model for women, Frances made her influence felt in other ways. She supported a charity called the Needlework Guild that helped clothe the poor. Along with an African American woman, she helped charter the Washington Home for Friendless Colored Girls. She tried to organize a charity devoted to poor black children, but it ultimately faltered for lack of support. Nonetheless, she became involved with a group that distributed Christmas gifts to impoverished African American youth, dispensing the presents herself.

Frances seemed to sympathize with workingwomen in a way that suggested they should achieve equality and be self-supporting. She held Saturday-afternoon receptions at the White House, because that was the only time when workingwomen—teachers, shop assistants, seamstresses, factory hands—were free to come. These Saturday receptions were frowned upon by some White House officials, who felt they drew too many lower-class women. Frances issued an instruction to the staff not to try to subvert her Saturday events by scheduling other functions.

She contributed to the Christian Women's Temperance Union, which supported women's suffrage. While she did not publicly embrace voting rights for women, she pointedly did not disavow her support for women's suffrage, as Lucy Hayes had done. This left the movement free to infer her commitment to them, which was not always true. When the organization asked her to stop wearing low-cut gowns because it set a bad example for young women, Frances ignored their puritanical dictate. They in turn pretended that she had agreed to their demand, and printed up flyers for a women's conference stating that the first lady would no longer wear the immoral garb. Feminism was still in its nascency, but the now-familiar tension between liberation and those who felt their role was to guard against anything demeaning to or exploitive of women was already present. Whatever was inferred, Frances kept wearing her low-cut blouses.

She was wildly popular. White House receptions were thronged with guests—some observers called them "crushes"—because everyone wanted to meet Frances. After standing in line shaking hands for hours, she often had to have her arms packed in ice at night to reduce the aching. She received so much mail that she had to hire help to handle the correspondence, but even this was not sufficient. The Cleveland White House became the first to adopt the use of a form letter to manage the volume of letters.

Political foes began to worry that Frances's popularity would boost her husband's reelection prospects. Cleveland had been a controversial president because he vetoed so many laws passed by Congress. He grasped a fact of presidential power that few of his predecessors seemed to have fully appreciated: The Constitution gave him the power to govern in "the negative" by using the presidential veto.

Overriding a presidential veto is difficult for Congress. It takes a two-thirds majority—sometimes called a supermajority—to pass legislation over the president's veto. This gives the chief executive formidable power over a fractured Congress. During the Civil War, and especially through the impeachment trial of President Andrew Johnson, Congress had steadily asserted its power over the White House. Particularly in matters concerning the president's power to choose or dismiss his cabinet and other senior executive branch appointees, Congress had actually usurped power that properly belonged to the president.

Cleveland was also the first Democrat to hold the White House since before the Civil War. In a Congress dominated by Republicans, his political strategy was to use the veto. The twenty-one presidents before Cleveland used it a mere 132 times. In his first term as president, Cleveland used the power three hundred times!

He was unanimously nominated for a second term, and actually increased his narrow popular-vote margin, but Cleveland lost in the electoral college to Benjamin Harrison. Grover and Frances left Washington before the inauguration of the new president but not before Frances was said to have told the White House staff to take good care of the furnishings during their absence; they would be back in four years.

And they were. In 1892, Cleveland again won the Democratic nomination. His running mate was Adlai Stevenson, grandfather of the diplomat who would later run for president and become famous in the Kennedy cabinet as ambassador to the United Nations during the Cuban Missile Crisis. Cleveland's opponent was the incumbent, President Harrison, whose campaign for reelection lacked heart. Harrison's wife had died earlier that year, and he was depressed. The country was also mired in economic problems brought on by several factors, including a high tariff on imported goods that Cleveland had opposed. Grover Cleveland was swept back into office, becoming the only president to win two nonconsecutive terms in the White House.

Frances was no longer the ingenue, the fresh college graduate who had swept an aging bachelor and the nation off their feet. She was now a mother and had a more mature bearing, and a mother's caution. The public that had so adored the young bride half a decade earlier now was equally mesmerized by their baby daughter, Ruth. Frances was horrified by the eagerness with which visitors to the White House grounds swept the little girl up in their arms, handing her off into the crowd of eager admirers. On one occasion, an overzealous visitor tried to snip off a lock of the girl's hair as a souvenir. At that point, Frances had the White House policy changed to close the grounds to visitors. For greater privacy, the president and first family often stayed at their private residence near Georgetown instead of at the White House. As maturity grasped her, the Gay Nineties gave way to an economic depression.

She then confronted a family crisis that could have deepened the country's difficulties. Cleveland was only three months into his second term when a rough patch of skin on the roof of his mouth was diagnosed as cancerous. Doctors recommended surgical removal, and President Cleveland agreed to the procedure under strict conditions designed to assure secrecy. He didn't want the country, already at a low point in consumer confidence, to be further shaken by the news that he had a potentially fatal disease.

At the end of June 1893, Frances went to the family vacation home at Buzzards Bay, New York. She asked the now-ever-present newspaper reporters who met her there to hold off reporting news of her husband's absence until he arrived to join her, for fear of needlessly alarming the public.

The cover story was that he was having some teeth extracted. The truth was that he was undergoing a hazardous operation in New York Harbor on a yacht named the *Oneida*. Grover was losing more than teeth. The greater portion of his left jaw was being amputated.

The *Oneida* belonged to Cleveland's close friend, Commodore Elias C. Benedict. He and the crew were sworn to absolute secrecy. Medical equipment was brought on board the yacht, and a surgical unit was set up. On July 1, Grover underwent the operation. Externally, his cheek appeared normal. Inside, the missing jawbone had been replaced by a rubber jaw. He went back to work, and no one ever knew the facts about the president's brush with cancer until his death nine years later! Later that year, Frances gave birth to a little girl named Esther—who was the first child of a sitting president born in the White House.

The economic recession lasted throughout Cleveland's second term, which was marred by labor strife and protests. There were social highlights—visits by Hawaiian and Spanish royalty—and, despite being older and perhaps wiser, Frances remained popular. Although she wept when they left the White House for the second time in 1897, the couple happily settled in Princeton, New Jersey. Her family had continued to grow, and in her last years in the White House she was preoccupied with domestic concerns.

Grover Cleveland died in 1908. He left a sizable estate. Frances, now a forty-four-year-old woman with growing children, never needed to collect the five-thousand-dollars-a-year pension Congress had authorized. She remarried at the age of forty-nine. Her husband, Thomas Prexton, was a restless businessman who decided to make a midlife career change and become an archaeologist. No longer hampered by Grover Cleveland's view that a wife shouldn't bother herself about politics or public policy, Frances took on a public role. She was active during World War I, making public speeches on behalf of the war effort. She later appeared at campaign rallies for the Democratic presidential contender Alfred E. Smith.

One newspaper columnist said she had the "good nature and tact of Dolley Madison, the culture of Abigail Adams, the style and vivacity of Harriet Lane, and a beauty greater than that of any of the ladies of the White House still remembered by the old stagers [old-timers] of Washington." She lived until 1947, when she passed away peacefully in her sleep.

She owes her relatively high rating of 23 in the Siena Research Institute poll to the fact that she was a national celebrity and popular first lady who was therefore a political asset to the presidency. In the category of "public image," the academics polled by the Siena Institute rate Frances Cleveland No. 17.

Caroline Lavinia Scott Harrison

First Lady: 1889–1892
23rd Presidential Administration
Siena Research Institute Rating: 29

"Best housekeeper the White House had ever known."
—Frank Carpenter, *Cleveland Leader* Newspaper

Revisionists strain to portray Caroline Harrison as a supporter of the women's rights movement, but there is scant evidence to support this view. Other than pressing her husband to hire a female family friend as a stenographer—she did become the first woman on the White House staff—Caroline Harrison devoted her effort to the refinement of the White House living quarters. To the extent she was an activist, it was for civic causes, not political or feminist movements.

Caroline was just a teenager when she met her future husband, an aspiring attorney named Benjamin Harrison. He had the pedigree of a blueblood. He was the great-grandson of a signer of the Declaration of Independence, Virginia governor Benjamin Harrison. He was the grandson of former president William Henry Harrison, and for a short period of time after he and Caroline married they lived with his grandmother, the former first lady Anna Symmes Harrison.

Caroline also had a social pedigree, although it was not as politically illustrious as that of her future husband. She was the daughter of a prominent educator and Presbyterian minister, Dr. John Witherspoon Scott.

The Scott family was well known in Oxford, Ohio. Her father had founded an elementary school for girls as well as the more advanced Oxford Female Academy, where he served as headmaster. He was a professor at Miami University in Ohio, and he saw to it that Caroline was well educated. She was fond of music and the arts, and showcased her talent as a painter and in the decorative arts.

Benjamin Harrison was a college student at Miami University when they met. By the time he graduated in 1852, they were secretly engaged to be married. When he moved to Cincinnati, Ohio, after graduation in order to study law, the couple advanced their marriage plans. Caroline's father performed the dawn ceremony on October 20, 1853.

The newlyweds moved in with former first lady Anna Symmes Harrison at the family home, The Point. Benjamin was admitted to the bar the following year, and the young couple moved to Indianapolis, where he went into a law partnership. His new partner, Will Wallace, introduced Harrison to Indiana political circles and the Republican Party.

The law practice prospered, and Caroline took up the kind of cultural activities customary for an upper-middle-class woman of the times. She played the piano, joined church groups, painted watercolors, and decorated china and pottery in a home studio that had its own kiln. The Harrisons might have enjoyed an idyllic, prosperous, and uneventful life had it not been for the Civil War.

Benjamin was descended from Revolutionary War veterans, and it was inconceivable that he wouldn't join in the fray. In 1862, he raised a company of volunteers called the Seventieth Indiana Infantry and became its colonel. During Sherman's infamous march through the South, Harrison played a decisive role in the battle for Atlanta that would culminate with the burning of the city. After his men broke through heavily defended Confederate lines at Peachtree Creek, Harrison earned a field promotion to brigadier general. He was just thirty-two years old.

Unlike Julia Grant or Lucy Hayes, Caroline did not share the dangers of the field with her husband during the Civil War. Rather than expose the family to Confederate artillery fire, as Julia had done during the Vicksburg campaign, or care for the boys in uniform, as "Mother Lucy" Hayes did for the Twenty-third Ohio Volunteers, Caroline stayed in Indiana far from the fighting. She made occasional visits to Benjamin when his troops were in camps well away from the front lines, but confined her war relief efforts to fund-raising for the Ladies Patriotic Association and the Ladies Sanitary Committee, which helped treat wounded soldiers.

Harrison had risen in prominence because of the war, and in peacetime he rose rapidly in Republican Party ranks. His law firm income also rose, and the family soon built a sixteen-room home. Caroline took art lessons and literature classes. He ran for governor twice, and lost both times. Finally, in the election of 1880, the Indiana legislature chose him to be U.S. senator.

In 1881, the Harrisons moved to Washington. Caroline eagerly embraced the life of a political spouse, building goodwill by hosting the obligatory receptions and dinners throughout Harrison's six-year Senate term. When he lost his seat after only one term, Harrison boldly announced his candidacy for the presidency. He won the Republican nomination in 1888.

It was an era of "front-porch" politicking: Instead of traveling the country campaigning for votes, candidates stayed at home and let the press, politicians, and curious voters come to them. Harrison gave his stump speeches to crowds that assembled by the thousands, and Caroline hosted an endless throng of Republican officials, journalists, and well-wishers who literally wore out the carpets during the course of the campaign.

Grover Cleveland won the popular vote in the 1888 election, but Benjamin Harrison outdid him in the all-decisive electoral college tally by 233 to 168. Frances Cleveland had captured the country's heart, and her image appeared freely in Cleveland campaign materials. In response, Caroline Harrison's image was also used. After four years of exhaustive media coverage of Frances, however, Caroline was at a disadvantage. No one knew much about her.

It is only fitting, then, that her image became prominent in the campaign. Front-porch politicking, after all, meant that she had been by his side throughout most of the campaign. While candidates' spouses had often figured in previous campaigns, especially in political controversies like Rachel Jackson's disputed divorce, it had only recently become common practice for them to campaign openly in elections.

There is much evidence to support the contention that the Harrisons were a true political partnership. Benjamin consulted Caroline freely and relied on her advice. Perhaps she even shares some of the responsibility for history's verdict that Harrison's presidency was mediocre. Future president Teddy Roosevelt summed up the theme when he called Harrison a "cold-blooded, narrow-minded, prejudiced, obstinate, timid old psalm-singing Indianapolis president."

Harrison was an obsessive micromanager. He squandered the first one hundred days of his presidency—the period we now call the honeymoon—trying to personally interview candidates to fill some seventeen hundred political appointments or "plum" jobs. This not only was an incredible waste of presidential time but also alienated leaders from Harrison's own party whose power depended on their ability to serve as patrons to their loyal party supporters by rewarding them with government jobs. By taking that power into his own hands, Harrison irritated many party leaders.

His economic policies were also a failure. Harrison was a protectionist who wanted to use high tariffs to promote American industry, but to get the western states to go along he had to back a compromise called the Sherman Silver Purchase Act. The law required the Treasury Department to purchase four and a half million ounces of silver on the market each month. Western mining interests liked the law, because it had the effect of keeping the price of silver steady. To pay for the silver bullion, the treasury issued currency redeemable in silver or gold. So many people redeemed their paper currency for gold that the government's reserves were almost wiped out, destabilizing the value of the dollar. The act was an economic disaster and was repealed shortly after Harrison's presidency ended. Yet he believed it was such important legislation that he immediately wrote to Caroline about the bill.

They shared other misjudgments together. During his first year in office, Harrison's political appointee to the position of postmaster general, John Wanamaker, gave Caroline a twenty-room house at the seashore in

Cape May, New Jersey. There was an uproar when the press found out, and President Harrison insisted it was all a misunderstanding. There had never been any intention by the first lady to take the lavish gift; the Harrisons really meant to buy the property. To cover up the botched attempt to accept graft, President Harrison wrote out a check for ten thousand dollars to pay Wanamaker. To their credit, the Harrisons learned from this misstep. They either refused all bribes offered them in the future—or were careful enough not to get caught twice.

The first lady turned her attention to remodeling the White House. With the aid of an architect, she developed elaborate plans to transform it into an elegant Gilded Age mansion. Senator Leland Stanford of California introduced a bill in Congress to appropriate the $950,000 to carry out Caroline's plans, but the bill was killed by a Republican Party leader angered that President Harrison had rejected one of his patronage requests. Instead, Caroline received thirty-five thousand dollars from Congress to renovate the existing building.

While renovating, she came across the china patterns of previous first ladies in an old cabinet. Caroline had wanted to include an art gallery in her transformation of the White House, and recognized at once that the White House china collection had historical importance. She initiated the display of previous china patterns, which now form an important part of the permanent White House collection that is open to visitors on the public tour.

In an attic, she came across an elaborately carved but disused desk. It had been a gift from Queen Victoria to President Rutherford Hayes. Carved from the wood of the British ship HMS *Resolute*, it was brought back into use by Harrison. Most Americans would recognize the desk today as the one they see on television when presidents give speeches from the Oval Office. It has been used as a working desk by most presidents.

After her discoveries, Caroline realized that it was important to chronicle these pieces of White House history. The first lady was the impetus for the creation of an inventory that not only listed the pieces but also recorded as much of their history as was known.

Many of her renovations were more prosaic. Rats had infested the White House by the late nineteenth century, so Caroline used some of the money appropriated by Congress to replace wooden flooring with chew-proof concrete and to tile walls for less leakage and improved sanitation. She had the building wired for electric lighting, although neither she nor her husband understood the new marvel and were afraid that turning the lights off might electrocute them. If the staff didn't do it, they left them on all night.

Caroline canceled Frances Cleveland's innovative Saturday-afternoon receptions for workingwomen. This single act is strong evidence that Caroline wasn't deeply interested in women's advancement or working-women, although she did help raise funds for the medical school of Johns Hopkins University on the proviso that women would be admitted to study to become doctors. When it came to women of her own social class, Caroline could be generous in outlook.

Revisionists such as Charles W. Calhoun and Dorothy and Carl Schneider have interpreted her role in helping to create the Daughters of the American Revolution as feminist activism. She did become its first president while still first lady, but the record tells a somewhat different story.

The centennial of the Washington presidency in 1889 sparked renewed interest in the Revolutionary Era, and it was celebrated in New York with a re-creation of the first inaugural ball. Caroline Harrison and other former first ladies, including Julia Grant and Frances Cleveland, attended. Martha Washington became the first first lady to have a dollar bill bear her likeness when special commemorative currency was issued. The Revolution was in vogue, and it became a source of prestige to be able to claim a revolutionary ancestor.

Suddenly, women wanted to join the Sons of the Revolution, a long-standing organization whose members traced their lineage to the Revolution. In 1890, the year after the Washington Centennial, the Sons of the Revolution decided not to admit women into its ranks even if they could prove their lineage from a revolutionary ancestor. Caroline Harrison supported the creation of the Daughters of the Revolution because the Sons of the Revolution had snubbed her for membership. President Harrison, it will be remembered, was a direct descendant of a revolutionary ancestor, and was therefore eligible for this social distinction.

Superficially, the founding of the D.A.R. appears to strike a blow for equality between men and women. But there may have been an unwholesome motive for the sudden desire to claim membership in either group. The 1890s were an era of high immigration, and being able to trace one's ancestors to the *Mayflower* or the Revolution was really just another way to distinguish one's pedigree from the newly arrived, largely Catholic and non-WASP masses.

It was probably not a social honor of the type the workingwomen and shop assistants who attended Frances Cleveland's Saturday receptions would have cared about, and they certainly wouldn't have fought over it.

It takes a great deal of imagination to see Caroline's role in creating the Daughters of the American Revolution as a triumph of social emancipation—or as evidence that Caroline Harrison cared about equality for women. She did, however, manage to win a new badge of social superiority for status-conscious females. Caroline Harrison's lasting contribution to the growing body of White House precedent was that she became the first first lady to decorate the White House with a Christmas tree. In the century separating Martha Washington from Caroline Harrison, the role of first lady had evolved into one of Victorian gentility. While many first ladies exercised substantial power privately, in public their role was to be hostess of the White House and, every four years, join in political campaigning.

Toward the end of Harrison's term of office, Caroline became ill. One chronicler reports that she died of cancer; all others give the cause of death as tuberculosis. Her demise in 1892 left President Harrison badly dispirited. Some historians attribute his lackluster showing in the presidential campaign that year to depression over her death.

Even if he had campaigned well, however, the only issue that mattered in 1892, as during his initial election run in 1888, was the state of the economy. The tariff Harrison proposed when campaigning against Cleveland four years earlier had been tried as an economic remedy, and had failed. Harrison had run a clean campaign in 1888, and was widely admired for it, but the revelation of the gift house in New Jersey had irreparably harmed his reputation. Still, even this might have been overcome given a different economic climate. The president did have vision—Harrison saw six more western states admitted into the Union, he began a project to modernize the navy to include new steel ships, he pushed for better trade ties to Latin America and a canal through Central America—but he lacked the political skills to make most of his agenda a reality.

In the end, his second term was torpedoed by rising consumer prices. His reelection campaign was a classic pocketbook election, and he lost because he hadn't been able to deliver on his campaign promise from 1888 to restore economic growth.

Had Caroline Harrison continued the Saturday receptions, the shop girls and workingwomen might have given her early warning about the shifting public mood.

Ida Saxton McKinley

First Lady: 1897–1901
25th Presidential Adminstration
Siena Research Institute Rating: 32

"White House invalid."
—Col. W. H. Crook, "Memories of the White House"

Guests at presidential state dinners must have been befuddled when the ever-attentive President McKinley would suddenly throw a large handkerchief over his wife's head. Veiled by the cloth, what happened beneath was only part of the tragedy and enigma that enveloped the McKinley presidency.

She may have had epileptic fits. She certainly had seizures. Some of her outbursts suggest classic paranoia. Yet she was determined to fill the role of first lady and refused to relinquish it to another woman, not even a relative. Throughout his long political career—fourteen years in Congress, two terms as governor of Ohio, and two terms in the White House cut short by an assassin—William McKinley had become accustomed to adjusting to his wife's strange affliction. Bizarre as it may have seemed to new guests at the White House to see him suddenly shield his wife from view, to the McKinleys it was simply a normal accommodation to an abnormal condition.

With the exception of the 1896 election, the press also shielded Ida. When she fainted at the first McKinley inaugural ball and had to be carried from the room by her husband, it was noticed by the guests but underreported by the press. Her seizures were not the subject of press speculation or investigative reporting, although it became widely known that she was in some way an invalid. The details were simply left a mystery.

It was not always so. Ida Saxton was a vivacious and independent young woman during the first twenty-five years of her life. With auburn hair, striking blue eyes, and petite features, Ida was a beautiful woman born to privilege. Her father was a prominent banker in Canton, Ohio, who gave his daughter every advantage his affluence afforded.

She was born in June 1847 and attended boarding schools in Cleveland and New York. She was not college educated, but completed her studies at a finishing school for girls in Pennsylvania. Her father then sent Ida and a younger sister on an extended grand tour of Europe.

In what was otherwise an idyllic European romp—even if the girls chafed under the restrictions of their chaperone—death stalked Ida. Back home in Ohio, her beau died suddenly. They had exchanged letters, and he made plans to greet the girls in New York when their returning ship docked that fall. After that, in her letters home, Ida began to speak of severe headaches.

When she did return to Canton, her father gave her a job in his bank.

Although women of Ida's social rank rarely worked, contrary to popular misimpression, most women in the eighteenth and nineteenth centuries—poor women, farmers' wives, and women of the lower middle classes, that is—worked. Only the wives and daughters of the well-to-do could afford an idle existence, kept aloof from the sordid details of daily commerce by bevies of servants and men who wanted them kept like sheltered doves. Perhaps this was because these men of power and social standing knew how easy it was to exploit and abuse working-class people, especially women, and so wanted their own female relatives protected from the base impulses of fellow capitalists.

Albeit under the protective eye of her father, Ida progressed from clerk to cashier over a period of several years. She learned the banking business and attained a measure of economic self-sufficiency unusual for upper-class women of the time.

Like so many things about Ida, where and how she met her future husband, William, is something of a mystery. Some biographers say she was twenty-one years old when she met the promising young attorney at a church picnic. This seems improbable, since he was Methodist and she was Presbyterian and they didn't attend the same church. Others place the date of their meeting several years later, when she clerked at her father's bank and he came to transact business. Yet other accounts portray their meeting as a chance encounter on the Canton, Ohio, social circuit, where Ida and her banking family were the equivalent of local royalty.

What is known is that he was four years older than Ida. McKinley, a Civil War veteran, was just establishing his law practice. He had enlisted in the Union army while still a teenager. His commanding officer (and future president) Colonel Rutherford Hayes said of the young McKinley that he was "one of the bravest and finest young officers in the army."

Although his family was not as socially prominent as hers, McKinley must have seemed dashing to the young Ida. When he proposed to her on a moonlight carriage ride, she agreed.

One thousand guests attended their wedding ceremony on January 25, 1871. Ministers from his church and her church administered the vows. They honeymooned in New York.

For a while, it must have seemed that Ida's charmed life would continue. Her father gave the young newlyweds a house as a wedding present. McKinley's star was rising. He had recently been elected county attorney and had potential political prospects as a war veteran with ties to Rutherford Hayes, who was then governor of Ohio. Later that year, Ida bore her first daughter, Katherine, in the house her father had given them. They had a happy two years together before death struck further blows.

The first victim was Ida's mother, who died in early 1873. Ida was pregnant with her second child at the time, a frail girl who was born one month later. She and William christened the child Ida, but her birth was not the happy event of their first daughter's arrival.

Ida may have suffered from postpartum depression during the five months that the child lived. After her death in August 1873, Ida's afflictions worsened. Some writers depict what happened next as a mental breakdown; her doctors at the time diagnosed her condition as an inflammation of the circulatory system called phlebitis. Whatever it may have been, the headaches returned. Ida also began suffering from seizures and believing that she was being punished by God.

She became extremely protective of Katherine, refusing to allow the child out of her sight. Biographer Thomas Beer records that when an uncle invited the toddler to join him for a walk, the little girl said, "No, I mustn't go out of the yard, or God'll punish Mama some more." Despite Ida's protective efforts, the third death came in June 1875, when Katherine died of typhoid fever.

It may be that Ida was epileptic, and it is simply coincidental that worsening symptoms appeared after these tragedies. Or it may be that Ida's problems weren't simply a poorly understood illness, but rather a serious mental health condition. It is also quite possible that both diagnoses are correct. Epilepsy was not well understood at the time, and it would not be impossible for its characteristic seizures to unnerve a victim and trigger mental health problems.

Ida's behavior, however, transcends simple epilepsy. She became fixated on William. She kept a portrait of him placed where it could be seen from her bedroom. She demanded to know his whereabouts constantly. If he was away longer than expected, on his return she would be "sobbing like a child." It was as if she had transferred the anxiety she felt over Katherine's safety after little Ida's death to her husband. It was as if Ida's vigilance could somehow protect him from premature death, too.

His daughters dead, his wife's health shattered, William McKinley turned to politics. The year after Katherine's death, he was elected to the U.S. Congress. They sold the house her father had given them as a wedding gift and moved to Washington. Perhaps he hoped it would give them a fresh start.

His former commanding officer, Rutherford Hayes, was also going to Washington after the election of 1876, but this time as commander in chief. William and Ida were welcome guests at the Hayes White House. Ida rallied sufficiently to become a stand-in first lady for Lucy Hayes during a two-week period when Lucy was traveling. She joined in the city's social life along with other congressional wives, and traveled with her husband on congressional business to states as far away as California.

McKinley's congressional career was a success. He rose through party ranks to become chairman of the powerful House Ways and Means Committee. However, when he pushed through the McKinley Tariff of 1890, raising the cost of thousands of imported items, the voters retaliated by voting him out of office.

William and Ida returned to Ohio, where he campaigned successfully for governor. In Columbus, Ida seemed to thrive. She hosted parties, entertained at dinners, and stood at reception lines greeting guests, although she shielded herself from the physically painful ordeal of shaking hundreds of hands by holding a bouquet of flowers. They attended the opera and theater and outwardly lived a normal life.

Their only setback came in 1893 when a business partner with whom McKinley had cosigned a loan ran into trouble and went bankrupt. Governor McKinley was left saddled with the obligation. It was $130,000, a fortune at the time. Ida's father had died in 1887, leaving her with a sizable inheritance and independent means. She offered to use her money to repay the debt, but McKinley was bailed out by the generosity of affluent political backers. It was not a transaction that would escape political scrutiny today—especially since the organizer of McKinley's financial rescue, Mark Hanna, would later demand to be repaid by an appointment to the U.S. Senate—but in the laissez-faire atmosphere of the Robber Baron era it was ethically acceptable.

When McKinley ran as the Republican presidential nominee in 1896, Mark Hanna became his campaign manager. Hanna raised an astounding three million dollars, a huge sum for a political campaign at the time, investing much of it in political literature and campaign materials that seemed to Teddy Roosevelt as if McKinley were being marketed "as if he were a patent medicine." Democratic contender William Jennings Bryan, by contrast, had a mere fifty thousand dollars in his campaign war chest.

With its large advertising budget, McKinley's was the first media campaign in American politics. Today, it is normal for most of a presidential campaign budget to be spent on advertising, especially on television. Before McKinley, however, most of the campaign budget was spent on electioneering activities, getting money into the hands of supporters at the ward and district level so they could turn out (or buy, if necessary) the voters.

In addition to McKinley's image, Hanna made sure that Ida's face was prominently featured on political buttons. Front-porch politics still dominated the electioneering methods of the era, and as the crowds trooped to Ohio to see their candidate in the flesh, Ida was often withdrawn. This reclusiveness caused a minor campaign crisis when the press printed wild Democratic charges that Ida was in fact half African American, an English spy, and a Catholic to boot!

Outspent by a factor of sixty to one, the Democrats next accused McKinley of being a secret agent for the pope, a drunk, and a wife beater. At the time there was substantial anti-Catholic bias, and the charge that McKinley was a puppet of the Vatican was an effort to turn Protestant voters against him. There was dissension in McKinley's campaign over whether to refute the charges or ignore them. In the end, Hanna decided to produce an official biography of Ida McKinley, counting on the fact that if the McKinley campaign filled the information vacuum with a positive account the negative rumors would wither. It worked. McKinley beat William Jennings Bryan by a margin of almost one hundred electoral college votes.

Ida greeted news of his election victory with a dread born of intuition. "Oh, Major," she warned him, "they will kill you, they will kill you."

She was not the first of the incoming first ladies to have premonitions of her husband's death. Given her obsessions, one could easily discount this and discuss it as simply another manifestation of Ida's neurotic anxiety. That in fact is what William did, explaining away her fears by saying "this little woman is always afraid someone is going to harm her husband."

As White House hostess, Ida assumed the many duties of first lady to the best of her ability. Then, as now, there was no wardrobe allowance for a president or first lady. Using her inheritance money, Ida spent ten thousand dollars on formal gowns and arrived in Washington with a regal wardrobe. She attended formal White House events and state dinners, always sitting next to her husband with the ever-ready handkerchief. At receptions, she often received guests seated in a chair, or standing in line as she had done in Ohio at the governor's mansion with a protective bouquet of flowers in her hands. She would never become known as a lavish hostess or an elegant entertainer, but she wasn't particularly trying to become known as a glamorous first lady.

Visitors saw the strain upon her instead. One congressman's wife described an encounter with Ida when she called upon her in the White House:

She sat propped with pillows in a high armchair with her back to the light. Her color was ghastly, and it was wicked to have her dressed in bright blue velvet with a front of hard white satin spangled in gold. Her poor relaxed hands, holding some pitiful knitting, rested on her lap as if too weak to lift their weight of diamond rings, and her pretty gray hair is cut short as if she had had typhoid fever. She shook hands with us lightly, but didn't speak.

Ida's knitting could be manic. The Civil War had been over for twenty years, yet Ida was knitting literally thousands of slippers, blue for Union army veterans, gray for Confederates, brighter colors for orphaned children and widows. If her knitting was obsessive-compulsive, her focus on the long-ago conflict was somewhat bizarre. She gave away this macabre handiwork as quickly as she could create it, and then knitted more. It is impossible to say what motivated her.

She had free range over the White House. She interrupted cabinet meetings and staff conferences whenever she wanted anything from William. His instant responses to her whims became the subject of staff scorn. Many could not understand why a man handling the responsibilities of the presidency would literally wear himself out trying to simultaneously be nurse and butler to his invalid wife.

She resented any excess attention he paid to other people. When he became enthralled in a conversation while she was next to him in a receiving line, Ida tugged at his sleeve until he turned his attention to her. When he innocently remarked that a woman he had met at an event was attractive, she had one of her seizures. Whether it was feigned to attract his attention, or a real episode, is impossible to know. She mistrusted the motives of many around her husband, and vetoed one candidate for the president's military aide because of a petty dislike of his wife.

She had paranoid outbursts. She accused a cabinet secretary's wife of wanting to replace her. When a young Englishwoman told her she liked Washington but loved England best, Ida heard sinister undertones in the remark.

"Do you mean to say," she shot back, "that you would prefer England to a country ruled over by my husband?"

When visitors from the opposing political party, the Democrats, came to the White House Ida raged about her bizarre conspiracy theory that Grover and Frances Cleveland had misused their power in the White House by concocting a real estate transaction in which they received a disguised bribe by selling their Washington home for an inflated price.

There is no historical evidence to justify Ida's suspicions about the sale of the Cleveland residence.

In 1898, the U.S. battleship *Maine* exploded accidentally, probably because of a faulty boiler, in the harbor at Havana, Cuba, killing 266 Americans. Two months later, McKinley asked Congress for a declaration of war. The Spanish-American conflict received overwhelming approval from the American public, who had been fed a steady diet of largely false news reports of Spanish atrocities in their Puerto Rican, Cuban, and Philippine colonies. The war made McKinley extremely popular.

War also awakened a missionary zeal in Ida. She became fixated with sending Christian missionaries to save the souls of heathen children in the newly liberated Philippines by converting them to Christianity. When the war ended, the United States annexed the Philippines. Some historians believe it was due to Ida's influence.

In 1899, death struck close to Ida again. This time it was her only brother who fell. He was murdered by a jilted lover.

McKinley was easily reelected when he campaigned again for the presidency in 1900. The hero of San Juan Hill, Teddy Roosevelt, was his vice presidential running mate. Roosevelt replaced Vice President Garret A. Hobart, who had died in office in 1899. Ida was present along with Roosevelt and the rest of her husband's cabinet for a December 1900 celebration of the centenary of the White House. She was also present for the inauguration celebration and ball. Shortly thereafter, however, her seizures seemed to worsen. Instead of asking another to stand in for her as first lady, as Lucy Hayes had done with Ida in an earlier decade, Ida instead simply canceled all the White House social events of the season.

By early summer, she was able to travel to San Francisco with William, where an infection in an injured finger worsened. It posed a serious health risk as the infection spread throughout her body, causing the postponement of several previously planned presidential events.

One was the president's visit to the Pan-American Exposition in Buffalo, New York. It was rescheduled for September 6, 1901.

On the appointed day, as President McKinley worked his way through a crowd, a clean-shaven man in a black suit with a white cloth covering his right arm approached. As McKinley shook the man's left hand, he fired twice with a pistol concealed beneath the handkerchief. Leon Czolgosz, a self-professed anarchist, had become the third presidential assassin.

It was an act known as "propaganda of the deed," the nineteenth century's form of terrorism. Russian prince Peter Kropotkin, an anarchist theoretician exiled in London, coined the phrase to describe the revolutionary effect on the masses when a head of state or a king was assassinated. Kropotkin advocated such assassinations, and anarchists such as Czolgosz responded in countries as far apart as Spain and America.

McKinley lingered a week before succumbing to infection caused by the wound. It was Friday the thirteenth and a few minutes past midnight on the fourteenth when doctors pronounced him dead.

Ironically, Ida did not collapse into a nervous breakdown when her premonition came true. Instead, she pulled herself together and tried to maintain William's spirits throughout his weeklong battle to live. She rode the train back to Washington seated beside his coffin. Her composure was maintained during the official funeral, and for the solitary trip back to Ohio.

For the remainder of her life, Ida lived with her younger sister Mary, the companion of her European travels in happier times. No one reported any further seizures, although if she suffered from them, they may have been kept private out of respect for the widow. Some writers speculate that this disappearance of her symptoms means they were purely psychological. The true answer will never be known. She died in 1907.

Edith Carow Roosevelt

First Lady: 1901–1909
26th Presidential Administration
Siena Research Institute Rating: 14

"Quite a politician."
—Sir Cecil Spring-Rice

Shortly before nine in the morning on Monday, September 16, 1901, the Pennsylvania Railroad's special funeral train pulled away from the station in Buffalo, bound for Washington. It was carrying President McKinley's body. Teddy Roosevelt was in the third Pullman car. He had been mountaineering in the Adirondacks when news of McKinley's impending death reached him. Unexpectedly, the forty-two-year-old had become president. As they passed town after town on its way to Washington, bearing the assassinated McKinley's coffin, girls tossed flowers onto the train and tracks.

Edith Roosevelt had not wanted her husband to run for vice president in the 1900 campaign. At the Republican convention, they jointly wrote a statement that the couple planned to issue ruling Teddy out as McKinley's running mate. When she saw the enthusiasm the delegates had for the commander of the Rough Riders and the legend of San Juan Hill, however, her reluctance disappeared.

Edith Carow Roosevelt was a model political spouse. Like Sarah Polk half a century earlier, she played an important part in her husband's political success. In fact, she was involved in politics throughout her lifetime. Like Sarah, she read the newspapers avidly, noting items that Teddy needed to see. She was never a detriment in a political campaign like Rachel Jackson or a reluctant political spouse like Margaret Taylor or Jane Pierce; on the contrary, the young Mrs. Roosevelt and her growing brood of children fascinated the voters and the press. She was unpretentious, especially when it came to fashion. A sniping congressman's wife remarked that Edith never spent more than three or four hundred on her wardrobe for the year—and it looked like it.

She had known Teddy since early childhood. Edith was born in 1861 in Norwich, Connecticut, to a prominent family whose ancestors included the famous Puritan minister Jonathan Edwards. Their families lived close by in New York City, and Teddy's sister, Corinne, was one of Edith's playmates. He may have proposed to her more than once when he was still a student at Harvard, but Edith was not the first Mrs. Teddy Roosevelt. At Harvard, he met and became engaged to Alice Lee. They were married in 1880.

Nevertheless, it was Edith who threw Teddy a party to celebrate his election to the New York Assembly in 1881. Once Edith overcame her initial shock and, some say, disappointment over Teddy's marriage to Alice, she held a reception for the couple. Edith and Teddy continued to travel in the same social circles after his marriage to Alice. When Alice died from complications of childbirth on Valentine's Day three years later—his mother died in a different room of the same house that same day of typhus—Roosevelt left his newborn daughter in the care of his sister and went west. When he returned to New York, he and Edith rekindled their romance. They were secretly engaged one year and nine months after his first wife's death.

It was a long engagement. The following spring, Edith went with her mother and sister to find a place to live in Italy. It was a Gilded Age ritual for British and American elites to expand their cultural horizons by living in Europe for extended periods. While Edith was abroad, Roosevelt ran for mayor of New York City, and after his defeat joined her overseas. They were married in December 1886 at St. George's Church in London. The newlyweds spent the winter of 1886 in Italy and in France before returning to England.

Teddy's political career took a leap in 1889 when President Harrison appointed him civil service commissioner. Edith joined him later that year after giving birth to their second child, a boy named Kermit, who, along with stepchild Alice and firstborn Theodore, made a family of three. Leaving the children again in the care of Teddy's sister—a pattern that would continue before and after the White House—Edith joined her husband in Washington.

It was her first introduction to the White House, and she fit easily into the city's political and social circles. She also flouted convention by participating openly in the city's social life when she was pregnant with their third child, Archibald, at a time when women traditionally went into "confinement."

The Roosevelts returned briefly to New York in 1895 when he was appointed police commissioner, but an appointment as assistant secretary of the navy caused his return to the capital only two years later. Then war broke out with Spain, and Roosevelt resigned his office in order to form a troop of volunteers who became known as the Rough Riders, which made Teddy famous.

Edith was recovering from an abdominal tumor that had followed the birth of their fifth child, Quentin, when she made a trip to Florida to see his regiment off. Upon his hero's return to New York after the war, Teddy planned a run for governor. He won, and the family moved to Albany.

Edith adopted Ida McKinley's trick of holding flowers in her hands so she wouldn't have to cope with the bone-crushing, finger-bruising ordeal of shaking the hands of thousands of well-wishers at the gubernatorial inauguration. She enjoyed being first lady of the Empire State, a fact that may explain her reluctance to see Teddy run for national office as a vice presidential candidate in 1900.

When she and the five Roosevelt children moved into the executive mansion—it wasn't customarily called the White House until President Roosevelt himself began calling it that—Edith quickly discovered it wasn't as suited to family life as the spacious New York governor's mansion had been. The rooms on the ground floor of the White House were used for receptions and state dinners, and the living quarters on the second floor shared space with the offices for the president and his staff. It wasn't ideal for a young family. She had four active boys—Theodore, Quentin, Kermit, and Archibald—and two girls, Alice and Ethel. The children liked pets, so the White House also had to host a small menagerie that at one time or another included a kangaroo mouse, a pony, a bear, and assorted cats and dogs.

Edith actively managed the family, the White House social functions, and the expanding political role of first lady. She set important precedents in the political management of the presidency, particularly regarding her handling of the press and its boundless appetite for news about the first family. It was an extraordinary performance.

Her daily routine was daunting. No matter what the weather, she and Teddy liked to walk every morning for their daily "constitutional." Each morning, the family then breakfasted together. Edith next read her correspondence and the papers, taking notes on the articles of political importance. She continued by going over her schedule with Isabelle Hagner, a civil servant Edith had hired to help deal with reporters and to serve as social secretary for an annual salary of fourteen hundred dollars. Belle Hagner thereby became the first White House staff person exclusively assigned to a first lady. It was an important precedent that paved the way for the gradual expansion of the first lady's area of purview. President Roosevelt liked to use lunch as another occasion for work, and Edith joined him and his guests—many of them last-minute invitees—for the meals and conversation. In the afternoon she received callers until about four, when she and Teddy would ride horses. She devoted the remaining time before dinner to her children. Interspersed throughout the days, nights, and weeks were formal political events, receptions, diplomatic visits, and state dinners. Once a week, Edith also hosted a discussion group of the wives of cabinet members; the discourse turned more on current affairs and intellectual matters than fashions and gossip.

Edith's schedule for one month as first lady reveals the official demands of the job. In December 1902, she hosted a cabinet dinner. Twelve days later was the traditional New Year's reception. The following week was the Diplomatic Reception, followed by the Diplomatic Corps Dinner, and then the Judiciary Dinner and the Supreme Court Dinner. Congress's turn came next with the Congressional Reception, and then it was the military's turn with the Army and Navy Reception.

Edith also liked cultural events. She hosted musical performances that featured distinguished artists such as the Polish diplomat-pianist Jan Ignace Paderewski and the cellist Pablo Casals. She held lunches for artists such as the sculptor Augustus Saint-Gaudens and writers such as Henry James. She in effect turned the White House into a literary and cultural salon. Isabelle Hagner credited Edith's support for getting Congress to pass the legislation that created the National Gallery of Art.

Edith appreciated the building's historic heritage. She built on former first lady Caroline Harrison's collection of vintage White House china patterns and put the entire assemblage on permanent display in a public area of the White House. When the White House was renovated during Roosevelt's second year in office, at a cost of half a million dollars, Edith made room for a gallery to hang the portrait paintings of all the previous first ladies. It was this renovation that gave the White House the shape it has today. The East Wing is the first family's residence, and the West Wing houses the Oval Office and staff offices. The original building maintained its eighteenth-century style and is dedicated principally to formal events.

Like Frances Cleveland, Edith was in a constant tug-of-war with an increasingly intrusive press over privacy. The teenage Alice—a rebellious and free-spirited adolescent—particularly fascinated the press and the public. Paparazzi—"camera fiends," they were then called—stalked her every move. Enterprising merchants sold postcards featuring her photo. When she was photographed at a racetrack receiving money from a bookie, the Roosevelts finally intervened with newspaper publishers to prevent the photos from being printed.

Much like the Clintons would do almost a century later to shield their teenage daughter Chelsea, the Roosevelts, especially Edith, urged the media to respect her children's privacy. The Roosevelts also set a precedent by including first family members on exotic travels; Alice was the first daughter of a president to be made part of an official delegation, which in her case took her to the Far East. Arguably, such a tradition was carried to excess by Hillary and Chelsea Clinton.

Trying to manage the press's insatiable appetite for news about her family, Edith decided to feed the media fresh photographs of the children at regular intervals. The photos were taken by friendly photographers on contract to the White House. Not only did this expedient somewhat reduce the pressure from the press, but it also had the beneficial by-product of allowing the White House to control the images that appeared in the media. It was a huge stride in public relations management.

Roosevelt was easily elected in his own right in 1904. He was an activist president who, in his first term, got things done: He pledged to continue the assassinated McKinley's policies, but then declared war on the Robber Barons in his first message to Congress. Before Roosevelt, no president had taken on the monopolies. He backed the creation of a Department of Commerce and Labor with the power to police corporations. He named the first Jewish American to the cabinet when he placed Oscar Straus in charge of this new department. He ordered his attorney general to pursue an antitrust case against railroad baron John Pierpoint Morgan.

Roosevelt pushed through the creation of a Central American canal by backing a revolution. The narrow isthmus that engineers recognized as ideal for building the canal was part of Colombia. Roosevelt encouraged a group of Colombians to rebel, seize the isthmus, and declare themselves independent. He then recognized Panama as sovereign, and sent in the American fleet to defend it from Colombia. Panama in turn deeded the land and rights to build and operate the canal to the United States into perpetuity. (In 1978, President Carter negotiated a treaty to give the Canal Zone back to Panama in the year 2000. It is now Panamanian territory.)

In his second term, Roosevelt became the first American to win a Nobel Prize. Edith played an important, and secret role in his success. Mediating an end to the war between Russia and Japan in 1905, Teddy, with Edith's help, managed a diplomatic back channel—the first recorded incidence of a first lady playing a prominent role in secret diplomacy. Normally, governments communicate with one another through strict protocols and hierarchies. Presidents deal with the ambassadors sent by foreign countries; secretaries of states deal with foreign ministers; secretaries of defense deal with ministers of defense. These are normal channels. There are, however, times when a diplomatic initiative is so sensitive or risky that statesmen avoid normal channels and use unusual means to resolve problems. Indeed, the use of back channels in secret diplomacy is a basic element of statecraft. President Nixon had Henry Kissinger use back channels and secrecy to negotiate the reestablishment of diplomatic relations between the United States and China in 1972.

Teddy Roosevelt preferred the use of back channels to normal channels. To safeguard secrecy, he preferred to carry out negotiations during walks in out-of-the-way places like Washington's Rock Creek Park, and he didn't like writing down communications because they could be leaked or stolen by spies.

Japan wanted Teddy's help in mediating an end to the war with Russia. Britain was allied with Japan, and France was allied with Russia. Roosevelt recognized that both European countries would be key to a settlement of the war.

Teddy's former best man from his wedding to Edith, Sir Cecil Spring-Rice, was a British diplomat. Spring-Rice, known as "Springy" to the Roosevelts, was posted to the British embassy in St. Petersburg, then the capital of Russia. He was in an ideal position to provide insight into Russian and British intentions. Moreover, he was willing to help his old friend Teddy play a constructive role in ending the conflict.

Because it was risky for President Roosevelt to correspond directly with Springy—Teddy was going around the normal channels that involved the British ambassador to Washington and the Foreign Office in London —Edith played a crucial role as a "cut-out" who would act as the go-between for Teddy and Spring-Rice, while maintaining a position of deniability in case it became necessary to conceal the true purpose of her activities. Cecil Spring-Rice sent his intelligence reports to Edith under the guise of ordinary correspondence, and she passed them on to Teddy, who was able to help bring Russia and Japan to the negotiating table as a result. After Teddy brokered a peace treaty, Spring-Rice praised Edith for being "quite a politician." Her role remained secret. No wonder Edith ordered her staff to routinely destroy her correspondence once she had handled it. She may have had a hand in many more sensitive affairs of government; we will never know, because she not only sent her own correspondence to the shredders, but also destroyed most of the letters exchanged between her and Teddy.

Roosevelt mediated other simmering conflicts. He arranged an international conference in Spain in 1906 to forestall a war between France and Germany over the control of Morocco. When he was awarded the Nobel Peace Prize that same year, he and Edith discussed whether or not to keep the prize money of $36,735 that went with it. They rejected keeping the money as improper, although Teddy said he would have liked it as a legacy for their children to inherit. However, he believed that because he had won the prize for his efforts in public service, the money should be donated to charity instead. It was a principled stand that fore-shadowed the new sense of ethics in government, an end to the era of in-side deals and payoffs.

Roosevelt was America's first effective environmentalist, too. John Muir's writings about the Sierras had only begun to capture a large audi-ence, and Roosevelt—always a man of action—was already preserving wilderness. When he heard that there was no federal law to prevent him from establishing a bird sanctuary on Pelican Island, Florida, he created one. He added more than one hundred million acres to national forest land; made Crater Lake, Oregon, a national park; and created fifty-one new bird sanctuaries by executive order. Hunters, backpackers, and hik-ers today recognize the forests Roosevelt protected, among them Medi-cine Bow, Colorado; the Toiyabe in Nevada; the Cascade, Olympic, and Rainier forests in Washington; and Big Hole, Montana.

The two terms of the Roosevelt presidency were an extraordinary pe-riod in America's emergence as a mature industrial economy, a world power, and a unique nation that appreciated both its natural heritage and its growing cultural sophistication. The Roosevelts embodied both the spirit of the frontier, which had been so prominent a part of the country's formation and national character, and its future, as an equal partner with the old dynasties of Europe and Asia.

Edith was essential to the Roosevelt presidency. Observers noted that she often won converts to Teddy's causes, building on the political coali-tions he needed to make his activist brand of government succeed. Official visitors would stop and talk with her when he was running behind in his appointments to hear her views on the administration's policies.

Her political activism continued after his death in 1919. The elections the following year marked the first time women could vote, but Edith did much more than cast a ballot: She campaigned publicly for the Repub-lican ticket in the fall of 1920. Outliving Teddy by almost thirty years—she died in December 1948—she was outspoken until the end. For example, when her nephew-in-law Franklin Delano Roosevelt ran for the presidency in 1932 as a Democrat, Edith campaigned publicly against him.

HELEN HERRON TAFT

FIRST LADY: 1909–1913
27TH PRESIDENTIAL ADMINISTRATION
SIENA RESEARCH INSTITUTE RATING: 25

"I had always had the satisfaction of knowing almost as much as he about the politics and intricacies of any situation."

Former first lady Ida McKinley had fantasized about converting Philippine tribespeople to Christianity. Instead of dispatching missionaries, President McKinley sent William and Helen Taft. To a girl from Ohio, the country must have seemed exotic in 1900. Her mission was to help remake the Philippines in America's image, creating democratic institutions where none had ever before existed. She and her husband were to put into effect a wholesale cultural transformation and institutionalize the rule of law. Rudyard Kipling had called it the "white man's burden" to go out and civilize the natives. He might have added "white woman's burden" to that calling.

In her memoirs, Helen would write that living in the Philippines was "a big and novel experience, . . . I have never shrunk before any obstacles when I had an opportunity to see a new country and I have never regretted any adventure."

She was born in June 1861. Her father was a politically connected attorney who had been a schoolmate of future president Benjamin Harrison, as well as the law partner of another future president, Rutherford B. Hayes. She lived in a world of privilege.

Helen was exposed to the White House very early. She was still a teenager when the family made an extended visit to Washington during the Hayes presidency. Some biographers report that she decided during that trip to follow the example of first lady Lucy Hayes and marry a man "destined to be president of the United States."

Others present the young Helen as fiercely independent and determined never to marry. Her father gave her a good education that included attendance at Miami University in Oxford, Ohio, where she studied German and chemistry. After completing her formal studies, she worked at her father's law firm before becoming a teacher for two years. During this period, she speculated about writing a book so that she would never need to be financially dependent on a husband, and mused about living life as a single woman.

Instead of writing, Helen met her future husband William Taft. He was four years older than she, a law student who also came from a well-connected family. William's father, Alphonso Taft, was a local judge who had served in the Grant administration as attorney general and secretary of war.

Alphonso saw to it that his son was educated at an Ivy League college. William graduated second in his class at Yale and then attended law school at the University of Cincinnati.

Politically speaking, Helen and William's engagement made them a power couple from the start. Their combined connections would assure a prominent career for William and a "big and novel" adventure for Helen. They married on June 19, 1886, after a one-year engagement and set off for an opulent, three-month European honeymoon. When they returned to Ohio, William's family connections paid off with an appointment as a state superior court judge. It was the beginning of Taft's lifelong series of political appointments—none of which he campaigned for or had to struggle to achieve—which would culminate in the White House and finally the Supreme Court. Ironically, Taft attained high positions through his connections, but failed to achieve great distinction in any of them.

Taft's ambition was to be a judge. Left alone, he might have happily remained one his whole career. Helen's eyes were set on other goals. When her father's former classmate, Benjamin Harrison, became president, Helen's family connections paid off again for William. Taft was offered the appointment of solicitor general by Harrison. She reportedly had to persuade him to take the job; he wasn't sure a detour from the bench fit his career plans.

The young family moved to Washington. Helen, still just twenty-nine years old, was the wife of a senior administration official. The Tafts were welcome visitors at the White House, further whetting Helen's ambitions to become first lady. At the end of the Harrison administration, William Taft was taken care of with appointment to the federal circuit court in Ohio.

Being appointed a federal judge pleased William, but Helen was disappointed in having to leave Washington. She immersed herself in civic good works for the three years following her return to Ohio. She joined a kindergarten movement to promote early childhood education, and became active with the Cincinnati Orchestra Association. While she found civic involvement rewarding, it was no substitute for grand adventure.

President McKinley's offer to have Taft help create a new government in the Philippines gave William misgivings. Helen was eager for him to take it even though it meant uprooting their three young children for life in the tropics. Taft, who had opposed annexation of the Philippines, was persuaded to accept the appointment.

William went ahead to Manila, while Helen and the children took a more leisurely route. She had them stop in Hawaii, then Japan, and along the way she was welcomed on the diplomatic social circuit, even being received by the empress. It literally took months before she and the children arrived in the Philippines.

As a U.S. commissioner—a representative of the victorious nation—

Taft was treated like a bigwig in the Philippines. The spoils of war suited Helen. She liked the attention and the power and was determined to enjoy them guiltlessly.

"We are really so grand now it will be hard to descend to common things," she wrote to a relative. "We have five carriages and two smaller vehicles, and fourteen ponies, a steam launch and who knows how many servants."

When Taft's travels in the roadless islands required going long distances by horseback, Helen joined him. Later, she would boast that she had gone places that "no white woman" had been before. In 1901, Taft was appointed governor of the Philippines by McKinley, and the Taft family moved into Malacanang Palace. It would later become the presidential residence of the Philippines, notorious as the place where Imelda Marcos's hundreds of pairs of shoes were found after she and President Ferdinand Marcos were forced into exile in the 1980s amid charges of massive political corruption and conspiracy to murder their political rivals.

Perhaps such notions were already entrenched. Taft's mission to rid the Philippines of corruption was a noble cause, but political cultures are not easily transformed. The Philippines was corrupt before he arrived and remained corrupt after his departure. Then, after McKinley's assassination, President Roosevelt offered Taft an appointment to the Supreme Court. Taft wanted the job, but felt his work in the Philippines was unfinished and declined. Three months later Roosevelt offered Taft the post of secretary of war—the same cabinet position William's father had held under President Grant. He accepted.

As governor of the Philippines, Taft had enjoyed an immense amount of power and prestige. As expatriates the world over have found, to be on a remote outpost of empire is to attain an undeserved but exhilarating prominence. Back in Washington, Taft was just another member of the cabinet, one of hundreds of self-important political figures who populated the ego-ridden city. Helen sensed a comedown.

She wrote that it was not "at all like entering upon the duties and privileges of the wife of the Governor of the Philippine Islands. I thought what a curious and peculiarly American sort of promotion it was which carried with it such diminished advantages."

Nevertheless, she plunged into the social duties of cabinet wife. The Tafts entertained almost every night of the week. Helen made the rounds of social calls, now no longer as tedious a chore as in the days when Washington's unpaved streets had to be negotiated by horse and carriage, but still a burden. Whenever Taft's duties sent him abroad—and Roosevelt used him often as a negotiator and intermediary—Helen traveled with him, always delighted to discover a new country. One of Taft's special missions was to oversee plans for the building of the Panama Canal.

Helen's entertaining and William's gregarious personality attracted political allies. But there was little love lost between first lady Edith Roosevelt and Helen Taft.

Edith wanted Teddy to run for reelection in 1908, but Roosevelt had pledged not to seek a third term. He was so wildly popular, however, that any candidate he gave his blessing to would have a powerful advantage in winning the Republican nomination. Many wanted to be T. R.'s heir apparent, and Helen was determined that William be foremost among them.

Helen Taft met several times with President Roosevelt to urge him to support her husband. Taft himself was reticent; he didn't think he had the qualities to be a good chief executive. Roosevelt's own favorite was another appointee, Secretary of State Elihu Root. He had served as a political adviser to Roosevelt, and shared his taste for bold action. Roosevelt was confident that if Root became president, he would continue to carry out Teddy's reform policies. Roosevelt did not have the same confidence that Taft, a traditional Republican, would do so. Root's personality, however, had won few friends in Washington. Before he agreed to support Taft, Roosevelt sounded out his inner circle. When he found that not enough of them believed Root could win the nomination, Roosevelt reluctantly decided to back Taft. He did so warning Helen that Taft would need to fight for the presidency.

It was the ultimate political appointment. By getting the nod from President Roosevelt, Taft won the Republican nomination by acclamation. He easily defeated Democratic nominee William Jennings Bryan in an electoral college landslide.

When outgoing president Teddy Roosevelt decided not to ride in the inaugural parade with President Taft, Helen seized the opportunity to sit alongside her husband.

"No president's wife had ever done it before," she exulted.

She made immediate changes in the White House. She was the first first lady to bring in twin beds for herself and her husband. Many biographers have commented that Helen had an aversion to sex, but the twin beds might have been a simple expedient to get a good's night sleep. William Taft was morbidly obese as president, and he had always been overweight. He had to have a special bathtub built to accommodate his girth; postcard vendors took a photograph of four workmen sitting in the specially designed tub and made good money selling them to tourists. No doubt Taft also snored. Twin beds were probably a necessity.

She replaced the uniformed White House police with black servants dressed in blue livery. It was a peculiar choice, but perhaps it reminded her of her days in Malacanang Palace.

She also lobbied Congress for money to buy a presidential automobile. She wanted luxury cars, but the twelve-thousand-dollar appropriation was more suited to Fords. So she contacted executives of Pierce-Arrow and arranged for a presidential limousine in exchange for the company's ability to use the White House's commercial endorsement. Helen may have been inspired by the British example, where the royal household's use of a product entitles a merchant to display the words *by appointment to His Royal Majesty.*

Helen had been providing William with political advice for a lifetime and wasn't about to curtail the practice now. One White House staffer recalled that she "attended almost every important conference that was held in the White House proper. She would even walk in on private conferences, unheralded and unannounced."

At White House receptions, if the first lady saw President Taft talking to a prominent politician, she would hasten to his side and join in the conversation. "I do not believe in a woman meddling in politics or asserting herself along those lines," Helen wrote in her memoirs, "but I think any woman can discuss with her husband topics of national interest, and, in many instances, she might give her opinion of questions with which, through study and contact, she has become familiar. . . ."

One of her lasting contributions to Washington is familiar to anyone who has been fortunate enough to visit the city in the spring when the cherry blossoms are in bloom. Helen had admired cherry trees when she visited Japan, and wanted them used to decorate West Potomac Park. When the Japanese learned of her interest, they sent two thousand trees, but they arrived diseased and had to be destroyed. The next shipment consisted of three thousand trees, and enough took after transplantation to create the spring display enjoyed today.

Helen had been first lady for only a few months when she suffered a stroke that left her temporarily speechless and partially paralyzed. At social events her sisters and daughter stood in for her, although she recovered sufficiently by 1911 to resume the role of first lady in full.

It was an auspicious recovery: 1911 marked the twenty-fifth anniversary of the Tafts' marriage. Helen used the occasion for a White House extravaganza. Six thousand guests were invited. The leading industrialists of the day attended, offering lavish silver anniversary gifts, some costing as much as twelve thousand dollars. Guests showered the couple with sterling pieces as presents, so many that Helen later had the initials removed from many of the less desirable pieces and "regifted" them to others.

Teddy and Edith Roosevelt did not attend the Tafts' anniversary party. Friction had grown between the two men as Teddy began to feel that Taft was too cozy with rich industrialists. He called Taft a "fathead" and "puzzle-wit."

There were also personal slights. Helen had reportedly used her influence to deny Alice Roosevelt's husband, Congressman Nick Longworth, an appointment as minister to China.

"I could not believe you to be serious when you mentioned that man's name," she told William. "I won't even talk about it."

As the Republican convention of 1912 neared, the friction erupted into political combat. Roosevelt had sixty delegates pledged to him, and Taft had sixty-three, and for the next two weeks the convention was brokered. Finally, on August 1, Taft won the nomination. Four days later, Roosevelt formed the Bull Moose, or Progressive, Party and announced his independent candidacy for the presidency. The three-way split divided the Republican votes between Taft and Roosevelt, and Democratic candidate Woodrow Wilson won the election. A similar political dynamic eighty years later would result in George Herbert Walker Bush losing to William Jefferson Clinton in a three-way race with Ross Perot.

Helen Taft was said to be so distraught over the loss that she couldn't bring herself to say good-bye to the White House servants. Yet there were still good things ahead for Helen and William. Her ambition to be first lady had been fulfilled; his was to be a Supreme Court justice. In 1921, President Warren Harding appointed William to the position.

The Tafts used their influence and connections to create a political dynasty. Son Robert Taft became a prominent senator. Daughter Helen earned a doctorate in history from her father's alma mater, Yale, and went on to become president of Bryn Mawr college. Helen died in 1943, having outlived her husband by thirteen years.

Among the accomplishments of the Taft administration was the establishment of a Children's Bureau in the Labor Department to oversee child labor law enforcement, the near completion of the Panama Canal, and the admission of Arizona and New Mexico to statehood. Politically, however, Taft squandered the high level of public support that the Republican Party enjoyed during the two terms of Roosevelt's presidency.

Helen Taft was a full partner to her husband. Without her influence, he might never have broadened his career perspective beyond the law. She intervened to urge him to take more demanding assignments that opened new doors to him, including the presidency. She did not try to be a fashion trendsetter, but aimed her energies at their political partnership. She never was a popular first lady, it should be mentioned, but she had a hard act to follow after the Roosevelts' tenure in the White House. Her stroke also forced her into semiseclusion and set back her ability to emerge as an eminent White House hostess and trendsetter. Nonetheless, she ranks along with Abigail Adams as one of the more politically involved presidential spouses. In another era, she might have followed her tenure as first lady with a run for the Senate.

Ellen Louise Axson Wilson

First Lady: 1913–1914
28th Presidential Administration
Siena Research Institute Rating: 21

The artist in residence with the Association of Women Painters &
Sculptors.

Had Ellen Wilson lived longer, she might have left her artistic mark on the White House and the nation's cultural life; she wanted to become a professional artist before she married. But she died after less than two years in the White House, her tenure cut short at the age of fifty-four by kidney disease. The date was August 6, 1914, the day guns began to roar in Europe starting World War I. It would consume much of Woodrow Wilson's two-term presidency.

Ellen Louise Axson was born in Rome, Georgia, shortly before the outbreak of the Civil War. Her father was a charismatic Presbyterian minister who also suffered from mental illness and probably committed suicide. Ellen was an infant when her future husband, Woodrow Wilson, met her for the first time. He was only six years old.

Ellen was homeschooled until the age of eleven. She graduated from Rome Female College in 1876, at the age of sixteen. She hoped to study at Nashville University, but money was a problem for the Reverend Axson. Instead, Ellen enrolled again at Rome Female College as a graduate student, continuing her education by studying French, German, and art, and teaching herself trigonometry.

Her artistic talent showed even as a teenager, and she was able to earn money painting portraits. She was, at five feet, three inches and 115 pounds, trim and petite. When she wasn't painting or drawing, she enjoyed shooting guns.

Ellen's mother died in 1881 during childbirth. Her father died three years later, following a nervous breakdown that had caused him to be committed. During the interval between the two deaths, Woodrow Wilson came to hear the Reverend Axson preach. The young couple fell in love and were soon engaged.

He was a penniless academic studying for his doctorate, and unable to support a wife. They mutually decided to postpone marriage. When Ellen's father died in May 1884, she came into a small inheritance and decided to use it studying art.

Woodrow helped her find a boardinghouse in New York and accompanied her on the trip north. Ellen thrived in the metropolis. She joined the Art Students League, toured museums, attended lectures, and took in the city's cultural offerings voraciously.

The following year, Woodrow got a job offer from Bryn Mawr college. During their year apart, the two had corresponded regularly. Ellen knew that with hard work she could become a professional painter, but had chosen to spend her life with Woodrow even if it meant sacrificing her own prospects. They were married on June 24, 1885, thirteen months after her father's death.

In 1890, the Wilsons moved to New Jersey where Woodrow was offered a professorship at Princeton. When Wilson was a young scholar, Ellen helped translate academic articles from German into English, reviewed his manuscripts before he published them, and assisted in the preparation of his class lectures. They were full intellectual partners long before he entered the White House. By this time the couple had three daughters, Margaret, Jessie, and Eleanor Randolph, and Ellen found that even with domestic help she rarely had the time she needed to concentrate on her painting.

Woodrow's academic career prospered at Princeton. In 1902, he was elected president of the university. The family moved into the president's mansion, where she designed a special stained-glass window. His increased earnings allowed the family to afford travel, and Ellen eagerly visited Europe and its great museums. After he burst a blood vessel due to high blood pressure—an ominous warning of things to come—the family spent a summer in the Lake District of England so that he could rest. The region was then, and is still, a favorite haunt of British landscape painters and writers. Although Ellen studied with some of the leading American impressionists, in her own work she experimented, sometimes painting in a naturalistic style and sometimes in a more modern impressionistic manner.

Their marriage may have been marred by Woodrow's indiscretion with Mary Allen Hulbert Peck. Ellen spent the summer of 1908 in an artists' colony in Old Lyme, Connecticut. Woodrow's letters to Ellen and Mary during this period hint at infidelity. At the least, his correspondence with Mary Peck, then in the middle of a divorce, was indiscreet. The episode would come back to haunt him.

Woodrow's academic career, however, had always focused on politics. His first book was on government and the consequences of the tilt in the balance of power toward Congress and away from the presidency. In 1910, when the Democratic Party offered him the chance to run for governor of New Jersey, he could put the academic theory of his writing to the test.

The Republican Party had dominated New Jersey's political landscape for the past fourteen years. Wilson was an unlikely challenger. He had no political experience or track record. He was almost a sacrificial lamb. Nonetheless, he campaigned vigorously. His reward was a victory in the gubernatorial race by a margin of more than fifty thousand votes and a Democratic takeover of the legislature.

The surprising triumph made Wilson a rising star in Democratic Party circles. He and Ellen made official visits together to communities around the state. He was an activist governor who had a clear legislative agenda he wanted to accomplish. He wanted reforms in workmen's compensation, child labor laws, state election laws, and better regulation of public utilities. Wilson's popularity increased with each legislative success. In 1912, the Democratic convention, after six days of deliberations and forty-six ballots of the delegates, nominated Wilson to run for president. The three-way race between Republican William Taft, Bull Moose candidate Teddy Roosevelt, and Wilson gave the Democrats an advantage. When the election was over, Wilson, the newcomer to politics, had 435 electoral college votes; former president Roosevelt had won 88; and the veteran insider Taft won a mere 8 electoral college votes. It was a blowout landslide for Woodrow and Ellen Wilson. The bitter infighting between Taft and Roosevelt had made voters turn away from both candidates.

Ellen had been a valuable ally during the presidential campaign, it should be emphasized. When newspapers erroneously reported that she had spent $2,000 on clothes during a campaign tour of Georgia, she sent out a correction: The real amount was $140. (In fact, for the inauguration the Wilsons had to arrange a bank loan of five thousand dollars so that Woodrow, his wife, and three daughters could arrive with appropriate wardrobes for the Washington social season.)

To Woodrow, an inaugural ball seemed unnecessary. Instead, the Wilson family dined together in the White House to celebrate privately. The choice did not upset Washington society, which still was able to celebrate through the inaugural parade and swearing-in ceremonies.

Over the next three months, the new first lady more than made up for the lack of an inaugural ball. She held more than ten receptions a month, averaging more than five hundred guests for each. She had help from her three daughters and Isabelle Hagner, who had first been hired by Edith Roosevelt.

She also became politically involved in the new administration. The role of adviser was not entirely new to Ellen. Woodrow had sought her help in his academic career, so it is unsurprising that he continued to do so in government.

Ellen is credited with urging Woodrow to name three-time Democratic presidential candidate William Jennings Bryan to the position of secretary of state. She also advised on other cabinet appointments and helped work on Woodrow's speeches. One cabinet officer says she "knew the political situations and outlined them with grasp and judgment."

But her most important political projects were hers and hers alone. At the turn of the century, Washington was full of tenements, meant to be temporary housing for the workers who helped build the new federal city. They were overcrowded, fire-prone, and vermin-ridden. After the first lady and the chairwoman of the Women's Department of the National Civic Federation toured the slums together, Ellen determined that she would make it her project to clear the tenements and move their inhabitants into improved housing. She also lobbied to improve working conditions for civil servants, including the provision of adequate numbers of bathrooms for the growing number of women in the federal workforce. Her growing involvement in civic philanthropy, however, was cut short; a terse White House announcement obliquely referred to health problems. An unknown illness had robbed Ellen of energy throughout her first months as first lady, and the White House doctors prescribed rest.

Ellen contentedly spent the summer of 1913 at an artists' colony in New Hampshire, recovering her strength from the mysterious malady. She was invited to join the Association of Women Painters and Sculptors, and spent time with fellow artists such as Maxfield Parrish. There were spirited discussions, and even talk—which Ellen correctly dismissed as politically premature—of government support for the arts.

When she returned to the White House that fall, two of the Wilson daughters had weddings to arrange. The middle daughter, Jessie, was engaged to an attorney named Francis Sayre. They were married in the East Room of the White House on November 25, 1913. There were five hundred guests at the ceremony.

Ellen also attended Woodrow Wilson's first State of the Union address to a joint session of the Congress in April 1913 as well as his second joint session address in 1914. Previous presidents had simply transmitted the message to Congress, but Wilson wanted to emphasize that government was a cooperative undertaking between human beings, not institutions, and so he established the precedent of going to face Congress with his message in person. Every succeeding president would follow his precedent.

In the spring of 1914 came the May-December match of youngest daughter Eleanor to Treasury Secretary William McAdoo, with whom she had unexpectedly fallen in love. McAdoo was twenty-six years her senior.

The White House wedding was among the dominant social affairs of the season. Just before Eleanor's marriage, Ellen fell and injured herself. Nevertheless, she was still able to be of help in preparing for the wedding, assisting Eleanor in deciding details like floral arrangements and menus. The couple married on May 7, in a small event involving only about one hundred guests. There was little grousing among the socialites.

Ellen's health problems were by now well known. Throughout the spring, she gamely carried on, following political affairs and handling the duties of White House hostess.

It was June before Ellen's physicians realized the gravity of her illness. She had an incurable kidney disease. One of her last wishes was to see Congress pass legislation called the Alley Clearing Bill. It was her project to rid Washington of the tenements and replace them with modern housing. It passed on August 6, 1914. Ellen Wilson died at five P.M. that very day. Her tenure as first lady had lasted slightly more than seventeen months. Yet it was the period when President Wilson's legacy was created. This included tariff cuts despite the opposition of the Senate. He accomplished this, in large measure, because Wilson, the lifelong student of government, realized that by appealing to the people, he could force Congress to acquiesce to his will. Although special-interest lobbyists fought Wilson's cuts, the letters that poured into Congress overwhelmed the opposition. Tariffs were cut by an average of 25 percent and set the stage for further progress toward free trade internationally.

The tariff reductions covered items ranging from wheat and wool to steel and iron, and affected the prices of most goods consumers bought. However, the tariff cuts were accompanied by something else that is now familiar to every American—the federal income tax. To offset the loss of revenue from tariffs, Congress passed a law that taxed income at a rate ranging from 1 to 6 percent, depending on the size of one's income.

In June 1913, Wilson pushed for the Federal Reserve Act, a landmark piece of legislation that created the mechanism to help stabilize the economy's normal cycles of boom and bust. This law created the position of chairman of the Federal Reserve, the post now held by Alan Greenspan, with power to regulate the money supply and set interest rates. The Clayton Anti-Trust Act of 1914 helped give the federal government more power to regulate and control monopolies. After the outbreak of World War I in August 1914, Wilson's attention turned inevitably to foreign wars.

Ellen had been involved with Woodrow's principal domestic policy priorities in 1913 and 1914. Many historians believe that the Federal Reserve Act ranks as Wilson's top domestic accomplishment. Credit is due to her for the part she took in the administration while she lived; historians rank Wilson's presidency among the country's top ten.

Her term as first lady was incomplete, which makes it difficult to fully assess her evolving performance in her role. Based on her first seventeen months, however, it can safely be said that she would have been a formidable first lady had her health been better.

EDITH BOLLING GALT
WILSON

FIRST LADY: 1915–1921
28TH PRESIDENTIAL ADMINISTRATION
SIENA RESEARCH INSTITUTE RATING: 10

"Petticoat government"
—GOP Senator Albert Fall

If President Wilson's staff had had their way, he would never have married Edith Bolling Galt. The forty-three-year-old widow had met Woodrow through Helen Bones, a cousin of the president's who worked on the White House staff. They had a chance encounter with the president when Helen and Edith stepped out of the White House elevator. Edith later called it one of those days when you "turn a corner and meet your fate."

At first, Woodrow courted Edith by inviting her to join his cousin Helen and Dr. Cary Grayson, the White House physician and key presidential adviser, for tea. Soon there were dinner invitations. By May 1915, their courtship was in full bloom, and Woodrow announced to Edith that he intended to marry her.

His aides were aghast. Only nine months had lapsed since Ellen's death. They feared that the public would not accept a remarriage so soon. They wanted any remarriage postponed until at least 1916—safely after the midterm congressional elections. Wilson's cabinet and senior Democratic Party officials met secretly to debate what might happen politically if Wilson went ahead and remarried against their better judgment.

Historians say several aides decided to convince Wilson he must delay. They conspired to mislead the president into believing that his correspondence with Mary Hulbert Peck, the divorcée with whom he may have had an extramarital affair when married to Ellen, would be published in the newspapers if he persevered with his plans to marry Galt.

The story they spun was based on the age-old notion of the fury of a woman scorned. It held that Mary Peck had agreed not to publish her letters from then Princeton University president Wilson in exchange for a payment of money. In fact, Wilson had given Mary Peck a seventy-five-hundred-dollar loan. According to the story fabricated by Wilson's aides, the loan was being construed as payment of blackmail. As rumors of Wilson's relationship with Edith Galt spread throughout Washington, however, they alleged that Mary had decided to publish the letters anyway out of pique if he remarried. A chagrined Wilson reluctantly concluded he had no option but to postpone.

That spring, a German U-boat torpedoed the British ship the *Lusitania*. Wilson sought Edith's advice. Their unique political partnership had commenced. He sent her letters detailing classified matters and sensitive foreign policy issues.

He was also depressed by the turn of events that had marred his marriage plans. At least some of his advisers were worried about his frame of mind. He was despondent, and Dr. Grayson worried that Wilson's depression might deepen. Edith had been undeterred by the threatened publication of the Peck-Wilson letters, although she agreed to wait until 1916 to marry. By that fall, however, Woodrow decided to brave any impending scandal. In early October, Wilson himself typed out a wedding announcement. The marriage took place on December 18, 1915. It was primarily a family ceremony with fewer than fifty guests.

Edith Bolling was born in 1872, heiress to a fractured legacy. She was born into a southern aristocratic family that lost its plantation during the Civil War. She claimed to be a direct descendant of Pocahontas. Before becoming involved in a romance with a president, she had little interest in politics. She claimed not to have even known who was running in the 1912 presidential race!

Her life had been shaped by personalities that seem to belong in a novel. Edith had an eccentric grandmother who made her look after her twenty-seven canaries. The old woman schooled her in the Bible and home economics. Edith's other grandmother liked to sing songs and primed the girl with tales of romance. Her father read the classics to the family in the evenings. Her education was spotty, however, consisting of two interrupted years at different finishing schools. She was just fifteen when she had her first serious romance; he was a thirty-eight-year-old boyfriend of her sister.

She was twenty-four when she married her first husband, Norman Galt, one of the heirs to the well-known Washington store Galt & Company. It was once frequented with excess by the likes of Mary Todd Lincoln and Julia Grant; ultimately, Norman became the sole inheritor of the company. When he died in 1908, the store passed to Edith. She successfully oversaw the business for several years before selling out to the employees.

By her midforties, Edith Galt was an independent woman. She had means, was shapely, still attractive, and was enjoying the prime of her life. Dressed elegantly, she was socially active and traveled to Europe extensively.

Before she met Wilson, she had attended some of his speeches, although she failed to find them captivating. As her interest in him grew, however, so did her interest in his policies. In her memoirs, published in 1939 to defend her role as first lady against charges that she had assumed too much authority while Wilson was convalescing, Edith described her political education:

> . . . I followed day by day every phase of the mosaic which he was shaping into a pattern of statecraft . . . except for the formal inter-

views with officials, I always "sat in" when one or two people we knew came to discuss policies. In that way I was never a stranger to any subject and often able in small ways to be of help.

Although President Wilson did not seek a formal declaration of war from Congress until 1917, World War I had an effect on the Wilson White House. Diplomatic receptions became hopelessly complicated affairs, given that the ambassadors from many countries were now at war with one another, making joint invitations difficult if not impossible.

The immediate consequence was a prompt curtailment of White House entertaining. Liberated from the duties of social hostess, Edith was free to concentrate her energies on her new husband and a new world of politics and statecraft.

Their daily routine began shortly after dawn, when they would rise from the Lincoln bedroom. Frequently they began the day with a round of golf, followed by work with memos and correspondence until about nine o'clock. Edith would then walk with Woodrow to the Oval Office and sometimes stay with him for an hour or more.

In the afternoon, she took calls from visitors, ambassadors' wives, cabinet spouses, and the city's political elite. In the late afternoon, she and Woodrow might ride horses for a while or take a spin in Edith's electric car.

They often had lunch and dinner together. She tried to learn to ride a bicycle in the White House basement but gave up after too many falls. She and Woodrow also shot pool together, enjoyed going to the theater, and spent much time together going over official papers.

America entered the war in April 1917. A million men were immediately sent to the European front; a million more were readied. More than one hundred thousand died in the conflict.

Perforce, White House priorities shifted. Public tours and the annual Easter egg roll were canceled. So was the New Year's Day celebration, a presidential staple since Washington's era. Edith began making appearances at Washington's main railroad terminus, Union Station, dressed in a Red Cross uniform to greet the troops mustering for the fight. As first lady, she was invited not only to christen but also to name the growing fleet of navy ships. When she found that the British had already used many of the names she considered most inspiring, she began using Native American names like *Quistconck* for the new battle and transport fleet.

The war demanded austerity and sacrifice. The Wilson administration instituted immediate plans for rationing of food, fuel, and commodities needed for war production, such as copper and iron for weapons and armaments and cotton and leather for uniforms and boots. Wilson's cabinet agreed that a voluntary spirit of cooperation would inspire more than draconian controls.

Edith readily rose to the challenge. She changed the White House menus so there would be days without meat or wheat, and days when the consumption of energy was minimized. The first lady also brought a flock of twenty sheep onto the White House lawn and had a few pounds of their wool auctioned in every state for the benefit of the Red Cross war drives. She raised more than ninety thousand dollars with them. She sewed pajamas and blankets to help inspire other women to do the same, augmenting the war effort with free labor. Film stars like Charlie Chaplin and Mary Pickford joined with the first lady in fund-raising drives for war bonds.

Meanwhile, when she wasn't participating in events to motivate the public and inspire support for the war effort, she learned to translate the top-secret war codes given only to the president and top officials. This way she could help Woodrow decode incoming messages, and aid in coding his replies. The first lady became in essence a cypher clerk, a specialist in coding and decoding secret messages, but this was a cypher clerk who knew the president's policies intimately. The work gave her inside access to the details of American diplomacy and war in a way few other first ladies had experienced, with the possible exception of Martha Washington.

On November 11, 1918, an armistice was signed, formally ending World War I. More than thirty nations signed the armistice, which brought the fighting to an end but left the details of a comprehensive peace agreement to be worked out at the Paris Peace Conference. Now Woodrow Wilson's real challenge would commence.

Ever the scholar, Wilson had grappled with history's underlying lesson about the horrific slaughter of World War I. He wanted to prevent any recurrence, and what he finally envisioned was a League of Nations in which friction could be mediated without resort to war. He set about trying to persuade the major European powers to back his plan. It was in many ways a utopian vision that had one key difficulty: World War I had been a battle of empires, with France and Britain victorious over Germany and the Ottoman and Austro-Hungarian Empires. There were spoils to be divided and reparations to be paid.

Edith went with Woodrow to Europe in December 1918 for the presentation of his fourteen-point peace plan, the centerpiece of which was the proposal to create a League of Nations, at the Paris Peace Conference. The trip made her the first first lady to travel overseas.

Because no women were allowed in the all-male audience when Wilson addressed the delegates, she had to listen to his speech hidden behind a curtain. For five hours, Edith stood and listened to Wilson's speech and the delegates debating his proposals at length. They traveled together through Europe, staying at Buckingham Palace and visiting the king of Italy. They returned to Europe in June 1919 for the signing of the Treaty of Versailles, which established the terms for a comprehensive peace.

The treaty had 434 articles. The most controversial was Article 231, assigning blame for the war to Germany, which was required to pay heavy financial reparations. Germany also lost all of its overseas colonies. They were divided among the Allied powers. German territory was also given to Poland, including cities with large ethnic German populations, like Gdansk, then known as Danzig.

The punitive aspects of the treaty jeopardized Wilson's vision of a framework that would preserve European peace. But key points from Wilson's fourteen-point plan were intact, including the right to national self-determination and the League of Nations.

No president can commit the United States to an international treaty; the U.S. Constitution reserves that power to the Senate. Before a treaty can become binding, two-thirds of the Senate must approve it. This places presidents in the awkward position of negotiating treaties with foreign countries before they know whether the Senate will support the final result. Wilson's toughest challenge would prove to be persuading the U.S. Senate to adopt the Versailles treaty.

Senator Henry Cabot Lodge, a Republican from Massachusetts whose career had begun in journalism, had deep misgivings about any treaty that included the League of Nations. Isolationists were wary of being drawn into future European conflicts, which they perceived as battles over borders, markets, and empires bearing little on American national interests. Lodge and his supporters saw the league as inviting endless foreign entanglements, and they set out to defeat it. Before Wilson was able to return from signing the Treaty of Versailles, Lodge began campaigning against it.

Wilson turned to the public for support, as he had done in pressing for the tariff reduction in 1913 at the beginning of his presidency. Counting on an outpouring of public opinion to overcome resistance in the Senate, Woodrow and Edith set out on an eight-thousand-mile whistle-stop train tour involving more than forty speeches, each one lasting about an hour, outlining his vision and urging support.

After twenty-two days, Wilson had to cancel the tour. He had been stricken with headaches and one particularly tormented, sleepless night when Edith thought he was having a nervous breakdown. When she found him with one side of his face drooping, partially paralyzed, however, she knew it was a serious physical problem. Some medical experts today believe Wilson had encephalitis; at the time it was believed he had suffered a serious stroke.

Thus began a period sometimes referred to as Edith Wilson's "regency." This was a time when she assumed control of the affairs of state and took the full powers of the presidency into her own hands. It lasted from September 25, 1919, until mid-January 1920.

Woodrow Wilson was isolated in the White House from all but the medical staff. At first not even Vice President Thomas Marshall was allowed to see him. The gravity of his condition was kept secret from the public, the press, Wilson's own cabinet, and Congress.

For the first four days, if a White House officer or a cabinet official needed the president to make a decision, Edith would greet the official, hear the case, privately present the facts to Woodrow, and return with his decision. Sometimes, she would come back with no decision at all, as when Interior Secretary Lane wanted Wilson's approval to sign leases for oil drilling on government land. On other occasions, she gave directions that were incomprehensible, and officials would have to go through the process again to seek clarification. Secretary of State Lansing complained that his simple questions received "answers communicated through Mrs. Wilson so confused that no one could interpret them."

Not every matter brought to the president's attention received it. Edith used her own judgment as to whether matters were important enough to merit Wilson's limited energies; there were cabinet vacancies that only Woodrow could decide how to fill, but Edith wouldn't bother him with the matter until it became a serious political problem. In issues of lesser importance, she informed the cabinet that they were to make decisions on their own authority. Unless it was a matter that genuinely (in Edith's view) merited presidential attention, Woodrow should not be troubled. Edith's foremost concern was his health and recovery.

Then Wilson's doctor confided to a cabinet member that the president had suffered a stroke. The following day, the full cabinet met to discuss the matter. As rumors began to circulate that Wilson was disabled and therefore unable to discharge the duties of the presidency, Wilson's opponents in the Senate took note and began attacking Edith for assuming power.

"We have petticoat government," one senator fumed in a congressional hearing. "Mrs. Wilson is president."

When she drafted her memoirs, Edith explained the origins of this extraordinary state of affairs:

> Of course the burning question was how best to serve the country— and yet protect the President. . . . I talked with the Drs. and asked them to be brutally frank with me. . . . Dr. D leaned toward me & said, "Madame it is a grave situation but I think you can save it. Have everything come to you. Weigh the importance of them & see if it is possible by consultations with the respective Heads of each Dept. to solve them without the guidance of your husband. If not they of course must go to him."

Rather matter-of-factly, this most unlikely of women rose to the occasion and helped her husband recover his health while still running the presidency.

"So I began my stewardship," Edith wrote. "I studied every paper & sent for the different Secretaries or Senators. . . . I never made a single decision regarding public affairs myself . . . the only decision that was mine was what was important. . . ."

If Edith had actually been running the government on her own, she might have succeeded in persuading the Senate to accept Wilson's cherished League of Nations. A turning point came on November 17, when Democratic Senate majority leader Hitchcock came to the White House to meet with Edith. Hitchcock told her that unless Woodrow compromised with the isolationists, the White House would fall short of the number of votes required to ratify the treaty.

Edith's instinct was to compromise, and she pleaded with Wilson to agree. He refused, however, and on November 19, the Senate defeated Wilson's treaty. The League of Nations was dead. Wilson had failed to achieve the top presidential priority of his second term in office. It was a stunning setback.

In December, Wilson met with two senators in his sick chambers, with Edith taking notes. Because the meeting demonstrated that he had control of his faculties, the rumors and charges that Edith had usurped the powers of government were finally put to rest. When his State of the Union message was sent out with penciled changes in her handwriting in January, however, the grousing began again, albeit at a lower tempo, that "Queen Edith" was running the White House.

Wilson slowly recovered his health and faculties, but his political prospects were damaged by the stroke and its surrounding controversy. He had hoped for a third term in office, but the Democratic convention delegates nominated Ohio governor James Cox instead.

The second term of the Wilson administration, nevertheless, saw the passage of landmark constitutional amendments. In 1920, for example, eleven months after Wilson's stroke, the Nineteenth Amendment granted women the right to vote. Less auspiciously, the Eighteenth Amendment outlawing alcohol was ratified in 1919. Wilson had vetoed the legislation from his sickbed (although skeptics claimed the signature on the veto message was Edith's, not Woodrow's), but Congress had overridden it. The Roaring Twenties were on their way, complete with speakeasies, Prohibition, and rum-running gangsters.

Woodrow Wilson won the Nobel Peace Prize in 1919 for his efforts to pass the Treaty of Versailles and create the League of Nations. Because he was still convalescing, the medal was not formally awarded to him until 1920. By then he was a lame-duck president, waiting out the time between the election of his successor and the swearing-in of the new president. Congress did not formally ratify a peace with Germany until the following year, when Wilson was no longer in office.

He died in 1924, leaving Edith a widow for the second time. Politics was now in her blood. She campaigned publicly for the election of Franklin Delano Roosevelt. When one of the White House staffers who had tried to block her marriage to Woodrow published an unflattering book charging that she ursurped presidential powers during Woodrow's convalescence, she countered by penning her own side of the story, called simply *My Memoir*, published in 1939. That same year, as Hitler invaded Poland to reclaim the city of Danzig stripped from Germany by the Paris peace treaty, she accused Senator Henry Cabot Lodge of causing World War II by opposing the League of Nations. It is doubtful that the League of Nations, by itself, could have prevented World War II. There were ample diplomatic efforts to maintain peace between England, France, and Germany before Hitler invaded Poland and Czechoslovakia. It was not a lack of dialogue that caused World War II.

Like another first lady before her, Dolley Madison, Edith became a Washington institution. She was an honored guest in the Roosevelt White House, and attended her last presidential inauguration in 1961 as the guest of John Fitzgerald Kennedy. She died later that year of heart failure at the age of eighty-nine.

Florence Kling
DeWolfe Harding

First Lady: 1921–1923
29th Presidential Administration
Siena Research Institute Rating: 35

"The Duchess"
—President Warren Harding

If Florence Harding had written an autobiography about her childhood years, it might have been titled "Daddy Dearest." Amos Kling was a wealthy banker in a small town who was used to getting his way. When Florence, the only daughter of three children, clashed with him, he punished her by whipping. When she grew older and violated the curfews he set for her, he simply locked her out of the house, leaving her to find a friend with whom she could spend the night.

When she became pregnant and was determined to marry at the age of nineteen, Amos Kling opposed the match. So Florence eloped with the baby's father, Henry DeWolfe. Six months later, she gave birth to a baby boy the young couple named Marshall. The marriage lasted only a few years and, subsequently, Amos offered to care for the baby boy—but not Florence. He left her to support herself by giving piano lessons. Already estranged from her father, Florence thereafter rarely visited her son; during the presidential campaign of 1920, she tried to deny he even existed. When Marshall died at the age of thirty-five, leaving behind a widow and two children, Florence never invited her grandchildren to the White House, not even once.

Amos Kling opposed Florence's remarriage to Warren Harding also. Using his influence as a trustee at their local Methodist church, he successfully barred the couple from a wedding ceremony there. When they decided to marry in a private home, he blackballed the wedding guests by threatening to withhold bank loans from them and to use his influence to ostracize them. After the wedding, he wouldn't speak to Florence for seven years, and it was fifteen years before Amos visited the Harding household. Florence first had to lose a kidney and come dangerously close to death before her unyielding father relented and consented to visit her.

These character traits—vindictiveness, emotional coldness, rigidity, and a domineering will—were, finally, Florence Harding's legacy as well. As first lady, she kept a little red book that listed her enemies. She tended to imagine insults and snubs where none were intended at the White House. She displayed a petty vindictiveness not only toward her real and imagined enemies, but also toward those whom she simply envied. She tolerated her husband's many illicit sexual relationships because she didn't want to separate again and compromise her own political ambitions. She also saw nothing wrong with serving liquor in the White House during Prohibition, when even beer or wine were denied to ordinary Americans.

Yet she was in many ways the first of the modern first ladies in the sense that she understood that no matter how much power and influence she might exert privately, the first lady was also expected to fill a public role beyond that of White House hostess. Radio and mass-circulation newspapers combined to create the first mass media, and Florence learned to mask her dark side through cultivating relationships with the press. She learned to use the press to project a favorable image—often jarringly at odds with reality—by adopting socially popular causes such as the welfare of war veterans and the Animal Rescue League, and staging photo opportunities like posing for photographers with the "doughboys," as the war veterans were then known. She called the reporters who jostled to cover her activities "my boys" and held background press briefings. In a background briefing, Florence talked with reporters about political and social events, but under ground rules that barred the reporters from quoting the first lady, thereby enabling her to speak more candidly. No first lady had ever used these techniques to manipulate her press coverage. None, in fact, had even tried. Florence's handling of the press set a lasting White House precedent.

The image that Florence cultivated ensured public popularity, but as in all cases where appearances mask a conflicting underlying reality, it was to be fleeting. Harding was a popular president in his own time, and as first lady Florence was virtually revered. But that was only because the dry rot in their personal and their political lives was temporarily hidden from the public. Behind the public image lay a cesspool of corruption unlike anything the country had experienced since the Grant presidency. The old Lincoln adage applies to Warren and Florence Harding: You can fool some of the people some of the time, and some of the people all of the time, but not all of the people all of the time. Once the Harding administration's scandals became known, its reputation was irreparably damaged.

Today, Warren Harding ranks among the very lowest of presidents in every expert poll taken. Because Florence was his full partner throughout his political career—some say she was actually his puppet master—she must bear her share of history's condemnation.

The story of Warren and Florence Harding's peculiar relationship begins in Marion, Ohio; he was twenty five, she was thirty. She had just given a piano lesson to his sister. Warren came from a newspaper family, and at the age of twenty-five had managed to raise three hundred dollars to buy the failing *Marion Star* newspaper. Initially, Florence pursued Warren. He may have been attracted as much to her social status as Amos Kling's daughter as to Florence's other attributes. They married in 1891, and not long thereafter Warren suffered the first of his nervous breakdowns.

Warren went off to Battle Creek, Michigan, for an extended period of recovery. While he was gone, the newspaper's circulation manager resigned, and Florence stepped in for what she thought would be a temporary job. She ended up staying with the newspaper for fourteen years, and is credited with helping transform the struggling business into a financial success.

Florence's years as a newspaper executive gave her crucial insight into the daily operations of the press. As a result, she had a depth of understanding of public relations unlike any previous political spouse. She knew the appetite of the press for scandal, its need for information to fill a vacuum, its moods and vagaries, its capacity for a media frenzy, the difficulty of ensuring accuracy, and the constant need to cover the hot story of the moment under tight deadlines. It was invaluable political training for the role of first lady.

In 1899, she urged Warren to run for the Ohio legislature. When he announced his candidacy for the state senate, Florence became his campaign manager. She handled the schedule, acted as treasurer, and helped line up political supporters. It was the beginning of a political odyssey in which he handled the public speaking and she handled almost every other aspect of his political career.

He won, and the Hardings went off together to the state capital at Columbus. Florence never hesitated to join in meetings in his office, and enjoyed the endless socializing that is essential to a political career. He flourished in politics, rising to the office of lieutenant governor, and then the U.S. Senate.

In 1905, Florence fell ill with kidney disease. She was hospitalized for five months. Conveniently for Warren, his next-door neighbor and close friend Jim Phillips was being treated for a mental disorder. That left his friend's wife, Carrie, prey to Warren's legendary womanizing. They began an affair that lasted many years. Florence, in fact, didn't discover the infidelity until 1911, when she came across suspicious correspondence between them. She supposedly considered divorce, but rejected it on the rationale that it was better to put up with a cheating spouse than lose the prestige, status, and money to be gained from putting up with him. She was in her early fifties, and she didn't want to start over. This, too, was part of a lifelong pattern of trying to create a pretense to mask a sordid reality, especially when it came to political corruption.

In 1914, Harding was elected to the U.S. Senate. He soon began an affair with a teenager, Nan Britton, who worked for him. Years later, Britton wrote a book in which she claimed that Warren fathered her child. In addition to the affair with the blond-haired girl, Warren kept up his dalliance with Carrie Phillips, writing her erotic love letters when he wasn't in Nan's embrace, all the while living with Florence and keeping up appearances.

President Woodrow Wilson had made an error in political judgment in 1918, going against first lady Edith's advice to appoint a token Republican to the U.S. delegation to the Paris Peace Conference. Wilson was too partisan to take Edith's sage advice to co-opt the Republicans by making the delegation bipartisan. He compounded the error during the 1918 midterm congressional elections by issuing a statement warning that a Republican takeover of Congress would divide the nation's leadership. Edith had urged against the statement. The voters rebuked Wilson by giving control of Congress to the Republicans.

Emboldened by this political weakness, Ohio Republican kingmaker Harry Daugherty began urging Senator Harding to run for the presidency. Daugherty was a political operative (today we would call him a "consultant" or "strategist") who dominated state politics in Ohio, then a Republican stronghold. Over the years, Daugherty had built a network (they were called "machines" in the early twentieth century) of loyal supporters through party patronage and by doling out government jobs and contracts to reward political allegiance. He was in a position to deliver a substantial number of delegates to Harding at the Republican Party convention.

Wilson's stroke and lengthy incapacitation combined with the controversy over the League of Nations proposal and Edith's "regency" were fortuitous for Harding. Running on a campaign theme of "return to normalcy," he won the 1920 presidential race with 61 percent of the popular vote. It was the largest margin any president had ever won.

Florence had been instrumental. At the Republican convention at the Blackstone Hotel in Chicago, she had circulated among the five hundred all-male delegates urging the conventioneers to nominate her husband. It was unprecedented, but she pulled it off without alienating the men. Florence had learned how to be direct and work well with men during her career in the newspaper business. Harding won the nomination on the tenth ballot.

Florence was also instrumental in the presidential campaign of 1920. She helped stage photo opportunities for the press, schedule his appearances, edit his speeches, and spin the press. She met with his staff at cam-

paign headquarters on a regular basis, checking on the campaign's progress and urging refinements to the strategy. No presidential spouse had
ever been so active in a political campaign.

She became briefly controversial when a newspaper reported on her
previous marriage to Henry DeWolfe. Florence resorted to lying that she
had never had a child. Although her son, Marshall, had died in 1915, he
was survived by a wife and two infant daughters. The storm dissipated
when Republicans conveniently uncovered a divorce in the past of the
Democratic presidential candidate, James Cox. Not since Rachel Jackson
had a divorce figured so prominently in a political campaign. If Rachel
had lived, she would have become the first divorced first lady; instead
that distinction would fall to Florence.

In addition to front-porch campaigning, Harding made use of the whistle-
stop train tour. While he gave speeches at each stop, Florence watched
the reactions of the crowds so she could later make refinements in the
speeches. It was the first campaign in which women had the right to vote,
and her acuity was an asset to Harding and his male political managers.

Florence was sixty years old when Harding was elected president, and
at the height of her ambition. Almost thirty years earlier, at her wedding,
she had supposedly remarked that one day she would make him into a
president. A believer in destiny and the occult, Florence had consulted
Madame Marcia—a Washington, D.C., astrologer whose real name was
Marcia Champrey—about her husband's political future. Madame Marcia
confirmed Florence's belief in Warren's potential. After Warren became
president, Florence continued to consult her astrologer about cabinet
members and others who served the Harding presidency.

She relished the role of first lady, too. She had two maids to take care of
her wardrobe, and she received a facial and a massage daily to keep her
appearance youthful. Wearing scarves to hide the wrinkles on her neck,
she dressed brightly.

Florence reopened the White House to public tours and reinstated
public events such as the Easter egg hunt that had been suspended during wartime and ex-president Wilson's convalescence. During her first
New Year's Day reception, she shook six thousand hands in the receiving
line. At the end of the day, her hands were so swollen that her gloves had
to be removed with scissors.

Florence liked power. But she disliked Vice President Coolidge's wife,
Grace, who was much younger and far more attractive than she was.
There was no government-provided housing for the vice president at that
time; the Coolidges lived in rooms at the Willard Hotel. When a proposal

came to Harding to support a government mansion for the vice president, Florence vetoed it firmly.

"I just couldn't have people like those Coolidges," she said to Warren, "living in that beautiful house."

Warren consulted her on the choice of his cabinet officers, and collectively the couple made ruinous choices that would prove to be their political undoing. While a few Harding appointments were exemplary—Herbert Hoover was named commerce secretary and Andrew Mellon headed the Treasury Department—Harry Daugherty, the Ohio political operative, was given the post of attorney general. Another political crony, Albert Fall, was named interior secretary. Charles Forbes, a Congressional Medal of Honor winner, was named to head the Veterans Bureau.

Daugherty predated Bill Clinton's abuse of the powers of presidential pardons by opening up an office at 1625 K Street known as the "Little Green House"; it served as headquarters of the Ohio Gang, a group of political loyalists who colluded with Daugherty. Attorney General Daugherty himself orchestrated the illegal sale of almost any official papers the federal government could issue—immunity from prosecution, pardons, licenses—in a gigantic scheme to enrich himself and the other insiders in the Ohio Gang. Ironically, the "K Street Corridor" in contemporary Washington is known as the district where today most lobbyists and influence peddlers have their offices and conduct the same trade in political favors, although in somewhat more oblique terms. Daugherty and the Ohio Gang were not subtle. They viewed the federal government as no different than a corrupt city hall in a small town.

Interior Secretary Albert Fall got Harding to transfer oversight of valuable government oil deposits to his department. The reserves were being held for emergency use by the U.S. Navy at Teapot Dome, Wyoming, and Elk Hills, California. Today the country has similar reserves, called the Strategic Petroluem Reserve, in case of oil embargos or disruption of supplies caused by war. Once Fall had control over the oil reserves, he took bribes from oil barons to let them illegally drill the oil. It was the famous Teapot Dome scandal. Without soliciting competitive bids, Fall gave the rights to drill the reserves to two oil tycoons, Harry Sinclair of Mammoth Oil and Edward Doheny of Pan-American Petroleum. Both men had loaned Fall large amounts of money. A Senate investigation uncovered the scandal, and Fall was indicted and eventually sentenced to prison. In 1927, the Supreme Court invalidated both leases, and the oil fields were returned to the government.

Medal of Honor winner Charlie Forbes was the worst of all. After

World War I, the Veterans Bureau and its hospitals served the largest number of seriously injured vets this country had ever seen. Improvements in medical treatment since the Civil War meant that more men survived even horrible injuries. Florence Harding had made these veterans, especially those who were disabled or out of work, one of her favorite White House causes. Like the reporters, she called them "my boys" and liked to visit them in hospital wards and invite them to White House events. She had twenty of the "doughboys" ride in the Hardings' inaugural parade and hosted an annual garden party at the White House for wounded veterans from Washington's hospitals.

The veterans made great stage dressing for Florence's photo opportunities. The press covered her interest in their plight. When she learned of veterans facing financial hardship, she would graciously offer to arrange help.

Meanwhile, Veterans Bureau chief Charlie Forbes was stealing them blind.

Forbes submitted inflated orders for new supplies, medicine, and equipment for the Veterans Bureau, and then sold stocks from the bureau's warehouses to pharmaceutical companies and private medical suppliers. He took kickbacks from contractors who submitted inflated bids on new hospital construction. His schemes cost the government an estimated two hundred million dollars that should have been spent on the veterans.

Historians still debate whether Warren Harding knew the extent of corruption in his government. Because Florence eventually burned many presidential records, it's possible that Warren was implicated in the corruption—but proof of his involvement was covered up by Florence.

It is possible that Forbes preyed on Florence's weakness for the veterans, cynically counting on her support when he went to President Harding and Congress for more funding. It is also possible that Florence knew Forbes was bilking the government, and she may have been a willing participant in the corruption. Somehow, despite Florence's great interest in veterans, she never managed to visit one of Forbes's warehouses or learn the extent of his abuse of government wares.

Just as today some states permit the medical use of marijuana, during Prohibition the law exempted the "medicinal" use of alcohol. While it was a federal crime for an ordinary citizen to possess liquor, the Harding White House was constantly supplied with booze taken from government stocks under the medicinal use exemption. Florence freely entertained guests with alcohol, and President Harding made it a staple of his regular White House poker games with the Ohio Gang. Whether it came to his personal life or his political life, Harding was an unabashed hypocrite. He had voted for Prohibition because it was politically expedient, yet hired a White House staffer whose job was essentially to be the bootlegger to the presidency.

Was Harding a hapless stooge of his poker partners, who were freely looting the country? Most of the investigations into the various scandals arising from his presidency—Teapot Dome, Daugherty's Ohio Gang, Forbes's thefts at the Veterans Bureau—took place after his sudden death in 1923. Moreover, Florence removed crates of papers and memos from the White House after his death and systematically destroyed their contents. Harding apologists have maintained that she was looking for and burning letters and notes of his extramarital affairs, but it seems more likely that she was destroying evidence congressional committees might have used against him. Florence certainly failed to destroy a number of Warren's love letters to Carrie Phillips, which came to light in the 1960s. Florence later said she was destroying papers that might have been misunderstood or taken out of context. In sum, she was covering up.

She claimed that her husband "does well when he listens to me and poorly when he does not." Theirs was a lifetime political partnership in which she was at least an equal partner, and quite possibly the dominant partner. Harding himself acknowledged on many occasions that he could not make a decision until he had consulted the "Duchess," his pet term for her.

Was it Florence who advised Warren to let some of the key criminal suspects in the breaking scandals flee?

Close to the end of 1922, the corruption at the Veterans Bureau began to come to light. For reasons that will never be known, Harding permitted Forbes to resign and go to Europe to evade prosecution. When one of his associates in the scam committed suicide, Forbes returned to the States, confident that Harding would not permit his arrest. Forbes was unaware that Attorney General Daugherty had given Harding a dossier on the illegal activities that made prosecution inevitable. No doubt Daugherty needed a fall guy, and Forbes was tailor-made for the role. As a returning fugitive from justice, Forbes was already under suspicion. Daugherty's dossier would ensure that an investigation would center on Forbes.

Fortunately, there was a whistleblower at the Justice Department. Jesse Smith had been an aide of Daugherty's who had been forced out of the department because he had grown squeamish about the illegal activities at 1625 K Street. Smith managed to get an audience with the president in which Smith let it be known that the full extent of Daugherty's corruption could be exposed. Inexplicably, Harding gave Smith twenty-four hours' advance notice that he would be arrested. Perhaps Harding expected him to do as Forbes had done and flee the country. Instead, Smith returned to the apartment he shared with co-conspirator Attorney General Daugherty and shot himself, ensuring that the complete details of the scandal would never be known.

Smith's papers on the affair were found burned.

Realizing that they had a burgeoning crisis on their hands, Warren and Florence decided on an ambitious western tour to distract public attention from the scandals in Washington. First, however, Harding sent Nan Britton to Europe, presumably to keep her beyond the range of the now-inquisitive press corps. The intriguing possibility exists that she was privy to pillow talk with the president that might have been incriminating.

In June 1923, Harding set off for Alaska. He couldn't have possibly put more distance between himself and Washington, except perhaps by going to Hawaii. He kept up a schedule of public appearances and speeches, no doubt intended to give the press and wire services and radio correspondents presidential news to report.

At the end of July, Harding became ill. His doctors at first diagnosed it as a case of food poisoning, but he worsened almost immediately. The presidential entourage went south to California, where medical specialists met him at the train and went with him to San Francisco's Palace Hotel. He died there on the night of August 2.

Conspiracy theories about his death arose immediately. Florence wouldn't consent to an autopsy, which gave rise to suspicions that Harding had been poisoned, the latest in a string of mysterious deaths whose net effect was to hush up the Harding White House scandals. This particular conspiracy theory was the theme of a best-seller, *The Strange Death of President Harding*, written by one Gaston B. Means, a former government investigator. The implication was that Florence herself could have killed Warren in order to cover up not only the scandals but also her own involvement in the corruption.

Florence stoically rode the funeral train back to Washington with her husband's body. Then she cleaned out the contents of his office at the White House, as well as an entire bank vault, and systematically set about the destruction of their contents and the sanitizing—if such a thing was still possible—of his presidential legacy.

Congress conspicuously refused to give her the normal pension for a presidential widow. It didn't matter. She was now a wealthy woman, thanks to inheritances from her father and husband. She was also paid $13,300 a year—a huge amount at the time—to serve as a contributing editor to her old newspaper, the *Marion Star* in Marion, Ohio. She died on November 21, 1924, a little more than a year after Warren's death.

To her dying breath, she never publicly acknowledged the existence of her own grandchildren. She maintained her pretenses to the very end.

GRACE ANNA GOODHUE
COOLIDGE

FIRST LADY: 1923–1929
30TH PRESIDENTIAL ADMINISTRATION
SIENA RESEARCH INSTITUTE RATING: 19

"The man would not have been what he was without the woman."
—Gamaliel Bradford

Grace Coolidge's chief virtue was authenticity. She is among those first ladies who led an independent life before she married. For a brief time, Ellen Wilson had pursued a career as a painter, and Abigail Fillmore supported herself by teaching for almost seven years. Grace Coolidge became a teacher at the Clarke School for the Deaf in Northampton, Massachusetts, for two years before she married. By doing so, she formed a commitment to working with the deaf that sprang from genuine concern instead of an effort to adopt a cause. Two years after her tenure as first lady ended, she was voted among the country's top twelve women of all time. The National Institute of Social Sciences honored her with a gold medal for her work with the hearing impaired.

Unlike other political spouses, Grace Coolidge never coveted the White House. She would have been content had her husband remained governor of Massachusetts. But after Calvin Coolidge's handling of a police strike struck a chord with the nation, he was nominated by the delegates to the Republican convention to share the 1920 presidential ticket with Warren Harding. Coolidge had called out the state militia to guard public safety during a police strike, declaring, "There is no right to strike against the public safety by anybody, anywhere, anytime." The strike took place in Boston during the hot summer of 1919. Riots broke out when the police went on strike after the police commissioner cut nineteen jobs from the police force. Just as a later president, Ronald Reagan, had won public acclaim by firing striking air traffic controllers who had threatened to cripple the nation's air travel, Coolidge's replacement of the striking police with National Guardsmen was publicly popular.

When Harding died abruptly in 1923, the news reached Grace and Vice President Coolidge while they were vacationing at home in Vermont. To leave no gap in presidential powers, Calvin Coolidge was sworn in as president by his father instead of waiting until he could return to Washington. Grace reportedly wept.

She was already well liked in Washington, D.C., for her vivacity, conversational charm, and dapper style. In many ways, Calvin and Grace were flinty Vermonters, sparing with their money, and unaccustomed to extravagance of any variety. The sole exception was Grace's wardrobe. An attractive woman, Grace dressed well, earning her the envy and animosity of the dowdy Florence Harding. What was more, the country loved her; as the extent of the Harding administration's corruption became clear, Grace Coolidge's unaffected style and straightforwardness did much to help restore public confidence in the presidency. By the time Calvin Coolidge's second term of office ended in 1929, she was one of the most popular first ladies the country had known.

Grace Anna Goodhue grew up in Burlington, Vermont. She was an only child. Her parents, Andrew and Lemira Goodhue, saw to it that their daughter received a college education, and she graduated from the University of Vermont in 1902. The following fall she went to work at the Clarke School for the Deaf in Northampton, Massachusetts.

In Northhampton, she met Calvin Coolidge. He was a fellow Vermonter who had been raised in the village of Plymouth Notch, the son of a shopkeeper who was active in local politics and who had served three terms in the state legislature and in various local offices.

After graduating from Amherst College, Calvin began practicing law in Northampton, and he became active in Republican politics. After a two-year courtship, they were married in her parents' home on October 4, 1905.

Their political life began immediately. As soon as their honeymoon in Montreal ended, he was on the stump campaigning for election to the school board. Two years later, he was sworn in as a member of the Massachusetts State Legislature. It was the beginning of a meteoric political career that would climb rapidly from the legislature to the state senate, president of the state senate, lieutenant governor, governor, vice president, and finally the presidency itself, all within less than twenty years. Remarkably, it should be noted, Coolidge achieved his rapid ascendancy without family connections or wealth to propel him along the way.

Early in their marriage, Grace committed herself to a supporting role not only in Calvin's career, but also in terms of giving their children a stable home environment. Calvin agreed with this course of action. Calvin's mother had died when she was just thirty-nine. He was only twelve. His younger sister Abigail died when he was eighteen. These emotional losses may have made him value a stable family life for his children, even if it meant separations because of his political career.

It led them to have a commuter marriage. While Calvin was away in Boston during legislative sessions, Grace stayed behind and raised their two young sons in Northampton. Even when he was elected governor of Massachusetts in 1918, Grace tried to raise the boys at home while commuting to Boston for political and social events that required her presence. This pattern of marriage would be familiar to many women of the late twentieth century who chose careers that took them away from their spouses. Although Grace maintained the traditional role of homemaker, it left her to handle many of the family responsibilities alone.

Harding's victory in the 1920 presidential election sent Grace and Calvin packing for Washington. They enrolled their now-teenage sons in boarding school and settled in themselves a few blocks from the White House at the Willard Hotel.

Although Vice President Coolidge had sat in on regular cabinet meetings during the Harding presidency and was otherwise active in the affairs of government, he had not been corrupted by Harding's Ohio Gang. He did not play poker with Harding and Daugherty and the others and kept his distance from their illegitimate dealings. Now that he was president, Calvin terminated the use of the White House as a speakeasy. If other ordinary Americans had to endure the dry spell of Prohibition, so would he and the first lady.

The Coolidges entertained at the White House more than any previous presidency for the simple reason that they liked it. Grace used her afternoons to schedule meetings with delegations and visiting groups. She turned the White House into a cultural center, issuing invitations to film and theater stars like Douglas Fairbanks Jr. and John Barrymore, as well as performing artists as diverse as Sergei Rachmaninoff and Al Jolson. Her White House was at the cutting edge of popular culture. Hollywood silent-film icons like Tom Mix and Mary Pickford mingled with the political elite, as did wits like Will Rogers and national heroes like Charles Lindbergh. She handled the tedious duties of political calls by inviting groups of twenty-five to thirty people at a time to meet with her twice weekly for tea. Royal luminaries who visited included the Prince of Wales and queen of Romania.

Although many commentators have written about President Coolidge's famous reticence as a conversationalist—Coolidge was the quintessential man of few words—he was not aloof from the press. Calvin Coolidge held more news conferences than any previous president, and he was especially open to radio interviews. In 1924, the Republican convention that unanimously nominated him on the first ballot made history by becoming the first political convention to be broadcast by radio.

As first lady, Grace also knew how to cultivate the media. She didn't meet with groups of reporters or engage in news interviews in the same way that her predecessor, Florence Harding, had done. But Grace understood that a modern first lady had to be accessible to the press. She soon became adept at staging photo opportunities to feed the insatiable appetite the press had developed for covering the activities of first families.

Grace posed with visiting delegations, which included many groups representing professional women. She posed while riding in parades, cutting ribbons at ceremonies, and laying cornerstones. The photographs conveyed not only her activism as first lady, but also her youth and vitality. She was younger, prettier, and healthier than recent presidential spouses, and the contrast helped her. The same could be said for other first ladies to come, especially Jackie Kennedy and Hillary Clinton, both of whom followed on the heels of matronly first ladies. Grace's official activities—meeting with delegations, attending ribbon-cutting ceremonies, hostessing at state dinners—were widely reported by the media, especially on radio and in large-circulation magazines. The media interest helped make Grace a household presence, and the Coolidges' popularity soared.

Grace Coolidge's fondness for the color red soon set a trend. She rarely appeared in the same dress twice, and the variety of her wardrobe made her a style-setter. She made up for Calvin's legendary charisma deficit, boosting not only her own image but also his. When he ran for reelection in 1924, Coolidge won 54 percent of the popular vote; the popularity of his presidency owed much to his wife.

As a college-educated woman, Grace became a trendsetter for young women in more than a fashion sense. Those who aspired to an education and a career looked up to her as a role model. Aware of this, she invited thirteen hundred college women to the White House in 1924 for the unveiling of her official portrait.

She also opened the 1925 Woman's World Fair in Chicago by symbolically pressing a button. The button didn't really open anything; Grace's gesture merely signified the fair's opening for the press. Today, the same thing is done with the annual White House Christmas tree lighting. The president or frst lady pushes a button, but the button isn't connected to anything; it's all done for the sake of the cameras. While she generally refrained from voicing opinions and being quoted while first lady, Grace's actions spoke louder than words—especially when conveyed by photographs. When she did speak out on the subject of women and careers, she said that she believed it would soon be commonplace for women to have a working life outside of the home. The 1920s were an era of prosperity. America had a growing middle class. Fewer married women needed to work in order to help sustain their families, yet Grace foresaw that women who didn't need to would choose to work outside the home for personal fulfillment.

She also demonstrated she was a modern woman in other ways. Only a few decades earlier, in Harriet Lane's day, it had been considered unfeminine for women to engage in physical exercise or run in athletic races.

But in the Roaring Twenties, all sorts of physical fitness activities were in vogue. Grace took an interest in golf, then the latest rage. She learned to swim the backstroke after a woman, Gertrude Ederle, swam the English Channel using the technique. She earned the title "First Lady of Baseball" because of her knowledge of the sport, and she enthusiastically supported the Boston Red Sox and Washington Senators. All this was conveyed to the American people through photographs, establishing an indelible image of Grace as hip and trendy.

Within a year after becoming president, tragedy struck her family. The Coolidges' sixteen-year-old son Calvin Jr., died of blood poisoning from an infected blister. He had been playing tennis when the blister appeared, and he treated it himself with iodine because he didn't want to bother his parents by mentioning it. The infection worsened and septicemia set in, killing him. In his autobiography, President Coolidge said that losing his son caused "the power and glory of the presidency" to fade. He partially blamed himself for the boy's death because of his absorption in politics.

Grace Coolidge handled her grief by continuing in her commitment to other children, especially with regard to the handicapped. When she first came to Washington as Vice President Coolidge's wife, she was elected to the board of directors of the American Association to Promote the Training of Speech to the Deaf. She continued in that capacity as first lady while also serving as a trustee to the Clarke School for the Deaf where she had taught. As first lady, she invited Helen Keller to visit the White House. She also opened the doors of the White House to special tours by students from the Clarke School, and used her powers to advocate educational opportunities for the deaf and the blind.

President Coolidge joined his wife Grace in her commitment. Although he felt it was improper for him to sign fund-raising letters to create an endowment for the Clarke School, feeling that the prospect could lead to the trading of political favors, he allowed their name to be used when Clarence Barron, editor of *The Wall Street Journal*, proposed creating a two-million-dollar endowment for the school called the Coolidge Fund. By the time the Coolidge presidency ended its second term, the endowment was fully funded, with one-quarter of its revenues set aside for the study of the causes and psychological effects of deafness, areas of special interest to the first lady.

During her tenure in office, Grace Coolidge broadened her interest to other disabilities. She set a precedent by becoming the first first lady to open a fund-raising affair—an invitational event that sponsors pay money to attend—for Aid to Crippled Children. She joined in fund-raising for Christmas Seals, the Children's Hospital, and the Hospital for Joint Diseases.

It is difficult to fully assess the impact Grace Coolidge had on her husband's policies. Because the Coolidges considered the restoration of public confidence in the presidency the sine qua non of their White House tenancy, they deliberately set out to create a contrast with their predecessors. If Florence Harding had been outspoken with the press, Grace would make no comments for quotation or on the record. If Edith Galt Wilson had been suspected of usurping presidential powers during Wilson's stroke and convalescence, Grace would maintain more than an arm's length between the role of first lady and affairs of state. This leaves historians with a perplexity: Was she as removed from the official duties and policies of the presidency as the public image suggests, or was she a politically involved spouse whose role was shrouded by a very effective public relations effort?

In support of the belief that she was a political activist are a few intriguing facts that seem to belie the image of a housewife. Alongside President Coolidge, Grace attended government budget meetings. She was in the gallery for the Senate hearings on the Teapot Dome scandal. She met with political figures including New York governor Alfred E. Smith. But whether she did any of this because of her own political interest, or from the belief that it was her duty to take an active interest in her husband's affairs, simply isn't known. When President Coolidge, who could easily have won reelection, made the announcement in 1928 that he would not seek a third term, Grace was apparently caught off guard along with the rest of the nation. Still, a letter Grace wrote to a friend suggests that he had shared his decision with her in advance; perhaps it was only the timing of his announcement that surprised her. At least one writer who knew her at the time, William Allen White, believed that Grace Coolidge's influence over policy and political issues was more pronounced than was publicly known. "The whole union [of Grace and Calvin]," he wrote, "seemed cabalistic. . . ."

The Coolidge administration was not an activist presidency in the sense that Calvin sought to enlarge or extend the power of the federal government or the presidency. Coolidge believed firmly that the principal business of Americans is business, and he didn't favor unwarranted interference in the way people ran their lives. Like other politicians whose roots sprang from state and local government, Coolidge didn't believe all wisdom or solutions to pressing social problems originated in Washington.

Moreover, his presidency coincided with the economic boom years of the Roaring Twenties, when there weren't overt calls to Washington in the name of public welfare.

His major accomplishment as president was to successfully push for tax cuts in 1924 and again in 1926, while still reducing the national debt. Supply-side economists believe that history has badly underrated the effect of the Coolidge administration's tax cuts in creating the wave of prosperity America enjoyed in the 1920s. He also took an interest in the burgeoning aviation industry, signing several laws to promote and regulate civil aviation. Critics note, however, that President Coolidge did little to rein in the runaway speculation in the stock market that finally resulted in the collapse of 1929, the year after he left office.

Feminists deride Grace Coolidge for deferring to her husband's decisions in their marriage. She was of the belief that every household needs a head, and saw her submission to her husband's decisions as a natural consequence of marriage. She was in this respect the polar opposite of her predecessor Florence Harding, who by most accounts dominated her husband and made him submit to her will not only in marital matters but also in his career decisions. By her own account, Florence says that she and Ohio political operative Harry Daugherty pressured Warren Harding into announcing his presidential candidacy by backing him against a wall until he agreed to run. Harding himself often deferred political decisions, saying he had to ask Florence before he could make a commitment.

It's clear, however, that Grace didn't believe she had to be completely deferential to Calvin's decisions. Before they married, she had written that "marriage is the most intricate institution set up by the human race. If it is to be a going concern it must have a head. . . . In general this is the husband. His partner should consider well the policies he advises before taking issue with them." The fact that she reserved the right to take issue with her husband's views shows that she didn't consider marriage vows a pledge of blind obedience.

After the Coolidge administration ended, Grace broke her public silence. With her husband's active encouragement, she began writing articles for publication in *Good Housekeeping* and other magazines. She kept up her efforts on behalf of the deaf and the handicapped long after Calvin's death from a heart attack in 1933, eventually devoting more than fifty years of her life to her passion.

On the eve of World War II, when isolationists in the Republican Party urged the United States to refrain from involvement, Grace used her public prominence to speak out publicly urging the country to side with

England and France against Hitler. Then, when fighting broke out in Europe, she turned her energy to fund-raising to bring Jewish refugee children from Germany and to aid Dutch victims of the Nazi invasion of the Netherlands. After the United States entered the war, the sixty-two-year-old former first lady trained as an air-raid warden, participated in drives to sell war bonds, and donated her house to the navy for use during the duration of the war.

She died in 1957 of heart failure, outliving Calvin by almost twenty-five years. They were years marked by her continued commitment to the hearing impaired and to the social and political causes that inspired her most.

LOU HENRY HOOVER

FIRST LADY: 1929–1933
31ST PRESIDENTIAL ADMINISTRATION
SIENA RESEARCH INSTITUTE RATING: 13

"Bad men are elected by good women who stay away from the polls."

Silver- and gold-mining boomtowns were still springing up in the deserts and mountains of the American West in 1893 when Lou Henry decided she didn't want to be a teacher anymore and turned her attention to geology. It was an unorthodox field for young women in the 1890s, but that didn't stop Lou, the eldest daughter of Charles Delano and Florence Weed Henry, from entering Stanford University. When she graduated in 1898, she was one of the few women in the entire country with a geology degree.

Growing up in California after her family moved from Iowa exposed Lou to the unfenced, great western outdoors. Unlike Iowa and the settled farmlands of the East and Midwest, sparsely populated California contained vast expanses of wilderness. Her father was a banker who took his wife and two girls on camping, fishing, and hunting excursions. He taught them to hike and ride horseback, and he fostered in them a love of adventure and challenge.

Lou met Herbert Hoover, her future husband, at Stanford in 1894. She was a freshman and he was already a senior about to become a mining engineer. He was apparently smitten by the tall, willowy, blue-eyed Lou, who could outwalk any of the men in her class on field trips to collect rock specimens. He proposed to her before graduating, but she put him off so she could finish her degree. When he proposed to her in the fall of 1898 by sending a telegram from his mining job site in Australia, she agreed to marry him. The couple were wed in Monterey, California, in 1899. Instead of a wedding gown, Lou wore a double-breasted brown travel suit. That same afternoon, the bride and groom took a train to San Francisco, and then sailed to his next job assignment in China. They spent their honeymoon at sea.

It was the beginning of a lifetime of travel and adventure that would take the Hoovers to Sri Lanka, Burma, Siberia, Australia, Egypt, Japan, and Europe. It was a lifetime that made Lou Henry Hoover one of the most worldly, urbane, and intellectual of any woman to occupy the White House. If the voters had not scapegoated the Hoover administration for the Great Depression of the 1930s (the collapse of the stock market in October 1929 had nothing to do with Hoover's policies) and she had had a second term in the White House, Lou might easily rank as one of the foremost first ladies.

In China, Lou continued to indulge her intellectual curiosity and love of adventure. She studied Chinese culture and learned to speak the language. Lou helped find tracts and books on mining, and then translated them from the Chinese. When Herbert's mining work required travel to remote sites, some of them bandit-infested, Lou rode with him on mule-back. Not even the Boxer Rebellion fazed her spirit. This rebellion, which drew its name from a Chinese secret society called Righteous Harmonious Fists because its adherents believed ritual forms of boxing and martial arts would protect them from European weapons, began as a movement to violently drive foreigners out of China. The initital victims were Christian missionaries and churches in the Shandong area of China, but the rebellion soon spread to Beijing.

Instead of taking refuge in a safe haven, as her husband insisted, she spent the month of the siege taking tea to the soldiers defending the foreign compound. The foreigners lived clustered in an area of Beijing known as the Legation Quarter. Armed with a handgun for self-defense, Lou rode her bicycle throughout the compound ferrying tea. Although she had a bicycle wheel shot out from under her and her hometown newspaper prematurely published her obituary, Lou—like Winston Churchill, who once said there is nothing more exhilarating than to be shot at without effect—found the experience of living through a siege exciting.

After the Boxer Rebellion, the Hoovers moved to London. As it had been throughout most of the California gold rush, British venture capital was critical to the development of mining industry in all parts of the world in the early twentieth century. From London, Herbert traveled to remote regions in search of valuable minerals. Lou frequently accompanied him, even after the birth of their first son, Herbert Clark Hoover Jr. In his first year of life, the infant circled the globe not once, but twice, as mother and baby trekked the planet alongside Herbert.

The family's fortunes prospered in London. As he helped develop and operate mines all around the world, he was handsomely rewarded. He was still a young man when he became a millionaire.

Lou had been more than Herbert's mate: Her expertise in geology and her intellectual drive made her an equal partner in his business enterprises. She not only studied cultures and collected artifacts in her world travels, but also studied local mining laws, labor relations, and the political environments of the countries where she lived and traveled, and she applied that knowledge to their careers. When she was researching in the British Museum, for instance, Lou came across an obscure sixteenth-century German mining treatise. Together, she and Herbert translated the work and published it in a scholarly edition.

The Hoovers were in London when World War I began. Tens of thousands of Americans were suddenly stranded in Europe and couldn't get home. Lou, who had been president of the American Women's Club, organized a group to help find shelter and book passage for their stranded countrymen, especially women and children who were traveling without men. In the era before the euro, credit cards, and automatic teller machines, this was a formidable undertaking. Most countries accepted only their own currency, and negotiating bank drafts and cash advances from America under wartime conditions was difficult. In a mere three weeks, their efforts helped forty thousand Americans return to the States. In many cases, the Hoovers advanced their own money to help fellow Americans.

Two months after the war began, Lou took their sons back to Palo Alto, California. Herbert stayed behind in Europe to run relief efforts for Belgium. When Lou returned to London, she too became involved in war efforts, helping set up free food and beverages for soldiers at London's train stations, and handling accounting for the American Women's War Relief. Herbert's success in the mining industry had made them independently wealthy, and they were able to devote all their attention to the relief efforts.

War relief became the couple's first experience in civic affairs. Their efforts in Europe did not go unnoticed in America. When the United States joined the fray in 1917, President Woodrow Wilson turned to Herbert Hoover to coordinate food supplies and distribution. The Hoovers moved to Washington, D.C., where Lou undertook the job of persuading American women to use less food and to plant gardens, making her own home an example for the rest of the nation. The family remained in Washington until the war's end in November 1918, when Herbert Hoover returned to Europe to oversee postwar relief efforts. President Harding named Hoover to his cabinet in 1921. Hoover was with Harding on the Alaska trip when the president was stricken and died.

It was during their time in Washington that Lou became involved with national women's organizations. Always athletic, she lent her support to the formation of the National Woman's Athletic Association, became national president of the fledgling Girl Scouts organization in 1922, and encouraged women to become politically active with their new voting rights. "Bad men are elected by good women who stay away from the polls," she said.

Hoover stayed on as commerce secretary in the Coolidge administration. When Coolidge decided not to seek another term of office in 1928, Lou was delighted that Herbert was going to run. She toured the country by his side and as often alone, stumping for the ticket. Hoover won in a landslide. The couple had become prominent during the wartime drive to conserve food. Lou's first public speech, in 1917, was publicized all over the country. Soon people spoke of their efforts to conserve as "hooverizing." By the time of the 1928 election, *hoover* had become a household word. Herbert and Lou went on a six-week tour of South America between the election and the inauguration, and prepared themselves for the rigors and the pleasures of the White House.

The elation of victory was to be short-lived, however. Although Hoover had warned against irrational exuberance in the stock market—stock prices were rising every month, far outpacing the underlying value of the companies whose shares were being traded speculatively—his warnings fell on deaf ears. Hoover had been in office only seven months when the stock market crashed on October 30, 1929. The Great Depression had begun. It would plunge twelve million Americans into joblessness, cause five thousand banks to fail, and lead to more than thirty thousand businesses going bankrupt.

Not since the Civil War had the country faced so severe a crisis. Herbert Hoover's response was to work incessantly on measures for public works programs and job creation, but he and his cabinet misjudged the depression to be just a severe recession. Hoover badly hurt his credibility when he predicted that the worst of the economic slowdown would be over in sixty days. Perhaps because he believed the recession would be brief, Hoover resisted federal aid to the unemployed. He vetoed the Bonus Act, which would have provided almost a billion dollars in aid to World War I veterans. These policies made Hoover appear callous to the plight of millions of Americans.

During World War I, the Hoover name had been turned into a praiseworthy verb—*to hooverize*, meaning "to conserve food for the war effort." Now in a cruel reversal the name came to symbolize all that was wrong with the country. Shantytowns that sprang up alongside railroad tracks and roads to accommodate the millions of men moving aimlessly around the country seeking work were called "Hoovervilles." A newspaper used to keep a homeless person warm was dubbed a "Hoover Blanket."

The mockery turned to rage when, acting under Hoover's general orders, General Douglas MacArthur burned the makeshift dwellings in a Hooverville in Washington, D.C., where thousands of unemployed and destitute World War I veterans were camped out. Historians agree that President Hoover wanted MacArthur to peacefully disperse the men, but his failure to later discipline MacArthur for exceeding his orders seemed to voters as though Hoover approved of the brutal methods.

Lou shared Herbert's incomprehension of the political requirements of the moment. She maintained a no-comment, no-quotation rule in dealing with the media, precisely at a time when the Hoovers needed to connect with the nation and reassure people on a human level. Herbert Hoover had never been an inspiring public speaker, and both Lou and Herbert were reluctant to engage in self-promotion by drawing attention to the many charities they had assisted or their philanthropic work. They simply could not grasp what the nation needed, and squandered their political popularity in a series of calamitous political and policy blunders.

As first lady, Lou continued to promote causes she believed in strongly. She gave many speeches to the Girl Scouts, joined the girls in outdoor camping and activities, and met with individual troops at the White House. She was chairwoman for the first national Conference on Athletics and Physical Education for Women and Girls in 1923.

She was also the first first lady to deliver a radio broadcast. She gave speeches on the occasion of the dedication of the Daughters of the American Revolution's Constitution Hall, and to a National 4-H Club assembly. These prepared speeches for largely ceremonial occasions were not a substitute for a sustained effort to reach and reassure the American people, though. The next president, Franklin Delano Roosevelt, would understand the intimacy of radio and its unique ability to reach people through an informal "fireside chat."

Among Lou Hoover's positive contributions as first lady was a unique appreciation of the history of the White House. Together with an assistant, she inventoried the building's historic contents and documented White House traditions, building on the work begun by Caroline Harrison and Edith Roosevelt. She restored historic and period furnishings to the White House and used private funds to create replicas of some of the furniture of President Monroe and his wife, Elizabeth, to decorate what is now known as the Monroe Room.

She also appreciated the White House's ability to be a cultural center. As Grace Coolidge had done before her, Lou invited artists and performers to White House events. The acclaimed pianist Vladimir Horowitz was among those who accepted her invitation to play.

Before Lou Hoover, pregnant women were not expected to attend White House events or appear in receiving lines. This world-traveling woman who hadn't hesitated to take her infants into the jungles of Malaysia or traipse around the globe while pregnant considered the notion of a woman's prenatal "confinement" absurdly medieval. Lou insisted that expectant mothers be allowed to accept White House invitations. But she ended the long-standing tradition of White House celebrations on New Year's Day that any citizen could attend without an invitation, primarily because she felt it was too great a strain on Herbert to shake thousands of strangers' hands for hours on end. It had the unintended consequence of making the Hoovers seem aloof.

Lou caused a controversy when she gave an invitation to an African American woman to join her for tea. Never mind that Jesse DePriest was a congressional spouse, and that one White House tradition was for the first lady to entertain all congressional spouses at least once a year. Congressman Oscar DePriest, a Republican from Illinois, had, in fact, made history by becoming the first black politician elected to the House of Representatives in the twentieth century, and Lou was determined that his wife should come to the White House for tea. Because the first lady had the foresight to seat Mrs. DePriest among a group of open-minded women who willingly accepted her presence, there was no incident to mar the event. But afterward Lou was criticized severely by a partisan press, especially in the solidly Democratic southern states.

As first lady, Lou also influenced the hiring of women in the federal government by pushing her husband to sign an executive order that put women on an equal footing with men for civil service jobs. In addition, she pushed Herbert to name women to top politically appointed positions. As a result, Hoover named seven women to high-level positions and appointed three dozen more as federal commissioners.

No incumbent president ever performed worse in an election than Herbert Hoover did in the presidential contest of 1932. Franklin Delano Roosevelt won 57 percent of the popular vote. Hoover got 40 percent. Despite this, it was not the end of public life for either Lou or Herbert Hoover. She continued her efforts on behalf of the Girl Scouts and women's athletics. She remained politically active through the California League of Women Voters and Republican women's organizations. She was even asked by new first lady Eleanor Roosevelt to become vice chairwoman of the Women's Committee on Mobilization for Human Needs, but she declined.

She worked with Herbert on various relief efforts for countries overrun by the Nazis during World War II. When the Salvation Army launched an effort to clothe a million European refugees, Lou accepted the challenge of becoming chairwoman of the drive's Western Women's Committee.

Almost up to his death in 1964 at the age of ninety, Herbert Hoover remained active. In addition to his joint projects with Lou, Herbert wrote nine books after leaving the presidency. When World War II ended, President Harry Truman put Hoover's formidable talents for organizing war relief efforts to work. Truman also tapped Hoover to chair the Commission on Organization of the Executive Branch of the Government, adopting hundreds of the commission's recommendations. President Eisenhower used Hoover for a commission on government reform. Lou died of a heart attack on January 7, 1944.

In more normal times, Lou Hoover's activism on behalf of women, her cultured interest in the White House, and her prowess as a hostess would certainly have made her a popular first lady. However, the depression was not normal times, and it demanded a different kind of leadership that simply eluded Lou and Herbert. They shared the belief that the depression was just a normal recession that would soon end. In the early stages of the depression, that was a reasonable belief. No one comprehended that the collapse of the U.S. stock market would be followed by bank closings that spread as far as Europe, turning a Wall Street calamity into a global catastrophe. It was an unprecedented event, in strictly economic terms, and it is therefore little wonder that it was bewildering to the Hoovers at first. In hindsight, we can all see easily the outlines of history, but when you're living in the moment it is difficult to glimpse the outlines of what is to come.

Still, Lou Hoover scored a very respectable rating of 13 in the Siena Research Institute poll of academics.

Anna Eleanor
Roosevelt Roosevelt

First Lady: 1933–1945
32nd Presidential Administration
Siena Research Institute Rating: 1

"People can be brought to understand that an individual, even if she is a President's wife, may have independent views . . . but actual participation in the work of government we are not yet able to accept."

Eleanor Roosevelt represents a watershed in the role of first lady. Before her, the boundaries of a first lady's activities had expanded gradually. After Eleanor, it would be possible for her successors to do virtually anything they wanted in the role of first lady, short of declaring themselves co-presidents.

There had always been something subtly different about Eleanor Roosevelt, something that suggested she would not follow the normal social expectations for a woman of her era. Instead of sensing her strength, the older women in Eleanor's life viewed her differences as weaknesses. Her own aunt called her an "ugly duckling" as a child. Her mother, sensing Eleanor's lack of youthful femininity, called her by the nickname "Granny" and compounded the hurt by showing favoritism to Eleanor's two brothers. First Lady Edith Roosevelt considered that the teenage Eleanor, whom she called a "poor little soul," had few prospects in life.

Eleanor's childhood was difficult. Her alcoholic father was in a sanatorium when Eleanor's mother died. She was only eight years old. Eleanor and her brothers were then shuffled between relatives. Her father died from delirium tremens, a brain disorder caused by alcoholism, in 1893.

Her grandmother Mary Hall became Eleanor's guardian. In 1899, the family sent her to Allenwood, a feminist and socially progressive boarding school in England. The fifteen-year-old spent three years in the all-girl boarding school, a period she later called the happiest in her life. When she returned to America in 1902, she was introduced as a debutante in New York and expected to begin dating men. The prospect brought her to the verge of a mental breakdown, then politely called a "nervous collapse."

Her cousin Alice Roosevelt thought that the five-foot, nine-inch, eighteen-year-old Eleanor was really "rather coltish-looking, with masses of pale, gold hair rippling to below her waist, and really lovely blue eyes." Another cousin, Franklin Delano Roosevelt, also saw Eleanor's attractions. He began courting her and by Christmas 1903 proposed marriage.

Although she outwardly conformed to the conventions of her era by marrying and bearing children, first lady Eleanor Roosevelt also, according to biographer Blanche Wiesen Cook, had a female lover whose bedroom was just across the hall from hers in the White House. There is no evidence that Eleanor had acknowledged her sexual orientation at the time, or that Franklin considered her anything other than heterosexual. Eleanor never spoke openly about her lesbianism, although her private letters leave no doubt that her attachment to other women was physical as well as emotional. There is also an intriguing entry Eleanor wrote into her journal in 1925: "No form of love," she said, "is to be despised." The courtship between Franklin and Eleanor has the appearance of a true romance. Franklin's mother, Sara Delano Roosevelt, thought the couple were too young to marry. She wanted them to keep their relationship private for a year, so Eleanor and Franklin secretly corresponded with each other and met behind Sara's back. After a sixteen-month engagement, the fifth cousins were married on March 17, 1905. Her uncle, President Theodore Roosevelt, gave the bride away. Eleanor was twenty years old.

After the wedding, they took a three-month honeymoon in Europe. When she returned to the States, Eleanor was already pregnant with the first of their six children, one of whom died in infancy.

In 1910, the Democratic Party drafted Roosevelt to run for the New York State Senate. Despite the handicap of running in a heavily Republican district, Franklin won the race. Eleanor warmed to the role of political spouse, sharing in the substantive work of politics and policy, but she disliked the many purely social events to which Senator Roosevelt was invited, especially those where drinking was involved. One of the first significant compromises of their marriage involved their joint decision that he could accept as many social invitations as he wished and stay at the parties as long as he liked, while she was free to decline. This may have reflected her understandable distaste for drinking, given her father's death from alcoholism. It could also have been the start of the distancing between Eleanor and Franklin, a distancing that would eventually exclude marital intimacy while each partner tolerated the other's infidelity. By the time Franklin was president, Eleanor had a lesbian lover living with her in the White House. Franklin openly referred to the woman, Lorena Hickok, as Eleanor's "she-man."

In 1912, Eleanor attended her first national political convention, where Roosevelt threw his support to Woodrow Wilson. When Wilson won the election, he rewarded Roosevelt with the position of assistant secretary of the navy in return for his help in the election campaign. It was the same post Teddy Roosevelt held under the McKinley administration, and it signaled that Franklin Delano Roosevelt was on the political escalator.

Eleanor was delighted to move to Washington. Thanks to Teddy, the Roosevelt name carried cachet and opened doors politically as well as socially. Eleanor dutifully made the rounds calling on the spouses of cabinet members, Supreme Court justices, and those in Congress. She and Franklin entertained frequently, but he continued to be able to accept party invitations she reserved the option to decline.

After the birth of their son Franklin Jr. in 1916, after eleven years of marriage, Eleanor considered her conjugal duties completed. She told Franklin she no longer wanted to have intimate relations with him. For his part, Franklin soon began an affair with Eleanor's attractive young social assistant, Lucy Mercer; it would last a lifetime. It was Lucy Mercer, in fact, not Eleanor Roosevelt, who was at Franklin's side when he died in 1945.

In 1918, Eleanor discovered love letters Lucy had written to Franklin and contemplated divorce. Then she decided it would compromise his political career. Franklin already had been elected to the New York State Senate, and he had aspirations to run for higher office. Like many another political spouse, Eleanor believed it was better to keep up the public pretense of a normal marriage rather than go through a divorce that would not only shatter their nuclear family but also compromise the couple's future prospects. In 1920, Franklin campaigned as vice president alongside Democratic nominee James M. Cox, but Republican Warren Harding won the election. Had Eleanor sued for divorce, Franklin would probably never have been chosen for the Democratic ticket that fall.

When the Roosevelts returned to New York at the end of the Wilson administration in 1921, Eleanor became active in women's groups. That summer, Franklin contracted polio. For a year, he battled the crippling disease with Eleanor bravely at his side and managing the family. Then in 1922, he went to Florida to recover, accompanied by Missy LeHand, who had become his assistant during the 1920 presidential campaign when Roosevelt ran as vice president. Although Eleanor had remained politically loyal to Franklin, emotionally the pair had grown distant. Franklin's battle with polio and temporary retirement from an active political life liberated Eleanor to enjoy a seven-year period she called her "private interlude."

Eleanor found her public voice by writing newspaper columns and radio broadcasts. She also decided to build her own house on the Roosevelt property at Val-Kil, near Hyde Park. Two other women—Marion Dickerman and Nancy Cook—moved in with Eleanor. Franklin, without a trace of bitterness, referred to their house as the "love nest" and "honeymoon cottage." For a period of seven years, the relationship among the three women was very close. They collaborated in journalistic enterprises, publishing the *Women's Democratic News*, which Eleanor edited, in running a school, and in a business that sold handmade crafts and pottery at the height of the "arts and crafts" movement. The relationship only collapsed in the early 1930s, just before Eleanor's relationship with a (female) journalist she met during the 1932 presidential campaign commenced.

It was during this period that Eleanor became a political activist. On her own, independently of Franklin's stalled political career, she made public appearances and raised funds for causes as diverse as mass transit, public recreation facilities, public housing, workers' rights, and education. She learned from Franklin's political strategists how to handle public speaking and make a powerful impression through body language at the podium. She became involved in election campaigns.

She also learned to fight hard. When her cousin Theodore Roosevelt Jr. ran against incumbent New York governor Al Smith, Eleanor decided that his Achilles' heel was involvement in the Harding administration's financial scandals. In fact, he had been unfairly implicated in the Teapot Dome scandal by the press, and was innocent of wrongdoing. But Eleanor knew it would be politically damaging if the voters believed, even falsely, that he had been involved in the scandal. To remind them of his alleged role in the Teapot Dome scandal, Eleanor improvised a media stunt. She designed a car that had a steam-billowing teapot and drove around the state following Teddy Roosevelt Jr., to draw critical media attention. Everywhere he campaigned, Eleanor followed, and the press and voters took notice of the teapot—and thought about Teapot Dome and Theodore Roosevelt Jr. Eleanor herself admitted that it was "rough stuff" and an unfair tactic, but it worked.

Eleanor reassured Franklin that her political activism was only intended to temporarily fill the vacuum created by his convalescence, and not to eclipse him. The battle with polio had delayed, but not destroyed, his political ambitions. By the time he returned to politics, however, with a bid to become governor of New York, her name had become well known in the state's political circles. He won in the close 1928 election with Eleanor's active help throughout the campaign. Franklin was reelected governor in 1930 by a wide margin.

Just as Eleanor had discovered the power of radio, Franklin, too, grasped the importance of the new medium. He gave his first radio "fireside chat" while still governor of New York. With Eleanor's encouragement, Franklin named Frances Perkins as his labor commissioner. As president, he would name her his labor secretary, making history by appointing the first female cabinet member.

Polio prevented him from traveling throughout the state easily, so

Eleanor became Franklin's "eyes and ears," attending political and cere-monial events in his stead and reporting back to him in great detail. Dur-ing the 1928 campaign for governor, he had a car specially built with hand controls to allow him to drive. Franklin also traveled by train. People were aware of his impairment, but his press appearances were carried out sit-ting down in a normal chair, and he was almost never photographed in a wheelchair. Because Eleanor had become a well-known public figure throughout the state in the 1920s, her appearance in his stead was widely accepted. Their political partnership meant that his impairment was never an issue to the voters. Together they hosted events and strategy sessions at the governor's mansion, and they became the inseparable power couple, even if when it came to the intimate details of their mar-riage they had grown apart. They were literally halves of a whole in which the whole was larger than the sum of its parts.

The Great Depression was exactly the kind of crisis this political duo was made to tackle. Eleanor Roosevelt's concerns about the conditions of workingpeople and their plight was sincere. She had given the issues se-rious attention, intellectual study, and tireless political energy for the bet-ter part of a decade. It was not a "cause" that she embraced for political expediency or public relations value like Barbara Bush's advocacy of liter-acy programs, which came about only because she realized that as first lady she needed a cause. Rather, it stemmed from sincere convictions that sprang from deep in the wellsprings of her psyche.

Political conventions of the era might have kept her in the background had it not been for Roosevelt's handicap. Whether or not she would have emerged from his shadow had he never suffered polio is a question open to debate, but when she did emerge she did so with a power and a pres-ence unequaled in political history.

When Roosevelt ran for president in 1932, Eleanor was a critical part of the campaign. Behind the scenes she coordinated grassroots efforts of the Women's Division of the Democratic Party, while in public she campaigned with the ticket and gave public speeches. She participated in photo op-portunities and helped write campaign materials and would have stumped the country more extensively, except that Roosevelt's campaign strate-gists feared she would overshadow him. They joked that their problem was to "get the pants off Eleanor and onto Franklin."

Eleanor attracted notice wherever she went. Lorena Hickok of the New York bureau of the Associated Press—the sole female reporter in the campaign press corps—wrote a flattering series of stories about Eleanor. Eleanor understood the importance of Hickok's precedent and began to give her scoops. When the tide of the presidential campaign seemed poised to turn in Roosevelt's favor, her chiefs at AP assigned Hickok to cover Eleanor regularly. It was the beginning of a relationship that would continue into the White House.

Franklin Delano Roosevelt won the 1932 presidential race, beating incumbent president Herbert Hoover. His margin of victory increased in the 1936 reelection campaign against Alf Landon, where Eleanor now campaigned openly with Franklin. Cautious as ever, his political advisers wanted to restrict her presence in campaign stops, but the crowds wouldn't hear of it. They clamored to see Eleanor, and she obliged. This time Roosevelt won 523 electoral college votes to the Republicans' 8. The campaign had been a referendum on the New Deal (there were really two "New Deals," each of which referred to landmark legislation passed by the Roosevelt administration, with the first New Deal of 1933–1934 dealing with the need to reinvigorate the economy, and the second New Deal of 1934–1935 dealing with social reform), and Roosevelt's mandate was overwhelming. When Roosevelt campaigned for an unprecedented third term in 1940, Eleanor gave a speech to the Democratic national convention delegates. She was no longer in the background, and in the future no successor first lady would be either, except by choice.

The Roosevelt administration lost no time in facing the economic crisis that Herbert Hoover had mistakenly believed to be a short-term problem. So active was the Roosevelt presidency in sending the Republican Congress legislation that the tradition of the "First One Hundred Days" was born, the period when a new president is presumed to have a brief window of opportunity to capitalize on the voters' mandate by initiating change.

In the first year of the twelve-year Roosevelt presidency, Roosevelt's Civilian Conservation Corps—a public works program funded by the federal government—put three million young people to work on flood control, road building, and forestry. The Agricultural Adjustment Administration sought to boost crop prices for America's hard-hit farmers. The Tennessee Valley Authority was created to electrify a seven-state region and control floodwaters. The National Industrial Recovery Act created the Public Works Administration, which sponsored projects like the building of the Hoover Dam and the Works Progress Administration which employed artists and photographers to paint murals in public buildings and chronicle the era by creating a visual record for history. The Federal Emergency Relief Administration was also established to channel federal funds into state and local governments caught in the double whammy of plummeting tax revenues and the growing legions of the unemployed and impoverished. Taken together, these bills became known as the New Deal.

As unemployment rose to 25 percent at the beginning of the Roosevelt presidency—one in four Americans was made jobless by the depression—Eleanor was tied down with the traditional hostess duties of a first lady. At a reception for the Daughters of the American Revolution, she shook more than three thousand hands in a single session. When she could, she used the White House hostess role to advance her political aims, sponsoring conferences in the East Room and hosting gatherings of women federal workers. In New York during the 1920s, she had built networks of women active in politics by creating women's Democratic clubs throughout the state. Now Eleanor was creating networks of women active in government.

The Roosevelts also understood the popular appeal of celebrities. Franklin had become committed to the fight against polio and championed the March of Dimes. Now they both sought the support of movie stars to endorse the March of Dimes. They were pleased by the response. So many celebrities came to the White House, in fact, that it earned the nickname "Little Hollywood." They included Errol Flynn, Shirley Temple, Clark Gable, Bette Davis, Elizabeth Taylor, Bing Crosby, and Bob Hope, the leading stars and entertainers of their day. Eleanor even made a cameo appearance in a newsreel film short with comedian Jack Benny to promote a charity.

But when she openly invited the public to write to her about their concerns, she discovered her true calling as first lady. In the first year of the Roosevelt administration, she received more than three hundred thousand letters. She answered as many as she could personally, sometimes writing up to fifty replies a day. Soon she began speaking out on radio and in speeches and in a newspaper column she wrote, empathizing with the poor and the powerless. She appeared in the newsreels that preceded feature films in the 1930s, giving her more mass exposure than any prior first lady. Eleanor soon became the symbolic connection between the people and the White House at a time when faith in all institutions had been badly strained by the economy's collapse and the shattered lives of millions.

Much has been written about Eleanor Roosevelt's flirtations with socialism. She once told a friend she would have voted for a socialist candidate, Norman Thomas, if her husband hadn't been running for office in the same election. She even expressed some sympathy with the ideals of communism, calling it a system closer in spirit to democracy than fascism.

Many political theorists would agree with Eleanor's assessment, at least in terms of the classic utopian Marxist theory. In practice, however, Soviet-style Marxism had more features in common with fascism than democracy, according to leading intellectuals like Hannah Arendt, who characterized both communist and fascist governments as totalitarian regimes. It was politically risky for Eleanor to liken democracy to Marxism. Critics seized on her statement and charged the Roosevelt administration with undermining the American tradition of rugged individualism and the capitalist system.

In truth, the Roosevelt administration saved American democracy. Other industrial countries hard hit by the depression succumbed to class warfare, as with the Spanish Civil War in the 1930s, or social upheaval, as in Germany and Italy, turning alternately to Marxism and to fascism. By facing the immediate crises of hunger and despair and meeting the need with food, work, and ultimately hope, the Roosevelt administration prevented the kind of social unrest that led to the rise of dictators like Stalin in the Soviet Union and Hitler in Germany.

Eleanor's calling at this time of national crisis was to bridge the gap between the government and the people. Just as they had done during Herbert Hoover's administration, thousands of unemployed war veterans gathered in Washington to press their demands for government welfare benefits. So many combat veterans gathered together prompted fears of rebellion. Instead of sending the army to restore order, Roosevelt dispatched Eleanor, who met with the men and listened to their grievances.

Soon Eleanor was sent on the road, seemingly everywhere, with Franklin's direct encouragement. Some missions she chose on her own, as when she decided to visit West Virginia after reading Lorena Hickok's account of conditions in a coal-mining town. Others were suggested by presidential advisers, including the president himself. On a visit to California's San Joaquin Valley, where many had found work in the fields as migrant laborers, Eleanor had her car stop by a shantytown. She was accepted by the inhabitants, who recognized her immediately and seemed to think it was perfectly normal for the first lady to show up in their "Hooverville" to see how they were faring.

While Eleanor's public presence demonstrated that the Roosevelts cared about ordinary people, when it came to policy she was equally active. She gave regular reports to Franklin through "the Eleanor basket," kept at his bedside, with policy and personnel recommendations. She especially urged the appointment of women and recommended individual candidates for federal jobs.

Throughout this period, Lorena Hickok, called "Hicks" by Eleanor, lived in the White House. She had a bedroom just across from Eleanor's. She had resigned her job at AP in order to become an adviser to Eleanor, but missed her independence. At Eleanor's suggestion, Hicks was hired by the Federal Emergency Relief Administration to carry out fact-finding missions for its administrator, Harry Hopkins. Hopkins was one of Roosevelt's key architects of New Deal welfare programs and an able and energetic administrator. Over time, he would rise to become a top Roosevelt aide during World War II, and an important go-between for Roosevelt in dealing with America's wartime allies, Churchill and Stalin. Hicks used her reporting skills to travel around the country to see firsthand how the New Deal programs worked—or didn't work—and wrote confidential reports for Hopkins, the president, and the first lady.

Eleanor and Lorena, says biographer Blanche Wiesen Cook, had a stormy and intimate relationship that lasted almost a decade. It came to an end after Hickok had an affair with another woman in 1942, while still living in the White House. In 1966, Lorena confided to Eleanor's daughter Anna that she had destroyed many of the letters written by the first lady, because Lorena considered their contents to be indiscreet. But after her death in 1968 at the age of seventy-five, Lorena donated the surviving letters from Eleanor to the Franklin D. Roosevelt Library.

Most of these letters were exchanged when the two women were separated because of Eleanor's or Lorena's official travels. Although they sometimes traveled together on official trips, such as the trip to Puerto Rico in 1934, and vacationed together privately in Yosemite and Maine, Eleanor's heavy travel schedule after her first year as first lady meant frequent separations from Lorena. The two women spoke often by telephone, with Eleanor sometimes waking up Lorena at two A.M. just to hear her voice. They also wrote letters.

The surviving letters chronicle the women's physical and emotional intimacy. Eleanor complained of being "empty" without Lorena, and wrote longingly of her desire to kiss and caress Lorena.

"I love you deeply, tenderly darling & I would like to put my arms around you," the first lady wrote in January 1934. In another letter Eleanor said, "Oh! How I wanted to put my arms around you in reality instead of in spirit. I went and kissed your photograph instead & the tears were in my eyes." In a letter of 1933 Eleanor wrote: "Hick darling, All day I've thought of you & another birthday I *will* be with you, & yet to-night you sounded so far away & formal, oh! I want to put my arms around you, I ache to hold you close." The imagery in another is more erotic: "A cigar may not always be a cigar, but the 'northeast corner of your mouth against my lips' is always the northeast corner."

In other letters, the two women planned a life together after the White House. It would not have been Lorena's first "Boston Marriage," as lesbian relationships were then called. As a young reporter, she and another woman had lived together in an open lesbian relationship. Eleanor speculated about whether she and Hicks would live together in a country cottage, and whether they would fight over how to furnish it. But it was not to be.

Lorena became involved with a woman named Marion Janet Harron, a federal tax judge ten years her junior. Judge Harron visited Lorena at the White House so frequently that the guards came to know her. Janet was admitted to the building without being asked for identification. Letters between Hicks and Harron at the FDR Library document their lesbian relationship. Lorena sometimes taunted Eleanor by flaunting her affair. Although she and Eleanor remained in contact for many more years, the first lady's relationship with Lorena cooled after Lorena's affair with Janet Harron.

Eleanor Roosevelt also gets credit for introducing Harry Hopkins to Franklin. Hopkins performed ably in his relief work and became a presidential emissary for Roosevelt on the eve of World War II, carrying out shuttle diplomacy between Winston Churchill and Joseph Stalin in developing the Lend-Lease program. After the fall of the Soviet Union in 1991, archives from the Soviet intelligence service surfaced that portray Hopkins in a fresh light. It appears that he was a top spy for the Soviets. Toward the war's end, Hopkins had used his influence with Roosevelt to advance Stalin's aims of dominating Eastern Europe. Her embrace of Harry Hopkins may have been a rare lapse in Eleanor's judgment about people.

No sooner had the crisis of the depression abated in the late 1930s than an international crisis loomed. Adolf Hitler had been elected chancellor of Germany in 1933, and spent the remainder of the decade surreptitiously building up Germany's military in violation of the Treaty of Versailles. In 1939, he invaded Poland. It was the beginning of World War II. Roosevelt believed the United States would inevitably be drawn into the fighting, and initiated the Lend-Lease program in 1941 to help arm future allies Great Britain and the Soviet Union, so they could withstand the Nazi juggernaut until the U.S. entered the war.

Eleanor threw herself into relief efforts for war refugees, helping British children cross the Atlantic safely, so that they could stay in the United States until the war's end. She fought to expand immigration quotas for

Germany so that Jews could flee the anti-Semitic regime for the safety of America by lobbying Congress to increase the quotas while she also pressed the State Department to issue more visas. Eleanor worked with Jewish leaders pressing Congress to pass a bill that would increase the U.S. immigration quota for Germany by twenty thousand so that Jewish children could be admitted. The bill failed to pass Congress. Her efforts to pressure the State Department paid off with visas for several hundred Jewish children to come to America, but to the end of her life she spoke candidly about her regret that she couldn't save more people from the Holocaust.

When the United States entered the war after Pearl Harbor, Eleanor once again reached out to touch the people whose lives were most affected—the troops. Less than a year after the Japanese attack, Eleanor was on the road in Europe visiting American soldiers. On the home front, she toured the headquarters of the Women's Army Auxiliary Corps and military units, including the Army Air Corp's first African American combat pilots. She went to the factories and shipyards where a new largely female workforce filled the gap created by the mobilization of the men into the military. Once again she became a morale builder and a symbol of hope to a nation gripped by crisis.

Franklin Delano Roosevelt died of a cerebral hemorrhage while vacationing at Warm Springs, West Virginia, in April 1945. Lucy Mercer, his longtime mistress, was at his side instead of Eleanor. The fighting in Europe was almost over. Vice President Harry Truman became president, but Eleanor's political career was far from over.

As first lady, she had broken all barriers. As a former first lady, she continued to expand the role a presidential spouse could play in the country's life. While it is true that almost every aspect of Eleanor Roosevelt's role as first lady built on precedents established by her predecessors, she brought the powers of the role together in a focused way no other woman had done before her. Eleanor chose political goals such as advancing legislation or expanding the budgets of programs that worked, and then used her powers as first lady to build public support while also using her skills at networking to build inside political support. She leveraged her power to achieve concrete policy goals. In so doing she set a standard that all future first ladies would be measured against.

In 1945, President Truman named Eleanor the U.S. delegate to the newly established United Nations. She was instrumental in the assembly's passage of the Universal Declaration of Human Rights, and was posthumously given the U.N.'s first Human Rights Award for her achievement.

After Franklin's death, Eleanor resumed her radio broadcasts and embraced the new mass medium of television with enthusiasm. By the late 1940s, she was writing prolifically. She had resumed her newspaper column, began publishing her three-volume autobiography, and wrote a column in *McCall's* magazine.

Throughout her White House years, the first lady had been especially receptive to blacks and concerned about segregation and racism's corrosive effects on democracy. Many times she had been criticized for appearing in public with African Americans and for supporting the work of the National Association for the Advancement of Colored People. Now that she was free to pursue her own political interests without fearing the impact on Franklin, she accepted invitations to join the board of directors of the NAACP and the Congress of Racial Equality.

Eleanor remained active in partisan politics, reluctantly endorsing Harry Truman for election in the 1948 campaign, aware that he was backing away from her cherished New Deal policies. In 1952, Democratic activists tried to draft her to run for president. Instead, she supported Illinois governor Adlai Stevenson, who ran twice for the presidency without success. In 1960, she lent her support to Senator John Fitzgerald Kennedy after he made a commitment to civil rights, and she campaigned actively for his election. When he created the Peace Corps, Eleanor accepted his offer to become a member of its advisory council; later she chaired the Kennedy Commission on the Status of Women.

Eleanor Roosevelt died of tuberculosis on November 7, 1962, at the age of seventy-eight. With Franklin she became part of a successful political partnership in a country that demanded activism. During Franklin's terms of office, the United States and its allies prevailed in a world war, overcame the Great Depression, and created the foundation of the modern American government with its substantially greater federal role in every aspect of life. Many historians believe that great challenges create great presidents; the same can be said of first ladies. Eleanor Roosevelt served at a time of national crisis, and showed her greatness through untiring work. She connected with common people in ways that inspired them to believe the best about their leadership in the worst of times. It remains an exceptional accomplishment that took stamina, intellect, and above all genuine empathy.

Elizabeth Virginia Wallace Truman

First Lady: 1945–1953
33rd Presidential Administration
Siena Research Institute Rating: 11

"The independent lady from Independence."
—*New York Times Magazine*, 1946

The first documented terrorist attack on American soil happened in 1950, in broad daylight, right on Pennsylvania Avenue. It almost made first lady Bess Truman a widow. During repairs to the White House, the Trumans had moved across the street to stay in Blair House, a historic guest residence usually reserved for visiting heads of state. On a November afternoon in 1950, two men attempted to carry out a plot to advance Puerto Rican independence by assassinating President Truman.

Bess was upstairs when gunfire rang out. When she raced down to find out what was happening, one of the terrorists lay dead and the other had been wounded. On the sidewalk also lay the body of a policeman who had been killed in the gunfight. Although a spokeswoman said the terrorist attack had been deeply shocking to Bess, she said little about the matter publicly and carried on with her duties as first lady as though nothing had happened. Privately, she wept.

It was a typical reaction from a woman who valued privacy for herself and her family, and submitted to the highly public role of presidential spouse with a degree of reluctance. Had Bess Truman been able to be Harry's political partner without the pomp and ceremony and media scrutiny of life in the White House, she would have preferred it. On one occasion while dining in Washington's Mayflower Hotel, Bess requested a chair facing the wall so that she wouldn't be made uncomfortable by the gawking and curious stares of other diners—a reaction that would have been unthinkable to a more outgoing first lady such as Eleanor Roosevelt. When pressed to give her opinions on public matters, the first lady would often tell reporters her views didn't matter because she didn't hold office.

The contrast between her predecessor, Eleanor Roosevelt, and Bess could hardly have been stronger. Eleanor coveted a public role; Bess wanted to be left alone. Eleanor would descend into coal mines to see the working conditions the men faced for herself; Bess publicly announced she wouldn't be touring any. They were both Democrats, but Bess came from a midwestern, Farm Belt background that was distinctly conservative; Eleanor was an unabashed Northeast liberal.

The two women had met when Bess was a Senate wife, and reportedly she admired Eleanor Roosevelt. But she had no intention of copying her as first lady. During the eight years of the Truman administration, Bess would reshape the role in her own way, limiting her public role to that of White House hostess, refusing to adopt any specific cause as her own, and staying out of the public debate over policies and politics. Yet in important respects, she exercised even more influence over presidential policy than Eleanor Roosevelt, though her power was carefully shielded from public view. Bess was best behind the scenes.

Harry and Bess Truman were childhood sweethearts. They met in a Sunday school class at the First Presbyterian Church, although Harry was actually Baptist. She was five and he was six years old. Family lore has it that he developed an immediate and lasting crush on the blue-eyed, flaxen-haired Bess. Throughout elementary and high school, they shared classes and he doted on her. The feeling was not mutual. Although Bess sometimes let Harry carry her books, she wasn't romantically interested in the bookish boy with the thick glasses.

Bess Truman graduated from high school at age sixteen, but did not attend college because of financial difficulties. When she was eighteen, her father killed himself. Her maternal grandparents assumed responsibility for raising Bess and her three brothers while also supporting their grief-stricken mother. Because of the stigma then attaching to suicide, the tragedy was rarely discussed within the family. To avoid dealing with it socially, the grandparents sent her mother, brothers, and Bess away to Colorado for a year. The trauma of her father's suicide, coupled with the emotional state of being unable to discuss it, threw a shadow of darkness into the teenage Bess's life and reinforced a need for privacy.

After she returned from Colorado, Bess was enrolled at a college preparatory school in Kansas City. She not only excelled academically at the Barstow School but also played on the basketball team and competed in track and field. When she finished her studies, however, instead of going on to college, as did many of her classmates, Bess returned to Independence.

By 1910, Harry Truman was back in the courtship game. He was now a partner in the family farm, and began dropping by to visit Bess. When he didn't call, he wrote her letters—literally hundreds of them. Three years later when he proposed to her, she accepted, but the couple kept their engagement secret because of opposition to the match from Bess's mother.

As a Baptist, Harry Truman was of the wrong religion. The Wallaces were Presbyterians who had become Episcopalian as they rose in the narrow social hierarchy of Independence. Bess's father had pretensions of a career in politics and membership in the town's elite. He won election to minor offices such as treasurer of Jackson County, Missouri, and was appointed deputy U.S. surveyor of customs for the port of Kansas City, Missouri. When Bess was very young the family moved to the most exclusive neighborhood in town as soon as he could afford it. Her father's social aspirations, however, didn't match his means, and he was often deeply in debt. Believing himself a failure, he sought solace in saloons. Despondent over his debt and his self-perceived failure, he shot himself at home on June 17, 1903. In contrast, Harry Truman's father had been a mule trader, a profession looked at askance by the town's elite. Although her father's suicide had changed the family circumstances, Bess's mother refused to abandon her social pretenses. She thought Harry was unworthy of her daughter.

The engagement dragged on for six years. When the United States sent troops to fight in World War I, Harry—like many farm boys throughout history—thought it would be the adventure of his lifetime and enlisted to fight. Now it was Bess who wanted to be married before he went overseas, but Harry wouldn't risk making her a widow or saddling her with a husband who might return maimed or crippled.

By the time he returned, Harry had distinguished himself as a competent artillery officer who saw combat action in the "war to end all wars." He was advanced to the rank of major, a distinction that no doubt helped soften his future mother-in-law's objections to the match.

Bess and Harry were married on June 28, 1919, twenty-nine years after Harry had first been smitten by her in Sunday school! She was thirty-four and he was thirty-five years old.

Truman's political career began in 1922, when he ran for a county judgeship and won the election. Two years later, the couple had a baby daughter, Mary Margaret. Bess was almost forty and had suffered two miscarriages before giving birth to the child they called Margaret. During most of the rest of the decade, Bess was a devoted mother to her daughter. She was not active in Harry's political campaigns when he ran unsuccessfully for reelection in 1924 but victoriously in 1926 and 1930. Bess had made the choice to nurture her daughter instead of her husband's fledgling political career.

Harry was not content with state or local office. In 1934, he ran for the U.S. Senate. Bess stumped with him, making campaign appearances with Harry near home and in the vicinity of Kansas City. But she didn't give speeches or media interviews, believing that the only role she needed to play was to be seen seated next to her husband.

Behind the scenes, she was more active. Like other political spouses, she paid close attention to the newspapers and clipped newspaper articles she thought Harry should see. She handled political correspondence and served as his secretary. He began calling her "the Boss," a term he meant affectionately, not in the sense that Warren Harding might have said the same thing about Florence. The driving force in Truman's political career was Harry, not Bess.

Nonetheless, when he won the election and the family moved to Washington, she enjoyed being a senator's wife. She was active along with other wives in the Congressional Club, but the Trumans did not try to entertain extensively or become major players in Washington's social scene. Bess listened to debates in the Senate and stayed abreast of political and legislative developments.

During the muggy Washington summers, Harry drove Bess and Margaret back to Missouri. He would return to Washington, but stayed in touch with Bess by writing as frequently as he had done when courting her before World War I. He sent her the *Congressional Record* so she could stay current, filled her in on the backroom jockeying and vote trading, and candidly told Bess what was on his mind. Her responses were thoughtful and full of questions, which forced him to clarify his own thinking.

At the end of Harry's first Senate term, he faced a tough challenge in the primary election. This time, she plunged into the crowds with him at campaign rallies, enthusiastically greeting voters and shaking the hands of supporters. Behind the scenes, Bess helped map Harry's campaign strategy and doctor his speeches, inserting gentle but effective homespun verbal barbs poking fun at the opposition. For Truman's Senate race against primary opponent Lloyd Stark, who owned apple orchards, Bess came up with this line: "Any farmer who is dang fool enough to vote for another farmer who's losing money farming ought to have his head examined!" Her next line took on Truman's other primary challenger, District Attorney Maurice Milligan: "And any farmer who's dang fool enough to vote for a lawyer who never sees a farm ought to have his head examined twice!" Many of Harry Truman's now-famous one-liners were in fact coined by Bess.

When Harry won, he put Bess on the office payroll as a Senate staffer. She was paid twenty-four hundred dollars annually. Predictably, there was grumbling that she was overpaid and that spouses didn't belong on the congressional payroll. In fact, Bess was creating an important precedent—that political spouses do often work as hard as candidates and elected officeholders and deserve to be compensated in return. While other political spouses had been put on Capitol Hill office payrolls before, care was usually taken not to draw attention to the fact. In this case, Harry and Bess did nothing to conceal her work. In reply to criticism, Harry defended her by saying she earned every cent of her salary. As an example, when he traveled away from Washington to review defense spending on wartime fact-finding missions, it was Bess who managed the day-to-day operations of the Senate office. Today, it is commonplace for congressional spouses to hold salaried jobs not only in the House and Senate offices of their spouse, but in their political party organizations as well. Bess, however, was the first first lady to hold a paid political position before entering the White House.

Franklin Delano Roosevelt hadn't intended to seek a third term of office, but felt compelled to remain in the presidency because of World War II. When he ran for reelection in 1944, Truman was chosen as his running mate. Roosevelt's first vice president had been Texas congressman John Nance Garner, who served in that office until 1940. In that reelection race, Roosevelt dumped Garner in favor of Agriculture Secretary Henry Wallace. Roosevelt wanted Wallace to be on the ticket for the 1944 race, but the majority of the delegates to the Democratic convention were concerned that the left-leaning Wallace would be a poor replacement as president if Roosevelt's failing health resulted in his death in office. The compromise candidate was Harry Truman.

During the campaign, when Bess's Senate salary briefly became a political issue, she was the one who handled it. She told Harry to defuse it with one of his trademark one-liners, by simply saying that the Trumans weren't rich and that Bess had to pitch in and work to make ends meet.

When Roosevelt died unexpectedly in April 1945, Bess was catapulted into the job of first lady. Eleanor offered to hold a news conference to introduce Bess to "the girls," the female White House correspondents (no male reporters were allowed in Eleanor's press briefings, although many asked to be included). When Bess declined to continue the regular press briefings and announced her intention to quit the practice altogether, the troubles began.

Spurned, the women reporters responded with a torrent of criticism, comparing Bess unfavorably to Eleanor. The negative publicity hurt. Bess attempted to smooth over the problem by inviting female correspondents to a tea, but when she didn't make any newsworthy remarks the effort to conciliate was doomed. Thereafter, Bess Truman never had an easy relationship with the media. The White House press office instituted a practice of special briefings for "lady correspondents" on Bess's schedule of activities, and interviews were permitted with the first lady through written questionnaires. Still, it was no substitute for genuine access. By the end of Truman's presidency, less than one-third of the women with press credentials to attend the briefings bothered to come.

Nevertheless, the bad press did nothing to diminish Bess's power behind the scenes. Within months of being sworn in as president, Truman had to decide whether or not to use nuclear weapons against Japan. White House insiders report that after one particular closed-door meeting on the war, both Harry and Bess were uncharacteristically grim faced. While some historians maintain that Bess was not consulted by her husband about the decision to use the atomic bomb against Hiroshima and Nagasaki, there is persuasive evidence that Harry did ask her advice in helping him decide in favor of using atomic weapons.

Truman's public approval rating rose to an astronomical 87 percent in a Gallup poll taken after the Japanese cities were devastated. This was a level no president reached again until President George W. Bush briefly hit 92 percent during the military retaliation against the Taliban regime in Afghanistan in response to the terrorist attacks of September 11, 2001. Truman had finished what the Japanese had started at Pearl Harbor, and for a brief interlude he enjoyed a honeymoon with the voters.

Social events at the White House had been curtailed during the war years, but in January 1946, the first lady triumphantly restored the Washington social season. Once again there were formal state receptions, White House dinners, and afternoon teas. She developed a reputation as a gracious hostess, even if her conversation remained discreetly limited to small talk. Still, the press would not give Bess a break. When fashion reporters critiqued her dowdy appearance, Harry rose to her defense by saying that she looked exactly like a happily married housewife of twenty-five years should look. It was the housewife image that finally turned up favorable press coverage for Bess. As men returned from the fighting, their top priority was to make up for lost time with sweethearts and wives by settling down and raising families. It was the beginning of the Baby Boom, and family values were in vogue. When Bess invited the members of her hometown bridge club to the White House, the press covered the event positively. As the Latin craze hit America, Bess decided to learn conversational Spanish and enrolled in a thirty-two-week course along with many other Washington wives. When she offered to host her Spanish classes at the White House, the media loved it. The gathering of Washington wives was reported as if it were an ordinary get-together of a neighborhood women's group. Independence, Missouri, was an archetypal American town, and the press began to portray Bess as a product of her environment; Bess's hometown connections began to receive press attention as well. *The New York Times* ran a magazine feature in 1946 calling her the "Independent Lady from Independence."

After the long years of the depression and the war, Americans craved a return to domesticity, and homemaker Bess Truman embodied the values that were coming into vogue. Still, despite Bess's newly found popularity, the Truman presidency did not have an easy time in the immediate postwar period. Unemployment for discharged veterans was high, and while the G.I. Bill helped ease the pressure on job markets by giving ex-servicemen and -women money to attend college, the overall economic downturn hurt Truman's popularity. His domestic initiatives—legislation affecting civil rights, federal aid for education, and national health insurance, collectively called the Fair Deal—fared poorly in the Republican-controlled Congress. Before long, Truman's 87 percent approval rating had plummeted to 50 percent, and his chances of winning the 1948 presidential election were in doubt.

Without making her role public, Bess plunged into campaign planning. She might remain silent, even stony faced, among groups of political figures, but she was listening carefully and making her own assessments. Later, she would privately offer Harry her counsel. He acknowledged that she was often a better judge of character than he was, and had the capacity to detect phoniness in those who wanted to use him.

A handful of insiders knew the extent of her true influence. One was India Edwards, vice chairwoman of the Democratic National Committee. She thought that Bess was a shrewd political player. White House aide Clark Clifford also understood the extent of Bess's influence over Harry's decisions on people, policy, and political strategy. Clifford believed Bess's assessment of prospective appointees for domestic assignments as well as diplomatic posts was particularly keen, and Truman benefited from her counsel by selecting competent people to carry out his polices at home and abroad. Yet the Trumans were careful never to make a public statement about Bess's role even given the tremendous precedent set by first lady Eleanor Roosevelt.

Was it a conscious effort to differentiate between Bess and Eleanor? While she was beloved by the majority of the public, Eleanor Roosevelt's political activism had made her a lightning rod for criticism. When she reached out to African Americans, her detractors attacked her for debasing the White House and reopening sectional wounds between the North and the South. When she participated in organizations with socialist ties, Eleanor was accused of being a communist and even the FBI opened an investigation into her associations. The crises of the depression and World War II and Eleanor's remarkable role in restoring America's morale overcame the criticisms, but whether her brand of political activism would have been tolerated in more normal times is an open question. With a return to prosperity, homeownership on the rise, and suburbs blossoming across the landscape, America simply may not have been ready to embrace another Eleanor Roosevelt.

Any desire Bess might have had to emulate the former first lady dissipated quickly in Democratic Party infighting in the run up to the 1948 election. A movement to place Eleanor on the ballot as President Truman's running mate infuriated Bess, because the draft-Eleanor movement was widely touted as a remedy to Truman's perceived weaknesses. One of the factors panicking the Democrats was caused by the new science of political polling then still in its infancy. Polls consistently showed Truman running behind Republican challenger Thomas Dewey. The methodology these polls used, however, was faulty. They were primarily polls conducted over the telephone—at a time when many poor and rural voters lacked telephones. This led to an error known as "undersampling" of lower-income voters. Because many of Dewey's supporters had telephones, the polling methodology was skewed in his favor. If the polls had been conducted door to door, the results would have been more objective. (Author's note: Even with door-to-door polling, bias can still result. In the late 1980s, when Nicaragua held a presidential election, American pollsters were eager to see whether the ruling party's Sandinista candidate Daniel Ortega would win or whether his challenger, Violeta Chamorro, would triumph. To measure the poor population accurately, they used door-to-door techniques. But many of the interviewers who carried out the door-to-door polling wore T-shirts bearing the colors of the Sandinista political party. Many people being interviewed suspected that the pollsters were affiliated with the governing Sandinista party. As a result, many people falsely told the interviewers they would vote for the ruling party candidate, and the American pollsters inaccurately predicted that Daniel Ortega would win. Only one pollster, an Oxford-educated Argentine named Felipe Noguera, accurately forecast that Chamorro would win. Noguera had taken great care to ensure that his polling interviewers did nothing to bias the results, including making sure that none of their clothing reflected the party colors of either side.)

Even though the polls were wrong, Truman still had an uphill political battle on his hands. His Fair Deal civil rights initiatives angered southern Democrats and caused a split within the Democratic Party as the "Dixiecrats" broke away to form the States' Rights Party. They nominated South Carolina governor Strom Thurmond (until recently the oldest member of the U.S. Senate) to run for president as the States' Rights Party candidate.

To make matters more difficult, the Republicans had co-opted many of Truman's policies by voicing support for their own version of the Fair Deal legislation. Shrewdly, Truman guessed that the Republicans were only pretending to support his progressive legislation. To call their bluff, Truman convened a special fifteen-day session of Congress and challenged it to pass the legislation. When Congress did not go along, Truman had his campaign theme. He ran against the "do-nothing" Eightieth Congress.

Just when his election prospects appeared hopeless to all—even Bess— she rose to the occasion. When Truman decided to stump the country by train in his famous whistle-stop tour, speaking from the back of the Ferdinand Magellan railroad car in town after town, Bess and Margaret went with him.

Bess appeared alongside Harry at each stop, where he proudly introduced her as "the Boss." Other than to say a few words to welcome the crowds, Bess didn't make speeches. But she participated in the daily campaign strategy sessions with the inside advisers. She continued to edit Harry's speeches also, sharpening the prose, punctuating them with one-liners, and cutting the length because she thought they were often "too verbose."

When he won the election, it marked one of the most famous comebacks in presidential history. The whistle-stop campaign made the difference. On a tour of thirty thousand miles, Truman delivered more than three hundred speeches and reached six million people. As one of the unsung political strategists responsible for the outcome, first lady Bess Truman deserves credit for the Truman's comeback.

The second Truman term was rocked by the communist takeover of China and the Korean War. To the American public, the Korean War appeared to be a civil war between the communist North and democratic South Korea. After World War II, Korea, which had been occupied by Japan, was divided between North and South at the thirty-eighth parallel. After a series of border clashes in 1950, North Korea launched an invasion of South Korea. Outwardly, the war had the appearance of a domestic conflict. What the public was not told at the time was that the newly created Central Intelligence Agency knew that Soviet premier Josef Stalin had collaborated with China in attacking American troops on the Korean peninsula. Russian pilots were flying the MIG aircraft that fought the newly created U.S. Air Force in the skies. These intelligence secrets were not made public until the fiftieth anniversary of the Cold War in 1997. Truman's knowledge accounts for his speed in dispatching U.S. troops to South Korea. Within hours of the invasion by the North, Truman ordered U.S. Navy and Air Forces to begin moving to the combat zone. Later, the United Nations Security Council voted to send international troops to protect South Korea, but the United States provided the majority of the forces.

Bess and Harry Truman knew the truth behind the sudden surge of Marxist expansion around the world because of the CIA briefings. Truman had no illusions about the fact that the Soviet Union and China were collaborating against the United States and the West. The response was the Truman Doctrine, which committed the United States to a global defense of freedom. The Truman Doctrine is widely considered to mark the beginning of the U.S. response to the Soviet-initiated Cold War, which had evolved when Stalin reneged on agreements to hold democratic elections in Eastern Europe and commanded Soviet military aggression toward Turkey and Greece. Idealists such as Eleanor Roosevelt still believed that the goal of world peace was attainable through treaties and better mutual understanding. While Truman used Eleanor in the United Nations, however, he knew from personal experience in the trenches that America was facing a new and different kind of war that called for military strength.

Unfortunately for Truman, one legacy of the Roosevelt administration was a government bureaucracy staffed with political activists, many of whom were socialists and communists. The fall of China in 1949, in fact, was widely blamed on sabotage from within the American government. While it is true that the Soviet Union gave the Chinese communists large amounts of U.S. military equipment that had been given to Russia under the World War II Lend-Lease program to fight Germany, and that the United States did not similarly equip the Chinese nationalists fighting under Generalissimo Chiang Kai-shek, there were many reasons why Mao Zedong's communists triumphed. Even if some American officials sympathetic to the communists exercised influence to block assistance to Chiang Kai-shek, that would not have been a decisive factor in the final outcome.

Nonetheless, the debate over "Who lost China?" was politically potent. Soon the House Un-American Activities Committee and Senator Joseph McCarthy of Wisconsin began holding public hearings to expose

what they called "twenty years of treason." We know now, because of secret Soviet intelligence files released after the collapse of the Soviet
Union, that McCarthy was more right than wrong. There were Soviet
spies high in the Roosevelt administration, most notably presidential aide
Harry Hopkins. The Soviet Union tried to infiltrate Hollywood for the
purpose of influencing the mass media to undermine America's government, operating through the American Communist Party, which it subsi-
dized heavily with money, and other front groups to recruit sympathetic
directors, writers, and actors. (Author's note: The Soviet intelligence services were so convinced that Hollywood could be controlled that as late as
1986, a Soviet KGB officer operating under the pseudonym Sergei Zavarotniy argued with me that Reagan's friends in Hollywood were produc-
ing anti-Soviet films at the direction of the White House in order to whip
up "anti-Soviet" hysteria that would make the American public more
supportive of Reagan's defense buildup. Our conversation took place following a conference of Mexico's Institutional Revolutionary Party, the
PRI, in Guanajuato, Mexico. At the end of the conference, at which I was
one of two official U.S. observers, my travel plans back to Mexico City fell
apart when powerful Mexican labor leader Fidel Velasquez literally took
over the last flight of the weekend to Mexico City for his delegates to the
conference. Because I needed to urgently return to Washington, D.C., I
hired a car and driver to go to Mexico City. When Zavarotniy, who needed
to return to his embassy in Mexico City, learned that I had a car, he asked
to ride with me. During our four-hour trip we debated a range of topics,
from Gorbachev's reforms policies—glasnost and perestroika, meaning
"openness" and "restructuring"—to Reagan's Central American policies.
As examples of his belief that Hollywood was being used to propagandize
the American public, Zavarotniy cited the films *Red Dawn, An Officer and a
Gentleman,* and *Top Gun.*) Given the Soviet Union's handling of its own
film industry in order to propagandize the Soviet people—even film titans
such as Sergei Eisenstein were never free of Stalin's editorial control—it
is unsurprising that the Soviets would want to use similar techniques of
propagandizing through mass media in other countries.

The McCarthy and HUAC hearings ultimately hurt Truman's presidency, especially after the conviction of State Department aide Alger
Hiss for perjury. Hiss had passed top-secret U.S. government documents
to Whittaker Chambers, a spy for the Soviet Union, in 1938. Hiss had lied
about his role when called before the committee, and was prosecuted
twice for perjury. His second trial in 1950 resulted in a conviction and a

five-year prison sentence. (Although Hiss supporters for many years defended his innocence, recently disclosed Soviet archives show that Hiss
was in fact a Soviet agent.)

Against this background, Truman quarreled with his top military commander over Korea. General Douglas MacArthur had become a hero during World War II by liberating the Philippines. He staged an unorthodox
but brilliant military maneuver in Korea. Instead of landing his troops far
to the south in territory still held by South Korea's defenders, MacArthur
chose the risky tactic of landing at Inchon in the the middle of the country, behind the North Korean lines. The surprising assault initially drove
back North Korean invaders, who had advanced far enough to occupy the
South Korean capital of Seoul before MacArthur's counterattack. Then
Chinese troops invaded.

MacArthur knew that the secret intelligence showed China and the
Soviet Union had been allies in the war all along, and that the real enemy
wasn't in North Korea's capital of Pyongyang but in Beijing and Moscow.
He pushed for an all-out war against China. Truman didn't believe that
Korea was worth starting a third world war over. He was furious when
MacArthur disobeyed his order not to speak out publicly about their differences, and fired the popular general in a famous encounter. In April
1951, Truman flew to the Pacific to meet with MacArthur, who also arrived by aircraft from the Far East. At the airport, General MacArthur, in
a war of wills with the president, initially refused to leave his airplane and
tried to make Truman come to him.

MacArthur's insubordination didn't last long. He relented and left his
airplane to meet Truman, who relieved him of command. Truman's own
mother-in-law questioned the wisdom of dismissing such a competent
general, but Bess defended Harry's action. There is little doubt that she
and Harry discussed the move in advance and mutually agreed on its necessity.

Another matter of less urgent necessity arose when the leg of first
daughter Margaret's piano busted through the floor. One of Bess's main
contributions to the White House itself was a thorough renovation during
Truman's second term. After the piano incident, Bess began a concerted
campaign to secure funds to restore the building. She was genuinely worried that its historic character not be lost and was fearful of its collapse.
Structural engineers certified her concerns, and Bess began lobbying for
funds, even calling House Speaker Sam Rayburn for support.

The most expensive proposal involved saving the original walls of the
White House, while lining the interior with steel beams for strength. The

cheaper alternative—favored by many in the media and Congress—was to simply bulldoze the White House and replace it with a new structure. Bess would not relent and allow the historic building to be destroyed. She lobbied congressional spouses she knew from the Congressional Club, called on former first ladies, and even made one of her rare public statements urging public support. She prevailed, securing eighty-five million dollars for the renovation of the White House.

In keeping with Dolley Madison's instinct to save White House furnishings from being burned by the British, Bess Truman protected the White House itself from being destroyed.

The Trumans retired from politics in 1953. The combination of the Korean War and the domestic inflation it caused had taken a toll on his public approval, and when he left the White House his popularity was at an ebb. Heavy government defense expenditures drove up prices for many commodities, resulting in inflation on the home front. Although Congress gave him power to reinstitute wage and price controls, it was too late to check the runaway inflation—though the controls did lead to riots in steel mills by angry workers. He withdrew from public life to write his autobiography. He and Bess traveled to Hawaii and Europe, but made Independence their home. Harry Truman died in 1972.

Bess lived for another decade. Truman's reputation was revived posthumously, to her delight. In 1974, Bess accepted the post of honorary chairwoman in the reelection bid of Missouri senator Tom Eagleton. Two years later, at age ninety-one, she did the same for Congressman Jim Symington in his Senate campaign. In a Gallup poll, Bess was named one of the twenty most admired women in America—and professed not to understand the reasons why she had been included.

Bess Truman died in 1982 at the age of ninety-seven.

Mamie Geneva Doud Eisenhower

First Lady: 1953–1961
34th Presidential Administration
Siena Research Institute Rating: 17

Pretty in Pink

For the second time in less than one hundred years, a victorious military commander became president. Like the Grant administration, the new administration that came to the White House in 1953 brought a first lady who had not ascended through the political ranks. There the similarities between the two women ends.

Julia Grant aspired to high society and accepted bribes and gifts from her Robber Baron consorts. Mamie Eisenhower had developed a strong sense of ethics. Although she had been born to easy affluence, the majority of her twenty years as a military spouse had been solidly middle class. As an officer's wife, she knew duty, self-sacrifice, and team camaraderie. To a nation whose middle class was finally on the rebound after the long years of depression and war, she was the perfect icon.

Mamie quickly became immensely popular. She set fashion trends for other women to follow. Her name and image were used more extensively in merchandising than those of any previous first lady since Frances Folsom Cleveland. She was deluged with mail, averaging seven hundred letters a week, each of which she tried to personally answer. She was a political asset on the campaign trail and in the White House.

Mamie learned early in her marriage the shape her life would take. As a newlywed, Ike returned from work at Fort Sam Houston to quickly pack his gear for a training deployment in the field. When she protested the long absence, his response was terse. "Mamie, there's one thing you must understand," he told her. "My country comes first and always will. You come second."

Mamie Eisenhower was born in Boone, Iowa, in 1896. Her mother was a Swedish immigrant whose family spoke their native language at home. Her father's family had come to America in 1639 and counted among its ancestry one of the founders of Guilford, Connecticut. The family had prospered in the livestock trade. When doctors advised John Doud to move to a more temperate western climate for the sake of his wife's health, he was able to retire from business at the age of thirty-six and pay cash for a large home in Denver, Colorado.

Mamie was ten years old at the time and spent the rest of her childhood in the West, alternating between the family's summer home in Colorado and a winter home in San Antonio, Texas. She was educated in public schools and showed no interest in attending college. Popular and pretty, she was more interested in social pursuits than in academics.

She met Dwight Eisenhower in October 1915 in San Antonio, Texas, during a visit to Fort Sam Houston. Ike was the officer of the day and volunteered to personally escort the vivacious eighteen-year-old around the grounds. Their attraction was immediate and mutual.

Second Lieutenant Eisenhower soon started courting Mamie regularly. Mamie's father liked Ike, although he doubted his daughter's ability to live on a lieutenant's pay of $167.67 a month. Financial realities, however, would not deter Mamie. They were engaged on Valentine's Day, 1916, only five months after their initial meeting at Fort Sam Houston. In July, they were married in Denver at a small ceremony in the Doud residence. She was nineteen, and he was twenty-five.

In the summer heat, Mamie and her husband moved into the quarters for married junior officers at Fort Sam Houston. During the next four and a half decades of Eisenhower's public service, by Mamie's count, the couple had thirty-seven different homes.

From the start, Mamie was determined to prove the couple's self-reliance. She took over managing the household spending and the family finances. She could easily have asked her wealthy father for financial help, and probably would have received it. Throughout the years, he delighted in periodically giving the young couple new cars. But Mamie didn't want to rely on her family for their support. To cut back on Ike's mess bills from the officers' club, she quickly learned to cook meals and pared forty dollars a month in expenses. She selected clothing carefully so that it would be stylish, but not faddish, and therefore wouldn't need to be replaced so soon. Some months they had only a quarter left when payday rolled around, but Mamie delighted in her ability to stretch the military pay.

It was a pattern she would continue as first lady. When she took over management of White House social functions and events, one of the staff members presented a dinner menu to the president for approval before showing it to Mamie. When he subsequently presented it to her along with the explanation that the president had seen it, she quickly set him straight. Mamie explained firmly that she would make all such decisions in the future herself. She managed White House entertaining and menus and social functions as she had done throughout Ike's military career, by taking charge and handling every detail meticulously.

During Eisenhower's prewar military career, Mamie and Ike were stationed across the United States, in Central America, and the Philippines. At Fort Meade, Maryland, their three-year-old son Doud Dwight Eisenhower, nicknamed "Icky," died of scarlet fever. Mamie was only twenty-four, but death had already been a frequent visitor in her life. All of her grandparents and two of her sisters had died. When their second son, John Sheldon Doud Eisenhower, was born the year following his elder brother's death, Mamie's protective instincts verged on obsessive.

Icky's death strained the Eisenhower marriage. For a while, Mamie's behavior became extremely giddy, bordering on mania. Ike worried that she was verging on a nervous breakdown. His response wasn't entirely healthy, either. To avoid further pain from the loss of a child, Ike distanced himself emotionally from his second son, John. Statistics show that 70 percent of couples who lose a child suffer marital problems, many ending in divorce. But under the guiding hand of Virginia Conner—the wife of Ike's commanding officer in Panama, General Fox Conner—the couple bridged their differences. Mrs. Conner helped Mamie face the crisis in their marriage. She encouraged Mamie to immerse herself in the social duties of an officer's wife and to schedule more time alone with Ike. Mamie changed her hairstyle, adopting the bangs that became her trademark. The emotional and physical makeover signified Mamie's resolve to reengage in her marriage, and in Ike's career. Meanwhile, General Conner tutored the promising young Eisenhower in military history and strategy. By the time they left Panama in 1924, Eisenhower was a better officer and the marriage was once again vibrant.

Part of Mamie's determination was to be a partner in her husband's career. Military life places a high value on cohesion and bonding among the individuals who make up any military unit—at the level of the infantry squad, the platoon, the company, the battalion, and the overall life of the base. In peacetime, this means spouses must be an active part of the military base's social life. Cohesion in combat is the difference between a military unit that can fight and one that falls apart under stress. Between wars, the camaraderie is maintained through parties, dinners, entertainment, and galas at the noncommissioned officers' clubs and the officers' clubs, in which spouses play a part.

Mamie turned each Eisenhower home into a gathering place for other military couples. Since youth, her personality had been suited to social activities. Now she took naturally to the role of hostess, welcoming newcomers, putting guests at their ease, conversing easily and with a sincerity that made people feel she had a genuine interest in them. At base after base, wherever they lived became known as "Club Eisenhower" because of their frequent entertainment.

Mamie's embrace of the duties of a military spouse helped Ike climb through the ranks, but opportunities for advancement in the peacetime military were few. On the eve of World War II, he was still a lieutenant colonel. By 1942, however, Eisenhower was made commanding general of all U.S. forces in Europe.

His promotion made Mamie a subject of interest to the press and the public. She spent the war in Washington, D.C., where as Ike's wife she could easily have had access to the top political circles and the social elite. Instead, she declined most invitations to parties and dinners, convinced that it would show an extreme insensitivity at a time when Americans everywhere were making sacrifices for the war effort.

She devoted her days to helping in war drive efforts like the American Women's Voluntary Services. For the three years between 1942 and 1945, she saw her husband only once. They wrote volumes of letters, to each other, but correspondence couldn't fill the void entirely. Although many Eisenhower defenders contest the truth of Kay Summersby's assertion that she and Ike had a romantic affair when she served as his military aide during the war, her 1975 book *Past Forgetting: My Love Affair With Dwight Eisenhower* is explicit. She was a pretty young Irish woman many years Mamie's junior. She never asserts that they had a sexual relationship—by her account, Eisenhower was impotent throughout the war years—but makes clear that it was a romantic love affair, which she believed would end with Ike divorcing Mamie to marry her. At the time she wrote *Past Forgetting*, Eisenhower was dead and Kay herself had terminal cancer. She had run into Eisenhower only once after the war, and it was just a brief encounter near his New York office in 1948. He told her continuing their affair was "impossible," according to Kay's account. Although Mamie forgave Ike, rumors of the affair would dog the couple for years. To counter Kay's assertions, Mamie authorized her son to publish the intimate correspondence between her and Ike during the war. The result was *Letters to Mamie*, which clearly shows Eisenhower's love for her. Eisenhower biographer Stephen Ambrose believes that while Ike was attracted to Summersby, his commitment to Mamie was stronger.

After the war, Eisenhower served as the army chief of staff for three years, and then retired to accept the offer to become president of Columbia University. Their hard-earned prominence made the couple fixtures on the New York social scene, and for the first time Mamie moved in the circles of high society.

In 1951, President Truman pressed Eisenhower back into service as commander of the North Atlantic Treaty Organization, and Mamie and Ike made another move—this time to Paris. As NATO supreme commander in war-ravaged Europe, the Eisenhowers were sought after by heads of state and the royal families of Europe. Her social skills, which Mamie had polished so well during a lifetime in the military and in New York's academic, financial, and social circles, were now expanding to include entertainments with foreign dignitaries and diplomats. No first lady ever entered the White House better prepared for the social duties of the office.

During his entire military career, Eisenhower had carefully followed the constitutional dictate that separates the military from political affairs. When he retired in 1948, both political parties tried to recruit him as a presidential candidate, because neither knew whether he was a Republican or a Democrat! He didn't disclose his political affiliation until 1952, when he ran against Democratic nominee Adlai Stevenson as the Republican presidential contender. Eisenhower beat Stevenson with 55 percent of the popular vote in an electoral college landslide of 442 to 89. He was the first Republican president since 1933.

Mamie was an asset to the GOP ticket during the presidential campaign of 1952, although she didn't give political speeches and kept a relatively low profile with the press. Nevertheless, wherever she appeared at Ike's side, the crowds shouted for Mamie. One columnist who covered the campaign guessed that Mamie's popularity with the voters added an extra fifty electoral college votes to the Republican column. At campaign whistle-stops, Mamie greeted supporters who came to the Eisenhower train and shook hundreds of hands. When she appeared before a crowd, she might not have said much, but she communicated with hearty waves and full-voiced greetings to supporters that came across as heartfelt. Press photographers loved her willingness to pose for photographs. She enjoyed campaigning before the crowds, and the crowds thrilled to her.

Mamie gave her first—and only—press conference as first lady in March 1953. Normally, she preferred more controlled media access by granting one-on-one interviews to reporters. She had learned during her long years as a military wife to publicly separate her opinions from those of her officer-husband, never commenting on affairs under his command. She carried this practice into the White House, avoiding controversial issues and deferring public comment on politics and policy. She refused a publisher's offer to write a regular newspaper column like Eleanor Roosevelt's "My Day," because she didn't want to be drawn into the same political role Eleanor had played. Mamie believed her role as first lady was to help her husband entertain visitors at the White House, to support him in his campaigns, and to let him and his advisers handle political and policy decisions. She saw the role of first lady as an extension of the role of an officer's wife that she had fulfilled throughout her adult life.

Even as first lady, Mamie remained down-to-earth. When she was com-
plimented on a hat assumed to be a Paris original, she remarked offhand
that she had purchased it mail-order for $9.95. Her favorite television
shows were *As the World Turns* and *I Love Lucy*. The show's cast—Lucille
Ball, Desi Arnaz, William Frawley, and Vivian Vance—became the first
television actors invited to the White House when they came to a reception in 1953. Like the Reagans, the Eisenhowers often preferred to eat
dinner from trays while watching television shows. The first lady was
mentioned in an episode of *I Love Lucy* (Mamie did not appear on the
broadcast), which purported to show that Lucy and Mamie weren't part of
the golfing set. It was an imaginative fiction. Mamie had become an accomplished golfer while stationed in the Philippines before the war. But
it was part of the developing bond between the middle class and the unpretentious first lady, who actually seemed not to belong to the country-
club set.

She soon became a fashion icon. Her favorite color was given a special
name by the Textile Color Institute, "First Lady Pink." It soon became
the most popular color of the decade, extending beyond clothes to paint,
linoleum, and ceramics. Her bangs—a style she adopted in the mid-1920s
in Panama—again became fashionable in the '50s. Merchants used her
image to promote their products aggressively—without any compensation to Mamie.

She drew a firm line between the West and East Wings of the White
House. The East Wing was her domain, and she didn't tolerate any interference from the West Wing in her affairs. When one Eisenhower policy
aide thought it made sense to hire a woman liaison to all the women's organizations the first lady supported, the chief of staff didn't even broach
the idea with her. He knew Mamie would not be managed by the White
House staff.

In turn, Mamie stayed out of presidential affairs. She entered the Oval
Office only four times during the eight years of the Eisenhower presidency, and then only when she was invited. While she had a reputation
among the staff for expressing her views behind the scenes, sometimes in
strong terms, she drew a firm line between Ike's duties as president and
her own convictions. She did sometimes send notes to the spouses of
White House staffers or cabinet members, expressing the president's satisfaction in their performance, but this was no different from what she
had learned to do with subordinate officers' spouses during their military
life. It was part of the job of building cohesion and morale.

During her tenure as first lady, health matters affecting Mamie were kept from the press and public. When she underwent a hysterectomy and dropped from public view, she was accused of "inactivism." She also had an inner-ear imbalance that sometimes caused her to sway uncontrollably when she walked, to the point of lurching into walls and doors. The public was never told, and when vicious rumors that she was often drunk were spread about, some people believed them. Had Mamie not considered her health her own private affair, she might have been spared the criticism.

In fact she liked cocktails and parties, especially theme parties. She was the Martha Stewart of her era when it came to holidays. For a Halloween event, she decorated the White House with cornstalks, had orange bulbs put in the chandeliers, and even included witches' heads in the decor. She hosted similar theme parties for St. Patrick's Day and Easter. The Eisenhowers set records for entertaining, handling seventy official state visits in their two terms in office.

She had unusual, but effective, working methods. Because of her health, Mamie had to schedule herself carefully. She found that she could work best by scheduling blocks of activity interspersed with periods of rest. She typically spent mornings in her pink bed, holding meetings with staff to discuss scheduling matters, going over invitations and menus, and handling the correspondence she felt obliged to answer personally. She often stayed in bed this way until noon.

But the pattern of one of her work weeks shows how busy Mamie managed to be. In just one week, she met with the Women's Forum on National Security, the National Association of Real Estate Boards, the National Institute of Catholic Women, the National War College Officer's Wives Club, the National Association of Medal-Winners of the French Resistance, the Women's Group of the American Savings and Loan Institute, and the National Federation of Business and Professional Women's Clubs. There were so many requests for meetings with the first lady that she could hardly accommodate them all. In 1953, she became honorary chair of the Crusade Against Cancer.

When Eisenhower ran for reelection in 1956, Mamie was again an asset on the campaign trail. He was reelected with 57 percent of the popular vote in a second face-off with Adlai Stevenson. Several months before the election he had a heart attack, but it didn't harm his reelection prospects.

Mamie now added the American Heart Association to the health-related causes she championed. As a result of her efforts, Mamie was praised by the organization for helping increase donations by 70 percent and increasing the number of AHA volunteers by three-quarters of a million people.

One of the most notable developments of the Eisenhower presidency involved advances in civil rights. In Eisenhower's first term, the Supreme Court ruled that "separate but equal" schools violated the Constitution. School integration became the law of the land. When Arkansas governor Orville Faubus defied federal court orders, President Eisenhower sent federal troops to Little Rock to enforce desegregation. It was also in his second term that Eisenhower signed federal legislation to enforce voting rights. These were the first significant civil rights enforcement actions since Reconstruction.

Mamie played a role in the new era of civil rights. She had fully supported Ike's controversial decision to send federal troops to Arkansas. Publicly, she expressed thanks to African Americans at public events. She sent a handwritten note to a ninety-four-year-old former slave. She endorsed the hiring of E. Fred Morrow, the first black man appointed to a nonclerical job in the White House. She wanted black singer Marian Anderson to sing the national anthem at their inaugural ceremony—the first black woman ever to perform at a presidential swearing-in. Anderson's rendition of the anthem won powerful applause. When Mamie revived the White House Easter egg hunt after its wartime suspension, she made it an integrated event for the first time, so that Washington's African American children were welcome to come. These are only a few among many instances in which the first lady used her power to set an example of social change for the rest of the country to follow. Other first ladies, notably Eleanor Roosevelt, had tried to reach past the barriers separating the races, but none did so as persistently and publicly as Mamie Eisenhower.

Ike was seventy years old when he left office. Mamie was sixty-four. Their eight years in the White House had featured growing tension with the Soviet Union, a CIA-backed coup in Guatemala, a CIA plan under way for the invasion of Cuba at the Bay of Pigs, and the embarrassment of seeing pilot Francis Gary Powers being shot down over Soviet airspace in a U-2 spy plane. The last two years of Eisenhower's presidency were clouded by these developments, and he left the presidency with a speech warning about the power of the military-industrial complex and its influence over the political system.

The prime-time farewell address was broadcast on radio and television on January 17, 1961. Eisenhower recapped the historic changes that had taken place during his lifetime. The Cold War had put the country on a permanent war footing, with a large standing army and an arsenal of weapons always on alert. Eisenhower viewed the development with alarm. "This conjunction of an immense military establishment and a large arms industry is new in the American experience," he warned. ". . . We must guard against the acquisition of unwarranted influence, whether sought or unsought, by the military-industrial complex. The potential for the disastrous rise of misplaced power exists and will persist."

Despite the ominous tone of the speech, Eisenhower's farewell address went down well with the public and the press. America was entering a new age of superpower status, and the soldier-politician warned that not all enemies were external. The changes inside America required to keep up the Cold War were, in his view, also potentially threatening to our democracy. Presidential scholars rank Eisenhower No. 9 among all presidents.

In the Siena Research Institute poll, Mamie does not rank among the top ten first ladies. The academics give her an overall score that ranked her as No. 17. It is unsurprising that the professoriate ranks her rather low compared to her husband. Mamie was a populist first lady who embodied the traditional mores of her era, especially when it came to sex roles. These 1950s values are precisely what many see as Mamie's deficiency. This colors most people's perspective on Mamie Eisenhower's accomplished handling of the job of first lady, and downplays her genuine contribution to the progress of civil rights.

Dwight Eisenhower died in 1969. Mamie outlived him by a decade. She died of a stroke on November 1, 1979. One month before her death, Barbara Walters asked her in a television interview how she wanted people to remember her.

"As a good friend," she said.

Jacqueline Lee Bouvier Kennedy

First Lady: 1961–1963
35th Presidential Administration
Siena Research Institute Rating: 7

"I think the major role of the President's wife is to take care of the President and his children."

Not since Elizabeth Monroe and Louisa Adams in the early nineteenth century had the White House so resembled a royal court. It was even given the nickname "Camelot," the royal household of Arthurian legend. Throughout the history of the republic, there had been two dramatically different approaches to the job of first lady: There were the "democratic" first ladies, like Abigail Fillmore and Frances Cleveland; and there were the "four-year queens," like Harriet Lane and Helen Taft. Then there was Jacqueline Kennedy. Arguably, no first lady had ever achieved her level of glamour, erudition, and cosmopolitan savoir faire.

Jacqueline Lee Bouvier's early life was characterized by affluence and privilege. She was born on July 28, 1929, in Southhampton, New York. Her father, John Bouvier, was a well-to-do stockbroker who claimed to be descended from French aristocracy. Because of his womanizing, her parents divorced when Jacqueline was eight years old. In 1942, her mother, Janet Lee Bouvier, married Hugh Auchincloss, a wealthy, twice-divorced stockbroker who welcomed Jacqueline and her sister, Lee, into his life. Jackie began dividing her year between summers at the Auchincloss estates in Virginia and Rhode Island and the academic year at Miss Porter's School, a private boarding facility in Farmington, Connecticut. Her peers at Miss Porter's gave her the cruel nickname "Jacqueline Borgia," for the infamous Borgia family known during the Renaissance for ruthlessness toward rivals, but perhaps their intention was merely to highlight something regal in the teenage Jackie's bearing.

Jackie was tutored in all the social graces expected from a young lady of the upper class at the time. She had riding lessons—English, not Western—and became an accomplished equestrienne. She was taught ballet, given art lessons, and learned dances suitable for cotillion and the coming-out parties of young debutantes. The polishing paid off. She was named Debutante of the Year for the 1947–1948 social season in New York.

After Miss Porter's School, Jacqueline went to Vassar. She made the dean's list, but reportedly focused more of her attention on boys and dating than academic pursuits. Her junior year was spent abroad in Paris, studying at the Sorbonne and perfecting her French. For the first time in her life, she enjoyed a degree of independence. Later she would call this year in Paris—not the White House, not her time with multimillionaire shipping magnate Aristotle Onassis, nor her days working in publishing in New York—the high point of her life. She dated a young Bohemian with few prospects and dreamed of living in Paris. When she returned to the

States to complete her senior year in college, she attended George Washington University instead of Vassar.

The following year, Jacqueline made an effort to relive her dream. *Vogue* magazine held a Prix de Paris contest in which winning essays would be rewarded with a year's scholarship to the Sorbonne. She succeeded, but Jacqueline's parents opposed her choice, fearing that if she returned to Paris she might become entranced by the life of an expatriate and never return to the States. They wanted Jackie to take her place in American society. As a consolation prize from her parents after she agreed not to go to the Sorbonne, Jacqueline and her younger sister were given an all-expenses-paid summer vacation in Europe.

With her stepfather's help, Jacqueline landed a job with the *Washington Times Herald* as a photojournalist. It gave her invaluable perspective into the workings of the press—knowledge that would serve her well not only in the White House but also in her later life, when dealing with inquisitive reporters and intrusive paparazzi. Between 1951 and 1953, she had her own daily column in the paper. Called "The Inquiring Photographer," it featured light questions such as "Do women marry because they are too lazy to go to work?" along with a photograph of the person being featured. One of her subjects was six-year-old Tricia Nixon, whose father was then Eisenhower's vice president.

She was twenty-three when she began dating Congressman Jack Kennedy in 1952. He was a rich, handsome World War II veteran twelve years her senior. It was the kind of match her parents and, more important Kennedy patriarch Joseph, approved of readily. Joe Kennedy saw in the refined, elegant Jackie the ideal mate to match his son's political ambitions. The couple married on September 15, 1953, in a large ceremony followed by a reception at an Auchincloss estate. Jackie's father, John Bouvier, was supposed to walk her down the aisle but reportedly was too drunk. Her stepfather, Hugh Auchincloss, stepped in to give away the bride. They honeymooned in a villa at Acapulco owned by the president of Mexico.

Jacqueline quickly became an asset to Jack's political career. When he campaigned for reelection to the Senate in 1958, they made joint appearances, including a thirty-minute television broadcast from their home. Jackie's education had included several foreign languages; she was evidently a gifted linguist. She aided Jack in his Senate race by appealing to ethnic voters in Polish and Spanish, calling on them to register to vote and support her husband's candidacy.

Some aspects of campaigning did not come naturally to her. She was initially reticent and reportedly sometimes fearful in large crowds, and she didn't like campaigning with women's groups and the Democratic women's clubs Eleanor Roosevelt had helped create. When Jack won election to the Senate, however, she dutifully joined the Senate wives in their volunteer activities for the Red Cross. Privately, she had a dislike of most politicians and found many of the Senate wives to be too dowdy for her taste.

During the following year and for part of 1960, she was on the presidential campaign trail with Jack during the Democratic primaries. Jackie tirelessly attended the rallies, worked the crowds in small diners in New Hampshire, and met with farmers in Iowa, diligently helping her husband campaign.

She was an immediate hit with the political press. At one event where she wore an electric orange sweater and pink pedal pushers, her appearance riveted reporters. Jackie exuded glamour. Like Eleanor Roosevelt had done, Jacqueline authored a political newspaper column, which was called "Campaign Wife." Jacqueline made television appearances, and appeared in Jack's stead when his Senate duties prevented him from going on the campaign trail. After he won the Democratic nomination, however, she scaled back her political activities. She had had miscarriages in the past, and was pregnant with John Kennedy Jr. at the time; she didn't want to compromise the pregnancy. "John-John" was born on November 25, shortly after the election that his father and vice presidential candidate Lyndon Johnson won by a mere 0.2 percent, then the closest popular-vote margin yet. In the electoral college, the Democratic ticket fared better, with 303 votes to the Republicans' 219.

The Kennedys were the first young couple with a growing family to occupy the White House since Teddy and Edith Roosevelt, and they fascinated the public and the press. Jackie was only thirty-two years old when she became first lady. At forty-three, Jack was the youngest president ever elected. Their children, daughter Caroline and son John Fitzgerald Kennedy Jr., were frequently photographed at play in the White House and on the grounds, capturing public affection.

Jackie quickly emerged as one of the country's most glamorous first ladies. Although Mamie Eisenhower had been a fashion trendsetter, she was nonetheless thoroughly in sync with the middle-class values of her time. The appeal of Jacqueline's glamour represented more than a desire to copy her fashion tastes. With her cultured refinement, self-confident presentation, elegant entertaining, handsome husband, attractive family, facility in French, and ability to dazzle even Charles de Gaulle with her worldly savoir faire, Jacqueline Kennedy embodied the Cinderella fantasies of millions of American women. She lived in what was later nostalgically referred to as "Camelot," and women everywhere envied and idolized the image she projected.

Her fan mail averaged eight thousand letters a week. Her trademark pillbox hats became a fashion rage. Her bouffant hairdo and sleeveless two-piece outfits were copied everywhere. The poet Robert Frost compared her to another great first lady, Dolley Madison.

Not everything about the new first lady was as superficial as beauty and fashion. Beginning when he served in Congress, Jackie had used her language skills to translate foreign articles and books for Jack, including French texts on "Indo-China," as Vietnam and the surrounding countries were then called. President Kennedy told selected aides to go to Jackie when they needed his attention on an important matter they didn't want to share with other White House staff. There is no record of her substantive involvement in the great political crises of the Kennedy presidency, the botched invasion of Cuba at the Bay of Pigs or the tense standoff with the Soviet Union known as the Cuban Missile Crisis. But it would be misleading to suggest that she did not play some role in White House affairs, even if it was to serve as a conduit to her husband for selected advisers.

The Kennedy White House projected an appealing cultural image. While Ike and Mamie entertained television actors such as Desi Arnaz and Lucille Ball, President Kennedy preferred Hollywood stars like Angie Dickinson and Marilyn Monroe or performers like Frank Sinatra. Jacqueline hosted cultural events like the performance of cellist Pablo Casals and violinist Isaac Stern. Teddy Roosevelt's daughter Alice Roosevelt Longworth was a guest of the Kennedys for Pablo Casals's performance. She had first heard him play in the White House in 1904, when her father was president.

On becoming first lady, Jacqueline Kennedy surveyed the condition of the White House and said that it appeared to have been furnished from "a wholesale furniture store during a January clearance." It was not an exaggeration. The White House that is familiar to contemporary Americans, with its classic eighteenth- and nineteenth-century early American furnishings, exists largely because of Jackie Kennedy's efforts.

She formed a Fine Arts Committee to collect museum-quality pieces of period furniture from around the country. The committee was chaired by a connoisseur of early American furniture, Henry Francis Du Pont. The fourteen-member committee also helped raise funds to buy the furnishings.

Jackie showed off her results to the entire nation on February 14, 1962, when CBS televised a tour of the White House hosted by the first lady. Ratings showed that forty-six million people tuned in for the broadcast. Her renovation of the White House has endured over the years. Her efforts were so successful that soon there were enough authentic eighteenth- and nineteenth-century furniture and objets d'art to decorate other ceremonial government rooms such as the State Department's seventh-floor diplomatic reception rooms.

Jackie also helped establish the White House Historical Association, a nonprofit organization created to educate people about the White House and its traditions. It was established on November 3, 1961. Over the past forty years, the association has raised an additional nine million dollars through the sale of books, White House Christmas ornaments, and tour guides. The money is used for the continued upkeep of the White House's historical furnishings. Jackie was the inspiration behind the sale of White House guidebooks.

As first lady, she also supported the arts and culture. She persuaded de Gaulle to exhibit Leonardo da Vinci's priceless masterpiece, the *Mona Lisa*, in the United States. She was chairwoman of the Washington School of Ballet Foundation, served as an advisory board member of the American Symphony Orchestra, and held special events at the White House for noted performers and artists.

But in some respects, Jackie could be a temperamental first lady who valued time spent riding horses in the country or waterskiing with friends over the incessant duties of a presidential wife. Jacqueline occasionally refused to attend state dinners in honor of visiting foreign dignitaries and heads of state. She often missed scheduled events she had previously agreed to attend, leaving Vice President Johnson's wife, Lady Bird, to stand in for her, sometimes at the last minute. Her behavior verged on becoming a political liability. When a group of congressional spouses threw a lunch in the first lady's honor, she snubbed them to attend the ballet instead.

Still, when she traveled overseas with the presidential entourage for foreign summits, the multilingual Jackie was a diplomatic asset. She dazzled crowds in Colombia and Venezuela by addressing them in Spanish, and charmed adversaries such as the Soviet Union's Nikita Khrushchev.

She rarely traveled with her husband for domestic political trips. She made an exception for a trip to Dallas, Texas. November 22, 1963, was to become Jackie Kennedy's defining moment as first lady. Unlike Mary Lincoln, who was literally prostrated for more than a month by her husband's assassination, or Margaret Taylor, who was too grief-stricken by President Zachary Taylor's sudden death in office to attend his funeral, Jackie Kennedy's poised reserve throughout the ordeal of John Kennedy's assassination helped reassure a stunned nation.

Never before had a presidential assassination and the subsequent state funeral been a televised event. The powerful new medium carried the sensation of shock into homes across America with unprecedented immediacy and personal impact. It gave millions of Americans a participatory role in the events surrounding the Dallas shooting and made the entire nation eyewitness to tragedy.

The thirty-four-year-old widow began planning the details of the funeral for the slain president before Air Force One had even returned to Washington. Using the funeral for Abraham Lincoln as a model, she directed that her husband's body would lie in state in the East Room just as Lincoln's had done.

Jackie's almost serene, stoical poise and John-John's salute as the caisson carrying his father's coffin passed were unforgettably etched in the American mind. The young widow's loss of innocence, the children suddenly fatherless, created two paradoxical feelings among the public. One was a lasting public sympathy and protectiveness for her and her offspring; the other was an insatiable appetite for news about them. During these times, on television, the mythical Jackie was created. The image transcended the flesh-and-blood woman who had served as first lady for the previous twenty-two months.

It is difficult to assess a myth. Legends and fables have a powerful role in any culture. Americans craved them after the Kennedy assassination, and one that emerged to fill their need was the myth of Camelot, a calculated glorification of the Kennedy presidency. Another is the myth of Jackie, whose glamorous life would fill newspaper tabloids and gossip columns for the rest of her days.

The Kennedy presidency was tragically incomplete. In foreign policy, Kennedy displayed great presence of mind and extraordinary presidential leadership during the Cuban Missile Crisis of 1962, easily the most dangerous confrontation of the Cold War. But he also bungled badly with his halfhearted execution of the CIA's plan to invade Cuba at the Bay of Pigs in 1961, and then continued ill-advised covert actions to assassinate Cuban leader Fidel Castro. He made the first extensive commitment of U.S. troops to Vietnam, opening the way toward what would become one of the costliest, deadliest, and ultimately most futile military engagements the United States undertook throughout the fifty-year-long Cold War. Yet he also created the Peace Corps and challenged Americans to put a man on the moon by the end of the decade, rallying the nation's idealism and spirit of achievement.

In domestic policy, Kennedy's most noteworthy initiatives remained unfulfilled at the time of his death. Like Eisenhower, Kennedy faced opposition from southern politicians—most notably Alabama governor George Wallace—to desegregration. Kennedy didn't hesitate to send federal troops to enforce integration. It would fall to his successor to pass the domestic Great Society legislation Kennedy might have pushed had he lived.

Jackie Kennedy remarried in 1968. Aristotle Onassis, whom she had known when she was first lady, was twenty-three years older than she. He died in 1975, leaving her with a share of his estate valued at more than twenty million dollars. She pursued a part-time career in publishing, working for Viking Press and later Doubleday. In early 1994, she was diagnosed with non-Hodgkins lymphoma. She died in May of that same year, a few months short of her sixty-fifth birthday.

The Siena Research Institute poll ranks Jackie Kennedy among the all-time top ten first ladies, at No. 7. This is considerably higher than the overall ranking of 15 that presidential historians assign to President Kennedy. If one rated Jacqueline Kennedy's role as first lady entirely by the power of the image that she projected, she would rank even higher. In fact, on this sole attribute the Siena Research Institute survey ranks Jackie as No. 2. But her rating for integrity is 18. Eleanor Smeal of the Feminist Majority Fund believes the low rating for integrity stems from Jackie's remarriage to Onassis and the belief among many that this in some way betrayed John Kennedy's memory. Professor Tom Kelly of the Siena Research Institute agrees.

Nonetheless, Jacqueline Kennedy remains revered by millions of Americans for whom the myth of Camelot will always exert a strong appeal.

CLAUDIA TAYLOR "LADY BIRD" JOHNSON

FIRST LADY: 1963–1969
36TH PRESIDENTIAL ADMINISTRATION
SIENA RESEARCH INSTITUTE RATING: 6

"It is a good time to be a woman. It is a good time to be alive."

Lady Bird Johnson was well practiced in the social role of first lady even before Lyndon Baines Johnson was sworn in as president aboard Air Force One as it returned from Dallas, Texas. She was even more practiced as a politician. Jackie Kennedy was first and foremost a socialite for whom politics had never exercised great attraction. Lady Bird Johnson was the opposite. Not since Eleanor Roosevelt had a first lady with such vast political experience served in the White House.

Claudia Alta Taylor was born three days before Christmas in 1912. Her eccentric mother died when she was only five years old. Claudia was raised by her father, Thomas Jefferson Taylor Jr., an African American nurse who gave her the lasting (and detested) nickname "Bird," and a spinster aunt from Alabama named Minnie.

Lady Bird—the prefix was added later when Claudia entered public life, although the nickname stuck immediately—had a privileged upbringing despite the loss of her mother. Thomas Taylor was an affluent businessman who had married up the ladder socially, and Lady Bird's mother's relatives doted over her. She grew up splitting her time between East Texas and Alabama, summering at health spas in cool northern climates and spending her school years in Texas. She was only fourteen when her father gave her a car to drive to school; during the next summer vacation, Lady Bird and a teenage friend drove the car to Alabama to visit her relatives.

Lady Bird showed precocious intelligence. She graduated from high school at the age of fifteen. Because she was considered too young for college, she spent the next two years at the St. Mary's Episcopal School for Girls in Dallas.

By the time she enrolled at the University of Texas in the state capital of Austin, Lady Bird had not only her own car but also an open-ended Neiman-Marcus charge account, courtesy of her father. She completed a bachelor's degree with honors in 1933 and also received a teaching credential. The following year, she added a journalism degree and learned shorthand.

A mutual friend introduced her to Lyndon Baines Johnson in 1934. He was twenty-six years old but had already embarked on a political career in Washington, D.C., working for a member of Congress. He was brash and self-confident, and he proposed to her on the same day they met! To impress her with his seriousness, he took her to meet his parents. Within a few days, he had to go back to Washington, but he deluged her with letters and telegrams. When he found an excuse to return to Texas a few weeks later, he pressed her to marry him immediately.

While other women might have been put off by Johnson's obsessive behavior, Lady Bird was fascinated and attracted to him. She thought him the most handsome man she'd ever seen and introduced him to her father. He, too, was impressed by Johnson, advised his daughter that some of his best deals had been done quickly, and gave the match his blessing.

They were married in San Antonio, Texas, on November 17, 1934. The wedding ring, hastily purchased at Sears, cost $2.50. That left them with a few days for a short honeymoon in Mexico before the couple returned to Washington by train. A unique political partnership had begun with a whirlwind courtship and romance.

Her new husband expected Lady Bird not only to keep house but also to serve as a political asset in his ambitious career plans. Johnson worked for Congressman Kleberg and drilled Lady Bird in details about the congressional district, the issues that mattered to Kleberg's constituents, and the names and personalities of his major contributors and network of political players.

In 1935, Johnson was appointed director of the National Youth Administration's Texas programs. The National Youth Administration was one of Eleanor Roosevelt's favorite New Deal programs. Along with Harry Hopkins, Eleanor had helped create the NYA to help keep children in school throughout the depression, when parents couldn't afford basics such as school supplies or clothes and were tempted to put children to work to help the family survive. The NYA gave aid to poor children through state governments and provided work opportunities for young people. In one of her letters to Lorena Hickok, Eleanor gushed about a "terrific" day she had meeting with and entertaining sixty NYA staff and administrators.

The chance to demonstrate management skill with the NYA was a great opportunity for the young congressional staffer as well. Although she liked Washington, Lady Bird was delighted to return to Austin. Together, the Johnsons decided to make construction of roadside parks in the often parched and barren Texas landscape the focus of their energies. The NYA projects presaged the highway beautification campaign Lady Bird would embrace almost thirty years later when she became first lady.

Johnson made two crucial decisions in 1937. The first was to take the next step in his political career by running for Congress; the second was his affair with Alice Glass, the mistress of one of Lyndon's wealthy political backers. Lady Bird found herself at a crossroad.

Alice Glass and her friends snubbed and ridiculed Lady Bird to her face; Johnson himself made no effort to hide the infidelity from her. Had she divorced Johnson at this time, the scandal would have dimmed his prospects for winning the congressional seat. Lady Bird, therefore, chose to accommodate her husband's sexual adventurism—the Alice Glass affair was neither the first nor the last throughout their thirty-nine-year marriage. She also gave him the one thing that none of his mistresses could offer Johnson. She shrewdly determined to become indispensable in the arena of his life that mattered most to him—politics.

After consulting Texas politicians about Johnson's chances, Lady Bird determined that he could win the campaign with enough money. Using part of what she had inherited from her mother, she put ten thousand dollars into Johnson's race. Lady Bird's father ponied up another twenty-five thousand. These were enormous sums of money at the end of the depression, and Lady Bird's actions had given Johnson an incalculable advantage over his opponents.

In addition to becoming her husband's chief fund-raiser, Lady Bird threw herself into every aspect of the campaign. In public, she appeared as the dutiful wife; behind the scenes, however, she courted backers whose political endorsements carried clout, and worked with Lyndon on campaign strategy. On Election Day, she was still campaigning for him, making get-out-the-vote phone calls. He won.

From then on they were a political partnership. Lady Bird became a model political wife, currying favor with potential political allies, courting constituents, reaching out to potential adversaries who had become alienated by Johnson's intemperate personality and frequent outbursts. In 1941, he made a bid for the Senate and lost, but Lady Bird recalled it fondly as a "*we* campaign." Politics had become her career, too.

Congressman Johnson decided it was important for his political career to join the military after the bombing of Pearl Harbor. While in the House of Representatives, Johnson held the honorific title of lieutenant commander in the naval reserves. He had no navy experience or combat training. Nevertheless, President Roosevelt dispatched him on a fact-finding tour of the Pacific. It was not a safe job. One plane he flew in came under Japanese fire, and another crash-landed. One year later, President Roosevelt realized he needed to get the politician-soldiers out of the way of the professionals and recalled all members of Congress serving in military units to Washington.

While he served on active duty, Johnson kept his congressional seat. During his absence, Lady Bird not only ran the congressional office but also served as de facto congresswoman. She also took over responsibility for the Johnsons' personal fortunes at this time as well. Lyndon had come under fire for taking illegal campaign contributions and using his influence to get government contracts awarded to political cronies. It was Lady Bird who conceived of a way to create a business that would ease the financial pressure.

Using money inherited from her family, she bought a radio station in Austin. Now Lyndon Johnson's political backers could pay advertising fees to the station instead of giving money directly to him, enabling Johnson to use "personal" funds as his own contributions to his campaigns. It was a perfect subterfuge. In 1951, Johnson used his political clout to get a government monopoly—only the Federal Communications Commission could grant a license to set up a television station—for Lady Bird's broadcast business when she was awarded the only such license for Austin. Eventually, Lady Bird's broadcasting businesses made the Johnsons rich.

A rising political star in the postwar Congress, Johnson was elected to the Senate in 1948 by a margin of just eighty-seven votes. At the age of forty-six, he became the youngest Senate majority leader ever. In 1960, he ran against John F. Kennedy for the Democratic presidential nomination.

When Kennedy won, Lady Bird wept. At first she counseled Lyndon not to accept Kennedy's offer to run as vice president. Like an earlier first lady, Edith Roosevelt, Lady Bird worried that her husband would be eclipsed in the secondary job of vice president. But when he agreed to run, she gave the effort her complete backing. Jacqueline Kennedy was in the late stages of her pregnancy with John Jr. and couldn't keep up with the strenuous demands of a political race. Kennedy asked Lady Bird to campaign in her stead. She did so, making public appearances jointly and with her husband a total of more than 160 times. She hired a veteran newswoman who was loyal to the Democratic Party to coach her in media appearances. She stumped the country, supervised get-out-the-vote efforts, and gave public speeches.

Her role as a stand-in for Jacqueline Kennedy would continue after the election. As first lady, Jackie's interest in presidential events waned when the purpose was purely political. She frequently asked Lady Bird to stand in for her and assume the duties of first lady. At other times, Jackie's abrupt disappearances required Lady Bird to hastily fill in for the absent first lady. Lady Bird developed a reputation among insiders as a capable "pinch hitter."

For five days following President Kennedy's assassination and funeral, Lady Bird and President Johnson respectfully kept a low public profile.

In his first address to Congress as president, Johnson called for the continuation of Kennedy's New Frontier policies. But in his first State of the Union address three months later, Johnson launched his own domestic policy initiative—the Great Society program. It would become the centerpiece of his 1964 election platform.

The Great Society program remains the most sweeping and ambitious domestic policy agenda of any presidency since Franklin Delano Roosevelt. Declaring a War on Poverty, Johnson called for new approaches ranging from the Head Start program for early childhood education to dramatic increases in Social Security and health care along with massive welfare spending. President Johnson also pushed passage of the Civil Rights Act of 1964, which he deemed the most significant civil rights legislation since Reconstruction. The act barred racial discrimination in employment and public accommodations. Over time, it would be enlarged to include affirmative action policies redressing past discrimination.

As she had throughout their partnership, Lady Bird set out to be indispensable to the success of the Johnson administration. She chose for her role model not the glamorous Jackie Kennedy, on whose terms she could scarcely have competed even if she had been inclined to try, but rather Eleanor Roosevelt. While Eleanor had understood social and political causes, Lady Bird understood grassroots politics, the business of courting constituents and building support at the county and congressional district levels, as well as how to get things done in Washington. One was a policy intellectual; the other was a practical politician.

Lady Bird posted a sign on her desk that said CAN DO and set out to help Lyndon achieve his goal of creating the Great Society. She made political appearances in the South in support of the controversial civil rights legislation while insisting in the North that regional biases still lingering from the days of the Civil War not be permitted to make the South "the whipping boy of the Democratic Party." She deserves credit for the passage of the landmark 1964 Civil Rights Act.

During Johnson's 1964 presidential campaign, Lady Bird undertook to unify his support in the South, where resentment against the Johnson administration's civil rights initiative threatened to undermine him. On a train dubbed the Lady Bird Special, she made a whistle-stop tour through the southern states of North and South Carolina, Mississippi, Louisiana, Georgia, Alabama, Tennessee, and Florida. She was careful to call governors and senators in advance of her appearances, seek their advice, and ask them to appear with her. It was a masterful strategy of co-optation. She humbly masked the mission by passing out her recipes for pecan pie, along with campaign buttons in support of her husband, taking great care not to alienate anyone by being too overt about her political role. Meanwhile, her public appearances and speeches reached more than one million voters. It was a subtle balancing act, and she succeeded brilliantly. Political analysts credit her with helping Johnson carry the eight states where she campaigned on the Lady Bird Special.

The Democratic Party knew it had an asset in Lady Bird. Several of her speeches were collected in a small volume and published for Democratic activists and conventiongoers. When President Johnson defeated Republican challenger Barry Goldwater by a margin of sixteen million votes—the largest popular-vote margin ever—Lady Bird deservedly shared in the victory.

Before Johnson's term of office began, Lady Bird launched the beginnings of the campaign for which she would be most recognized as first lady. It began as an effort to beautify America's landscape by eliminating the clutter of advertising billboards and automobile junkyards radiating from the perimeters of America's towns and cities through amendments to the Federal Highway Act. Beautification also included urban areas, where trees and ornamental plants replaced barren lots and scattered trash, often through the efforts of volunteers and youth-employment programs. It was half a decade before the first Earth Day, and there were still no "environmentalists"; the handful of people who cared about the environment in the late 1960s, generally limited to academics and scientists, referred to themselves as "ecologists." Some observers credit the first lady for sparking awareness of the need to balance environmental concerns against other public policy goals. Lady Bird thought jobs and development and growth were important, but not at the expense of destroying the country's natural beauty. She never spoke in the modern environmentalist language of "sustainable development" and similar terms, but she shared in the basic concept.

When the Land and Water Conservation Act of 1964 was amended late in Johnson's term, funding from taxes and fees on mining companies was earmarked for conservation. Lady Bird considers this a groundbreaking precedent that paved the way for environmental legislation in later decades.

In addition to beautification, Lady Bird took special interest in the administration's new Head Start program. Like Eleanor Roosevelt, she enjoyed seeing programs in action. While Eleanor would descend into coal mines or visit relief projects in the field, Lady Bird went to schools to see the Great Society programs at work. She publicized their effectiveness by bringing the press with her as she toured, and then reported her own private impressions on the programs back to Lyndon, who was increasingly occupied with the Vietnam War.

Protestors were now shouting chants like "Hey, hey, L-B-J! How many kids did you kill today?" at demonstrations on campuses and in cities across the country. One of the antiwar protests that embarrassed the first lady most occurred at one of her own events.

To encourage women's active participation in all fields, Lady Bird regularly hosted special White House events she called "Women Doer Luncheons." The guest of honor on one occasion was the African American singer Eartha Kitt. The topic was supposed to be street crime, but Eartha didn't stick to the White House script.

Instead, she brought the protest against Vietnam directly into the White House. Lady Bird was mortified when Kitt accused Johnson of callously slaughtering young American men in Vietnam. Lady Bird rose to the challenge and defended her husband. After the outburst, the Johnson administration retaliated against Kitt by opening an FBI investigation against her. She believed the Johnsons punished her for speaking out by using their political influence to damage her entertainment career, blacklisting her just as Senator McCarthy had done two decades before to others in Hollywood. Newly declassified FBI files support Kitt's contention.

Johnson had inherited the problem of American military involvement in Vietnam from the slain President Kennedy. Defenders of Camelot like to speculate that Kennedy would have curbed American involvement before allowing the war to escalate to more than half a million men in the field. There is no proof for this belief. Columnist Garry Wills, author of *The Kennedy Imprisonment,* notes that the national security advisers who counseled escalating the war under Johnson were the same men who served during the Kennedy administration. Wills concludes that Kennedy would have followed their advice, just as did Johnson.

President Johnson certainly feared that there was no politically viable way for him to disengage from the Vietnam War. Recently disclosed tape recordings of Johnson's Oval Office phone conversations show that he escalated the war simply because he could conceive of no way to end the American engagement that would not also mean the end of his political career. In Johnson's mind, it seems, the real quagmire wasn't in Vietnam; it was in America. He feared being branded soft on communism should he pull out, but in the face of a growing antiwar movement he hesitated to use enough military power to win the war. Ultimately, he kept sending young men to fight knowing that they didn't have enough support to win the war, simply to maintain his own political viability. Johnson's own political survival was what mattered; if fifty thousand young men had to die for the sake of Johnson's political standing, it was a fair trade. Eventually, Johnson's frustration with the futile war and sense of entrapment between bad political alternatives doomed his presidency. Unable to find a way out, humiliated by the Tet Offensive that the Vietcong had launched on January 30, 1968, by simultaneously attacking more than one hundred South Vietnamese towns and the American embassy in Saigon—all targets the U.S. military had thought secure from the enemy—seeing no light at the end of the tunnel, Johnson announced he would not seek reelection.

The legacy of the Johnson presidency has recently undergone reassessment. The administration was initially marked by idealistic activism to tackle deep social inequities. However, the Great Society programs he introduced failed to significantly cut poverty rates and have now cost more than seven trillion dollars in federal spending. Head Start has failed to close the education gap between minorities and the majority, despite ever-increasing budgets. Johnson expanded Social Security and health care for the elderly and the poor, but both programs are now in serious jeopardy given the cost of expanded benefits and the failure of revenues to keep pace. Many of Johnson's Great Society laws were so-called entitlement programs, which created political constituencies who came to think of the government funds they received from the programs as their "entitlement." People believed, for example, that their expanded Social Security benefits came from the money withhold from their own earnings before retirement, when in fact Social Security and Medicare—just two examples among dozens of Great Society entitlements—were expanded so fast that the only way to pay was to tax younger workers more heavily. The constituencies created by these programs resulted in political pressure on subsequent presidents and congresses to keep the benefits level with inflation. Politically, these pressures have been impossible for politicians eager to win reelection to resist. The result is that the political system has been rendered helpless to cut costs or trim benefits until programs reach the crisis point. The combination of relentless increase in entitlement program spending and the escalating cost of the war in Vietnam made the 1970s an extremely difficult era from an economic standpoint, with interest rates that ultimately reached levels unseen since the Civil War. Judged unsentimentally, the Johnson presidency was a failure that keeps on failing, as the nation still has not been able to find ways out of the built-in fiscal crises inherent in his programs. The impending bankruptcy of the Social Security and Medicare systems are cases in point. If the federal government were required to do its bookkeeping under the same laws that apply to publicly traded corporations after the reforms of 2002, the results would show the government has a current annual deficit of $580 billion.

Lyndon Johnson retired to his Texas ranch after leaving the White House. He died in 1973. In May 2002, Lady Bird Johnson was hospitalized in Austin, Texas, after suffering a severe stroke. As a measure of her continuing popularity, thousands of get-well card and letters were sent to her at the Lyndon B. Johnson Presidential Library.

She ranks No. 6 in the 1993 Siena Research Institute poll of academics. But in 1983, Lady Bird Johnson ranked No. 3. The decline in her position reflects the ongoing reevaluation of the Johnson presidency. Still, she has twice been ranked among the top ten first ladies of all time. Her substantial achievements in pioneering new ideas and getting legislation passed to make them realities are extensive enough as to almost constitute an independent political career. It is therefore no exaggeration to say that Lady Bird Johnson took the role of first lady to a new level. She was almost a co-president—not equal in power to Lyndon, but closer than any other first lady since Eleanor Roosevelt.

PATRICIA THELMA CATHERINE RYAN NIXON

FIRST LADY: 1969–1974
37TH PRESIDENTIAL ADMINISTRATION
SIENA RESEARCH INSTITUTE RATING: 18

"Our success as a nation depends upon our willingness to give generously of ourself for the welfare and enrichment of the life of others."

As a teenager, Pat Nixon had the pinched face of a down-on-her luck figure in one of Dorothea Lange's famous photo essays on depression-era families. The first lady—nicknamed "Pat" by her father because she was born the day before St. Patrick's Day—was seventeen when William Ryan, the son of Irish immigrants and a onetime silver miner, died of black lung disease. Three years earlier, when Pat was fourteen, her mother had died from cancer.

It was the middle of the Great Depression. From the time of Pat's mother's death, the adolescent girl had to help bring up her younger siblings, cook and keep house for the family, and labor in farm fields to earn a living.

She had been born in a tent in the mining town of Ely, Nevada, at the eastern fringe of the state during the winter of 1912. Although Ely is geographically in the Great Basin Desert, it can be a bitterly cold place in the winter.

When she was just a toddler, the family moved to a farm in Cerritos, California. Their house was little better than a shack, with no running water or electricity. When Pat was old enough, she joined her parents laboring in the fields, picking fruits and vegetables. In time, so did her younger siblings.

"As a youngster, life was sort of sad," she said in an interview years later. "So I had to cheer everybody up. I became that kind of person."

It was a grim beginning from which education was her only way out. She managed to study hard despite the domestic burdens. When she graduated from high school, she was in the top of her class.

No one paid her way through school, but she dreamed of a college education. It was a ticket for her to escape the poverty of her youth and travel beyond the confines of her narrow world. For a short period, she worked at odd jobs while trying to put herself through junior college, until in 1931 one odd job promised adventure and a chance to expand her horizons.

An elderly couple needed help driving their Packard automobile across the country from California to New York. Although the proposed pay for the three-thousand-mile road trip was paltry, Pat jumped at the chance. In addition to covering her expenses on the road, the couple bought her a bus ticket back to California for the return trip. The result transformed her life.

Her intention was to return to California at the end of the road trip, but once she saw New York she decided to explore its opportunities. She stayed for two years and found work, first as a stenographer. To land a job as an X-ray technician, she took a course in radiology at Columbia University. With the money she was able to save from this job, Pat returned to California to complete her college studies in 1933. This time, instead of going to junior college, she enrolled at the University of Southern California.

It took her another four years to complete her degree, but when she graduated it was with honors. Despite her savings, she still needed to earn money while studying at school. She held odd jobs as varied as a dental assistant and store clerk, and even had small film roles. Armed with her degree, Pat began teaching high school in Whittier, California.

There, she decided to join an amateur theatrical group called the Whittier Players. At an audition, she met a young attorney named Richard Milhous Nixon. He fell in love at first sight. He told her she would marry him one day.

"I thought he was nuts," she said later. But, similarly to Lady Bird Johnson, apparently she didn't think he was so nutty as to not be worth seeing again. It was the beginning of a courtship that lasted two and a half years. Nixon was right about the outcome. They married on June 21, 1940, in a Quaker ceremony. After their honeymoon in Mexico, they moved into an apartment near his law practice in Whittier.

Pat continued to teach after the wedding to augment their income. When the Japanese attacked Pearl Harbor in December 1941, the couple moved to Washington, D.C., where Dick went to work with the Office of Price Administration, which set prices throughout the economy as a wartime measure to keep inflation under control. Pat landed a job there as well. After giving it very serious thought, Dick decided—despite his Quaker upbringing—that he needed to do his part in the war. He enlisted in the navy in 1942.

For a while, she moved with him to military posts around the country while he underwent training. When he was sent to the South Pacific on a combat tour, however, Pat went back to work at the Office of Price Administration. When the war finished, Nixon had risen to the rank of lieutenant commander. The thirty-two-year-old was being courted by California Republican Party officials to run for Congress before he was even out of the navy. They believed his status as a war veteran with experience working in Washington would make him an attractive candidate.

When he agreed and ran for the House of Representatives in 1946, Pat was enlisted in the campaign. It was a tough race against incumbent Congressman Jerry Voorhis, a liberal Democrat who had formerly been a member of the Socialist Party. Pat handled research into Voorhis's record, helped write and type campaign materials, stuffed envelopes, mailed brochures, and even went door to door canvassing, talking to voters to see if they had made up their minds yet, taking note of those who were still undecided and what issues they cared about most. She managed to devote herself full time to the campaign work even though she was pregnant with their first child, daughter Tricia, who was born in February 1946.

Nixon beat Voorhis in a campaign many consider unfair because of Nixon's charge that the liberal Democrat was a communist. Although Voorhis was a socialist, he had never been a member of the Communist Party. It was the beginning of the Red Scare that would culminate in McCarthyism. In Congress, Nixon built his national reputation as a member of the House Un-American Activities Committee investigating Alger Hiss, a Soviet agent who worked for the State Department. At the time, clear evidence of Hiss's complicity as a spy could not be established, but Nixon's skillful questioning managed to trap Hiss in perjury. Hiss was thereafter sentenced to five years in prison. KGB documents released after the collapse of the Soviet Union remove any doubt about Hiss's guilt, but at the time many considered him an innocent victim of Nixon's prosecutorial zeal.

Pat was a partner in Dick's rising congressional career. She not only fulfilled the obligations expected from a congressional spouse but handled office work as well. She typed memos, fielded political phone calls, and helped make the congressional office work smoothly. Nixon was reelected easily in 1946.

In 1950, Nixon decided to run for the U.S. Senate. There were now two young children in the Nixon household—four-year-old Tricia and two-year-old Julie—and Pat was again pressed into campaign service. His opponent was Helen Gahagan Douglas, a minor celebrity who had performed in the opera and on Broadway and was married to a movie actor. He attacked her for having links to the Communist Party, dubbing her the "Pink Lady" and printing his campaign attacks as "pink sheets." Nixon's campaign tactics created controversy, and although he won a lopsided victory it tainted his reputation and earned him lasting enemies among those sympathetic to Douglas.

Senator Nixon was just thirty-seven years old when the Republican Party then drafted him to run as Dwight Eisenhower's running mate in the 1952 presidential election. By now Pat had developed a fear and loathing of politics. She detested the need to attack political opponents, believing that politics brought out the most vicious traits in people. She tried, unsuccessfully, to deter Nixon from accepting the vice presidential nomination.

Her concerns about political attacks were eerily prophetic. During the 1952 campaign, Nixon's career was almost torpedoed by allegations that he had an eighteen-thousand-dollar slush fund at his personal disposal, contributed by Republican fat cats. The only way to counter the charge was to open the Nixon family finances to press and public scrutiny. Pat initially objected at the intrusion into their privacy, but realized that there was no alternative.

In a risky strategy, the family made a televised public defense now known as the "Checkers Speech." The name comes from the Nixons' pet dog, Checkers, who had been given to their daughters as a present. Nixon archly defended himself, noting that his wife, Pat, wore a modest cloth coat instead of fur, and depicting his family as living within their means while being falsely accused of taking what amounted to bribes. It was an emotional performance that went over well with the public and saved Nixon's career. Sixty million people—at the time the largest television audience ever—tuned in to see it. Throughout, Pat stood proudly by Dick's side. He mentioned her three times in the speech, noting that she wasn't on the Senate payroll like many other congressional spouses, including Bess Truman, and that she had a fighting Irish spirit that wouldn't quit. The Checkers Speech introduced Pat Nixon to the nation. The Eisenhower-Nixon ticket went on to win the 1952 election and won re-election in 1956.

As Eisenhower's vice president, Nixon went on fifty-four goodwill tours. Pat often accompanied him on the international trips. They were not easy ones. The Cold War was in its early stages, and in many countries communist agitators disrupted the visits with violent tactics verging on terrorism. During a trip to Venezuela, a communist mob surrounded the vice president's limousine, pummeling it with stones, trying to smash the windows with pipes while Dick and Pat sat trapped inside. Similar tactics were repeated in Lima, Peru. Pat met the attacks so coolly that journalists caught in the mob violence were amazed and impressed by her courage. She was the one reassuring the veteran reporters not to panic!

In Japan, Pat gave a special conference for female correspondents, the first such news conference ever held for women in that country. She did so consciously knowing that she was helping to knock down barriers. On the same Asian visit, she agreed to an invitation to a men's club for the same reason.

By the time the two terms of the Eisenhower presidency ended, Pat's political and diplomatic skills were well honed. As the wife of the vice president, she had functioned as a goodwill ambassador. During a groundbreaking visit to Moscow, she mingled with ordinary Russians at every chance, and engaged in repartee with Soviet Premier Nikita Khrushchev. It was an extraordinary metamorphosis given her background, and *Time* magazine called her "one of the U.S.'s most remarkable women . . . a public figure in her own right."

After losing in the 1960 presidential race against Democratic candidate John F. Kennedy, Nixon returned to his practice of law. Pat moved the family to Beverly Hills, California, and looked forward to privacy for herself and her daughters. Nixon, on the other hand, had the political bug. In 1962, he ran unsuccessfully for governor of California. After the loss, the Nixon family moved to New York.

In 1968, Nixon competed against Ronald Reagan and Nelson Rockefeller for the Republican presidential nomination. He won it on the first ballot. By now, Pat was a campaign veteran. The Democratic Party was badly splintered by the Vietnam War at the end of the Johnson presidency. The Democratic convention in Chicago that year was a police riot, mired in protests. The Democrats nominated Vice President Hubert Humphrey as their presidential contender. Lady Bird Johnson's efforts to keep the South united behind the Democratic Party had been successful in 1964, but now in 1968 the fissures between the party's northern liberals and southern conservatives erupted when Alabama governor George Wallace mounted an independent campaign for the presidency. Nixon's popular-vote margin was extremely narrow, but he won handily in the electoral college in the three-way contest.

Pat was first lady. She seemed first to use Mamie Eisenhower as a model. Although the volume of mail was more than she could handle personally, she managed to reply to several hundred letters each week. Sometimes it took her as much as five hours a day to read and respond to her mail. She handled it as she would have done in a congressional office. If a correspondent had a problem with a particular agency or department or needed assistance, the letter would be routed to the proper offices. If the mail expressed an opinion or voiced support, she would answer in a substantive way that let the writer know the effort to write a letter had been taken seriously. She understood how meaningful it was for average Americans to have direct contact with the White House, and the power a reply had.

In 1969, Pat made the cause of volunteerism her own White House initiative when she launched a national program to encourage Americans to help solve common problems. She visited successful volunteer programs to highlight and publicize their impact on social problems.

More than any previous presidency, the Nixon White House tried to stage the first lady's press coverage to amplify the activities of the president. When President Nixon gave a speech about an energy crisis, for example, the first lady would then tour an energy-conserving model home. When his topic was crime, she visited a juvenile facility. One day the newspaper would report the president's policy speech and proposals; the next day's coverage would feature the first lady illustrating the human dimension of the issue. The idea was to prolong the media coverage so that more people learned about the Nixon administration's actions, while at the same time giving people a concrete example of how a policy would work in their community. There are many instances illustrating this unique coordination between presidential policy priorities and the first lady's scheduling of media events. For the first time, White House planners realized the first lady could be utilized to shape media coverage in ways that were consonant with the president's themes.

Pat continued her international travel as first lady. In 1972, she made a three-nation African goodwill tour on her own. Publicly, she was presented as a presidential "ambassador." Despite the hostile reception during her first trip to Peru, the first lady insisted on returning in 1970 when a devastating earthquake struck the country. The mission to accompany relief flights of volunteer aid to Lima won her great respect from the Peruvians, and she was awarded a special honor, the Grand Cross of the Sun.

Behind the scenes, she was also politically active. Throughout their marriage, the Nixons had functioned as a political team. She shared her advice and views with him openly, attending Nixon's first cabinet meeting and questioning the biting tone of some of Vice President Spiro Agnew's heated rhetoric. She pressed her husband to appoint a woman to the Supreme Court.

Although she had always been reluctant to speak in public, during the 1972 presidential campaign Pat addressed the Republican national convention. She stumped the country making campaign appearances jointly with her husband and by herself when the campaign strategy so dictated.

Pat Nixon was on her way to becoming a high-profile, politically involved first lady when fate intervened. Two years before the landmark 1973 Supreme Court decision legalizing abortion, *Roe v. Wade*, Pat openly endorsed abortion, calling it a woman's personal choice. She backed a movement to amend the Constitution by mandating equal rights for women, and reporters sensed her second term could be a turning point for her. They began writing about the emergence of a "new Pat Nixon."

It all changed one night during the 1972 presidential campaign, when Washington police arrested five men in the act of burgling the Democratic Party headquarters at the Watergate Hotel. At first the act attracted little attention. Then two determined investigative reporters, Bob Woodward and Carl Bernstein, kept digging, and they uncovered links between the men arrested in the Watergate break-in and the Nixon reelection effort. Soon the trail led directly into the White House and the Oval Office itself, where President Nixon was orchestrating a clumsy cover-up, ordering his staff to tell the FBI director that the Watergate break-in was really a a CIA operation that the FBI should not investigate further lest it compromise national security. The scandal grew.

Then Congress opened hearings. On Friday, July 13, 1973, a witness named Alexander Butterfield disclosed that Nixon kept tapes of his Oval Office conversations. The White House tried to stonewall, claiming executive privilege. Nixon continued to fight even after the Supreme Court ordered that the tapes be provided to a special prosecutor investigating the affair. The Democratic-controlled House of Representatives began pushing articles of impeachment. Nixon knew the tapes held conclusive evidence that he himself had directed the Watergate cover-up. As demands for his impeachment grew louder in the House of Representatives, Nixon thwarted the opposition against him by resigning in August 1974.

Pat shared her husband's conviction that his political enemies had unfairly used the Watergate scandal to destroy his presidency. Nixon believed that most politicians spied on one another, and that the Watergate break-in at Democratic headquarters was simply how the game was played. As late as July 1974, she told him not to resign but to fight the House articles of impeachment and, if necessary, keep fighting through a Senate trial.

In the two decades between his resignation and death, Nixon's reputation underwent some rehabilitation. He authored a number of policy books and was active in politics behind the scenes—for example, Reagan's reelection managers Ed Rollins and Lee Atwater privately met with Nixon to seek his views on campaign strategy in 1984.

A balanced view of the Nixon administration's record has to take note of his significant foreign policy achievements. Whereas Johnson had been paralyzed by Vietnam and unable to find a way to disengage, Nixon succeeded in signing a peace agreement between North Vietnam and the United States in 1973. Under Nixon, the United States and Soviet Union signed a landmark agreement, the Strategic Arms Limitation Treaty, to cap nuclear weapons. Nixon's diplomacy, after twenty years of estrangement, paved the way for the reestablishment of relations between the United States and Maoist China.

On the domestic policy front, Nixon created the Office of Equal Employment Opportunity to start affirmative action programs throughout the federal government, expanding on Johnson's Civil Rights Act of 1964. His administration created the Environmental Protection Agency and Congress passed the National Environmental Policy Act, the nation's first significant environmental legislation.

Even after Watergate, the threat of impeachment, and Nixon's resignation, Pat Nixon remained one of America's most admired women, according to a *Ladies Home Journal* poll. Except for rare appearances—accompanying Richard on a return trip to China as private citizens and participating in a few events at the Reagan Library in the early 1990s—Pat withdrew from public view when she left the White House.

She died of lung cancer in June 1993. Nixon outlived her by another ten months.

Scholars rate Nixon's administration in the bottom quarter of U.S. presidencies, at No. 32. Pat Nixon, with a rating of 18 among all first ladies, fared much better than her husband among academics in the 1993 Siena Research Institute poll. However, at that time she had just died, which may have biased the results. In 1982, the Siena Research Institute poll of first ladies put Pat Nixon near the very bottom of the list with a rating of 37.

ELIZABETH BLOOMER
FORD

FIRST LADY: 1974–1977
38TH PRESIDENTIAL ADMINISTRATION

SIENA RESEARCH INSTITUTE RATING: 9

"At one time during my husband's administration I made the smart-aleck remark that a First Lady ought to be paid, she had a fulltime job, and I'm not sure I wasn't right."

After she left the White House, Betty Ford acknowledged that much of her time as a first lady was spent in a mental "fog that was sometimes euphoric, sometimes depressed." It was due to her abuse of prescription medication. Yet more than two decades after leaving the White House, Betty Ford remains proud of her work as first lady.

"My days in the White House left me with many happy memories," Betty wrote in 2001 in a letter of advice to Laura Bush. "I had no qualms about voicing my opinions. . . . Being First Lady is a job without concrete guidelines. Yet, it offers endless possibilities."

In 2001, a panel of academic experts and former staff to various first ladies was convened under the sponsorhip of the National First Ladies Library to assess the job requirements for twenty-first-century first ladies. The experts issued a report on the history of the role with recommendations for incoming first lady Laura Bush. Betty Ford broke almost all the rules set forth in *Laura Bush: The Report to the First Lady.*

The report advises against differing in public with the president. Betty publicly criticized President Ford on policy issues. The report cautions that a first lady should not be controversial or she will detract from the presidency. Betty was deliberately controversial, embracing positions that went beyond the safe zone of political consensus. She went her own way as if she had been independently elected, when neither she nor Gerald Ford had actually been elected at all. Neither Gerald nor Betty had a mandate from the voters. Unlike an elected president and first lady, they had no national base of support. In fact, Nixon had chosen Congressman Ford to replace his previous vice president, former Maryland governor Spiro Agnew, in the cynical belief that the House of Representatives would never vote to impeach him because Ford's congressional colleagues wouldn't want to make him president!

Despite—or perhaps because of—her free-spirited independence, Betty Ford won accolades for her work as first lady. Feminists loved her embrace of the women's liberation movement. She helped erase the stigma of breast cancer, paving the way for open discussion of the disease and its treatment. Her spontaneity at social events also introduced a sense of "dolce vita" into a White House beleaguered by two years of the Watergate scandals. Combined with her husband, Gerald Ford's, penchant for pratfalls, like beaning fellow golfers with stray balls or bumping his head on airplane and helicopter doors, the president and first lady gave the nation respite from the intensity of the Watergate years.

Elizabeth Ann Bloomer was born in Chicago in 1918 and grew up in Grand Rapids, Michigan. Her family was affluent, and Betty's childhood was privileged. While her predecessor, Pat Nixon, had worked as a teenager to support her orphaned siblings, Betty enjoyed summer vacations by a lakeside retreat, was given dance lessons starting at the age of eight, and earned money modeling dresses for a fashion store.

When she was sixteen, Betty's father died of carbon monoxide poisoning. He was well insured, however, and Betty's mother was able to raise the family without any major lifestyle changes. When Betty wanted to continue her study of dance, her mother enrolled her in Bennington College in Vermont.

For two years, Betty pursued her talent. During the summers, she modeled and, befitting a young woman of her social class, joined the Junior League. She already knew she wanted to become a professional dancer at the earliest opportunity and auditioned for Martha Graham's dance troupe. To her delight and surprise, she was accepted. Betty and a college roommate moved to Manhattan.

The starting pay as a dancer was a meager ten dollars per performance, so Betty "moonlighted" as a model with the John Powers Agency. The lithe young dancer, at five feet six inches and 108 pounds, may have been the first professional model with the waif look. Betty's mother sent money to help with her expenses, and she was able to continue taking dance classes at night.

Trouble came when her socialite mother tried unsuccessfully to coax Betty back to Michigan. During a two-week visit to New York, the older woman realized Betty's intent to become a professional dancer would mean she would never return to Grand Rapids to take her rightful place in society. A war of wills ensued in which finally the young Betty caved in to her mother's wishes. She moved back to Michigan on the premise that if she disliked it after six months, her mother would help her return to New York.

It was a fatal derailment. Back in Grand Rapids, Betty hit the party circuit, taught dance, and went back to the department store where she had modeled as a teenager to become a fashion coordinator. She had traded the unpredictability of an artist's life for the security of familiar surroundings.

In 1942, at the age of twenty-four, Betty married William C. Warren, who had been her escort to her first cotillion dance at the age of twelve. A doctor's diagnosis of diabetes kept him out of the military during World War II. After the war, he was completely disabled by diabetes for a two-year period. When he suddenly recovered in 1947, Betty divorced him.

She first began dating Gerald Ford, a war veteran who was just starting out as an attorney, before her divorce was final. By 1948, they were engaged to be married. Gerald ran for the House of Representatives that fall, and barely made it on time for their October wedding because he was out campaigning for votes. They spent their honeymoon campaigning for Congress.

Ford won the election, and he and Betty moved to Washington, where she would live for the next three decades. As Ford's congressional career prospered, Betty was a dutiful political spouse. She stayed in Washington and raised their growing family—between 1950 and 1957 the couple had three boys and one girl—while Congressman Ford's increasing responsibilities had him on the road as much as two-thirds of the year. In 1965, he was elected by the Republican caucus to the position of House minority leader.

As his career flourished and the demands on his time increased, Betty silently resented being left with most of the domestic duties. After being confined to bed after pinching a nerve in her neck the summer before Gerald's election as minority leader, she started taking medication for the pain. The physical injury combined with a strained marriage led to alcohol abuse—and the combination of pills and alcohol amounted to a serious substance abuse problem. Ironically, the Rolling Stones' hit song "Mother's Little Helper," about a homemaker's abuse of medication in order to make it through the day, came out right at the time that Betty Ford began sinking into her mental fog. Her life had become a cultural paradigm—or parody—without her even knowing it, and it was the fate of many others, too.

Her reserve broken down by the drinking and drugs, Betty began to cry uncontrollably. Craving to draw attention to herself, she began fantasizing about getting into a car and driving away from her children and husband. Although she sought help, she managed to keep her substance abuse problem hidden from her psychiatrist. Had she been open about her addiction in these twice-weekly sessions, she might have gotten help earlier and been sober as first lady.

We will never know what a sober Betty Ford would have done as first lady. She told an interviewer that she was a great admirer of Eleanor Roosevelt and wished to have a strong public presence like the older woman. After the torturous Watergate ordeal, the public gave President Ford a honeymoon and, for a brief period, there was a real chance to make an impact. His approval rating, in fact, was 71 percent. Then, almost overnight, Ford's approval rating dropped to under 50 percent after his decision to grant a presidential pardon to the disgraced Richard Nixon.

Almost immediately after Nixon's pardon, Betty faced her own crisis: She was diagnosed with breast cancer. It is difficult to realize this now, given our widespread public awareness of the disease, but in 1974 the stigma of cancer meant that most women didn't discuss it publicly—especially breast or ovarian cancer. Betty decided to break the rules by being candid about her mastectomy. She was a groundbreaker in bringing breast cancer and the need to find a cure to the forefront of public awareness.

In an odd way, she had just found her cause as first lady. It hit while recuperating from the radical mastectomy in Bethesda Naval Hospital. As first lady, she had within her grasp a tremendous ability to reach people. She began thinking of other women who were in the same position as she was in, cancer victims who had just had a breast removed, fearful about their prospects for survival, their attractiveness. She wanted to motivate women to go in for checkups.

It was an epiphany. All she did was mine her own life, be candid, and a repressed and taboo subject was brought into the public dialogue. When she gave a speech to a convention of psychiatrists and acknowledged the help she received through her own therapy sessions, she was given a standing ovation—and it became easier for others to seek help and openly admit their psychological problems. She had finally found her voice.

In 1975, *Time* magazine named Betty one of its "Women of the Year" for her courage in speaking openly about forbidden subjects. She was the first first lady to ever be so honored. Soon polls showed that the first lady was more popular than the president.

Political experts advise that any first lady should not wander into political minefields unnecessarily. In an interview with CBS's top-rated newsmagazine *60 Minutes* later that year, she literally touched on every sensitive political topic imaginable. She suggested that premarital sex might reduce divorce rates. She emphasized her support for the Equal Rights Amendment and legalized abortion. She said that marijuana smoking was as normal as drinking beer. She said it wouldn't surprise her if her teenage daughter Susan was sexually active.

It was too much. Betty's voicing of her opinions so candidly touched off a political maelstrom. A torrent of mail hit the White House, with the letters running two to one against her. A New Hampshire newspaper highly influential in Republican political primaries, the *Manchester Union-Leader,* called her a "disgrace to the White House." Still, many women rallied to her support. One poll showed her climbing from a 50 percent to a 75 percent approval rating. But she had yet to talk about her substance abuse problems.

Like other first ladies, Betty also voiced some opinions privately to her husband. She urged him to appoint more women to high positions in the executive branch. Among those whose selection she influenced was Ford's choice of Anne Armstrong as America's first female ambassador to the Court of St. James, and the naming of Carla Hills to the cabinet as secretary of housing and urban development.

Ford had assumed the mantle of the presidency from Nixon with a promise to the Republican Party that he would not run for the presidency, but in 1976, a presidential election year, he did so anyway. His toughest primary challenger was former California governor Ronald Reagan.

Reagan was against ratification of the Equal Rights Amendment, supported abortion only under limited circumstances, and otherwise was anathema to most of the causes Betty embraced so openly. The first lady threw herself into the political arena, campaigning in all the key primary states, wearing a VOTE FOR BETTY'S HUSBAND campaign button. It was a bitter primary that left the Republican Party badly divided.

Ford went on to face former Georgia governor Jimmy Carter in the fall election. Ford began badly behind Carter, who led him in some polls by as much as 30 percent. Betty campaigned hard for the ticket, and Ford cut steadily into Carter's impressive start, briefly pulling ahead of his Democratic challenger. But in a televised presidential debate, Ford slipped with an answer that seemed to imply that he believed Poland and the other Eastern European nations then dominated by the Soviet Union were in fact free. As the media harped on the gaffe over a period of several days, Ford's slim lead collapsed. Carter beat him by 1.7 million votes, with an electoral college tally of 297 to 240.

Because her husband's voice had given out, she delivered his concession speech to Carter. The distinguishing fact of the Ford presidency was the outspokenness of first lady Betty Ford.

After they left the White House, Betty at last was free to reveal the problem she had kept hidden so many years for fear that it would hurt Gerald's political career. In 1978, after a family intervention forced her to confront her addiction, she checked into the Long Beach Naval Regional Medical Center for drug and alcohol treatment. Once again, her personal experience provided an epiphany. While under treatment, Betty realized many others faced the same addictions. She resolved to use her own experience to try to make a helpful difference for others.

When word leaked out that she was in recovery, the media responded sympathetically. Betty began to receive letters from well-wishers around the country. After she was discharged, she began raising funds to establish a treatment center. The actor-comedian Bob Hope joined her efforts, as did millionaire tire maker and recovering alcoholic Leonard Firestone. The result was the Betty Ford Center for Drug and Alcohol Rehabilitation at Rancho Mirage, California. Since its creation in 1982, the Betty Ford Center has become the treatment facility of choice for celebrities and the wealthy with drug and alcohol problems.

Betty Ford broke many barriers and social taboos as first lady, and has continued to be a groundbreaker after her life in the White House. She has helped remove social stigmas. By so doing, she has taken personal tragedies and made them the basis for helping others. Her accomplishments have paved the way for others whose social consciousnesses transcend class boundaries.

She lives in Palm Springs, California, in retirement with Gerald Ford.

ELEANOR ROSALYNN SMITH CARTER

FIRST LADY: 1977–1981
39TH PRESIDENTIAL ADMINISTRATION
SIENA RESEARCH INSTITUTE RATING: 5

"Choose how you will spend your time, select a few key projects, stand by your convictions, and ignore the criticisms."

Under Rosalynn Carter, the office of the first lady completed its twentieth-century metamorphosis from a mere extension of the presidency into a vital White House organ. Previous first ladies had blazed the trail by campaigning, adopting special projects, using mass media, influencing policy decisions, and taking an increasingly active role in the nation's life. Yet none had approached the job with the discipline and professionalism of Rosalynn Carter and her staff.

For the first time, the first lady hired a chief of staff whose government salary and rank were equal to the president's chief of staff. Under Rosalynn, the full-time East Wing positions grew by almost 20 percent, but more important, she used the staff differently, reorganizing the workings of the office to expand beyond traditional social and entertainment functions.

Rosalynn established a press office and her own research division to keep her informed about policy issues. The all-important roles of scheduling and advance—the detailed work of coordinating the first lady's public appearances and travel—formed a separate branch. Another was devoted to social and personal business. There was also a division for projects and community liaison. Rosalynn's structured approach to the working of her staff was equaled by a focus on clear goals she wanted to achieve as first lady. She utilized her time and resources to their utmost. It made her one of the most successful first ladies ever.

Rosalynn viewed her relationship to her husband, James Earl Carter Jr., as that of political partner rather than political spouse. She realized this long before arriving at the White House. Whether it was during his short-lived navy career, running the family peanut business, or campaigning for and winning a progressive series of elections culminating in the presidency, Jimmy and Rosalynn worked together on terms of equality and mutual respect.

Eleanor Rosalynn Smith was born in August 1927 in Plains, Georgia. Her childhood was happy and uneventful until her father died of leukemia at the age of forty-four. Rosalynn was just thirteen years old when she had to help her mother shoulder the burdens of supporting and caring for herself and her three siblings.

As a teenager, Rosalynn made friends with Ruth Carter, Jimmy's sister. It was World War II, and many of the young men in her age bracket were away fighting. Jimmy, for one, was a student at the Naval Academy at Annapolis. They met in 1945 when Ruth invited Rosalynn to a picnic lunch while her brother was home for a visit.

Jimmy was smitten by the seventeen-year-old Rosalynn, and for months the couple corresponded while he was away at Annapolis. He proposed while at home for a Christmas vacation, but Rosalynn turned him down on the grounds that she was still too young. She was attending a nearby junior college and commuting from home. By February, she changed her mind and accepted his proposal.

When they married in July 1946, Rosalynn became not only Jimmy's wife but also a navy wife. Their home base was at the naval port in Norfolk, Virginia, but Jimmy was often away at sea for long voyages, leaving his teenage wife to manage the household and their first child, Jack, who was born in July 1947. Although she was not yet twenty years old, Rosalynn was learning to be organized and self-sufficient. Through the frequent separations, she was also developing emotional independence.

Other navy assignments took the young couple and their growing brood to Hawaii, California, Connecticut, and finally New York, where Jimmy had won a coveted berth in legendary Admiral Hyman Rickover's fiercely competitive nuclear submarine command. The young Annapolis graduate was marked as one of the navy's rising stars, and no doubt would have climbed through the ranks to the top of the navy's hierarchy had it not been for family problems.

When Rosalynn's father-in-law died, Jimmy felt obligated to resign his naval commission in order to take over the family peanut warehouse business. Although Jimmy's sense of duty prevailed, Rosalynn had gotten a taste of the world, and she thought a return to Plains would be too confining. She enjoyed the life of a navy spouse and wanted her children raised with broader horizons than had been open to her during her childhood in a small town.

Rosalynn and Jimmy began running the peanut warehouse business and expanding its facilities together. They took an active role in Plains's civic and social affairs. In 1962, their life took another fateful turn when he decided to run for the Georgia State Senate.

Rosalynn managed the family business while he campaigned for office, but in her spare time she tried to telephone all the voters in the state senate district and canvassed door-to-door for him. Jimmy lost, but it was a highly irregular election. A missing ballot box was discovered under the bed of a local political party boss's daughter—opened and empty. When Jimmy challenged the voting fraud in the Democratic Party primary (the South was still solidly Democratic in the 1960s, and the outcome of elections was basically decided in the primaries), he was met with heavy-handed intimidation tactics from party insiders that included death threats. He won his court challenge, though, and after a write-in election went on to take a seat in the state senate.

In 1966, Jimmy set his sights higher and made an unsuccessful bid for governor. Rosalynn turned over management of the peanut business to her brother-in-law Billy and became a full-time campaign staffer for her husband. Together they tutored themselves in the political skills they thought important for success. They developed a system to recall the names of people they had met, so that they gave a sense of personal touch to the important backers and contributors they encountered. Instead of campaigning side by side, they often split up to be able to go to more events and meet more voters. When she sighted a radio antenna as she traveled around the state, Rosalynn would drive up to the station and introduce herself as available for an interview. They lost the election, coming in third, but honed the political skills necessary to succeed the next time.

In 1970, Jimmy ran for the governorship a second time. He moderated his campaign themes to the extent that he presented himself as a conservative southern Democrat who nonetheless favored improved race relations. Rosalynn campaigned as aggressively as she had in 1966. She attended campaign events as diverse as a rattlesnake roundup, a tobacco auction, and a hot-air balloon ride. Rosalynn learned to memorize a short set of remarks to use when she was called on to speak publicly. This time Jimmy won.

Rosalynn's initiation into the role of a political executive's spouse came in the Georgia governor's mansion. At first she felt lost, as if her schedule and security requirements dictated what she could and couldn't do, but in time she managed to take charge of her schedule and make it work for her. It seems a simple transition, but many politicians and public figures never manage to fully gain control over their schedules given the multitude of competing demands on their time and energy. Yet every political expert knows that the schedule is the heartbeat of a political life. You either control it, or events control you and your prospects for success are left to chance. Political insiders carefully weigh every public invitation, proposed attendance at a ceremonial event, speaking opportunity, and request for a press interview against the strategic demands of their agenda. If the proposed event helps further the agenda, it is put on the schedule. If it does not advance the agenda, it is declined or shunted off to a staff member or political supporter—called a "surrogate" in political scheduling—to handle. If this system were not in use, political figures would be simply overwhelmed by the volume of demands on their time.

After six months, Rosalynn was ready to take on a visible public role. Her first major appearance involved presenting the governor's mental health program to the Georgia Association for Retarded Children. One of Carter's early initiatives was the creation of a state commission to explore how to improve the state's mental health services. As a member of the commission, Rosalynn toured state and private mental health facilities, building an awareness that would serve her well in the White House.

She also established a populist theme in the governor's mansion that would carry over into the Carter White House. The couple dubbed the executive mansion the "People's House," and to emphasize their accessibility to the voters they scheduled special receptions that anyone could attend. To manage the crowds, open invitations were issued by radio and newspaper announcements to residents of specific political districts, who were then welcome to attend a Sunday-afternoon reception.

Then, in 1975, Governor Carter decided to make a run for the Democratic presidential nomination the following year. As she had done in his gubernatorial campaigns, Rosalynn set out to campaign on his behalf, beginning with the state of Florida. She met with party activists and potential supporters, showed up at local radio stations to seek interviews, and acted as a personal emissary for her husband. It was the beginning of a grassroots campaign that many pundits and Washington insiders dismissed as a hopeless long shot. They had their eyes on better-known Democratic candidates. Carter was derisively dismissed as "Jimmy Who?" by many in the media, but Jim Allen, a dogged political reporter who wrote for United Press International, correctly projected that Carter would win the Democratic nomination.

Carter went on to defeat incumbent President Gerald Ford, the consummate political insider, by a 1.7-million-vote margin and a comfortable 297 to 240 in the electoral college. It was a humbling defeat for Ford, who believed he would easily win the contest, and he and first lady Betty Ford left Washington with great bitterness because they couldn't comprehend how the nation could have chosen a relative political outsider over a veteran career politician. Their mood had probably not been seen since the Hoovers.

The 1974 election was a disaster for the Republican Party. Registered Republican voters, disillusioned by Watergate and unenthusiastic about Ford's candidacy, stayed home in record numbers. Their absence from the polls not only caused Ford's defeat but also rebounded into the House and Senate, where the newly elected "Class of '74" congressmen and senators were decidedly more liberal than the incumbents they defeated. Carter was able to take office with a slate of newcomers in Congress who were politically in tune with his agenda. It was an auspicious beginning for the Carter administration.

Sensing that the nation was in a mood for a fresh tone, the Carter presidency opened on a populist note. The Carters dubbed their inauguration the "People's Inaugural" and walked down Pennsylvania Avenue to the White House instead of riding in a limousine. Rosalynn Carter wore the same blue gown she used when Jimmy was sworn in as governor of Georgia, setting a decidedly unostentatious tone.

The Carter administration continued its populist themes with a series of edicts that combined symbolism with frugality. President Carter wanted the White House staff to use their own cars to come to work, instead of being chauffeured in government automobiles. Thermostats were set at sixty-five degrees inside the White House to conserve energy. Hard liquor was banned from official White House state dinners because by serving only wine the Carters could shave a million dollars annually off the entertainment budget.

Although Rosalynn had her separate staff in the East Wing, the operations of the first lady were well coordinated with those of the president's staff in the West Wing. She attended cabinet meetings, had a weekly working lunch with Jimmy, and acted as his sounding board and political adviser. Publicly, she didn't disagree or push her positions to the exclusion of his agenda, as Betty Ford had done in the Ford White House, but privately she was candid and forthright. This deprived the press of many good stories showing conflict or distance between the president and the first lady, the kind of politically damaging stories that had been a staple during the Ford administration. Rosalynn understood what Betty Ford had not: It did no good for the first lady's polls to soar above the president's if the way she achieved it was to have a separate, and conflicting, political agenda.

As she had done while first lady of Georgia, Rosalynn continued her commitment to mental health issues. Betty Ford had destigmatized visits to the psychiatrist for those affluent enough to afford the fees; Rosalynn Carter wanted public services for the neediest improved. Beginning in 1977, she served as honorary chairwoman of the President's Commission on Mental Health. As first lady, she held public hearings, drafted papers on mental health needs, and issued recommendations for changes in government funding for state mental health programs.

To publicize her commission's work, Rosalynn took her mental health campaign to Hollywood. She lobbied the film and television industry to portray mental illness realistically and with sensitivity, and to use their power to focus attention on the special needs of the mentally ill. Back at the White House, she held meetings and receptions for advocacy groups and urged them to lobby Congress for change. Two months before the 1980 presidential election, Rosalynn's persistence paid off when Congress passed the Mental Health Systems Act, a comprehensive bill that over-hauled federal aid to the states for mental health care.

The Carter administration embraced the Equal Rights Amendment, a proposed amendment to the Constitution that would specifically guaran-tee every woman equal rights to men in all aspects of life from education to employment to social welfare benefits. Rosalynn joined in efforts to pass the controversial constitutional amendment. She also used her influ-ence as first lady to push for the appointment of more women to senior government positions. A record was set when almost one in four political appointments during the Carter administration went to women.

Another precedent was set when the Carter administration dispatched Rosalynn to Latin America in the summer of 1977 as the president's spe-cial representative. Never before had a first lady traveled with this kind of official status. Questions were raised about whether Latin American lead-ers would welcome a presidential spouse whose mission included sub-stantive affairs of state. Yet with some ability to speak Spanish, natural intelligence, and a keen political awareness, Rosalynn pulled off the mis-sion with aplomb.

Although she did not hold regular news conferences for the press, as Eleanor Roosevelt had done, Rosalynn was accessible to the media. In her first year as first lady, she gave almost three dozen individual press in-terviews and held twenty-two press conferences. Rosalynn was sometimes irritated that the media wanted to focus more on what she considered trivial issues—fashion or the social and entertainment aspects of the job—but she generally had good relations with the press.

The promising beginning of the Carter administration, however, soon gave way to events beyond Jimmy's and Rosalynn's control. The high cost of the Vietnam War, coupled with the growth in federal entitlement spending and the damage done to the American economy by the Arab oil embargo of 1973 and rising energy costs, proved disastrous. Interest rates rose as high as 21 percent, while double-digit inflation raged. The result was "stagflation"—a combination of low growth and rampant inflation—that undermined the Carter presidency.

In 1979, Carter was further diminished from within his own party. Senator Ted Kennedy mounted a primary campaign challenge that badly divided the Democratic Party, and though Carter eventually prevailed in winning the nomination to run for president again, his reelection bid was handicapped from the starting gate. He was perceived as being politically weak.

As a result, Rosalynn and Jimmy agreed on a political campaign strategy against Republican challenger Ronald Reagan that was the most negative since Lyndon Johnson's campaign against Barry Goldwater. Just as Johnson had used television to raise fears that Goldwater would start a nuclear war if elected, the Carter team charged that it wasn't safe to have Reagan in the White House. In a town hall meeting at North High School in Torrance, California, Carter warned that the election would "decide whether we have war or peace." Two hours later, to make sure the political reporters who covered the president got the news right, he repeated the same words almost verbatim in a speech to the AFL-CIO convention in Los Angeles.

The lowest blow to Reagan came when, under authorization of President Carter, the cabinet secretary for housing and urban development, Patricia Roberts Harris, delivered a hard-hitting speech that accused the Republican nominee of racism. In the speech, Harris said that Reagan would "divide black and white, rich and poor, Christian and Jew." She finished her race-baiting diatribe by saying that whenever she heard Reagan speak, she was "reminded of the specter of the Ku Klux Klan."

The negative attacks backfired when Carter met Reagan in a televised presidential debate. Polls showed that most voters had decided against Carter, provided that they considered Reagan a good alternative. When Carter returned to the attack in front of a nationwide television audience of millions, trying to invoke his daughter Amy's fears of nuclear war to make his challenger seem dangerous, Reagan responded with a devastating one-liner.

"There you go again," Reagan said, responding to a charge that Reagan opposed Medicare. Polls later showed audiences had interpreted the line as a rebuke to all of Carter's attacks. The same polls showed it was the most memorable line of the debate, and that voters had made their decision; with just four words, Reagan defeated Carter.

Like the Fords before them, the Carters left the White House embittered by defeat. But they had some notable successes in which Rosalynn shares full credit. The most noteworthy was the 1979 Camp David summitry between Israeli prime minister Menachem Begin and Egyptian president Anwar Sadat. In a marathon negotiating session, President Carter brokered a peace agreement between the two nations that stands to this day as a landmark achievement in the war-torn history of the Middle East. In his memoirs, Jimmy credited Rosalynn as a partner who helped him think through every twist in the difficult negotiations that ended thirty-one years of war. His foreign policy leadership is also remembered for an emphasis on human rights.

Both Jimmy and Rosalynn have remained active in political and humanitarian affairs since the presidency. Their work in Habitat for Humanity, mobilizing volunteers to help build homes here and abroad for the poor, has become well known. Former president Carter has also served as a special envoy in delicate diplomatic engagements in such war-ravaged places as Somalia during the Clinton administration.

In the spring of 2002, Rosalynn traveled with Jimmy to meet communist leader Fidel Castro in Cuba. The trip set a new precedent. No U.S. president, sitting or former, had traveled to Cuba since the forty-year-old embargo had been imposed.

In a groundbreaking speech broadcast live and unedited on Cuban television and radio, Carter called for extensive democratic reforms in that nation. After challenging Castro to reform, Jimmy called on President George W. Bush to lift U.S. trade and travel sanctions against the Caribbean nation. As she has been throughout his lifetime, political partner Rosalynn was at Jimmy's side throughout the historic trip. In 2002, Jimmy was awarded the Nobel Peace Prize. The Carters continue to live in Plains, Georgia.

Nancy Anne Frances
Robbins Davis Reagan

First Lady: 1981–1989
40th Presidential Administration
Siena Research Institute Rating: 36

*"Did I ever give Ronnie advice? You bet I did . . . I was the only person
in the White House who had no agenda of her own except helping him."*

Nancy Reagan is the most underrated first lady of the postwar presidencies. Scholars and academics consistently rank her near the bottom, despite the fact that she embodies many of the strongest attributes of the
women who had gone before her. She was an assertive woman determined to use her power inside a White House dominated by conservative
men who, for the most part, were not accustomed to treating women as
their equals. She was active in presidential policy making, the management of White House personnel, and in campaign politics. Her antidrug
campaign set new precedents for her office. During her tenure as first
lady, the White House was a glamorous place visited by artists and performers as diverse as Michael Jackson and Cary Grant. If her role is as-
sessed without partisan bias, she would have to rank among the country's
top first ladies.

At the height of the Iran-Contra crisis—the congressional investigations and independent counsel probe into whether laws were broken
when the Reagan administration sold weapons to Iran and used the financial proceeds to fund Nicaragua's Contras at a time when Congress had
cut off their aid—it was Nancy's intervention that restored the stability of
Reagan's presidency. At the peak of the Iran-Contra crisis, Congress suspected a cover-up at the White House. By moving decisively to bring
Howard Baker into the White House—a respected Washington insider
best remembered for his famous line during the Watergate inquiry, "What
did the president know and when did he know it?"—Nancy quelled talk
of a cover-up.

Her involvement in the firing of Chief of Staff Don Regan was controversial, with the first lady being blamed by many for interfering in White
House personnel decisions that were beyond her scope. But the untold
story is that by the time Nancy acted to convince her husband to fire
Regan, there already was a widespread movement in Reagan's inner circles to oust the chief of staff.

In early 1985, Regan put himself on a collision course with the first
lady. She expected to be treated as an equal in decisions affecting her and
the president, especially in the scheduling of events and speeches.
Regan, however, tried to shut her out. In White House senior staff meetings, the chief of staff openly boasted, "I never let a woman push me
around"—and the first lady wasn't going to be an exception.

By summer, Regan's high-handedness had alienated Vice President
George H. W. Bush. For eight hours in July 1985, Bush was made "acting" president when Reagan underwent an operation for the removal of a
tumor. During Reagan's convalescence, the vice president was expected

to monitor important policy decisions. Friction arose when Regan arbitrarily scheduled two important policy meetings, on South Africa and trade policy, when Bush was slated for travel outside Washington. When Bush asked Regan to reschedule the meetings, the chief of staff refused.

Long before Nancy took action, many in the White House and cabinet had concluded that the chief of staff was trying to usurp power. When one assistant to the president was asked if Regan had ambitions to run for office himself one day, he replied: "Why should he? He's already running the country!" In mid-November 1985, then treasury secretary James A. Baker III held a secret meeting at the Treasury Department to discuss the Regan problem. In attendance was longtime Reagan confidant Michael Deaver. Still, Nancy did not express her concerns about the growing lack of confidence in Regan to her husband.

Nancy, who had long acted as eyes and ears for her husband, was kept aware of the growing discontent. When the Iran-Contra crisis broke in late 1986, Vice President Bush went to the first lady to urge her to persuade the president to make Regan resign. Instead, she urged Bush to tell the president himself. As matters escalated, Regan became more of a liability. Regan thought the political crisis would blow over and opposed conciliatory actions to defuse it. When Reagan wanted to go on television and apologize for selling weapons to Iran, the chief of staff fought unsuccessfully to change his mind. Regan's combative attitude toward Congress threatened to escalate the crisis. At one point former president Richard Nixon talked with Nancy and offered to intervene to get Regan to resign. By the time President Reagan finally ousted him in late February 1987, Regan had made so many political enemies that Nancy Reagan's pressure for his resignation simply represented the consensus view among White House insiders.

Nancy Reagan is a model of a modern first lady. She didn't hesitate to involve herself in decisions affecting the presidency, whether they were over people, policy, or politics. Had Don Regan heeded longtime Reagan aides who cautioned that the first lady was a force to be reckoned with, and listened to warnings about the "icy stare" that foretold Nancy's belief that an aide wasn't loyally serving the Reagan's best interests, he might have fared better.

Long before she arrived in the White House, Nancy had developed a reputation as Ronald Reagan's political guardian. Politics is a realm where it is difficult to find someone who can absolutely be trusted. A running joke among insiders is that in the White House you can tell your friends from your enemies because your friends stab you in front, not in the back.

Even the closest aide or cabinet member has an agenda. Sometimes it's a personal or political ambition; sometimes a deep desire to change policy. Political leaders are always on their guard against being used or manipulated. Reagan's decision-making style favored having strong advisers around him and letting them openly argue their views, so that he could have the benefit of competing ideas before making a decision. In this environment, strong differences among advisers flourished, and Reagan often turned to Nancy as the one person he could absolutely trust.

Nancy used her power in a way many traditional men found upsetting: She was direct. If she had questions about someone's actions or a presidential aide or cabinet member was in conflict with Nancy, there was no uncertainty about it. She confronted people directly and made her views known in clear terms. Through the years, this quality earned her many enemies who didn't hesitate to leak unflattering stories about her to the press. As a result, her public image suffered. Long before she arrived in Washington, resentful men on Reagan's staff derisively called her "Queen Nancy" or the "Belle of Rodeo Drive." Another name that was meant to be demeaning, "Iron Butterfly," can also be construed as a compliment. In an age when many men were still chauvinistic, Nancy was a strong woman who didn't hesitate to use her power. Had she been first lady in the 1990s, this same trait might have been seen as a strength.

She was born in Manhattan in 1923, the only child of Kenneth and Edith Luckett Robbins. Her mother was an actress. The couple separated when Nancy was only five years old and because of the demands of her mother's acting career, Nancy was raised by an aunt and uncle in Bethesda, Maryland.

In 1929, Nancy was reunited with her mother and new husband, Dr. Loyal Davis (he later adopted Nancy), in Chicago, Illinois. At this point, Nancy's childhood took a bright turn. Dr. Davis was prosperous, and the family lived on prestigious Lake Shore Drive. Although her mother no longer acted, friends from her stage career often visited. Nancy was exposed early to celebrity friends such as Spencer Tracy and Katharine Hepburn.

In 1939, Nancy made her own stage debut in the high school production *First Lady*. She was cast in the title role. When she enrolled at Smith College in Massachusetts, Nancy followed her mother's career path and chose to study drama. She graduated in 1943, and returned to Chicago. Dr. Davis was serving in the army in Europe, and Nancy took a job at the Chicago department store Marshall Fields to be near her mother during the war. She also decided to begin her acting career in earnest. She landed roles in touring troupes around Chicago, and eventually was cast in a Broadway production, *Lute Song*, with Yul Brynner. In 1949, with Spencer Tracy's help, Nancy got a Hollywood screen test at Metro Goldwyn Mayer studios.

When they signed her to a seven-year contract that paid $250 a week, she was on her way to an independent career as an actress. She was cast in eleven films and won good reviews for her work. Her film credits include *East Side, West Side, Night Into Morning*, and *It's a Big Country*. In 1950, she met Ronald Reagan. He was then president of the Screen Actors Guild and already politically active not only in industry affairs but also in Washington's growing interest regarding communist influence in Hollywood. When "Nancy Davis" was posted on a list of actresses suspected of having communist ties, Nancy sought Ronald's help in clearing her name within the industry. Nancy's fears turned out to be baseless; another actress of the same name was the "Nancy Davis" in question.

Nancy and Ronnie were married in 1952. He had achieved success in Hollywood entirely on his own merits. He paid his way through college by washing dishes in the women's dormitory and worked as a lifeguard. Upon graduation from Eureka College, he began a career in radio broadcasting. An earlier marriage to actress Jane Wyman failed when she felt he was being drawn too heavily into politics, and Nancy became not only a bride but also a stepmother to two children, Maureen and Michael. They had two more children of their own, Patricia Anne and Ronald Jr., over the next six years.

Reagan's transition from acting to a political career coincided with his marriage to Nancy. In 1952, he became a television spokesman. The job gave him weekly television exposure introducing *General Electric Theater*, and widespread public exposure as he toured the country delivering speeches on public policy issues of the day. Although he was a registered Democrat, Reagan began to grow uncomfortable with the increasingly liberal direction his party was taking. He switched his registration to Republican after endorsing Richard Nixon in the 1960 presidential campaign.

In 1964, Republican presidential candidate Barry Goldwater sought Reagan's endorsement in his challenge to incumbent president Johnson. When Reagan gave a nationally televised speech on Goldwater's behalf called "Rendezvous With Destiny," he became an overnight political sensation. The speech was filled with idealism about America's destiny, and its optimistic tone and delivery was vintage Reagan. Goldwater's presidential bid failed, but Reagan was now a star in Republican circles. The following year he was approached by California industrialists who wanted to back Reagan in a gubernatorial campaign against incumbent Pat Brown.

Reagan accepted the challenge to run in the 1966 California governor's race. It was Nancy's first real introduction to politics. She took an active role in the campaign, making independent appearances on his behalf as well as by his side, and freely fielding questions about his views and positions on the issues. Reagan's campaign manager in the race was Stu Spencer, a veteran political operative who would later mastermind Reagan's 1984 landslide reelection.

Reagan defeated incumbent governor Pat Brown in a landslide. Nancy was now first lady of California. Immediately she established the modus operandi that would characterize her role as a political spouse for two terms of the California governorship, and a further two terms in the White House. She didn't hesitate to question the staff about the rationale for engagements that appeared on the governor's schedule, especially if she thought Ronnie was being overcommitted. She voiced her views on the performance of the people who worked for him, policy issues, and political allegiances. While she was careful in public not to exceed the public's expectations of a political spouse, deferring to her husband, being careful not to disagree publicly or in the press, she was soon recognized by political insiders as an independent woman who didn't hesitate to exercise her powers of judgment. Ronald in turn appreciated her candor, support, and involvement. They were a partnership.

As California's first lady, Nancy made the Foster Grandparents Program her project. It brought together the elderly and children to bridge a mutual need for involvement on the one hand, and parental-style nurturing on the other. Nancy was thirty years ahead of her time in championing the program; it would be the late 1990s before General Colin Powell made a similar appeal for a national mentoring program that worked along identical lines. Another cause she served was to draw attention to the fate of soldiers listed as missing in action in the Vietnam War.

Controversy dogged Reagan's two terms as California governor. The Free Speech movement, which advocated campus "sit-ins" and "teach-ins" and other nonviolent but confrontational tactics, took root in Berkeley and other California campuses as discontent with the Vietnam War widened. There were riots and acts of symbolic terrorism, such as the burning of the Bank of America branches on college campuses at Santa Barbara and Berkeley, with an attempted arson against the bank even in conservative Orange County at the Irvine campus. As governor, Reagan frequently went to the colleges, where he confronted student protestors face to face. The resulting publicity earned Reagan ongoing national attention.

(Author's note: Reagan had help from FBI director J. Edgar Hoover in his efforts to quell campus radicalism. During the 1966 gubernatorial race, Reagan had promised to restore order on California campuses; on January 16, 1967, FBI agents met with Reagan at the governor's mansion in Sacramento. Reagan asked for regular FBI briefings on student protestors, calling them "beatniks, radicals and filthy speech advocates," according to newly declassified FBI files. The documents regarding FBI activities on California campuses and Reagan's relationship with Hoover were released in 2001 as a result of a seventeen-year-long lawsuit filed by the *San Francisco Chronicle* under the Freedom of Information Act.)

In 1976, Reagan made his first serious bid for the White House, running against incumbent president Gerald Ford. Nancy joined wholeheartedly in the campaign, appearing jointly with Reagan as well as independently. She didn't enjoy giving political speeches, but she did participate in question-and-answer sessions and give interviews to the media.

Unfortunately, Stu Spencer was not advising Reagan in the 1976 campaign. A Rockefeller loyalist, Stu had agreed to work with the Ford campaign when Nelson Rockefeller became vice president. Spencer was responsible for the political attack strategy that halted Reagan's advance against Ford. He lost the Republican nomination challenge, but his strong showing in the primaries and among the GOP delegates created a strong foundation for the future.

Over the next four years, Nancy remained active in Reagan's political action committee, Citizens for the Republic (CFTR). She often joined him on the road—he had an active travel schedule making public speeches and campaigning on behalf of Republican candidates for the House and Senate. She also had her own scheduling staff at CFTR's Santa Monica, California, headquarters. They were now building the momentum to run another long-odds campaign against a second incumbent, this time Democratic president Jimmy Carter.

· When Ronald Reagan announced his presidential candidacy in 1980, Nancy was more involved in his political career than she had ever been. She met with his top strategists and advisers in political planning sessions. She traveled to the key primary states, and even overcame her skittishness at making political speeches. When there was trouble in the early campaign and liberal Republican George Bush surged ahead of Reagan in the Iowa caucuses, Nancy was involved.

The 1980 campaign was extremely negative. Reagan's opposition depicted him as an out-of-touch B-grade movie actor. They called him a warmonger whose strong anti-Soviet views might cause a nuclear war. The Carter team charged that if Reagan were president, he would "divide the nation, white from black, rich from poor, Christian from Jew."

Nancy came in for her share of criticism as well. A slip of the tongue during a speech in Chicago—she made a comment about "looking out over all these beautiful white faces"—opened her to charges of racism. When her habit of passing out chocolates to reporters on the campaign plane was ridiculed by a female reporter, who wrote that the retaliation if the offer of candy was refused was to deny any interview requests with candidate Reagan, Nancy's response was revealing because the charge was wrong.

In a self-deprecating gesture, the next time she came down the airplane aisle dispensing chocolates she had a sign around her neck that said TAKE ONE—OR ELSE! It was Stu Spencer's idea. But while most members of the press were smiling at the joke, campaign staff at Reagan-Bush headquarters were told to instruct political supporters to flood the female reporter's newspaper with a torrent of critical letters-to-the-editor and phone calls.

Reagan defeated Carter in the fall election, and for a brief period the Reagans enjoyed a political honeymoon. Trouble began when plans for the inaugural celebrations were announced. The tone was formal, and it was carried out from the swearing-in through the inaugural parade on into the inaugural balls. The style strongly contrasted with the Carters' populist approach, and the media began to report unfavorably on the Reagans' desire to restore an aura of glamour to the presidency. The total cost of the inaugural activities was estimated at sixteen million dollars.

Nancy's inaugural gown reportedly cost more than five thousand dollars. Jackie Kennedy had been praised for her fashion sense, but Nancy was criticized as being too extravagant. When Nancy raised eight hundred thousand dollars in donations to refurbish the White House, instead of being praised as Jackie had been, she was attacked for spending money on new White House china during a recession. It didn't matter that a double standard was at work; the political reality is that Nancy's debut as first lady was disastrous.

Less than three months into Reagan's presidency, John Hinckley wounded

Reagan and several others in an assassination attempt designed to impress the movie actress Jodie Foster. Reagan's humor during the ordeal generated widespread admiration and briefly made the president politically untouchable. That left Nancy as the lightning rod for criticism.

After the inauguration, Reagan staffers entered a White House that was a wreck. Desk drawers held half-eaten meals and molding sandwiches on plates that had been shoved deep into the recessions of drawers. Campaign brochures and pamphlets were left littered on the floors and in boxes strewn throughout offices. Carter's austerity measures meant the White House and Executive Office Building hadn't been maintained for years. Cracking paint peeled away from the walls and ceilings, exposing bare plaster. Threadworn rugs barely covered the floors.

Nancy came under intense criticism for renovating the White House quarters during the ongoing economic recession. Now that Reagan was off limits to partisan attacks, she was fair game. From her selection of a new china pattern to the designer clothes she wore, it was open season on Nancy. By December 1981, Nancy's overall approval rating in a *Newsweek* poll was only 26 percent, although 57 percent approved of the way she handled the duties of first lady.

No first lady has ever come under such intense criticism and rebounded politically. She used a combination of self-deprecating humor and steely determination. To defuse the criticism over her clothes, Nancy appeared at the annual Gridiron Dinner for the Washington press corps and, dressed in old clothes, performed a skit in which she sang lyrics to the tune of "Second Hand Rose." It was a bravura performance from a veteran actress, and the media loved it.

Throughout the latter half of 1981, the White House had been quietly working on a drug policy review initiated by the first lady's interest. Reagan appointees at the Education Department had discovered a promising approach to antidrug education efforts that relied on peer groups to encourage other students not to use drugs. In contrast to other advertising or classroom-based efforts to scare teenagers away from drugs that relied mainly on dire warnings about the long-term effects of drug abuse (research shows these approaches are minimally effective with the young people most at risk), the peer-group approach was highly effective. It was also labor-intensive, requiring a lot of work at the school district and community levels. But peer pressure succeeded where other approaches failed.

After White House presentations of the peer-group approach, the administration embraced the program. So did Nancy. The result was the first lady's "Just Say No" campaign. It was widely mocked by many who misunderstood its intended purpose of reinforcing federally funded grass-roots peer-pressure programs, but it was a public success. The first lady appeared on twenty-three television talk shows to promote the campaign, and convened a first-ever international conference of first ladies to coordinate antidrug efforts. By the beginning of the second term, Nancy's approval rating had soared to 69 percent.

During the 1984 reelection campaign, Nancy was deeply involved. Campaign manager Ed Rollins recounted in 1985 that he had sparred with Joe Frazier for eight weeks at Olympic boxing training camp and "never been so beaten up" as he had by Nancy during an hour-long meeting to discuss planning for the GOP convention. Stu Spencer was in the meeting along with Rollins, Mike Deaver, Lee Atwater, and other senior aides.

"She smelled fear all over you," Spencer told Rollins. From that point forward, Spencer took all the phone calls from the first lady about the campaign. Rollins told his receptionist that if the first lady called, to put the call through to Spencer. Sometimes the receptionist would tell Rollins, "She wants Stu. Stu's not in, so she wants you." Rollins's pat reply was, "Say I'm with Stu."

The first lady's calls came frequently after the Democrats nominated Geraldine Ferraro as their vice presidential candidate. When reporters asked Ferraro how she could reconcile being a practicing Catholic with her pro-choice views on abortion, Ferraro shot back that the press ought to question Reagan's Christianity, because of his lack of compassion for the poor.

The first lady soon got a tip from Roy Cohn that Ferraro's husband, John Zacarro, should be investigated. Spencer soon had a secret operation under way inside the Reagan campaign to delve into every detail of Geraldine Ferraro's and John Zacarro's lives. Nancy called Spencer almost daily to keep abreast of its progress. The result was a barrage of unfavorable publicity for Ferraro and Zacarro, a House Ethics Committee investigation, and eventually a criminal conviction for John Zacarro. Throughout the months-long operation, the first lady was kept fully informed, although most of the Reagan-Bush staff knew nothing about what was happening in the offices adjacent to campaign director Ed Rollins's suite where the anti-Ferraro operation was conducted.

When the campaign ended, Reagan won reelection by the second largest electoral-vote landslide in history—525 to 13.

Nancy was also influential in foreign policy. She and British prime minister Margaret Thatcher sensed at about the same time that the new Russian premier Mikhail Gorbachev presented an opportunity to change the course of U.S.-Soviet relations. She urged Reagan to seize the opportunity to meet with Gorbachev in a summit and try to achieve a breakthrough in nuclear arms control. Reagan's personal aide, James Kuhn, said at the time that this was one of only three issues Reagan cared about deeply. The other two were the Nicaraguan Contras and the Soviet economy. Nancy had a pivotal role in bringing about the thaw in relations between the U.S. and the Soviet Union at a time when many of Reagan's advisers were still urging him to keep Gorbachev at arm's length.

She set a precedent when she gave a speech at the United Nations urging international cooperation in the war on drugs. Nancy was the first incumbent first lady to do so, but this wasn't her only White House precedent. She broke a gender barrier when she chose James Rosebush to serve as her chief of staff. It was the first time a man had worked for a first lady in a substantive position. It was a breakthrough: The job was no longer "women's work."

Even the Reagans' closest aides often sensed a reserve. Carole Kuhn, who along with her young daughter Caitlin often accompanied her husband to Camp David while he served as Reagan's personal aide, noted that the Reagans seemed to have few close attachments. Caitlin called Reagan "the boss," and he seemed to show an interest in the infant, but Nancy was reserved even with the child. Ultimately, there was a change in 1987. Nancy became friendlier to those around her, playing with Caitlin as if she were her grandchild.

Two things happened in Nancy's life that many agree brought new warmth to her. First her mother died. Then Nancy was diagnosed with breast cancer and underwent a mastectomy. She had to cope with her grief and personal health crisis while juggling the demands of the presidency and an upcoming summit with Gorbachev, while enduring a fresh round of criticism in the press from second-guessers who felt that she should have chosen a lumpectomy instead of a mastectomy. Nancy was resilient, but this time something surfaced through the ordeals in addition to her toughness. Carole Kuhn noted that Nancy was a warmer person afterward, as if she had undergone a metamorphosis.

The two terms of the Reagan administration marked eventful years in the nation's life. When Reagan took office in 1981, the Cold War seemed intractable. When he left in 1989, the Berlin Wall had fallen, much of Eastern Europe was free for the first time since World War II, and the Soviet Union itself was beginning to disintegrate. Domestically, the years of stagflation were replaced by economic growth and new prosperity. When the Reagans returned to California after eight years in the White House, Nancy might have thought their days ahead would be calm.

In 1994, however, she faced a new challenge when the former president was diagnosed with Alzheimer's disease. She had written in her autobiography, *My Turn*, that when he was wounded in the assassination attempt and later when he faced an operation for cancer, she feared losing Ronnie and didn't know what she would do without him. But she has been brave in facing the gradual loss that comes with Alzheimer's disease.

Today she devotes her time to helping her husband and raising funds for the Reagan Presidential Library. In the spring of 2002, she received a medal from Congress for her work in the war on drugs.

BARBARA PIERCE BUSH

FIRST LADY: 1989–1993
41ST PRESIDENTIAL ADMINISTRATION

SIENA RESEARCH INSTITUTE RATING: 8

". . . It rhymes with rich."

Beneath Barbara Bush's grandmotherly facade beats the heart of a shrewd political infighter. There are two distinct levels on which to comprehend Barbara Bush: the superficial image, and the underlying reality. Her greatest contributions as first lady have come on the second level, not the first, although her carefully burnished image has served her well on the public relations front. Fresh disclosures in *George* magazine during the 2000 presidential campaign about Barbara's role in her husband's 1988 presidential campaign against Massachusetts governor Michael Dukakis show that she was behind what veteran political reporters Jack Germond and Jules Witcover called "the most mean-spirited and negative campaign in modern day political history."

Americans got their first glimpse of the unvarnished Barbara during the 1984 Reagan-Bush reelection campaign. After Vice President Bush was pitted against Democratic congresswoman Geraldine Ferraro in a vice presidential debate, he foolishly made a boast while within range of a reporter's microphone that he had "kicked a little ass" in the debate. Barbara soon followed up with her own assessment of Geraldine Ferraro, letting the world know that she thought the Democratic challenger was a bitch by coyly saying, "It rhymes with *rich.*"

Although her role was a closely guarded family secret for more than a decade, Barbara's intervention made the crucial difference in the 1988 strategy, according to Bush campaign insider Michael J. Bayer. George Bush could not have won the 1988 presidential race without her. The issue before them was the release of convicted Massachusetts murderer Willie Horton on a weekend furlough program. During his weekend release, Horton viciously attacked a Maryland couple in their own home, repeatedly raping and sodomizing the woman and torturing the man with a knife.

Although Dukakis led Bush by more than 20 percentage points in the polls and appeared headed for a landslide, Bayer says that Bush's chief of staff Craig Fuller resisted making Horton a campaign issue because Horton was an African American and his victims were white. Vice President Bush, an affirmative action supporter whose record in Congress included an early commitment to civil rights, didn't want to exploit the interracial aspects of Horton's crime as Fuller saw it.

The 1988 Bush-Quayle presidential campaign was eldest son George W.'s first presidential election; he worked on the campaign staff. His role, insiders say, was to enforce loyalty and keep an eye on Bush's campaign manager, the late Harvey Lee Atwater. Atwater and George W. saw eye to eye on the need to attack Dukakis as too liberal, with the Willie Horton case serving as their prime evidence. George W. met with his father and mother to persuade them that the strategy meant the difference between winning or losing the presidential race. Barbara agreed with George W., and persuaded her reluctant husband that he needed to use hardball tactics against Dukakis in order to win.

Vice President Bush began citing Horton's crimes in campaign speeches. The infamous Willie Horton television ad was produced by an outside political group with close ties to the Bush campaign. The strategy worked. Dukakis began dropping in the polls. Bush's use of the race issue, however, was so loaded with controversy that Republicans later tried to hide the genesis of the attack strategy. They claimed that they got the idea from Al Gore after he cited Horton in the New York Democratic primary debate against Dukakis. Gore did, in fact, raise the weekend furlough program in the debate, though he never mentioned Willie Horton.

Dukakis was never to recover politically from the attacks. In the fall, Bush won 54 percent of the popular vote and defeated Dukakis in the electoral college by 426 to 111. After the election, Democrats complained of illegal coordination between the National Security Political Action Committee (NSPAC), the outside group that produced the Willie Horton ad, and the Bush campaign. The Federal Election Commission opened a preliminary investigation and concluded that "there were opportunities for coordination between NSPAC and the Bush Committee" and that "several factors would appear to support a finding that NSPAC's expenditures were not independent." But when it voted on a full investigation, the FEC split evenly along partisan lines, so no complete probe ever took place. Two and a half years after the election, when he was mortally stricken with brain cancer, Bush campaign manager Lee Atwater issued a deathbed apology to Michael Dukakis for the underhanded campaign tactics.

Barbara Pierce was born into an affluent life in June 1925 in New York City, the third of four children of Marvin and Pauline Pierce. Her father was the publisher of *Redbook* and *McCall's* magazines. From birth, Barbara was part of a political dynasty: Her great-great-great-uncle was President Franklin Pierce, and her grandfather was an Ohio supreme court justice. She was a child of power and privilege.

She attended public school through sixth grade, and then went to the private Rye Country Day School, in Rye, New York, until her junior year of high school. Her parents sent her to an exclusive private finishing school, Ashley Hall in Charleston, South Carolina, for her final two years of high school education. After her graduation in 1943, she studied for three semesters at Smith College in Massachusetts.

She was just sixteen when she met her future husband, George Herbert Walker "Poppy" Bush, at a dance at the exclusive Round Hill Country Club in Greenwich, Connecticut. Barbara was entranced by the tall prep school student, whom she says rendered her literally breathless. Barbara and George came from similar social backgrounds. His father was a wealthy investment banker who would launch his own political career and win election to the U.S. Senate in 1952. Both George's and Barbara's families emphasized the fact that high public office was the birthright of the rich, although they liked to think of it as "public service," and believed contributing their time and talents to the country was an act of noblesse oblige.

The country-club romance blossomed, and Barbara was "Poppy's" date for his senior prom at the private Phillips Academy in Andover, Massachusetts. Following his graduation from Phillips in 1942, George enlisted in the navy. Their romance continued long-distance while he completed flying school. While on leave, Poppy invited Bar to the family compound at Kennebunkport where the Bushes summered. The teenage couple spent two and a half weeks together. At the end of the vacation, they told their respective families that they were engaged. Bar was eighteen, and Poppy was just nineteen. They set a wedding date for late December 1944.

Anticipating marriage, Barbara dropped out of college. George was sent to the South Pacific, where he began flying combat missions against the Japanese. On September 2, his plane was damaged during a raid and had to be crash-landed into the ocean. Although he was quickly recovered by a submarine, George was briefly listed as missing in action. Bar was sheltered from worry, as George's protective parents withheld the news until they received confirmation that Poppy was alive. She never was aware that her in-laws feared that her fiancé was lost at sea. The couple were married in January 1945. Bar considers it the turning point in her life.

Poppy had deferred his college admission to Yale University when he joined the navy. When he was decommissioned in the fall of 1945, he and Bar moved to New Haven so he could begin studying. At Yale, he joined the Delta Kappa Epsilon fraternity, was inducted into the Skull and Bones Society, and played varsity baseball. Their first child, George W. Bush Jr., was born in 1946. George H. W. also began his lifelong commitment to improving race relations by becoming active in the United Negro College Fund.

Bar and Poppy moved to Texas after his Phi Beta Kappa graduation from Yale in 1948. He went to work in the oil business for the International Derrick and Equipment Company in Odessa, Texas. George was soon promoted and worked as an oil equipment salesman in California, where their second child, a daughter named Pauline Robinson ("Robin") Bush, was born in 1949.

The following year the Bush family moved to Midlands, Texas. Using family money to finance the Bush-Overbey Oil Development Company, Poppy went into the oil business with a partner. A third child, John Ellis ("Jeb") Bush, was born in 1953.

Bar was less than enchanted with the role of mother and housewife. She said later that she often felt as if she'd "never, ever be able to have fun again" and that "George Bush, in his excitement of starting a small company and traveling around the world, was having a lot of fun...."

Then in 1953, three-year-old Robin was diagnosed with leukemia. Barbara and George went to heroic lengths to find treatment that could save their daughter's life, but she died in October after a seven-month battle with the disease. Both parents were devastated by the loss, and Bar began to show it outwardly when her hair began to gray prematurely. The couple had three more children in the 1950s—Neil Mallon Bush in 1955, Marvin Pierce Bush in 1956, and Dorothy ("Doro") Walker Bush in 1959. Meanwhile, George's oil business prospered, and the Texas branch of the Bush family enjoyed the same privileged life as its New England clan.

Bush's political career began in 1962 with a run for chairman of the Harris County Republican Party. Bar enjoyed the give-and-take of politics, although she found she had to curb a combative tendency to speak too openly and attack George's opponents. In his first run for the U.S. Senate in 1964, he lost. Setting his sights lower in 1966, Bush ran successfully for Congress.

Bar's first project as a political spouse was a slide show on Washington's gardens; she presented it to groups of Texas constituents. While Poppy served two terms in Congress, Bar went to social activities for congressional wives, attended briefings at the State Department, and participated in Republican Party events. She also wrote a monthly column that was distributed to Houston newspapers about life in Washington. In 1970, Bush ran again for the U.S. Senate and was defeated.

During the Nixon administration, Bush remained in public service through a series of political appointments beginning with U.S. ambassador to the United Nations in New York. As chairman of the Republican National Committee, Bush was one of embattled President Richard Nixon's most vocal defenders throughout the escalating Watergate crisis. When

Ford assumed the presidency, he sent Bush to China as head of the U.S. Liaison Office in Beijing.

Bar enjoyed her year in Beijing, where she studied Chinese language and culture and enjoyed the diplomatic lifestyle of embassy receptions and the prestige of being the wife of the top American official in the country. With the children back in the United States enrolled in private boarding schools, college, or on their own, the couple had more time for one another. It was a happy time that made them reluctant to return to Washington. Then a second Ford appointment made Bush head of the Central Intelligence Agency in 1975. Before he accepted the job as CIA director, Poppy and Bar called eldest son George W. and asked what he and his brothers and sister thought about the controversial new assignment. The children agreed that their father should accept the job offer.

Bar was depressed after returning to Washington. Poppy spent long hours at CIA headquarters. As her depression deepened, he suggested she seek professional help. She had suicidal urges and long crying spells. Even after first lady Betty Ford publicly acknowledged seeing a psychiatrist, Bar refused to seek help. It was a period of estrangement in their marriage that remains mysterious today. Some biographers have suggested that menopause or a thyroid condition called Graves' disease may have contributed to Bar's depression, but during the Bush presidency rumors would surface in Washington that Poppy had an extramarital affair. One of the names attached to the unproven allegations is that of a woman who worked closely with Bush when he was director of the CIA. Whatever the true cause of Bar's depression, she eventually overcame it and their marriage endured.

In 1979, when Poppy decided to run for the Republican presidential nomination, Bar was an enthusiastic supporter. She maintained a rigorous schedule of events and campaigned in every state but Alaska, presenting her trademark slide shows to audiences eager to learn more about Bush's candidacy. The campaign gained momentum after Bush won the Iowa caucuses, and for a while it seemed the Republican nomination was in hand. But the Bush strategists miscalculated badly in New Hampshire, where a showdown with Ronald Reagan backfired on Bush.

After he won the Republican nomination at the 1980 Detroit convention, Reagan didn't want Bush as his running mate. According to Germond and Witcover's comprehensive account of the 1980 race, *Blue Smoke and Mirrors*, Reagan considered Bush too preppy and wimpish for the job. He tried to broker a deal to have Gerald Ford become vice president, and considered his longtime supporter Nevada senator Paul Laxalt or

Congressman Jack Kemp for the post. When the arrangement with Ford broke down because the ex-president insisted on too much power sharing, Reagan reluctantly agreed to accept Bush as his running mate.

Bar and Poppy were not enthusiastic about Ronnie and Nancy, either. Bush looked down on the former California governor as lacking the Washington experience he had, and Bar resented Nancy's stylishness and Hollywood glamour. During the eight years of the Reagan administration, Nancy wrote, the two couples had dinner together privately on only a handful of occasions and never became friends.

When Bar became first lady in 1989, she and George wanted to make clear that their presidency would be different. The Reagans were badly offended when Bush's speechwriter, Peggy Noonan, chose the phrase *kindler and gentler nation* to describe his agenda, believing it was an indirect slap at the Reagan administration. When he received the Republican nomination in 1988, Bush had promised the delegates that he would continue Reagan's successful policies. When he took office, however, his first act was to dismiss all political appointees put in office by Reagan.

Barbara also learned to avoid the mistakes Nancy had made when she first became first lady. She avoided any display of ostentation, and made self-deprecatory jokes about how she, with her matronly figure, would never be a fashion sensation. She cultivated the public image of a grandmotherly woman who would not interfere with the men running the White House as Nancy had done.

Shortly before Bush's 1980 bid for the presidency, Barbara realized she needed a project if she were to become first lady. Her former chief of staff, Susan Porter Rose, says that Barbara chose literacy after long and careful reflection because she believed that many other pressing social problems—from joblessness to homelessness to crime—stemmed from illiteracy. It was a subject in which she had no background or special expertise. Some biographers claim that Bar's interest in literacy began because her son Neil was dyslexic, but Susan Porter Rose says that is "absolutely wrong." Barbara thought about how she could use the platform of first lady to accomplish the greatest good without getting into controversial subjects that would detract from the presidency.

As first lady, she worked for Literacy Volunteers of America and Laubach Literacy International on the problem of adult literacy. Studies had shown that an alarming number of adults could not read or write English with minimum proficiency. In fact it was a pseudo-problem; the country's record-high immigration rate in the 1980s and '90s meant that the adult population had a constant influx of new immigrants without a solid knowledge of English. As fast as these people graduated from English studies and learned to read and write in their new language, they were replaced by newly arriving immigrants. Yet the media was fascinated by the millions of supposedly illiterate adults (many had fine command of reading and writing in their native languages), and they didn't understand that high immigration rates were distorting the statistics. The first lady's campaign was a popular success.

Bar gave the royalties from books about the Bush family dogs—*C. Fred's Story* and *Millie's Book*—to a literacy organization she founded. She attended literally hundreds of events designed around literacy programs. She also championed Head Start, a federally funded preschool program for poor children.

In the summer of 1990, widespread abuses and bankruptcies in the savings and loan industry created a series of political scandals in Washington. House Speaker Jim Wright, a Texas Democrat, resigned rather than face investigation after his involvement with a corrupt Texas savings and loan became public and questions arose about financing of a book deal that appeared to break House ethics rules. The "Keating Five" scandal linked five U.S. senators, including Republican John McCain of Arizona, to a savings and loan executive named Charles Keating, who contributed to their campaigns and allegedly violated federal election law rules in providing private aircraft owned by the S&L for the senators' use. There were many more revelations of political contributions given to lawmakers in exchange for support of legislation sought by the industry. Democrats and Republicans traded charges over which party was to blame. Neil Bush came under criticism because of his involvement in a failed S&L in Colorado. This brought out Barbara Bush's maternal instinct and she came to the fore when Neil was, in her view, singled out for unfair scrutiny. She said it was because he was the son of a sitting president.

Barbara's overreaction to criticism of Neil that summer was a contributing factor in Bush's reelection defeat. In a brilliantly written speech to the executive committee of the Republican Party, meeting in Chicago in 1990, veteran strategist Ed Rollins had attacked the Democrats for creating the S&L crisis. The speech was carried on all three television networks and created an immediate sensation. But when Rollins appeared on a Sunday talk show and was asked about Neil Bush's involvement, he gave a defensive answer suggesting that the president's son probably regretted his actions. Barbara was furious and demanded that the Republican Party stop using Rollins as its spokesman. Later that fall Rollins had a second falling-out with the White House after Bush broke his "read my lips, no new taxes" pledge and made a deal with the Democratic Congress to increase taxes. Rollins, who was working to elect Republicans to the House, openly advised candidates to distance themselves from the Bush presidency. Rollins believed—correctly, as it turned out—that breaking the tax pledge would be politically disastrous for Bush, and he feared that if Republican congressional candidates backed Bush's tax increase, they, too, would suffer at the polls.

The breach between Bush and Rollins became irreparable in 1992, when maverick billionaire H. Ross Perot decided to mount an independent campaign for the presidency. Rollins and former Carter insider Hamilton Jordan, a Democrat, joined the effort. Perot's sudden surge in the polls coupled with the political defections of two top strategists from the Republican and Democratic Parties dominated television and newspaper coverage for weeks, weakening Bush's presidency. Ironically, a simple overture from the Bushes asking Rollins to help in the Bush reelection drive early in 1992 would have prevented Rollins from defecting to Perot, but the Bushes' blind fixation on loyalty prevented it.

Barbara worked hard for Poppy's reelection, campaigning around the country and delivering an address to the Republican national convention. But for Bar, politics had become all too personal. In 1988, when rumors about George's alleged infidelity had to be refuted, George Jr. told the press that he had personally confronted his father about the charges and been assured they were baseless. In 1992, when Perot attacked the Bush family's use of political connections to make personal fortunes, Bar resented her children's lives being dragged into the campaign and wanted the Bush team to strike back.

Republican opposition researchers—specialists whose job it is to study opponents and find ways to attack them—began work on Perot. Briefly, Perot pulled out of the 1992 race, only to reenter later in the year, when he feared that the Bush campaign planned to disrupt his daughter's wedding with nude streakers. Many derided Perot's fear as a paranoid fantasy, but in fact the 1972 Nixon campaign had used nude streakers to interfere with Democratic candidate George McGovern's political receptions as part of the "dirty tricks" operation that culminated with the Watergate break-in.

Despite an overwhelming approval rating of 89 percent following the four-day Gulf War in early 1991, Bush lost his 1992 reelection bid. Perot's candidacy cut deeply into his support among Republicans and independents, and cost him the reelection. Ross Perot won almost 20 percent of the popular vote, leaving incumbent President Bush with 37 percent.

Democratic challenger Bill Clinton won five million more votes than Bush. It was a crushing defeat, and made the Bush presidency, along with those of Carter and Ford, the third one-term presidency in a span of eighteen years.

It is difficult to measure the first lady's impact on presidential policies. Barbara's former chief of staff, Susan Porter Rose, insists that she did not see her role as first lady as involving policy-making decisions. She openly supported the use of women in combat, but the Bush administration didn't embrace the idea. However, President Bush did change his position on gun control and banned dozens of types of guns after the first lady called publicly for stronger regulations. Although she didn't participate formally in campaign planning sessions the way Nancy Reagan or Rosalynn Carter had done, Bar campaigned actively and influenced political strategy at decisive turning points such as the 1988 decision to use the Willie Horton issue. She and the president discussed political issues and personalities, but they did so privately, in keeping with their penchant for secrecy. In the fullness of time, we will learn how influential she truly was as first lady.

Barbara benefited from this low profile in matters affecting presidential policy and staffing of the cabinet and White House. Unlike Nancy Reagan, who had drawn criticism for supposedly overstepping her bounds with her involvement in policy and personnel decisions, Bar was careful not to be seen as meddlesome. As a result of the care she took to avoid public controversy, Bar was an immensely popular first lady who remains so today.

Bar and Poppy now live in semiretirement in Houston, Texas. She has the distinction, shared with first lady Abigail Adams, of being both the wife and the mother of a president. Bar reportedly earns between forty and sixty thousand dollars a speech on the lecture circuit, setting a record among former first ladies for income.

Hillary Rodham Clinton

First Lady: 1993–2001
42nd Presidential Administration
Siena Research Institute Rating: 2

". . . practice politics as the art of making what appears to be impossible, possible."

Hillary Rodham Clinton's conduct in the White House could have landed her in prison. This is according to the federal prosecutor who probed her handling of files pertaining to Whitewater and Madison Guaranty and Loan. The documents had been subpoenaed, but the first lady told investigators that there were no records to produce. She claimed—as Enron and Arthur Andersen would half a decade later—that the records had been routinely shredded in the mid-1980s to make room for new files at her law firm. In January 1996, however, some of the missing documents suddenly reappeared in the White House living quarters. In 2002, the prosecutor said that although he declined to issue an indictment, there was "credible evidence" that Senator Hillary Clinton had obstructed justice.

Controversial, combative, and polarizing, Hillary Rodham Clinton is among the most complex of the first ladies to occupy the White House. She is also the only first lady to launch an independent political career after leaving the presidency. Like Florence Harding, and Jackie Kennedy, and Lady Bird Johnson, she seemed to have decided early in her marriage to tolerate her husband's infidelity. At first, she pushed the boundaries of the first lady's role in ways no one had done since Eleanor Roosevelt. She is the closest any first lady has come to acting as co-president, and for a while it appeared she would expand the first lady's role in sharing presidential powers. But Hillary had to retreat to a more traditional role as scandal and criticism threatened the very existence of the Clinton presidency.

Attorney Barbara Olson investigated Hillary as part of the House Government Reform and Oversight Committee. Olson—who died on September 11, 2001 on the hijacked aircraft piloted into the Pentagon— wrote a best-seller about the first lady called *Hell to Pay: The Unfolding Story of Hillary Rodham Clinton.* Olson said:

> I have never experienced a cooler or more hardened political operator than Hillary Rodham Clinton. The investigators working for Independent Counsel Kenneth Starr found, as we did, that in one White House scandal after another, all roads led to Hillary. To investigate White House improprieties and scandals, the evidence necessarily led to *her* hidden hands guiding the Clinton operation.*

From a different political perspective, Olson might have praised Hillary as a brilliant strategist and tactician whose defense of her embattled

---

*From the book *Hell to Pay* by Barbara Olson. Copyright 1999 by Henry Regnery Publishing. All rights reserved. Reprinted by special permission of Regnery Publishing, Inc. Washington, D.C.

husband saved him from impeachment. She also helped him triumph over a succession of Republican efforts to destroy his presidency. Precisely how much credit Hillary is owed will not be known for many years. It takes a long time, with any presidency, before the White House insiders stop writing canned, self-promoting memoirs and start writing candidly. But from the available facts, it's not premature to conclude that Hillary Rodham Clinton is no ordinary political spouse. She has been a critical component of Bill Clinton's political career from the very beginning. In November 1992, when Hillary excitedly told *The Washington Post* that the country had "voted for the Clintons," she meant it in a way that no previous first lady would have conceived.

Hillary Rodham came into the world on October 26, 1947, the second year of the Baby Boom. She was raised in Park Ridge, an affluent suburb in Chicago, Illinois. Her father was a successful Republican businessman whose young daughter was a "Goldwater Girl," one of the young women who dressed in campaign outfits as a sort of cheerleader for the Republican candidate in the 1964 presidential campaign. As a young teenager she met Martin Luther King Jr., after he made an appearance in Chicago. She also met Senator Barry Goldwater after reading his book, *Conscience of a Conservative.*

Politics infected her from an early age. In high school, when asked about her ambition, she said she would "marry a senator." She ran for school office and was elected vice president of her junior class. Her classmates voted her "Most Likely to Succeed."

After high school, Hillary wanted to attend an all-female college. She chose Wellesley College in Massachusetts, enrolling in the fall of 1965. She broke free of her family's Republican politics at Wellesley when she went to work on Democratic senator Eugene McCarthy's 1968 presidential campaign. Hillary joined the ranks of college students protesting the Vietnam War, and took part in public protest marches in Boston. Her 1969 commencement speech, which mingled youthful idealism with 1960s radicalism, earned her a photograph on the cover of *Life* magazine. In the speech, instead of defining the goal of politics as the art of the possible, as it is more conventionally defined, she stood the idea on its head. She said it was to "practice politics as the art of making what appears to be impossible, possible." It was a subtle but important distinction. If politics is the art of "the possible," its limits are the boundaries of consensus. But if politics is about achieving goals others see as impossible, it is about change that seems unthinkable to others, change that goes beyond the consensus view, change that from a consensus view would be described as radical.

Hillary had fallen under the influence of radical thinker and political organizer Saul Alinsky at Wellesley. Alinsky was a veteran at confrontational political tactics. One of his dictums for political attacks was to "pick the target, freeze it, personalize it, and polarize it." Alinsky advocated going after a person, not an impersonal policy; hence, to oppose the war in Vietnam it was better to oppose "Nixon's war" than simply to be antiwar. Political polarization means finding what strategists today call "wedge issues" that divide people into opposing—polar opposite—camps. During the Vietnam War, the right wing in America polarized dissent with bumper stickers that read, AMERICA—LOVE IT OR LEAVE IT!

Hillary's commencement address immediately followed remarks by African American Republican senator Edward Brooke. When the senator spoke out against violent protest, Hillary abandoned her prepared text to speak spontaneously, making Brooke the target for her remarks by charging that he bore personal responsibility for the country's problems. It was Hillary's maiden voyage in the "politics of personal destruction," which would come to characterize the bitter partisan warfare of the 1990s.

Hillary entered Yale University to study law in the fall of 1969. She met Bill Clinton in the cafeteria when a mutual friend, Robert Reich—later to become Clinton's labor secretary—introduced them. (In other accounts there is a more dramatic story about catching one another's gaze while studying at the library, but the Reich introduction preceded the library encounter.) During the summers, Hillary worked as an intern in Washington, D.C., for the Children's Defense Fund and as a staffer on Senator Walter Mondale's subcommittee.

They began living together at Yale, and Hillary put off completing her law degree so that she could stay until Bill's graduation in 1973. In 1972, she and Bill took time out from law school to work on Democratic nominee George McGovern's campaign against the incumbent, President Richard Nixon. Bill was Texas coordinator for the campaign, putting him in charge of all of McGovern's election activities in the state of Texas. He was based in the state capital of Austin, while Hillary managed a voter registration drive in San Antonio. It was their first campaign as a couple.

After they graduated from Yale in 1973, Bill and Hillary separated for professional reasons. He took a job teaching law in Arkansas, while she accepted a position as counsel on the House Judiciary Committee. Her job was to develop the legal arguments for the impeachment of Richard Nixon. (Author's note: When the committee later voted articles of impeachment, it was one of the final acts preceding Nixon's resignation. Once the committee voted in favor of the articles of impeachment, it sets a trial into motion. The next step is for the entire House to vote for or against impeachment. If the House approves impeachment, the Senate is where the trial takes place. Nixon short-circuited the proceedings by resigning, rather than face a vote in the House that might have resulted in an impeachment trial.)

Hillary Clinton followed the protracted legal battle over the Nixon White House tapes, and no doubt took note of then first lady Pat Nixon's view that her husband should simply have disposed of the evidence before the courts ruled the tapes were not his to destroy. It was the kind of Watergate lesson a shrewd political tactician would absorb.

Shortly after Nixon's resignation, the twenty-eight-year-old Hillary drove to Arkansas with a friend. Bill Clinton was making his first run for Congress, and Hillary became his campaign manager. She helped polish his speeches and manage his campaign, and he praised her for her organizational skills. Although he lost the campaign, it marked their second collaboration in an election. After the race, Hillary stayed in Arkansas to teach law despite more attractive career opportunities available to her in Washington or New York. When they married in October 1975, Hillary chose to keep her maiden name of Rodham.

The following year Bill ran for office again, but this time he set his sights on attorney general of Arkansas. Hillary was his partner in the campaign. When he won, she joined the Rose law firm in Little Rock. In 1978, Bill ran for governor. Hillary was his chief political adviser. She drew criticism for keeping her maiden name, among other things, but he won the race. The following year, President Carter appointed Hillary to the board of directors of the congressionally chartered Legal Services Corporation.

Their only child, Chelsea, was born in February 1980. In that same year, Hillary was made a partner in the Rose law firm. Bill lost his reelection bid: A voter backlash over his tax increase on cars combined with voter anger that Clinton, at President Carter's request, had allowed dangerous Cuban criminals from the Mariel boatlift to be detained in Arkansas. Several hundred of the prisoners had broken out of detention, causing a crime wave and widespread panic in western Arkansas.

Hillary responded to Bill's defeat with an image makeover. For the first time, she took the last name *Clinton* as hers. She dropped her nerdy eyeglasses for contact lenses, styled her hair, and shed her blowsy garb for tailored suits. When Bill ran for reelection in 1982, she was the model of a candidate's wife. He appointed her chair of the Arkansas Education Standards Committee, and together they overcame teachers' union opposition and won public backing for educational reform legislation, which included teacher competency testing. Hillary was no longer simply an advocate; now she was a practitioner of the art of making the impossible possible.

Publicly there was triumph, but privately there was pain in the Clinton partnership. Clinton, like Lyndon Johnson and Warren Harding, was a womanizer. Many years later, after the Monica Lewinsky affair was revealed in 1998, Hillary would publicly acknowledge Bill's sexual transgressions for the first time.

Among the more painful revelations was Juanita Broaddrick's allegation that Bill Clinton, while serving as attorney general, had raped her in a Little Rock hotel room. Broaddrick says that she had an encounter with Hillary Clinton not long after the alleged attack. In Broaddrick's account, Hillary stared fixedly at her and made remarks about loyalty in a way that Broaddrick interpreted was intended to intimidate her to remain silent.

It was the beginning of a pattern of covering up for Bill's infidelity. In 1992, when Clinton was struggling to win the Democratic primaries and presidential nomination, Hillary stepped forward publicly to deny Gennifer Flowers's account of a long-running sexual relationship. Political experts credit her televised performance on *60 Minutes* with saving Clinton's campaign. When he went on to win the Democratic nomination, strategists for incumbent president George H. W. Bush understood her political importance and took aim at Hillary.

She made a misstep in May 1992. In an interview with *Vanity Fair* magazine, she mentioned rumors that President Bush had a mistress. The remark infuriated Barbara Bush, who demanded an apology through her staff. Hillary did apologize, but now the Bush family considered her fair game. What they had done to Dukakis over Willie Horton in 1988, they tried to do to Hillary in 1992.

No first lady's character had figured so prominently in campaign attacks since the nineteenth century (Rachel Jackson, for example). Hillary was denounced at the 1992 Republican national convention by speaker after speaker, from Marilyn Quayle to Pat Buchanan. She was accused of comparing marriage to slavery and wanting to give children the right to sue their parents in court. But when the votes were counted in November, the Clintons had won five million more votes and sent George and Barbara Bush home.

As first lady, Hillary took an office in the West Wing and a seat at the table in Clinton White House policy meetings. She had signaled her role as a partner in December 1992 at a summit of economists in Little Rock by appearing with President-elect Clinton for the meeting. She took an active role in staffing the new administration, recommending many who would fill the cabinet and the White House. She helped draft and edit White House speeches, deliberated over policy and political priorities with the president and his advisers, and spearheaded an ambitious initiative to overhaul the nation's health care system and give every American health insurance coverage.

While some first ladies had been extensively involved in policy making behind the scenes, none had ever had so open a role. Eleanor Roosevelt had sat in on meetings regarding the National Youth Administration with Harry Hopkins, but aside from asking a few questions she limited her discussion of policy decisions; her chief objective in appearing was to signal her support. Hillary's involvement was far greater. She took her own seat at the table, sometimes on the opposite side from the president. She asked questions, made suggestions, vetoed proposals, and served as a kind of co-president. For a brief period of time, it appeared that Hillary Rodham Clinton would legitimize the power sharing that so often exists between spouses in a political partnership by being so open about her involvement. Had she been able to win popular support for some of the policies she was associated with in the first year of the new presidency, such as the initiative to provide national health insurance, she would have broken the final barrier to a first lady's public involvement in policy making regarding matters of the utmost national importance.

Controversy, in any event, soon eclipsed her efforts. It began with her role in the firing of career White House travel office employee Billy Dale and five others. The first lady's role is amply documented in notes from White House administrator David Watkins, who warned that there would be "hell to pay" if Hillary's wishes were not met. Hillary wanted the career civil servants who worked in the travel office replaced with political appointees loyal only to the Clintons. She also wanted the business of the travel office run by a firm owned by Clinton supporters. These were minor political patronage concerns, and they pale in comparison to Hillary's historic effort to reshape the nation's health insurance system. It is puzzling that she even considered it worth her time to bother over how the White House travel office was run and staffed.

In any event, she provoked a needless controversy. Billy Dale, a thirty-two-year veteran of many presidencies, was widely admired by Democrats and Republicans alike for his character and capabilities in managing strenuous presidential trips. When Catherine Cornelius, a junior White House employee who was the president's cousin, alleged financial irregularities in the handling of travel office funds, the stage was set for the sacking of Dale and his associates.

Although a report from the accounting firm Peat Marwick had found sloppy bookkeeping in travel office accounts but no evidence of embezzlement or misuse of funds, the Clinton White House called in the FBI to launch a criminal probe. White House press secretary Dee Dee Myers released the news to the press, breaking FBI protocol by discussing an investigation before an indictment had been issued. Two years later, a jury acquitted Billy Dale of felony charges stemming from the final FBI probe.

The first lady's health care task force also generated controversy. Meetings that involved nongovernment employees as advisers were held in secrecy, leading to charges that the first lady was violating a sunshine law called the Federal Advisory Committee Act of 1974. *Sunshine law* is a phrase used to describe laws that require openness in government so as to prevent private interests from abusing their access to policy makers. Today, *transparency* is used similarly. The idea behind the Federal Advisory Committee Act was that if private individuals were called on to give policy advice to government officials, the nature of their advice should be public knowledge. The law, therefore, was very specific in requiring that meetings of task forces and the business they transacted be open to the public except for cases involving national security.

Hillary included many people ranging from academics to advocacy groups in her task force meetings, but she excluded many insurance and health care industry interest groups. The existence of the task force was widely publicized, but its deliberations were kept secret to all but the insiders. Those who were excluded from the task force meetings demanded to know what was under debate. When the White House refused to open the deliberations to public review, the Association of American Physicians and Surgeons sued Hillary, alleging that the sunshine laws had been violated. The court ruled against the first lady.

When Hillary was announced as chair of the task force, she declared that her reform plan would be finished in one hundred days. Instead, the process dragged on for most of 1993. By the time the proposal was before the Democratic-controlled Congress, its opponents had mobilized against it. Hillary's health reform was dead on arrival.

There were other problems as well, ranging from cabinet nominees such as Zoe Baird dropping out over ethics issues to the controversy over Clinton's plan to openly allow gays and lesbians in the military to disappointment that in lieu of the middle-class tax cut promised in the campaign, Clinton had raised taxes instead. By the end of Clinton's first year and a half, there was a growing political backlash. The discontent culminated with historic midterm elections in 1994 that gave control over both the House and the Senate to the Republicans for the first time in forty years.

Hillary responded by retreating from her openly activist role. She lowered her public profile in policy making so as not to draw attention to the co-presidency that she shared with Bill. She sought out a more traditional project that the public would accept. Her lifelong interest in policies affecting children was a safe haven for a first lady, and Hillary went to work on her book *It Takes a Village*. In 1995, she and daughter Chelsea toured Asia in a trip focusing on women's rights, economic development, and sight-seeing that made for sympathetic photo ops. The first lady spoke at women's conferences in New York and Denmark, toured South America, and was an outspoken critic of China's population control policies—which limited each couple to one child and were enforced through compulsory abortion or sterilization—at a United Nations World Conference on Women in Beijing. Her new focus on women and children helped restore her popularity just in time for the 1996 presidential election.

As she had in every other campaign, Hillary took a proactive role in the reelection drive. Republican candidate Robert Dole ran an ineffectual campaign, while President Clinton adroitly maneuvered toward the political center. The result was a healthy reelection margin of 379 electoral college votes to Dole's 159.

In the first year of Clinton's second term, the country had a balanced federal budget for the first time since the 1960s. But a series of scandals and investigations stemming from the Clintons' Arkansas dealings and probes of cabinet members led to the appointment of multiple independent counsels. The president and first lady were personally under the microscope in cases ranging from Paula Jones's sexual harassment suit to Whitewater.

For a while the investigations proceeded with relatively low intensity and only an occasional media frenzy when there was some new development, such as the jailing of Susan McDougal—the wife of one of the Clintons' Whitewater business partners—for her refusal to cooperate with prosecutors. Public interest was muted. Then twenty-one-year-old White House intern Monica Lewinsky's sexual relationship with President Clinton was revealed. A firestorm erupted.

Once again, Hillary rose to Bill's defense. She made an appearance on the *Today* show to defend her family's right to privacy. Behind the scenes, Hillary took charge of the defense. White House staffer Sidney Blumenthal spread the word among Washington reporters that Monica Lewinsky was a deluded stalker. The president denied before the entire nation that he had had an affair with "that woman, Ms. Lewinsky." The first lady and president were in full denial. This time, however, secret tape recordings made by one of Lewinsky's confidantes, Linda Tripp, and a semen stain on a blue dress that matched Bill Clinton's DNA, blew the Clinton cover-up.

When statements under oath made by the president in the Paula Jones case showed that Clinton had committed perjury, demands for his impeachment grew. Independent counsel Kenneth Starr referred a report to the Republican-controlled House that featured Clinton's sexual conduct with Lewinsky and his efforts to obstruct the investigation. On a party-line vote—not one Democrat voted for an impeachment trial—the House voted to impeach on December 18, 1998.

Hillary had already launched Clinton's defense with her famous accusation that a "vast right-wing conspiracy" was to blame for her husband's political predicament. Following the dictum of Saul Alinsky, she found a target, froze it, personalized it, and polarized. The target was special prosecutor Ken Starr, a Republican judge who had taken over the probe two years earlier.

First Ken Starr was thoroughly demonized and made to seem like a puritanical zealot. Hillary's strategy essentially put the Republican Party, and especially Starr, on trial in the court of public opinion for persecuting Clinton over a matter of private morality. Hillary, an astute political strategist, realized that the Senate would only impeach the president in a case like this if public opinion so demanded. The key was to divide public opinion and polarize it along partisan lines. By the time the Senate trial began in January 1999, the White House war room had been at work for months undermining the Republicans' case with the public. In the Senate, Republicans alleged high crimes and misdemeanors ranging from perjury to obstruction of justice. Democrats responded that a mere sexual peccadillo didn't reach the constitutional threshold for impeachment. With public opinion running in his favor, President Clinton survived the impeachment trial.

President Clinton believes his vindication in the Senate trial set an important constitutional precedent that helps preserve the powers of the presidency against excessive encroachment by the legislature. Hillary Clinton was instrumental in that outcome, and deserves her share of the credit. But the victory did come at a steep price. For the better part of the eight-year Clinton presidency, the investigations and scandals and ultimately the impeachment ordeal distracted from Clinton's agenda and his ability to push initiatives. He laments it as "lost time."

There may have been another price, yet to be paid in full. The first al-Qaeda-linked terrorist attack in the United States happened in 1993 with the bombing of the World Trade Center. Other Osama bin Laden attacks included bombings on two American embassies and the near scuttling of the USS *Cole*. When President Clinton responded to one Bin Laden terrorist attack by firing cruise missiles at a suspected biological weapons factory in Sudan and at a training camp in Afghanistan, the timing coincided with an August 17, 1998, grand jury appearance. Critics accused him of launching the attacks in order to divert attention from the grand jury testimony. Some former Clinton aides believe the criticism of the cruise missile attacks made Clinton cautious about a more robust war on terrorism. If this is true, it means that the excessively partisan atmosphere in Washington during the latter years of the Clinton administration may have helped Bin Laden by making Clinton reluctant to act aggressively against him for fear that it would only lead to more criticism that he was cynically trying to divert attention from the domestic scandals.

As the Clinton presidency drew to a close, Hillary announced her candidacy for the Senate seat being vacated by New York's Daniel Patrick Moynihan. In a hard-fought campaign against Republican congressman Rick Lazio, Hillary battled her way through charges of carpetbagging and taking campaign contributions from Palestinian radicals as well as using her influence to win pardons for Puerto Rican terrorists. The only first lady to have launched an independent political career, she won and became New York's junior senator.

The Clinton presidency ended on a final note of scandal when the Clintons took expensive gifts of furniture and other household items to fill the separate houses they purchased in New York, Washington, and the former president's New York City residence. Then only hours before President-elect George W. Bush was sworn in, Clinton issued pardons and clemency orders to 177 felons and prisoners, including fugitive financier Marc Rich, who was under indictment for evading forty-eight million dollars in taxes. Rich's estranged wife Denise was a major Democratic fundraiser who backed Hillary Clinton in her New York Senate campaign and had contributed to the Clinton presidential library fund. At the time this book was being written, federal investigators were probing whether any of the pardons were issued in exchange for political contributions.

As a first lady, Hillary was a polarizing figure. Partisan Democrats absolutely love her; partisan Republicans positively loathe her. Her future as a senator seems politically secure if she stays in a state where the majority of voters are registered Democrats.

Hillary Rodham Clinton's political trajectory is not over. She is widely viewed as a potential Democratic candidate for the presidency. If she can win support from independent voters, she may be able to advance to higher office than the Senate. If she succeeds in a run for the White House, she'll set two precedents. She will be the country's first female chief executive, and her spouse will become the country's first squire. It may sound like a Hollywood sequel, but the Clintons may return to the West Wing yet again.

LAURA WELCH BUSH

FIRST LADY: 2001–
43RD PRESIDENTIAL ADMINISTRATION
UNRATED*

"Education can help children see beyond a world of hate and hopelessness."

Laura Bush was on her way to Congress to give a briefing on early child-hood education, the special project she had chosen to undertake as first lady. It was a crisp fall morning. Waiting for her at the Capitol were Senator Ted Kennedy and Senator Judd Gregg.

As the first lady's limousine approached Capitol Hill, the lead Secret Service agent guarding her heard an urgent radio report: An airplane had hit the World Trade Center. While the car neared Congress, the first lady speculated that it had been an accident. Then the Secret Service received word that a second plane had smashed into the adjacent tower.

"We knew then that it was terrorism," Laura Bush said. "I remember thinking then that nothing would ever be the same."

Senator Kennedy and his dog, Splash, were waiting for the first lady. Laura had been a senior at the Robert E. Lee High School in her home-town of Midland, Texas, when President John Kennedy was assassinated in Dallas. She got the news while sitting in a classroom.

"I remember feeling as if a blanket had been thrown over the school," she recalled, "suffocating all the usual sounds of scraping chairs and class-room chatter. People cried. The horror was . . . almost too much to bear."

To be standing next to Senator Kennedy, the slain president's brother, as the events of September 11 began to unfold struck her as indescribably eerie.

The day was still early, and there were further shocks in store for the first lady. The Senate briefing was speedily canceled as the dimensions of the attack became clearer. Another airplane smashed into the Pentagon, sending plumes of black smoke billowing into the air just across the Potomac River.

Laura Bush was quickly rushed by the Secret Service to a secure place whose location is classified. Now she had her husband, who was on Air Force One en route from Florida back to Washington, to worry about. In a confused communication from the Secret Service command post at the White House, a threat to attack Air Force One had been relayed to Vice President Cheney, who was already in a separate secure bunker. Cheney was told that the threat had used the code word *angel to* refer to the presi-dent's aircraft. In fact, a real threat had been received but the code word was not used. It would have been alarming had it been, because it would mean the attackers had inside information. The most probable explana-tion for the confusion is that someone inside the White House panicked

---

*Laura Bush will be rated in a Siena Research Institute poll to be released sometime in 2003.

and said something inexact like "we've received a threat against Angel," leading to the misunderstanding. In any event, Vice President Cheney called Bush on Air Force One to tell him the presidential aircraft would be attacked next.

The plane immediately diverted to Barksdale Air Force Base, where George was able to call Laura to reassure her. It was the second time they spoke during the morning of September 11. Believing that he was next on the terrorists' target list, he told his wife that he was heading to the U.S. Strategic Command Headquarters at Offut Air Force Base in Nebraska, where he would be able to convene a video conference of the National Security Council and take command of the crisis. Soon Laura heard another rumor, that an aircraft had plunged into Camp David and caused widespread casualties. For a full hour, she believed many of the staff people she and George had gotten to know at the presidential retreat were dead.

That same afternoon, CIA director George Tenet reported that several of the September 11 terrorists were linked to Osama bin Laden. The American public may have been surprised by the attack, but the White House was not. Although eight months would pass before the American public would be told, throughout the summer of 2001 U.S. security agencies suspected that Bin Laden was planning a terrorist attack against Americans somewhere in the world. Intelligence agencies had tried, but failed, to discover when and where it would happen. FBI headquarters had botched several promising leads from its field offices about Middle Eastern men attending flight schools. One month before the World Trade Center and Pentagon attacks, President Bush had received a special CIA briefing about Bin Laden, and al-Qaeda, and the leads the United States had regarding plans to attack Americans.

"I was not on point," the president said in a May 2002 *Washington Post* interview, "but I knew he [Bin Laden] was a menace, and I knew he was a problem. I knew he was responsible, or we felt he was responsible, for the [previous] bombings that had killed Americans. . . . But I didn't feel that sense of urgency. . . ."

The day had been a wake-up call for Washington. After more than a decade of ineffective measures to combat terrorism, the country had paid a horrific toll for its complacency.

There was one last wake-up call, literally, for the Bushes on September 11. After he and Laura went to sleep in the White House living quarters, commonly referred to as the residence, late that night, the Secret Service received yet another report of a threatening airplane in the vicinity of the

White House. George and Laura were hurriedly awakened and rushed under guard through a tunnel into a secure bunker, where they braced for an airplane to crash into the White House. The president wore only a T-shirt and running shorts. Fortunately, it was a false alarm.

Laura Bush's initial reaction that things would not be the same was correct. She had planned to focus her energies as first lady on early childhood education. Instead, her focus would shift. She would become part of the war on terrorism.

Almost immediately, the first lady went to work planning a memorial service for the attack victims to be held on Friday, September 14, at Washington's National Cathedral. In what would be the beginning of their collaboration in the war on terrorism, White House aide Karen Hughes assisted the first lady. To emphasize bipartisan unity in the face of the attacks, former presidents Jimmy Carter and Bill Clinton were invited to attend. George and Barbara Bush also came, and were seated next to the president and first lady. To blunt fears of religious conflict, a rabbi, a Protestant minister, a Catholic cardinal, and a Muslim cleric officiated.

During his speech, Bush uttered the memorable lines that hinted at the coming war: "This conflict was begun on the timing and terms of others," he said. "It will end in a way, and at an hour, of our choosing."

The service ended with the entire congregation on their feet singing "The Battle Hymn of the Republic." Bush's national security adviser, Dr. Condoleezza Rice, felt that by the end, a wave of determination had swept over all the high government officials at the memorial service, washing away the sense of shock and sadness left in the immediate aftermath of the attacks. If Rice's reaction extends to the rest of Washington officialdom present that day, the first lady's careful planning paid off. She had helped boost morale, steeling government officials for a new kind of war.

Laura Welch was born on November 4, 1946, in Midland, Texas, the affluent town that is home to so many of the state's oil and gas entrepreneurs and corporate executives. Her father was a wealthy developer and her mother a full-time homemaker. The couple enjoyed local prominence. As an only child, Laura received her parents' undivided attention. She attended public school. Her childhood and adolescence were ordinary with one major exception. As a teenager, Laura killed Michael Douglas, her friend and high school classmate, when she ran a stop sign and collided with his car. No charges were filed in the accident, and the speed at which she was driving is illegible on the police report.

Her B.A. degree in education was from Southern Methodist University, where she joined the Kappa Alpha Theta sorority. After her graduation, she taught school in Houston for two years. She returned to college in 1971 to complete a master's degree in library science at the University of Texas at Austin. After a brief stint as a children's librarian in Houston, Laura returned to Austin, where she worked as a librarian in a public elementary school.

She met George W. Bush at a friend's barbecue party in Midland in 1977. Within a few months, they were engaged. On November 5, 1977, one day after Laura's thirty-first birthday, she and George were married.

George W. went on to run for Congress as a Republican. Laura, who considered herself a Democrat, switched allegiances after marrying into one of the country's most prominent Republican dynasties. She campaigned alongside her new husband, making appearances jointly with him and delivering political speeches when necessary. He lost the election.

In 1981, the couple's twin daughters, Barbara Pierce and Jenna Welch—named for their grandmothers—were born. Laura became a stay-at-home mom so she could devote her time to her babies. As she would later urge others to do when she became the first lady of Texas, Laura read to her children often, even in early infancy. One of her favorite books to read to her daughters was the 1947 classic, *Goodnight, Moon*.

Laura is credited with her husband's decision to stop drinking when their daughters were young, although she says he made the decision himself. The catalyst, if there was such an event, remains shrouded.

"I had the sense that was real," says Bush associate Jim Pinkerton about George W.'s alcohol abuse, "a genuine AA-like revelation, although he never told me the whole story. It was like, 'I've wasted a lot of time, I'm not going to do this anymore.'"

George W. then went to work full time in his father's 1988 presidential campaign with the energetic young Harvey Lee Atwater, a rising star in Republican circles known for his hardball tactics. Atwater was a disciple of renaissance philosopher Niccolò Machiavelli, who believed that ethics have no place in politics or statecraft.

George W. and Atwater "became fast allies," says another Bush insider. Lee's widow, Sally Atwater, says they were more than allies.

"They became good friends," she says, "We used to have them over, and Laura over a lot when Junior was out of town." George and Laura absorbed the lessons in tough political strategy from Lee Atwater. Sally recalls that George W. was "thrilled to have a ringside seat in the campaign."

After his father was elected to the presidency, George and Laura returned to Dallas. Critics have accused George W. of trading on his father's connections with a series of subsequent business ventures that earned him millions of dollars. He was a member of the board of directors when he sold Harken Energy stock in 1990 just before its value dropped steeply, raising suspicions of insider trading that were investigated by the Securities and Exchange Commission. No charges were ever filed, and the results of the SEC investigation are secret. The Harken stock was purchased by a mysterious private investor whose identity has never been publicly revealed. With the gains from the sale, George W. was able to pay off a loan that he used to purchase, along with a group of investors, the Texas Rangers baseball team. When the Rangers were later sold at a multimillion-dollar profit, George W.'s partners insisted he receive an equal share. These transactions made George W. a millionaire. With the family's growing affluence, daughters Jenna and Barbara switched from public to private school.

In 1994, Bush ran against incumbent Texas governor Ann Richards. This time he won. Laura soon emerged as a first lady of Texas who was involved and active. Although she worked in predictable public causes such as breast cancer research and fund-raising for an art museum, she felt passionately about reading for children and early childhood education.

Laura did not need to find a cause to make her own. Texas, with its constant infusion of Mexican immigrants, many poorly educated and needing to learn to read and write in English, presented special challenges for children. Laura launched the First Lady's Family Literacy Initiative in Texas and raised more than a million dollars in private contributions (her mother-in-law, Barbara Bush, helped substantially through money from her Foundation for Family Literacy) for statewide programs.

Another Laura Bush initiative was the creation of an annual Texas Book Festival. The original idea came from the Welsh town of Hay-on-Wye, where in 1988 the Guardian Hay Festival was launched; this annual book fair now attracts fifty thousand visitors and has transformed the small Welsh city into a book lover's paradise. (Former president Bill Clinton attended in 2001.) Other cities followed suit, including Los Angeles and Chicago, and Laura introduced the idea into Texas in the mid-1990s. Her inaugural festival included more than one hundred Texas writers, including Larry McMurtry and cable television talk personality Larry King.

In January 2001, following one of the most contentious presidential elections in history, Laura's initial actions showed she intended to pursue her passions for reading and education as first lady of the United States. During the inaugural ceremonies, Laura hosted a televised salute to eighteen American writers. Later, she and some of the authors toured public schools in Washington, D.C. For the next nine months, she was able to focus her time on projects dear to her heart. But everything changed after September 11.

Laura's first response as first lady was to encourage parents to talk openly with their children about the shocking events. She encouraged them to reassure their children, to take time to hug them and show their love and concern. On September 12, she wrote letters addressed to elementary school students for teachers to read in classrooms. A separate letter was sent to middle and high school students.

Five days later, she was in Pennsylvania at the memorial service for those who died on United Flight 93. The airplane's hijackers were trying to crash it into the White House when a passenger revolt interfered with their plot, causing the plane to crash into the ground.

"This has been a week of loss and heartache of a kind that none of us could have ever imagined," the first lady said at the ceremony, in a veiled reference to the fact that despite the summer's ominous warnings of a looming Bin Laden attack, neither the FBI nor the CIA were creative enough to imagine the tactics the terrorists would use.

As fighting began in Afghanistan, Laura and three other women at the White House—Karen Hughes, Mary Matalin, and Charlotte Beers—were shaping the public diplomacy response to the war. Taliban and al-Qaeda propaganda hostile to the United States was widely reported in global media, especially in the Muslim world, and President Bush assigned his longtime aide Karen Hughes the task of coordinating a response. Along with Madison Avenue advertising executive Charlotte Beers and vice presidential aide Mary Matalin, Hughes began to create a communications strategy to counter the propaganda.

In November, Laura Bush became one of the prime messengers of the campaign. Although Nancy Reagan participated in several joint radio addresses to highlight drug policy and her "Just Say No" campaign, Laura set a precedent by becoming the first first lady to deliver a Saturday radio address on her own. The syndicated Saturday radio address is normally delivered by the president, and a response is also broadcast by a spokesperson for the opposition party. Laura's topic was the Taliban's oppression of women.

"Only the terrorists and the Taliban forbid education to women," she said. "Only the terrorists and the Taliban threaten to pull out women's fingernails for wearing nail polish."

In January 2002, Laura spoke at Washington, D.C.'s, Ronald Reagan Building about the urgent need to help the children of Afghanistan. That country's new ruler, Interim Chairman Hamid Karzai, was by her side.

"Last November, I joined Americans in focusing on the brutality against Afghan women by the al-Qaeda terrorist network and the Taliban regime," she said. "And today, we continue to speak out on behalf of the women and children—especially girls—who for years were denied their basic human rights of health and education."

The first lady repeated the U.S. pledge to give Afghanistan $296 million in reconstruction aid, including money to rebuild and reopen schools.

In March 2002, as the new school year began in Afghanistan, the first lady continued her public diplomacy offensive by giving a speech before the United Nations Commission on the Status of Women on International Women's Day. Her remarks highlighted the international aid committed to rebuilding Afghanistan, with a special emphasis on women. She also underscored the goal of reopening Afghan schools, and her role in coordinating U.S. and international aid so that Afghan children would have books, supplies, and backpacks as they began the school year.

When she traveled to Europe in May 2002, accompanied by her twenty-year-old daughter Jenna, Laura not only talked about aid to Afghanistan but also discussed the NATO alliance with Czech president Vaclav Havel in a thirty-minute meeting. In an interview following the Prague meeting, the first lady voiced her agreement with Havel that Russia's role in NATO should be kept limited. It was a controversial position to take. For many Eastern European countries, such as the Baltics, Poland, and Hungary, NATO membership is viewed as insurance against any attempt by Russia to ever again subjugate their countries as it did during the Cold War. Some defense analysts believe, however, that Russia may one day become a full partner in NATO. George W. has spoken of the possibility that NATO may welcome Russia as a full member. Laura's remarks to President Vaclav Havel came just days before an official ceremony welcoming Russia into NATO in an advisory role.

During her trip, she made a thirteen-minute broadcast for Radio Free Afghanistan that was heard in twenty-eight countries. Her topic, the inclusion of women in Afghanistan's political system, was aimed at influencing the country's upcoming *loya jirga* meeting to organize a new government.

Laura also spoke out against Palestinian suicide bombers during the trip, frostily saying she had no sympathy for the mothers of Palestinian youths who kill themselves during terrorist attacks against Israelis.

In addition, the press and public finally learned what the Bush insiders had known all along: The U.S. government had numerous indications before September 11 that Bin Laden was planning an attack. Democratic senator Hillary Clinton held a press conference on May 16, 2002, and—paraphrasing Howard Baker's famous question at the height of Watergate—demanded to know what Bush knew and when he had known it. Sensing a chink in Bush's political armor, other leading Democrats including Tom Daschle and Dick Gephardt joined the former first lady in calling for probes.

Laura Bush rose to the defense. She issued a statement from Hungary:

We know—I know my husband, and all Americans know how he has acted in Afghanistan and in the war with terror. . . . It's sad to play upon the emotions of people as if there was something we could have done to stop it, because that's just not the case. . . . There was no way he could have predicted what would happen from this intelligence.

Clearly, the political management of the Bush presidency involves Laura. The first lady's influence over policy is difficult to measure, and she insists that she does not involve herself in the day-to-day operations of the West Wing. She also refuses to publicly discuss any policy differences she might have with her husband. But one incident reminiscent of Nancy Reagan's coaching of her husband during a news conference in which U.S.-Soviet relations were under discussion (Nancy whispered to Ronnie to answer a question by saying, "We're making progress") shows the depth of Laura's influence.

Early in the campaign against al-Qaeda, President Bush insisted he wanted Osama bin Laden "dead or alive." Some aides became concerned that the president had personalized the conflict and defined victory in such a way that it would lead to public disappointment if Bin Laden were not killed or captured. Nevertheless, Bush stuck to his tough rhetoric. At one event, when Bush repeated his line to reporters, Laura nudged him and spoke softly.

"Bushie, are you going to get him?" she was overheard whispering.

The president soon dropped his public statements about the necessity of killing or capturing Bin Laden.

Although she continues to try periodically to focus her agenda on reading and education in America, most notably with an early-March 2002

White House conference on teaching, Laura Bush's role as first lady has been defined for her by the events of September 11. Just as Eleanor Roosevelt's agenda was dictated by the Great Depression and World War II, Laura Bush's success as first lady will be measured to a large extent by how well she adjusts to the new reality. Great first ladies are relevant to their times in constructive ways; those who fail to realize that their public role extends beyond ceremony and personal agendas are doomed to mediocrity.

It is too soon to tell where Laura Bush will fall in the pantheon of first ladies. The Bush presidency was slumping badly in the polls just weeks before the attacks of September 11, but the president's and first lady's response to the terrorist challenge has been met with dramatic public approval. If that public support is sustained, and Laura Bush's activities remain relevant to the nation's concerns, the people will reciprocate. She may well be on her way to high ratings from the academic experts in future Siena College Research Institute surveys.

John B. Roberts II is a former White House insider who has advised presidents, heads of state, and first ladies in the United States, Ukraine, Costa Rica, South Africa, and Pakistan. He is currently a consulting television producer for *The McLaughlin Group*. His political writing has appeared in *George*, *The Washington Post*, *USA Today*, *The American Spectator*, *Campaigns and Elections*, and *The London Observer*.

He was educated at Oxford University in politics and philosophy and has a degree in fine arts from the University of California. He is an avid wilderness enthusiast, international pistol competitor, and aspiring novelist.

INDEX

NOTE: bold page numbers indicate main entries for first ladies

Abortion, 298, 305, 306, 326
Activism of first ladies. *See* Political
  activism
Adams, Abigail Smith, xii, **11–18**, 29, 40,
  117
Adams, Hannah, 4
Adams, John, 12–18, 21–22, 40, 117
Adams, John Quincy, 33, 38, 40–44, 48–49
Adams, Louisa Catherine Johnson, **39–44**,
  116
Affirmative action, 287, 300, 330
Afghanistan, 349, 357–58
Agnew, Spiro, 302
Agricultural Adjustment Administration,
  243
Air Force One, Bush and, 352–53
Alcohol, 207, 216, 223
  Bush and, 355
  Garfield and, 148
  Ford and, 304, 307
  Hayes and, 142–43
  Harding and, 216–17
  Pierce and, 92
  Polk and, 70, 73
Alien and Sedition Acts, 16
Alinsky, Saul, 341–42, 348
Allen, Jim, 312
Allenwood, 238
Alley Clearing Bill, 199
Al Qaeda, 349, 353, 357, 359
Ambrose, Stephen, 268
American Communist Party, 261, 295
American Heart Association, 271–72
American Revolution. *See* Revolutionary
  War
Anderson, Marian, 272
Anthony, Carl S., 90
Anti-Mason Party, 84
Arendt, Hannah, 245
Armstrong, Anne, 306

Arthur, Chester A., 148, 151–52
Arthur, Ellen Lewis Herndon, **150–52**
Arthur, Mary, 151
Articles of Confederation, 14
Assassination
  of Garfield, 146, 149
  of Kennedy, 279–80, 286, 352
  of Lincoln, 112, 118
  of McKinley, 175–76
Astor, John Jacob, 31
Atlanta, Battle of (1862), 163
Atwater, Harvey Lee, 299, 326, 330–31,
  355
Auchincloss, Hugh, 275, 276

Babcock, Orville E., 133
Baird, Zoe, 346
Baker, Howard, 318
Baker, James A., III, 319
Banks (banking system), 47, 65, 198
Barker, John, 4
Barron, Clarence, 225
Bayer, Michael J., 330
Bay of Pigs, 272, 278, 280
Beer, Thomas, 171
Beers, Charlotte, 357
Begin, Menachem, 315–16
Belknap, William, 134
Benedict, Elias C., 159
Benny, Jack, 244
Bernstein, Carl, 299
Betty Ford Center, 307
Bible, the, 43–44
Bin Laden, Osama, 349, 353, 357, 359
Black Friday, 132–33
Blaine, James G., 148, 154
Bland, Martha Dangerfield, 7
Bliss, Betty, 79, 80
Blumenthal, Sidney, 348
Bones, Helen, 200

Bonus Act, 233
Booth, John Wilkes, 112, 118
Boston Red Sox, 225
Boston Tea Party, 14
Bouvier, John, 275, 276
Box, Jacob, 131
Boxer Rebellion, 231
Breast cancer, 305, 327
Bristow, Benjamin, 133
Britain. *See* Great Britain
Britton, Nan, 212–13, 218
Broaddrick, Juanita, 344
Brooke, Edward, 342
Brown, John, 102
Brown, Pat, 322
Bryan, William Jennings, 172, 173, 189, 196
Bryn Mawr College, 191, 194
Buchanan, James, 95, 98–104
Bull Moose Party, 191, 196
Bush, Barbara Pierce, 329–38, 344, 354, 355
Bush, George Herbert Walker, xviii, 318–19, 324, 330–38, 344, 354, 355
Bush, George Walker, Jr., 316, 330–31, 332, 337, 349, 352–60
Bush, Jenna Welch, 355, 356, 358
Bush, John Ellis ("Jeb"), 333
Bush, Laura Welch, 302, 351–60
Bush, Neil Mallon, 333, 335, 336
Butterfield, Alexander, 299

Calhoun, John C., 43, 47, 166
Calhoun, Lucia Gilbert, 147
California, 86, 87, 95, 230, 245, 322
Camelot myth, Kennedy and, 275, 278, 280
Campaigning. See also Political attacks
    Adams (Louisa) and, 41–42, 43
    Bush (Barbara) and, 334, 337, 338
    Bush (Laura) and, 355
    Carter and, 310, 311, 312, 315
    Clinton and, 342, 343, 347, 349
    Eisenhower and, 269, 271
    Ford and, 306
    Garfield and, 147–48
    Harding and, 213–14
    Harrison (Caroline) and, 163–64
    Hoover and, 232–33
    Johnson (Lady Bird) and, 287–88
    Kennedy and, 276–77
    Lincoln and, 109–10, 113
    McKinley and, 172–73
    Nixon and, 294–95, 297, 298
    Polk and, 70, 71, 72
    Reagan and, 322, 323–24, 326
    Roosevelt (Edith) and, 178

    Roosevelt (Eleanor) and, 241, 242–43
    Taylor and, 79
    Truman and, 253–54, 257, 259
    Wilson (Ellen) and, 196
Camp followers, 138
Carpetbaggers, 121, 141
Carter, Eleanor Rosalynn Smith, 308–16
Carter, James Earl (Jimmy), Jr., 306, 309–16, 324, 354
Carter, Ruth, 309
Casals, Pablo, 278
Casey, James, 131, 134
Castro, Fidel, 280, 316
Central Intelligence Agency (CIA), 334, 353
Chambers, Whittaker, 261
Chamorro, Violeta, 258
Charitable causes
    Bush (Barbara) and, 335–36
    Bush (Laura) and, 356–57
    Cleveland and, 157
    Coolidge and, 225–26
    Eisenhower and, 271–72
    Hayes and, 139–40, 144
    Kennedy and, 279
    Madison and, 30
    Nixon and, 297–98
    Reagan and, 322, 325–26
    Wilson (Ellen) and, 196–97, 198
Checkers Speech, 296
Cheney, Dick, 352–53
Chiang Kai-shek, 260
Children's Defense Fund, 342
Childress, Joel, 69
China, 230–31, 259–61, 262, 300, 334
China, White House, 110, 165, 181, 324
Christmas tree, White House, 167, 224
Churchill, Winston, 247
Citizens for the Republic (CFTR), 323
Civilian Conservation Corps, 243
Civil rights, 258–59, 272, 281, 287
Civil Rights Act (1964), 287, 300
Civil War
    Garfield and, 146
    Grant and, 127–29
    Harrison (Caroline) and, 162–63
    Hayes and, 138–39
    Johnson and, 116, 118
    Lincoln and, 104, 110, 111, 112–14
    Polk and, 75
Clarke School for the Deaf, 221, 225
Clay, Henry, 41–42, 47, 78, 79
Clayton Anti-Trust Act (1914), 198
Cleveland, Frances Folsom, 153–60, 163–64, 166, 181

Cleveland, Grover, 154, 155–60, 163, 174–75
Cleveland, Oscar Folsom, 154
Clifford, Clark, 257
Clift, Eleanor, xx
Clinton, William Jefferson (Bill), 338, 342–49, 354
Clinton, Chelsea, 343, 347
--Clinton, Hillary Rodham, xii–xiii, xx, 12, 339–50, 359
Clothing. *See* Fashion
Cohn, Roy, 326
Cold War, xvii, 260, 272–73, 280, 296, 327
Coleman, Anne, 98
Colfax, Schuyler, 134
Colombia, 57, 75, 182, 279
Command of the Army Act, 122
Communism, 244–45, 259–61, 289–90, 295
Compromise of 1850, 86–88
Confiscation Act, 121
Congress on Racial Equality, 249
Conkling, Roscoe, 130, 131
Conner, Virginia, 267
Constitution, U.S., 13, 14, 75, 101, 204
Cook, Blanche Wiesen, 238–39, 246
Cook, Nancy, 240–41
Coolidge, Calvin, 221–28
Coolidge, Calvin, Jr., 225
Coolidge, Grace Anna Goodhue, 214–15, 220–28
Coolidge Fund, 225
Corbin, Abel, 132–33
Cornelius, Catherine, 345–46
Cornwallis, Charles, 5
Corruption scandals, xvii, 132–34, 140, 141, 215–18
Cox, James, 207, 214, 240
Crawford, William, 41
Cuba, 95, 175, 272, 278, 280, 316
Cuban Missile Crisis, 158, 278, 280
Custis, Daniel Parke, 6
Cutler, Manasseh, 22
Czolgosz, Leon, 175–76

Daily Telegraph, 42
Dale, Billy, 345–46
Dancing, 66, 73, 102, 303
Dandridge, John and Frances, 6
Daschle, Tom, 359
Daugherty, Harry, 213, 215, 217–18, 223, 227
Daughters of the American Revolution (DAR), 166–67, 234, 244
Davis, Jefferson, 80, 100
Davis, Knox, 80

Davis, Loyal, 320–21
Davis, Varina, 80, 90
Deaf Mute College, 144
Deaver, Michael, 319, 326
Decatur, Stephen, 33
Declaration of Independence, 14, 20
Definition of first lady, xv–xvi
De Gaulle, Charles, 277–78, 279
Delano, Charles, 230
Democratic Party, 195–96, 258–59
Dent, Frederick and Ellen Bray, 126–27
DePriest, Jesse, 235
DePriest, Oscar, 235
Desegregation, 272, 281
Dewey, Thomas, 258
DeWolfe, Henry, 210, 214
DeWolfe, Marshall, 210, 214
Dickens, Charles, 61
Dickerman, Marion, 240–41
Doheny, Edward, 215
Dole, Robert, 347
Donelson, Andrew, 46
Donelson, Emily, 45–50, 151
Doud, John, 265
Douglas, Helen Gahagan, 295
Douglas, Stephen, 94, 108, 109
Dove parties, 29
Draft riots, 113
Dred Scott decision, 101–2
Drug policy, Reagan and, 325–26, 327
Dukaki, Michael, 330–31
Du Pont, Henry Francis, 278
Duties of first lady, xv–xvi
  Adams (Abigail) and, 15
  Garfield and, 148
  Madison and, 28–29
  Monroe and, 35–36
  Polk and, 72, 74
  Roosevelt (Edith) and, 180–81
  Taylor and, 80
  Tyler (Letitia) and, 60–61
  Washington and, 5, 7, 8, 9, 10

Eagleton, Tom, 263
Easter egg hunt, White House, 144, 202, 214, 272
East Wing of the White House, 181, 270, 309, 313
Eaton, John, 49, 50
Eaton, Peggy, 49, 50, 52
Ederle, Gertrude, 225
Education (schooling)
  Adams (Abigail), 13
  Bush (Barbara), 331
  Bush (Laura), 354–55

Education (schooling) (*cont.*)
  Cleveland, 156
  Clinton, 341
  Coolidge, 222
  Fillmore, 83, 84
  Garfield, 146
  Grant, 129
  Harrison (Caroline), 162
  Hayes, 139
  Hoover, 230
  Johnson (Eliza), 117
  Johnson (Lady Bird), 281
  Kennedy, 275
  Lane, 98–99
  Lincoln, 107–8
  Nixon, 293, 294
  Polk, 69
  Roosevelt (Eleanor), 238
  Taft, 186
  Truman, 252
  Van Buren, 53
  Washington, 6
  Wilson (Ellen), 194
Edwards, India, 257
Edwards, Jonathan, 178
Edward VII, Prince of England, 103–4
Egalitarianism, 47
Eighteenth Amendment, 207
Eisenhower, Doud Dwight, 266–67
Eisenhower, Dwight D., 236, 265–73,
  295–96
Eisenhower, John Sheldon Doud, 267
Eisenhower, Mamie Geneva Doud,
  264–73, 277
Elections. *See* Presidential elections
Entertaining, xii
  Adams (Abigail) and, 15
  Adams (Louisa) and, 41
  Arthur and, 151–52
  Carter and, 312, 313
  Coolidge and, 223
  Donelson and, 46–47
  Eisenhower and, 266, 271
  Fillmore and, 85–86
  Ford and, 302
  Garfield and, 148
  Grant and, 126, 130
  Hayes and, 141–42
  Hoover and, 234–35
  Jefferson and, 22
  Johnson (Eliza) and, 119, 120, 123
  Johnson (Lady Bird) and, 289
  Kennedy and, 278
  Lane and, 100, 101, 102–3
  Lincoln and, 109, 110–11

  McKinley and, 173–74
  Madison and, 27–29, 35
  Monroe and, 33–34, 35, 37
  Pierce and, 90, 94
  Polk and, 72, 73
  Roosevelt (Edith) and, 180–81
  Roosevelt (Eleanor) and, 244
  Taft and, 190–91
  Taylor and, 80–81
  Truman and, 256
  Tyler (Julia) and, 64–66, 67
  Tyler (Letitia) and, 60–61
  Van Buren and, 52, 53–54
  Washington and, 8
  Wilson (Edith) and, 202, 203
  Wilson (Ellen) and, 196
Environmentalism, 184, 288, 300
Environmental Protection Agency (EPA),
  300
Epilepsy, McKinley and, 169, 171
Eppes, John, 23
Eppes, Mary Jefferson, **19–23**
Equal Rights Amendment (ERA), 305,
  306, 314

Faber, Doris, xiii, xiv
Fair Deal, 257, 258–59
Fall, Albert, 215
Fascism, 244–45
Fashion, xiii–xiv
  Bush (Barbara), 335
  Cleveland, 156
  Coolidge, 221, 224
  Eisenhower, 265, 270
  Kennedy, 277, 278
  Lane, 100
  Lincoln, 111–12
  McKinley, 173
  Madison, 27–28, 31
  Monroe, 37
  Reagan, 324, 335
  Truman, 256
  Van Buren, 54
Faubus, Orville, 272
Federal Advisory Committee Act (1974),
  346
Federal Election Commission (FEC), 331
Federal Emergency Relief Administration,
  243–44, 246
Federal Highway Act, 288
Federal income taxes, 198
Federalists, 12, 21–23, 38, 92
Federal Reserve Act (1913), 198
Feminism, 157, 166, 227. *See also* Women's
  rights

Ferraro, Geraldine, 326, 330
Fillmore, Abigail Powers, 82–88, 221
Fillmore, Millard, 83–88
Fireside chats, 234, 241
First Continental Congress, 14
First Reconstruction Act, 121
Fisk, Jim, 132–33
Flowers, Gennifer, 344
Folsom, Emma, 154–55
Folsom, Oscar, 154
Forbes, Charles, 215–16, 217–18
Ford, Elizabeth (Betty) Bloomer, xviii, 301–7, 313, 334
Ford, Gerald, 302–6, 312, 323, 334
Ford's Theater, 112
Foreign policy
    Adams (Abigail) and, 15–16, 18
    Bush (Laura) and, 357–59
    Carter and, 314, 315–16
    Fillmore and, 88
    Madison and, 29–30
    Monroe and, 34–35
    Reagan and, 326–27
    Washington and, 9
Fort Sam Houston, 265–66
Foster, Jodie, 325
Foster Grandparents Program, 322
France, 9, 15–16, 18, 21, 29–30, 34–35, 183, 203
Franklin, Benjamin, 20
Frazier, Joe, 326
Freemasons, 84
French and Indian Wars, 34
French Revolution, 16, 21
Frost, Robert, 278
Fugitive Slave Act, 86–87
Fuller, Craig, 330
Fund raising, 225–26, 285, 286
Future of the first lady, xx–xxi

Gadsen Purchase (1853), 95
Gallatin, Albert, 12
Galt, Norman, 200
Galt & Company, 111, 201
Gardiner, Alex, 63
Garfield, James, 146–49, 151
Garfield, Lucretia Rudolf, 145–49
Garner, John Nance, 255
George III, King of England, 21–23
Georgia Association for Retarded Children, 312
Gephardt, Dick, 359
Germany, 40, 183, 202–4, 207, 245, 247–48
Germond, Jack, 330, 334–35

G.I. Bill, 257
Gifts, 103–4, 111, 112, 164–65, 349
Girl Scouts, 232, 234, 235
Glass, Alice, 284–85
Gold, 74, 132–33, 164
Golden Spoon speech, 54–55
Goldwater, Barry, 288, 315, 321–22, 341
Goodhue, Andrew and Lemira, 222
Gorbachev, Mikhail, 327
Gordon, John Watson, 104
Gore, Albert, 331
Gould, Jay, 132–33
Governor, Samuel Lawrence, 33
Grant, Julia Dent, xiii, 125–36, 141, 142, 156, 163, 265
Grant, Ulysses S., 122, 126–35, 141, 142
Grayson, Cary, 200–201
Britain (England), 9, 14–16, 26, 29–30, 37, 52, 74, 99, 183, 203, 231–32, 247–48. *See also* Revolutionary War
Great Depression, xi, 230, 233–34, 242, 243–44, 245, 249, 293
Great Society, 287, 288–89, 290
Greene, Nathanael, 5
Gregg, Judd, 352
Grimke, Sarah, 43–44
Guiteau, Charles, 149
Gulf War, xviii, 337

Habitat for Humanity, 316
Hagner, Isabelle, 180, 181, 196
"Hail to the Chief," 64–65, 73
Halpin, Maria, 154
Hamlin, Hannibal, 118
Hampton College, 144
Hancock, Winfield S., 147
Hanna, Mark, 172–73
Harding, Florence Kling DeWolfe, xvii, 209–19, 226, 227
Harding, Warren, xvii, 191, 210–18, 221, 227, 232, 240
Harken Energy, 356
Harper's Ferry raid, 102
Harriet Lane (ship), 100, 102–3
Harris, Patricia Roberts, 315
Harrison, Anna Tuthill Symmes, 56–58, 162
Harrison, Benjamin, 58, 158, 162–67, 179, 186, 187
Harrison, Caroline Lavinia Scott, 161–67
Harrison, William Henry, 30, 54–55, 57–58, 162
Harron, Marion Janet, 247
Havel, Vaclav, 358
Hawthorne, Nathaniel, 94

Hayes, Lucy Ware Webb, **137–44**, 163,
   171–72, 186
Hayes, Rutherford B., 138–43, 146, 165,
   170, 171–72, 186
Head Start, 287, 288, 290, 336
Health care policy, Clinton and, 345, 346
Hell to Pay (Olson), 340
Hemings, Sally, 23
Henry, Florence Weed, 230
Hickok, Lorena, xiii, xvii–xviii, 239,
   242–43, 245, 246–47, 284
Hills, Carla, 306
Hinckley, John, 324–25
Hiram College, 146
Hiroshima, Japan, 256
Hiss, Alger, 261, 295
Hitler, Adolf, 207, 228, 245, 247
Hobart, Garret A., 175
Holloway, Laura, xiv, 49, 50, 90, 91–92, 98,
   99, 117, 127, 138, 143–44, 146
Hoover, Herbert, 215, 230–36, 243
Hoover, Herbert Clark, Jr., 231
Hoover, J. D., 90
Hoover, J. Edgar, 323
Hoover, Lou Henry, **229–36**
Hoovervilles, 233
Hope, Bob, 307
Hopkins, Harry, 246, 247, 261, 284
Horowitz, Vladimir, 234
Horton, Willie, 330–31, 338
House Un-American Activities Committee
   (HUAC), 260–61, 295
House Ways and Means Committee, 85, 172
Hughes, Karen, 354, 357
Humphrey, Hubert, 297

Ice cream, 28
I Love Lucy (TV show), 270
Immigration, 247–48, 335–36
Impeachment
   Clinton, 348–49
   Johnson, 122–23, 129–30, 158
   Nixon, 299, 342–43
Inaugurations, 46, 88, 91, 110, 196, 272,
   313, 324
   of Madison, 27–28, 29–30
Internal Revenue Service (IRS), 133
Iran-Contra scandal, xviii, 318, 319, 327
Irving, Washington, 29, 61, 86
Isolationism, 9, 204–5, 206, 227–28
Israel, 315–16, 359
It Takes a Village (Clinton), 347

Jackson, Andrew, 30, 41, 42, 43, 46–50, 52,
   84, 92

Polk and, 69, 70, 71
Jackson, Andrew, Jr., 49
Jackson, Rachel Donelson Robards, xiv, 46,
   48–49, 69, 214
Jackson, Sarah York, **49–50**
Japan, 182–83, 248, 256, 296
Jay's Treaty, 9
Jefferson, Martha Wayles Skelton, 20
Jefferson, Thomas, 17, 20–23, 30, 35
Jewell, Marshall, 131
Johnson, Andrew, 116–24, 129–30, 158
Johnson, Claudia Taylor "Lady Bird," 279,
   282–91, 297
Johnson, Eliza McCardle, **115–24**
Johnson, Lyndon Baines, 277, 283–91, 315,
   321–22
Johnston, Harriet Lane. *See* Lane, Harriet
Jones, Paula, 347, 348
Jordan, Hamilton, 337
Julia Waltzes, 66
"Just Say No" drug campaign, 325–26

Kansas, 101–2
Karzai, Hamid, 358
Keating Five, 336
Keller, Helen, 225
Kelly, Tom, xix, xx, 281
Kemp, Jack, 335
Kenmore Inn, 7–8
Kennedy, Jacqueline Lee Bouvier,
   274–81, 286
Kennedy, Joe, 276
Kennedy, John Fitzgerald, 208, 249,
   276–81, 286, 289, 297, 352
Kennedy, John (John-John) Fitzgerald, Jr.,
   277, 280, 286
Kennedy, Ted, 314–15, 352
Kennedy Commission on the Status of
   Women, 249
Khrushchev, Nikita, 279, 297
King, Martin Luther, Jr., 341
King, Rufus, 91
Kissinger, Henry, 182
Kitt, Earth, 289
Kling, Amos, 210
Know-Nothing Party, 88
Korean War, 259–60, 262, 263
Kropotkin, Peter, 175–76
Kuhn, Caitlin, 327
Kuhn, Carole, 327
Kuhn, James, 327

Ladies of the White House (Holloway), xiv, 90,
   146
Lady Adams Rangers, 17–18

Lady Madison (ship), 31
Lafayette, Marquise de, 34–35, 37
Land and Water Conservation Act (1964), 288
Landon, Alf, 243
Lane, Harriet, 97–105, 123, 224
Laxalt, Paul, 334
Lazio, Rick, 349
League of Nations, 203, 204, 206, 207, 213
LeHand, Missy, 240
Lend-Lease program, 247, 260
Lesbianism, Eleanor Roosevelt and, xiii, 238–39, 246–47
Letters to Mamie (Eisenhower), 268
Levees, 28, 36, 54, 60, 73, 80, 94, 123
Lewinsky, Monica, 347–48
Lewis and Clark expedition, 23
Liberia, 37, 139
Library of Congress, 23, 86
Lincoln, Abraham, 104, 108–14, 118, 120, 121, 128, 146, 280
Lincoln, Mary Todd, xiii, 106–14, 123, 128, 279
Lincoln, Robert, 114
Lincoln, Willie, 113
Lind, Jenny, 86
Lindbergh, Charles, 223
Literacy, 335–36, 356
Locke, John, 13
Lodge, Henry Cabot, 204–5, 207
Longworth, Alice Roosevelt, 179, 180, 181–82, 191, 238, 278
Longworth, Nick, 191
Lonnstrom, Doug, xix
Louisiana Purchase, 23, 35
Lusitania (cruise ship), 200

McAdoo, Eleanor Randolph Wilson, 195, 197
MacArthur, Douglas, 233, 262
McCain, John, 336
McCall's, 249, 331
McCardle, John, 116
McCarthy, Eugene, 341
McCarthy, Joseph, 260–61, 295
McDonald, John, 133
McDougal, Susan, 347
McGovern, George, 337, 342
McKinley, Ida Saxton, 168–76, 179–80, 186
McKinley, Katherine, 170, 171
McKinley, William, 169–76, 178, 187
McLean, John, 66
Madison, Dolley Payne Todd, 22, 25–31, 73

Kennedy compared with, 278
Lincoln and, 108–9
Monroe and, 35, 36, 37, 38
Polk and, 72–73
Tyler (Julia) and, 63–64, 65
Tyler (Letitia) and, 60
Van Buren and, 52, 53, 54
Madison, James, 26, 27–31, 35
Maine (battleship), 175
Manifest destiny, 74
Mann, Thomas Randolph, Jr., 21, 23
Mao Zedong, 260
March of Dimes, 244
Marion Star, 211–12, 219
Marshall, Thomas, 205
Marxism, 244–45
Matalin, Mary, 357
Means, Gaston B., 218
Media, the. *See* Press
Medicare, 290
Mellon, Andrew, 215
Mental Health Systems Act (1980), 314
Mentelle, Charlotte, 107–8
Mercer, Lucy, 240, 248
Metro Goldwyn Mayer, 321
Mexican War, 78, 79, 80, 93, 127
Mexico, 74, 78, 79, 95, 261
Milligan, Maurice, 254
Missouri Compromise, 37
Mondale, Walter, 342
Monroe, Elizabeth Kortright, 32–38, 234
Monroe, James, 33–38, 234
Monroe, Maria, 33
Monroe Doctrine, 37–38
Monticello, 20, 23–24
Morgan, John Pierpoint, 182
Morrow, E. Fred, 272
Mount Vernon, 7, 10, 29, 64, 103
Moynihan, Daniel Patrick, 349
Muir, John, 184
Munsey's Magazine, 72, 107
Myers, Dee Dee, 346
My Memoir (Edith Wilson), 207
My Turn (Nancy Reagan), 328

Nagasaki, Japan, 256
Napoléon Bonaparte, 21, 23, 35, 44
Napoleonic Wars, 15–16, 29
Narrative of a Journey From Russia to France, 1815 (Adams), 44
National Association for the Advancement of Colored People (NAACP), 249
National debt, 95, 227
National Gallery of Art, 104, 181
National Industrial Recovery Act, 243

National Institute of Social Sciences, 221
National Intelligencer, 28
National parks and forests, Roosevelt and, 184
National Security Political Action Committee (NSPAC), 331
National Youth Administration (NYA), 284
Needlework Guild, 157
Negative attacks, 294–96, 323, 324, 326, 330–31, 341–42, 344
New Deal, 243–44, 246, 249, 284
New Orleans, Battle of (1815), 30
News media. *See* Press
Nicaragua, 258, 318, 327
Nineteenth Amendment, 207
9-11 terrorist attacks (2001), 352–54, 357, 359, 360
Nixon, Patricia Thelma Catherine Ryan, 292–300, 303, 343
Nixon, Richard Milhous, 294–300, 302, 304, 319, 321, 333–34, 342–43
Nixon, Tricia, 276, 295
Nobel Prize, 182–84, 207
Non-Intercourse Act, 30
Noonan, Peggy, 335
North Atlantic Treaty Organization (NATO), 268–69, 358
North Korea, 259–60, 262

Ogle, Charles, 54–55
Ohio Gang, 215, 216–17, 223
Ohio Volunteers, 138–39, 163
Olson, Barbara, 340
Onassis, Aristotle, 281
Onassis, Jacqueline Lee Bouvier Kennedy, 274–81
Oneida (yacht), 159
Oregon Treaty (1846), 74

Panama Canal, 75, 182, 189
Paris Peace Conference (1913), 203, 204, 207, 213
Parker, Eliza, 107
Patterson, Martha, 119–20, 122, 123
Payne, John and Mary Coles, 26
Peace Corps, 249, 280
Pearl Harbor, 248, 256, 285, 294
Peck, Mary Allen Hulbert, 195, 200–201
Pentagon terrorist attacks (2001), 352–53, 357, 359, 360
Perkins, Frances, 241
Perot, H. Ross, 191, 337
Perry, Commodore, 88
Peru, 296, 298
Philippines, 175, 186, 187–88, 262

Philips, Sarah, 116
Phillips, Carrie, 212, 213, 217
Phillips, Jim, 212
Pierce, Benjamin (Benny), 91–96
Pierce, Franklin, 88, 91, 92–96, 331
Pierce, Frank Robert, 92–93, 94
Pierce, Jane Means Appleton, xiii, 89–96
Pierce, Marvin and Pauline, 331
Pinckney's Treaty, 9, 16
Pinkerton, Jim, 355
Polio, Roosevelt and, 240, 241–42, 244
Political activism, xv–xvi
  Adams (Abigail) and, 12–13, 29
  Adams (Louisa) and, 41–42
  Clinton and, 341, 346–47
  Coolidge and, 226
  Harding and, 214–15
  Hoover and, 235–36
  Lane and, 100–101
  Lincoln and, 111
  Nixon and, 298
  Roosevelt (Edith) and, 184
  Roosevelt (Eleanor) and, 241–42, 245–46, 257–58
  Taft and, 192
  Truman and, 256
  Tyler (Julia) and, 66
  Wilson (Ellen) and, 196–97, 198
Political attacks, 294–96, 323, 324, 326, 330–31, 341–42, 344
Political bias, xviii, xx
Political campaigns. *See* Campaigning
Political patronage, 48, 65, 131, 141, 345–46
Polk, James A., 31, 66, 67, 69–75, 79, 93
Polk, Sarah Childress, 31, 67, 68–76, 178
Polling (polls), xviii, 258
Powell, Colin, 322
Powers, Francis Gary, 272
Presidential elections
  1800, 17–18, 21–22
  1820, 38
  1824, 41–42, 48
  1828, 43, 46, 48–49
  1832, 84
  1836, 52, 84
  1840, 52, 54–55, 57
  1844, 66, 72
  1848, 78, 79, 85
  1852, 93
  1856, 88
  1860, 109–10
  1864, 112, 118
  1868, 130
  1876, 140–41

1880, 146, 147–48
1884, 154
1888, 163–64, 167
1892, 158, 167
1896, 169, 172–73
1900, 175, 178, 180
1904, 182
1908, 189
1912, 191, 196
1920, 210, 213–14, 221, 223, 240
1928, 232–33
1932, 184, 235, 242–43
1936, 243
1944, 255
1948, 249, 257, 258–59
1952, 269, 295–96
1956, 271
1960, 277, 286, 297
1964, 287–88, 321–22
1968, 297
1972, 298, 299, 342
1976, 306, 312, 323
1980, 314–15, 323–24, 334–35
1984, 326, 330
1988, 330–31, 335
1992, 337–38, 344–45
1996, 347
2000, 330, 356–57
Presidential pardons, 215–16, 349
Presidential veto, 157–58
Press (news media), xiii–xiv
    Adams (Abigail) and, 12
    Adams (Louisa) and, 42
    Bush (Laura) and, 357
    Carter and, 309, 314
    Cleveland and, 155, 156
    Coolidge and, 223–24, 226
    Eisenhower and, 269
    Ford and, 305
    Garfield and, 148
    Grant and, 131
    Harding and, 210–11, 216
    Harrison (Caroline) and, 163–64
    Hoover and, 233–34
    Johnson (Lady Bird) and, 288–89
    Kennedy and, 276
    Lane and, 102–4
    Lincoln and, 123
    McKinley and, 169
    Madison and, 28, 30
    Nixon and, 296, 298
    Reagan and, 325, 326
    Roosevelt (Edith) and, 181–82
    Roosevelt (Eleanor) and, 240–44, 249
    Truman and, 253–54, 255, 256–57

    Tyler (Julia) and, 66
    Washington and, 9
Prexton, Thomas, 160
Public policy. See also Foreign policy
    Adams (Abigail) and, 12
    Adams (Louisa) and, 42–43
    Carter and, 309, 313
    Clinton and, 344–45
    Hayes and, 140
    Johnson (Eliza) and, 119
    Johnson (Lady Bird) and, 288–89
    Kennedy and, 280–81
    Lane and, 100–101
    Lincoln and, 111
    Madison and, 29
    Polk and, 72, 74
    Reagan and, 318, 322
    Roosevelt (Eleanor) and, 245–46
    Taft and, 190
    Taylor and, 86–88
    Truman and, 251–52
    Tyler (Julia) and, 66
    Washington and, 9
Public Works Adminstration, 243

Qaeda, al, 349, 353, 357, 359
Quayle, Dan, 330–31

Radical Republicans, 120–22, 129–30, 135,
    140, 141
Randolph, James Madison, 23
Randolph, Martha Jefferson, 19–24
Randolph Mann, Thomas, Jr., 21, 23
Rating the first ladies, xvi–xix
Rayburn, Sam, 262
Reagan, Nancy Anne Frances Robbins
    Davis, xii, 317–28, 335, 338, 357, 359
Reagan, Ronald, 221, 297, 306, 315,
    318–28, 334–35
Receiving lines, 130–31, 148, 151, 173,
    234–35
Reconstruction, 139–41
    Eliza Johnson and, 121–22, 129–30
Red Cross, 202, 203, 277
Regan, Don, 318–19
Reich, Robert, 342
Reign of Terror, 16, 21, 34–35
Religious Liberty, Statute on, 20
Renovations, White House. See White
    House
Republicans (Republican Party), 21–22,
    110, 195, 312, 333
    Radical, 120–22, 129–30, 135, 140, 141
Revolutionary War, xii, 4–5, 14, 20, 34, 117,
    166

Adams and, 14
Washington and, 7–9
Rice, Condoleezza, 354
Rich, Marc, 349
Richards, Ann, 356
Richardson, William, 134
Rickover, Hyman, 310
Rights of women. *See* Women's rights
Robards, Lewis, 48
Robbins, Kenneth and Edith Luckett, 320
Rockefeller, Nelson, 297, 323
Roe vs. Wade, 298
Role model
 Adams as, 18
 Cleveland as, 156–57
 Coolidge as, 224
 Kennedy as, 277–78
 Lincoln as, 113
Role of first lady, xi–xiii, xxi
Rollins, Ed, 299, 326, 336–37
Roosevelt, Alice Lee, 178–79
Roosevelt, Anna Eleanor, xi, xiii, **237–49**, 340
 Eisenhower and, 269
 Hoover and, 235
 Johnson and, 284, 287
 Truman and, 251, 255, 257–58, 260
Roosevelt, Archibald, 179, 180, 181–82
Roosevelt, Edith Carow, xviii, **177–84**, 189, 191, 238
Roosevelt, Ethel, 179, 180
Roosevelt, Franklin Delano, 184, 207, 234, 235, 238–48, 255, 285
Roosevelt, Franklin Delano, Jr., 240
Roosevelt, Kermit, 179, 180, 181–82
Roosevelt, Quentin, 179, 180, 181–82
Roosevelt, Sara Delano, 238, 239
Roosevelt, Theodore, 164, 175, 178–84, 188, 189, 191, 196, 239
Roosevelt, Theodore, Jr., 179, 180, 181–82, 241
Root, Elihu, 189
Rose, Susan Porter, xvi–xvii, 335, 338
Rosebush, James, xvi, xx, 327
Rough Riders, 178, 179
Rush-Bagot Treaty (1818), 37
Russia, 42, 44, 142, 182–83, 260, 358. *See also* Soviet Union
Ryan, William, 293

Sadat, Anwar, 315–16
Saunders, James, 138, 139
Savings and loan (S&L) scandal, 336–37
Sayre, Jessie Wilson, 195, 197
Schneider, Dorothy and Carl, 65, 166

Schooling. *See* Education
Scott, John Witherspoon, 162
Screen Actors Guild (SAG), 321
Second Continental Congress, 6–7, 14, 20
Segregation, 249, 272, 281
Seminole Indians, 78
Semple, Letitia Tyler, 63
September 11 terrorist attacks (2001), 352–54, 357, 359
Sharpe, Alexander, 131
Shawnee Indians, 30, 57
Sherman Silver Purchase Act, 164
Siena College Research Institute, xix–xx
Sinclair, Harry, 215
Slavery, 16, 23, 37, 66, 95
 Buchanan and, 101–2
 Fugitive Slave Act, 86–87
 Lincoln and, 110, 112–13
Smeal, Eleanor, xvi, 18, 281
Smith, Al, 241
Smith, Alfred E., 160, 226
Smith, Benjamin, 120
Smith, Franklin, 120
Smith, Jessie, 217–18
Smith, Margaret Bayard, 27–28, 46
Smith, Samuel, 28
Smith, Walter, 78
Smith, William, 13
Social calls, 15, 35–36, 41–42, 60, 72–73, 188–89
Socialism, Eleanor Roosevelt and, 244–45
Social Security, 290
South Korea, 259–60, 262
Soviet Union, 259–62, 272, 295, 297, 299–300, 327. *See also* Russia
Spanish-American War, 175, 179
Spectator, The, 13
Spencer, Stu, 322, 323, 324, 326
Spoils system, 48, 141
Spring-Rice, Cecil, 183
Stagflation, 314
Stalin, Josef, 245, 247, 259–60, 261
Stanford, Leland, 165
Stanton, Edwin M., 121, 122, 129
Stark, Lloyd, 254
Starr, Kenneth, 348
State of the Union address, 197
States' Rights Party, 258–59
Stevenson, Adlai, 158, 249, 269
Stover, Mary, 120, 122
Strange Death of President Harding (Means), 218
Strategic Arms Limitation Treaty, 300
Strategic Petroleum Reserve, 215
Straus, Oscar, 182

Stuart, Gilbert, 26
Suffragism, 143–44, 157
Summersby, Kay, 268
Sunshine laws, 346
Symington, Jim, 263

Taft, Alphonso, 186
Taft, Helen Herron, **185–92**
Taft, Robert, 191
Taft, William, 186–92, 196
Taliban, 357–58
Tariffs, 42–43, 47, 164, 167, 172, 198
Taxes, 227, 336–37, 346–47
Taylor, Margaret Mackall Smith, **77–81,**
279–80
Taylor, Thomas Jefferson, Jr., 281
Taylor, Zachary, 78–80, 85, 86–88
Teapot Dome scandal, 215, 226, 241
Temperance movement, 142–43, 157
Tenement housing, Ellen Wilson and,
196–97, 198
Tenet, George, 353
Tennessee, 71, 116, 117
Tennessee Valley Authority, 243
Tenure of Office Act, 122
Terrorism, 251, 349, 352–54, 357–60
Texas, 66–67, 74, 95, 356
Texas Book Festival, 356
Texas Rangers, 356
Thatcher, Margaret, 326–27
Thomas, Norman, 244
Thurmond, Strom, 259
Tilden, Samuel J., 140, 141
Todd, John, 26–27
Todd, Robert Smith, 107
Treaty of Versailles (1919), 204–5, 207, 247
Tripp, Linda, 348
Truman, Elizabeth (Bess) Virginia Wallace,
xvii, **250–63**
Truman, Harry, xvii, 235–36, 248–49, 249,
251–63, 268–69
Truman, Mary Margaret, 253, 254, 259
Truman Doctrine, 260
Twain, Mark, 135
Tyler, John, 60, 61, 63–67
Tyler, Julia Gardiner, **62–67**
Tyler, Letitia Christian, **59–61**
Tyler, Priscilla Cooper, 60–61, 63

Underground Railroad, 101
United Negro College Fund, 332
Universal Declaration of Human Rights,
248
University of California, 322–23
University of Virginia, 20

Van Buren, Abraham, 52–53
Van Buren, Angelica Singleton, **51–55**
Van Buren, Martin, 47–48, 52–55
Velasquez, Fidel, 261
Versailles treaty (1919), 204–5, 207, 247
Veterans Bureau, 216, 217
Victoria, Queen of England, 53, 98, 99, 103,
104, 165
Vietnam War, 289–90, 322–23, 341, 342
Vogue, 276
Volunteerism, Nixon and, 297–98
Voorhis, Jerry, 294–95
Voting rights, 272
for women, xiv, 143–44, 207

Wallace, George, 297
Wallace, Henry, 255
Wallace, Will, 162
Waller, William, 64
Walters, Barbara, 273
Wanamaker, John, 164–65
War of 1812, 26, 29, 69, 78
War on Poverty, 287
Warren, William C., 303
Washington, Custis, 5
Washington, George, 5–10, 14, 15, 34, 35
Washington, Martha Dandridge Custis,
3–10
Adams and, 14, 15, 29
face on currency, 166
Jefferson and, 22–23
Madison and, 27
slaves and, 102
Washington City Orphans Asylum, 30
Washington Monument, 144
Washington Times Herald, 276
Watergate scandal (1972), 299, 333–34, 337,
343
Watkins, David, 345
Webster, Daniel, 46, 66, 88
Weddings, White House, 33–34, 64, 65,
155, 197
Wesleyan Female College, 139
West, Marian, xvi, 72, 107
Whig Party, 84, 85, 87–88
Whiskey Rebellion, 9
Whiskey Ring, 133
White, William Allen, 226
White House
Adams (Agibail) and, 13
Bush (Laura) and, 353–54
Cleveland and, 158–59
Coolidge and, 223
Fillmore and, 85–86

White House (*cont.*)
Garfield and, 148
Grant and, 126, 130
Harrison (Anna) and, 54, 57
Harrison (Caroline) and, 165–66
Hayes and, 141–42
Hoover and, 234–35
Jackson and, 46–47
Jefferson and, 23
Johnson (Eliza) and, 118–19, 120, 123
Kennedy and, 278–79
Lane and, 100, 101, 103
Lincoln and, 110–11, 113
Madison and, 26, 27–28, 29
Monroe and, 33, 36–37
Pierce and, 90, 94
Polk and, 72, 73–74
Reagan and, 318, 324, 325
Roosevelt (Edith) and, 180, 181
Roosevelt (Eleanor) and, 244
Taft and, 189–91
Taylor and, 80
Truman and, 256, 262–63
Tyler (Julia) and, 64–66
Van Buren and, 52, 54–55
Washington and, 8
White House Historical Association, 279
Whitewater scandal, 340, 347
Williams, George, 131
Wills, Gary, 289
Wilson, Edith Bolling Galt, 199–208
Wilson, Ellen Louise Axson, 193–98, 221
Wilson, Woodrow, 191, 194–98, 200–207, 213, 232, 239
Witcover, Jules, 330, 334–35
Woman's World Fair (1925), 224
Women's Christian Temperance Union, 142, 144, 157
Women's rights

Adams (Abigail) and, 12–13, 18
Adams (Louisa) and, 43–44
Cleveland and, 157
Clinton and, 347
Coolidge and, 224–25
Ford and, 302
Harrison (Caroline) and, 162, 166–67
Hayes and, 143–44
Hoover and, 235–36
Nixon and, 298–99
Woodward, Bob, 299
Workingwomen, 157, 166
Works Progress Administration (WPA), 243
World Trade Center terrorist attacks (1993), 349
World Trade Center terrorist attacks (2001), 352–53, 357, 359, 360
World War I
Cleveland and, 160
Hoover and, 231–32, 233
Truman and, 253
Wilson and, 202–4
World War II
Bush and, 332
Carter and, 309
Coolidge and, 227–28
Eisenhower and, 268
Hoover and, 235
Nixon and, 294
Roosevelt and, 246, 247–48, 249, 255
Truman and, 256
Wilson and, 207
Wright, Jim, 336
Wyman, Jane, 321

Yale University, 332, 342
Yandell, Enid, 136

Zacarro, John, 326